Applying Communication Theory for Professional Life

Applying Communication Theory for Professional Life

A Practical Introduction

Marianne Dainton
La Salle University

Elaine D. Zelley
La Salle University

Los Angeles | London | New Delhi
Singapore | Washington DC

Los Angeles | London | New Delhi
Singapore | Washington DC

FOR INFORMATION:

SAGE Publications, Inc.
2455 Teller Road
Thousand Oaks, California 91320
E-mail: order@sagepub.com

SAGE Publications Ltd.
1 Oliver's Yard
55 City Road
London EC1Y 1SP
United Kingdom

SAGE Publications India Pvt. Ltd.
B 1/I 1 Mohan Cooperative Industrial Area
Mathura Road, New Delhi 110 044
India

SAGE Publications Asia-Pacific Pte. Ltd.
3 Church Street
#10-04 Samsung Hub
Singapore 049483

Acquisitions Editor: Matthew Byrnie
Associate Editor: Nancy Loh
Editorial Assistant: Gabrielle Piccininni
Production Editor: Libby Larson
Copy Editor: Mark Bast
Typesetter: C&M Digitals (P) Ltd.
Proofreader: Dennis W. Webb
Cover Designer: Anupama Krishnan
Marketing Manager: Liz Thornton

Printed in the United States of America

Library of Congress Control Number: 2014931720

ISBN: 978-1-4522-7654-0 (pbk.)

ISBN: 978-1-4833-1179-1 (web pdf)

This book is printed on acid-free paper.

14 15 16 17 18 10 9 8 7 6 5 4 3 2

Brief Contents

Detailed Contents

10   Mediated Communication   175

11   Mass Communication   193

Preface

This book is designed to serve as a communication theory textbook for upper-level undergraduate and master's degree students. Although it is intended for upper-level students, we make no presumption that the students have previous knowledge or background in communication or communication theory. Rather, the text is meant to serve as a practical introduction to the topic for students pursuing (or currently working in) careers in communication-related industries.

We have found that the primary challenge of instructors teaching communication theory to career-oriented students is the abstract nature of the topic; many students have difficulty seeing the relevance of communication theory in their professional lives. Our goal for writing this book is to make communication theory tangible to students by explaining the theories in practical ways and by assisting students in seeing how theory can be used in professional life. The response to previous editions of this book has been overwhelmingly favorable, and we are grateful to have achieved our goal.

Based on reviews of the second edition, we have made several changes. First, in several cases we have returned theories that had appeared in the first edition but were eliminated or changed in the second edition. For example, attribution theory has been returned to the section on interpersonal/cognitive approaches, the narrative paradigm has been returned to the persuasion chapter, and groupthink has been returned to the section on group communication theories. Adaptive structuration theory has been reworked with a focus on virtual teams and also appears in the group communication chapter, and social learning theory (now called social cognitive theory) appears in the newly focused mass communication chapter. Finally, cognitive dissonance now appears in the intrapersonal/cognition chapter.

Second, we have added two chapters. Chapter 4 now addresses the debate between individualistic and social approaches to communication, framing the discussion around the nature and nurture debate. Chapter 10 focuses on media and communication. The theories included provide insights into the role social media play in our lives.

Finally, we have eliminated a specific chapter on leadership theory; as reviewers noted, several of the theories we had included were quite old, and many did not have a clear link to communication. Instead, we have included leadership implications and advice throughout the text. For example, in discussing social role theory (Chapter 4) we include implications for women and leadership. While examining emotional intelligence (also Chapter 4) we introduce transformational leadership. And a review of communication accommodation theory (Chapter 6) leads to a consideration of how leader-member exchange can be understood as an exemplar of in-groups and out-groups.

The net result is this edition does not include five theories covered in previous editions: social judgment theory (persuasion), interaction process analysis (group com), Likert's four systems (leadership), the contingency model (leadership), and the two-culture model of gender. These theories now appear on the instructors' site for the text. As described earlier, six theories eliminated in the second edition have been returned in this edition. Finally, five new theories are included in this text: the social role theory of gender (Chapter 4), anxiety/uncertainty management theory (Chapter 6), diffusion of innovations (Chapter 10), social network analysis (Chapter 10), and encoding/decoding theory (Chapter 11).

As a reminder to instructors and students, this textbook is not meant to provide a comprehensive survey of all communication theory, nor is it meant to focus only on particular contexts of communication. Instead, we have selected representative theories that have clear applicability to communication practitioners. Finally, we have not limited ourselves only to theories developed in the communication discipline because we believe all theories that address communication—whether developed within the field or not—are important tools for communication professionals.

A central pedagogical feature of this text remains the inclusion of a case study after each group of theories. In this edition we have sometimes chosen to keep the case study that appeared in the second edition. In other instances, we have returned to the case study published in the first edition. All cases associated with the previous editions of the text are available to instructors on the text website.

Acknowledgments

We would like to thank the reviewers for this edition, as well as the faculty members who have e-mailed us with their compliments and recommendations. We are very appreciative of their support and feedback, and we hope we have done justice to your recommendations.

We also would like to thank several of our graduate students, whose workplace stories serve as the foundation for some of our cases. Specifically, we thank Michele Langley, Vincent Haas, Maryam Ashfar, Janet Donovan, Lauren Zane-Virostek, Cristina Tosti, and Julie Pompizzi (all names and organizations listed in the case studies are pseudonyms).

We also would like to thank our students and colleagues at La Salle University. Our students continue to challenge us with the "so what" question, and we are pleased most of them are persuaded by our answers. Our colleagues in the Communication Department also deserve acknowledgment; they not only serve as outstanding instructor role models but also continue to greet our work with enthusiasm and provide us with much-needed social support. We particularly thank Katie Neary Dunleavy for her advice.

It often goes without saying (but shouldn't!) that we thank our family members and friends for their ongoing support. Both Marianne and Elaine are especially grateful to their husbands, Scott and Bryan, for serving as sounding boards and providing insight from the corporate world. More than a few of their experiences have made it into this text.

Introduction to Communication Theory

LEARNING OBJECTIVES

After reading this chapter, you will be able to...

1. Analyze a definition of communication, articulating the definition's level of observation, intentionality, and normative judgment.
2. Recognize the various contexts in which communication takes place.
3. Explain what is meant by communication competence.
4. Differentiate a communication theory from a concept and a model.
5. Discriminate between commonsense, working, and scholarly theories.
6. Use criteria for evaluating theory to determine the relative usefulness of a communication theory.

There are almost 400,000 web pages devoted to explaining that "communication is easy" (go ahead and search it!) and almost 80,000 YouTube hits for the same phrase. Of course, if mastering the communication process really only required viewing a 4-minute video, we would all be maestros of getting our messages understood. Unfortunately, much of popular culture tends to minimize the challenges associated with the communication process. Yes, in the 21st century we believe communication skill is important—you need only to peruse the content of talk shows, personal ads, advice columns, and organizational performance reviews to recognize that communication skills can make or break an individual's personal and professional life. Companies want to hire and promote people with excellent communication skills. Divorces occur because spouses believe they "no longer communicate." Communication is perceived as a magical elixir, one that can ensure a happy long-term relationship and guarantee organizational success. Yet, despite lauding communication as

1

the sine qua non of contemporary success, the secret to that success is treated superficially at best in our modern information environment. Clearly, popular culture holds paradoxical views about communication: It is easy to do yet powerful in its effects, simultaneously simple and magical.

We believe the communication process is complex. "Good" communication means different things to different people in different situations. Accordingly, simply adopting a set of particular skills is not going to guarantee success. Genuinely good communicators are those who understand the underlying principles behind communication and are able to enact, appropriately and effectively, particular communication skills as the situation warrants. This book seeks to provide the foundation for those sorts of decisions. We focus on communication theories that can be applied in your personal and professional lives. Understanding these theories—including their underlying assumptions and the predictions they make—can make you a more competent communicator.

WHAT IS COMMUNICATION?

This text is concerned with communication theory, so it is important to be clear about the term *communication*. The everyday view of communication is quite different from the view of communication taken by communication scholars. In the business world, for example, a popular view is that communication is synonymous with information. Thus, the communication process is the flow of information from one person to another (Axley, 1984). Communication is viewed as simply one activity among many others, such as planning, controlling, and managing (Deetz, 1994). It is *what* we do in organizations.

Communication scholars, on the other hand, recognize communication as more than just the flow of information. In a simplified world in which a short YouTube clip could explain to viewers why communication is "easy," we could handily provide you with a one-sentence definition of the term *communication*. Based on that simple definition, we would all understand the meaning of the term, and we would all use the term in exactly the same way. However, scholars disagree as to the scope of the process, whether a source or receiver orientation should be taken, and whether message exchange need be successful to count as communication.

DANCE'S DEFINITIONS OF COMMUNICATION

Fundamentally, communication is a complex process associated with sending, receiving, and interpreting messages. Beyond that, however, the concept of **communication** is just not that easy to delineate. Back in 1976, Dance and Larson reported 126 published definitions of the term *communication*. The variations in the definitions were profound. Table 1.1 highlights the ways the definitions varied.

In looking at the multitude of definitions of communication, Dance (1970) identified three variations. First, Dance argued that definitions varied based on the **level of observation**, which he described as the scope of what is included in the definition. For example,

Dance (1967, as reported in Dance & Larson, 1976, Appendix A) defined communication as "eliciting a response through verbal symbols." This definition limits what is considered communication in two ways. First, it limits communication to only that which elicits a response. Consider an example where you instruct a co-worker to fill out a particular form. If that co-worker doesn't respond in any way, by this definition communication hasn't occurred. The second way this definition limits communication is in saying communication is only verbal. So if your co-worker gives you the "okay" gesture when you've asked her to fill out the report, her response to your request would not be considered communication, as it was purely nonverbal. Definitions that make such limitations are said to have a relatively narrow level of observation; only specific types of message exchanges "count" as communication. These types of definitions might suggest messages that don't meet the requirements to be considered communication are *informative* rather than *communicative*.

Other definitions, however, try to be very inclusive about behaviors that might be considered communication. To illustrate, another definition identified by Dance and Larson (1976) says communication is "all of the procedures by which one mind can affect another" (Weaver, 1949, as cited in Dance & Larson, Appendix A). Notice that this definition does not give any indication of whether the mind is of a human, an animal, or even an alien (if there are such things). More importantly, it suggests *all* behavior can count as communication. Such definitions are considered to have a broad level of observation. As such, the first way to differentiate between theories is to consider what "counts" as communication.

A second distinction made by Dance (1970) is the stance the definition takes on **intentionality**. Some definitions explicitly indicate that for communication to occur, the exchange of messages has to be on purpose. For example, Miller (1966) defined communication as "those situations in which a source transmits a message to a receiver with conscious intent to affect the latter's behaviors" (as cited in Dance & Larson, 1976, Appendix A). Definitions such as this one are said to take a **source orientation**. So, for example, if your boss were to yawn while you gave a presentation, this definition would not consider the yawn as communication if your boss did not yawn on purpose (i.e., if she yawned as a physiological response to tiredness rather than to suggest you were boring her).

Table 1.1 Ways Definitions Vary

Differences in Definitions	Stance	Taken
Level of observation: *Are there limitations on what counts as communication?*	**Narrow** *Yes*	**Broad** *No*
Intentionality: *Do only messages sent consciously and on purpose count?*	**Source** *Yes*	**Receiver** *No*
Normative judgment: *Does the message have to be successfully received to count as communication?*	**Evaluative** *Yes*	**Nonevaluative** *No*

However, other definitions take a **receiver orientation** to communication. Such definitions buy into the notion that "you cannot not communicate"; anything you say or do is potentially communicative, regardless of whether you intended to send a message or not (see Watzlawick, Bavelas, & Jackson, 1967). For example, Ruesch and Bateson (1961, as cited in Dance & Larson, 1976, Appendix A) say that "communication does not refer to verbal, explicit, and intentional transmission of messages alone. . . . The concept of communication would include all those processes by which people influence one another." In this case, if you (as the receiver) were to interpret your boss's yawn as a message of boredom, it should be considered communication, regardless of whether the boss intended to send that message or not.

The final way Dance (1970) argues that definitions of communication vary is **normative judgment**, which is a focus on whether the definition requires an indication of success or accuracy. Some definitions would suggest that even if people misunderstand each other, communication has still occurred. Berelson and Steiner (1964), for example, say communication is "the transmission of information, ideas, emotions, skills, etc., by the use of symbols—words, pictures, figures, graphs, etc. It is the act or process of transmission that is called communication" (as cited in Dance & Larson, 1976, Appendix A). In this case, it is the transmission that is important, not the understanding. So, if a student has no idea what a teacher is talking about, by this definition communication has still occurred, it just may not have been very effective communication. Definitions like this are said to be nonevaluative.

Other definitions limit communication to only those situations where the receiver and the source share the same understanding after the communicative effort. These definitions, identified as being evaluative, require shared meaning in order to be considered communication; unsuccessful messages are not considered to be communication. To illustrate, Gode (1959, as cited in Dance & Larson, 1976, Appendix A) defines communication as "a process that makes common to two or several what was the monopoly of one or some." This definition suggests that if the message has not resulted in a common understanding, communication has not occurred. In the example of student-teacher interaction described earlier, if the student doesn't understand the teacher, then by this definition the teacher has not communicated. She or he may have lectured, cajoled, or presented, but she or he has not communicated.

By now you understand some of the complexities of the nature of communication. Throughout the book, different theorists likely use different definitions of communication. Sometimes these variations in definition will be obvious, sometimes they will be less so. For example, systems theory (see Chapter 9) spends a great deal of time articulating the nature of communication. In so doing, it becomes clear that this theory takes a broad level of observation, a receiver orientation, and is nonevaluative. However, other theories only imply what they mean by communication. Poole and colleagues, in their adaptive structuration approach (see Chapter 8), never articulate their definition of communication. Because the theory is grounded in Giddens's sociological approach, however, we can assume they define communication in a similar fashion to Giddens, who defines communication as "a basis for understanding and bridging experiences, a way of creating social reality" (Giddens, 1976, as cited in Putnam, 1983, p. 51). As such, this theory also takes a broad level of observation, but the focus is more on intentional acts (source orientation), and by stressing the notion of understanding, it is more evaluative in nature.

CONTEXTS OF COMMUNICATION

Although we hesitate to provide a single definition of communication, we can identify some specific **contexts of communication**. In fact, we have organized this book around these specific contexts. The first context that requires consideration is the cognitive context, by which we mean the influence our thoughts have on the way we communicate. Relatedly, the second context is the individual differences context. Here we consider the nature-nurture debate. In so doing, we continue to consider how individual differences and social roles play a role in the communication process. Third is the interpersonal context, which refers to the interactions between two individuals, who most often have a relationship with each other. Fourth is the intercultural context, which focuses on interpersonal communication when two people are from different cultures. The fifth context is not specifically focused on a setting for communication but on a particular type of communication: the persuasive context. Readers should know that persuasion actually takes place in a variety of settings, ranging from inside one person's mind to the mass media. The sixth and seventh contexts are closely aligned with the world of work: the group context and the organizational context. Finally, the eighth context is the mediated context, which is concerned with how technology influences our interpersonal, group, and organizational communication. The ninth and final context is the mass communication context, which focuses on the influence of mass-mediated messages. Table 1.2 provides an overview of these contexts and the theories associated with each, theories covered in this text.

Table 1.2   Contexts of Communication

Context	Theories
Cognitive	<ul><li>Attribution theory</li><li>Uncertainty reduction theory</li><li>Expectancy violations theory</li><li>Cognitive dissonance</li></ul>
Individual and social	<ul><li>Social role theory of gender</li><li>Emotional intelligence</li><li>Message design logics</li><li>An interactional perspective on workplace generations</li></ul>
Interpersonal	<ul><li>Politeness</li><li>Social exchange theory</li><li>Dialectical perspective</li><li>Privacy management theory</li></ul>
Intercultural	<ul><li>Hofstede's cultural dimensions</li><li>Communication accommodation theory</li><li>Anxiety/uncertainty management theory</li><li>Face negotiation theory</li></ul>

Context	Theories
Persuasive	• Elaboration likelihood model • Theory of reasoned action/theory of planned behavior • Inoculation theory • Narrative paradigm
Group	• Functional group decision making • Groupthink • Adaptive structuration theory • Symbolic convergence theory
Organizational	• Organizational culture • Organizational assimilation • Organizational identification and control • Organizing theory
Mediated	• Diffusion of innovations • Social network analysis • Media richness theory • Uses and gratifications theory
Mass communication	• Agenda-setting theory • Cultivation theory • Social cognitive theory • Encoding/decoding theory

COMMUNICATION COMPETENCE

Because we believe one of the goals of studying communication theory is to make you a better communicator, we should articulate more clearly the nature of **communication competence**. Research indicates that communication competence is most often understood as achieving a successful balance between effectiveness and appropriateness (Spitzberg & Cupach, 1989). *Effectiveness* is the extent to which you achieve your goals in an interaction. Did you get the raise? Were you able to convince a subordinate that timeliness is important? Did you persuade your spouse to clean the bathroom? *Appropriateness* refers to fulfilling social expectations for a particular situation. Did you assertively ask for the raise, or was it a meek inquiry? Were you insistent or wishy-washy when discussing your employee's tardiness? Was your interaction with your spouse demonstrative or did you passive-aggressively pile dirty towels on the floor? Many times a person is effective without being appropriate; consider a job applicant who lies on a resume to get a job for which he or she is unqualified. That person might be very effective in getting the job, but is such deceit appropriate? On the other hand, many times people are appropriate to the point of failing to achieve their goals. For example, a person who doesn't wish to take on an additional task at work, but says nothing because he or she fears causing conflict, might be sacrificing effectiveness for appropriateness. The key is that when faced with

communicative decisions, the competent commun
and appropriate. We believe the theories described
communication goals by providing an indication o
how you should do it.

CONCEPTS, MODELS, AND THEORIES

The term **theory** is often intimidating to students. We h
this book you will find working with theory to be les
expected. The reality is that you have been working with
your life, even if they haven't been labeled as such. The
understanding of the communication process (Miller, 200.
they move beyond describing a single event by providing a ...eans by which all such events
can be understood. To illustrate, a theory of customer service can help you understand the
poor customer service you received from your cable company this morning. Likewise, the
same theory can also help you understand a good customer service encounter you had last
week at a favorite restaurant. In a professional context, the theory can assist your organization in training and developing customer service personnel.

At their most basic level, theories provide us with a lens by which to view the world.
Think of theories as a pair of glasses. Corrective lenses allow wearers to observe more
clearly, but they also affect vision in unforeseen ways. For example, they can limit the span
of what you see, especially when you try to look peripherally outside the range of the
frames. Similarly, lenses can also distort the things you see, making objects appear larger
or smaller than they really are. You can also try on lots of pairs of glasses until you finally
pick a pair that works best for your lifestyle. Theories operate in a similar fashion. A theory
can illuminate an aspect of your communication so you understand the process much
more clearly; theory also can hide things from your understanding or distort the relative
importance of things.

We consider a communication theory to be any systematic summary about the nature
of the communication process. Certainly, theories can do more than summarize. Other
functions of theories are to focus attention on particular concepts, clarify observations,
predict communication behavior, and generate personal and social change (Littlejohn,
1989). We do not believe, however, that all of these functions are necessary for a systematic
summary of communication processes to be considered a theory.

Although similar to at least two other terms, we want to be careful to differentiate theories from other abstract notions. First, a **concept** refers to an agreed-upon aspect of reality.
For example, *time* is a concept, as is *love*, the color *orange*, and a *bitter* taste. All of these
notions are abstract, meaning they can be applied to a variety of individual experiences or
objects and can be understood in different ways. That is, you might love your cat in a different way than you love your mother; you might think time drags when in a class you
don't much like but that it speeds up over the weekend; and you might hate the color
orange and love the bitterness of certain foods. However, in and of themselves these concepts are not theories; they represent an effort to define or classify something, but they do

ghts into how or why we experience them in a particular way. Typically, ide a way to predict or understand one or more concepts. So, a definition of ication described earlier is a concept, but how that definition is used to explain mmunication process is a theory.

A second term you might confuse with theory is a **model**. Part of the confusion you might experience is because the term *model* is used in at least four ways (Gabrenya, 2003; Goldfarb & Ratner, 2008): as a synonym to the term *theory*, as a precursor to a theory (a model is developed and eventually becomes a theory), as a physical representation of a theory (i.e., a diagram such as the one that appears for expectancy violations theory in Chapter 3), or as a specific—often mathematical—application of predication (e.g., a researcher might develop a mathematical model to predict which job categories are going to be in high demand in upcoming years). Because of these varying ways of understanding a model, we believe the term *theory* is preferable when talking about systematic summaries of the communication process.

THREE TYPES OF THEORY

Of central interest is the importance of theory for people in communication, business, and other professions. Our definition of theory suggests that any time you say a communication strategy *usually* works this way at your workplace, or that a specific approach is *generally* effective with your boss, or that certain types of communication are *typical* for particular media organizations, you are in essence providing a theoretical explanation. Most of us make these types of summary statements on a regular basis. The difference between this sort of theorizing and the theories provided in this book centers on the term *systematic* in the definition. Table 1.3 presents an overview of three types of theory.

The first summary statements in the table describe what is known as **commonsense theory**, or theory-in-use. This type of theory is often created by an individual's own personal experiences or developed from helpful hints passed on from family members, friends, or colleagues. Commonsense theories are useful because they are often the basis for our decisions about how to communicate. Sometimes, however, our common sense backfires. For example, think about common knowledge regarding deception. Most people believe that liars don't look the person they are deceiving in the eyes, yet research indicates this is not the case (DePaulo, Stone, & Lassiter, 1985). Let's face it: If we engage in deception, we will work very hard at maintaining eye contact simply *because* we believe liars don't make eye contact! In this case, commonsense theory is not supported by research into the phenomenon.

A second type of theory is known as **working theory**. These are generalizations made in particular professions about the best techniques for doing something. Journalists work using the "inverted pyramid" of story construction (most important information to least important information). Filmmakers operate using specific camera shots to evoke particular emotions in the audience, so close-ups are used when a filmmaker wants the audience to place particular emphasis on the object in the shot. Giannetti (1982), for example, describes a scene in Hitchcock's *Notorious* in which the heroine realizes she is being poisoned by her coffee, and the audience "sees" this realization through a close-up of the

Table 1.3 Three Types of Theory

Type of Theory	Example
Commonsense theory	• Never date someone you work with—it will always end badly. • The squeaky wheel gets the grease. • The more incompetent you are, the higher you get promoted.
Working theory	• Audience analysis should be done prior to presenting a speech. • To get a press release published, it should be newsworthy and written in journalistic style.
Scholarly theory	• Effects of violations of expectations depend on the reward value of the violator (expectancy violations theory). • The media do not tell us what to think but what to think about (agenda-setting theory).

coffee cup. Working theories are more systematic than commonsense theories because they represent agreed-on ways of doing things for a particular profession. In fact, these working theories may very well be based on scholarly theories. However, working theories more closely represent guidelines for behavior rather than systematic representations. These types of theories are typically taught in content-specific courses (such as public relations, media production, or public speaking).

The type of theory we focus on in this book is known as **scholarly theory**. Students often assume (incorrectly!) that because a theory is labeled as *scholarly* it is not useful for people in business and the professions. Instead, the term *scholarly* indicates that the theory has undergone systematic research. Accordingly, scholarly theories provide more thorough, accurate, and abstract explanations for communication than do commonsense or working theories. The downside is that scholarly theories are typically more complex and difficult to understand than commonsense or working theories. If you are genuinely committed to improving your understanding of the communication process, however, scholarly theory will provide a strong foundation for doing so.

EVALUATING THEORY

Earlier we suggested that all theories have strengths and weaknesses; they reveal certain aspects of reality and conceal others. An important task students and scholars face is to evaluate the theories available to them. We are not talking about evaluation in terms of "good" versus "bad" but evaluating the *usefulness* of the theory. Each of you is likely to find some of the theories presented in this text more useful than others. Such a determination is likely due at least in part to your own background and experiences, as well as your profession. We would like to challenge you to broaden your scope and consider not just the

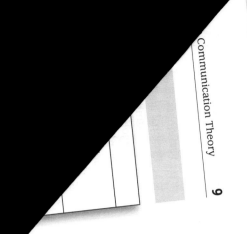

ı personally but the usefulness of the theory for people's
n general.

ards can be used to evaluate theories (e.g., Griffin, 2006;
007). All are appropriate and effective tools for comparing
heory. Because this text is geared toward working profes-
sh to soon be working in the profession of their choice),
ria outlined in Table 1.4 best capture the way to assess
nication theories in the communication, business, and
e talking about the *relative* usefulness of the theory. We
d or bad, weak or strong. Instead, we hope you look at
range from very useful at one end to not particularly

Table 1.4 Criteria for Evaluating Theory

Area of Evaluation	What to Look For
Accuracy	Has research supported that the theory works the way it says it does?
Practicality	Have real-world applications been found for the theory?
Succinctness	Has the theory been formulated with the appropriate number (fewest possible) of concepts or steps?
Consistency	Does the theory demonstrate coherence within its own premises and with other theories?
Acuity	To what extent does the theory make clear an otherwise complex experience?

The first area of focus is **accuracy**. Simply put, the best theories correctly summarize the way communication actually works. Recall, however, that we are referring to scholarly theories. As such, we do not mean accuracy in terms of whether the theory accurately reflects your own personal experience (although we would hope that it does!). Instead, when we use the term *accuracy* we are suggesting that systematic research supports the explanations provided by the theory. Thus, in assessing this quality, you should look at research studies that have used the theory to see whether the research supports or fails to support it.

A second way to evaluate theories is **practicality**. The best theories can be used to address real-world communication problems; in fact, Lewin (1951) said, "There is nothing so practical as a good theory" (p. 169). Clearly, some profound theories have changed the way we understand the world even though they aren't actually *used* by most people on a daily basis (Einstein's theory of relativity or Darwin's theory of evolution, for example). In terms of communication theories, however, theories that are accurate but can't be used in everyday life are not as good as theories that have great practical utility. For example, a theory that can help a person make better communicative decisions in his or her interactions with co-workers is better than a theory so abstract that it cannot be used by an individual in daily communication. Thus, a theory with more applications is better than a theory without practical uses. In assessing this criterion, you should look not only for how the theory has been used in the research literature but also whether the theory has made the leap to professional practice.

Succinctness is the third way to evaluate a good business or professional communication theory. *Succinctness* refers to whether or not a theory's explanation or description is sufficiently concise. Importantly, succinctness does not mean the theory is necessarily easy to understand or has only a few short steps; because the world is complex, theories trying to explain it are often fairly complex as well. Instead, what we mean by succinctness is whether the theory is formulated using as few steps as possible. The "three bears" analogy works here. Theories that have extra steps or include variables that don't help us understand real-world experiences would be considered overly complex. Theories that do not have enough steps, that don't delve beneath the surface, or that don't have enough variables to understand real-world problems are too simple. Theories that include no more and no less than necessary to understand a phenomenon thoroughly are considered just right; they are appropriately succinct. The best way to think of succinctness is to compare how much of the communication situation is explained by the theory in proportion to how many concepts are being used to explain it. The larger the situation and the smaller the number of necessary steps or concepts, the more succinct the theory.

The fourth way to evaluate a theory is to consider its **consistency**. The most useful theories have both internal and external consistency. By **internal consistency**, we mean the ideas of the theory are logically built on one another. A theory that proposes at one point that cooperation among team members guarantees success and at a different point proposes that competition is more effective than cooperation has a logical flaw. Similarly, theories that "skip" steps do not have much internal consistency. A theory predicting that age is related to the experience of jealousy and that one's expression of jealousy affects the future of the relationship, but then fails to tell us how the experience of jealousy is related to the expression of jealousy, has a logical gap. As such, it does not have strong internal consistency.

External consistency, on the other hand, refers to the theory's coherence with other widely held theories. If we presume that widely held theories are true, then the theory under evaluation that disagrees with those believed supported theories also presents a logical problem. As such, the notion of consistency, whether internal or external, is concerned with the logic of the theory. The most useful theories are those that have a strong logical structure.

The final area for evaluation is **acuity**. *Acuity* refers to the ability of a theory to provide insight into an otherwise intricate issue. Earlier we said theories evaluated as "succinct" are not necessarily easy to understand because the real world is often complicated. A theory that explains an intricate problem, however, is of greater value than a theory that explains something less complex. Think of acuity as the "wow" factor. If, after understanding the theory, you think "wow, I never considered that!" the theory has acuity. If, on the other hand, you think "no duh," the theory does not demonstrate acuity. To illustrate, a theory that explains a complex problem, such as how organizational cultures can influence employee retention, is a more useful theory than a theory that explains a relatively straight-forward problem, such as how to gain attention in a speech. Those theories that explain difficult problems show acuity; those that focus on fairly obvious problems demonstrate superficiality.

Summary

In this chapter, we discussed the popular perception of communication, which suggests that the communication process is paradoxically simple yet powerful. We identified three ways our understanding of communication can vary: the level of observation (what is included or not included in the definition), the role of intentionality (whether speaker intent is required), and normative judgment (whether success is required in order for an interaction to be considered communication). We then turned our attention to communication competence, indicating that competent communicators are those who can balance effectiveness and appropriateness. Next, we discussed the nature of theory. We differentiated between concepts, models, and theories. We also discussed the distinctions between commonsense theories, working theories, and scholarly theories. Finally, we provided a means by which scholarly theories of communication can be evaluated, namely accuracy, practicality, succinctness, consistency, and acuity.

Key Terms

Accuracy   10

Acuity   11

Commonsense theory   8

Communication   2

Communication competence   6

Concept   7

Consistency   11

Contexts of communication   5

External consistency   11

Intentionality   3

Internal consistency   11

Level of observation   2

Model   8

Normative judgment   4

Practicality   10

Receiver orientation   4

Scholarly theory   9

Source orientation   3

Succinctness   11

Theory   7

Working theory   8

Case Study 1: Education as Entertainment

Imagine a new theory has been proposed, described shortly. We challenge you to think critically about this theory using the concepts you have learned in this chapter.

In 1969 a radical new children's program appeared on television, one specifically designed to blend education with entertainment (characterproducts.com, 2004). *Sesame Street*, which has been on the air continuously for over 40 years, uses puppets, live action, and cartoons in an effort to teach children basic skills such as identifying colors, the ABCs, and counting. According to McMullin (2001), "The show employed principles of learning and developmental psychology in its presentation of academic and social skills" (para. 1). The show itself is highly researched, with a child psychologist in charge of research and evaluation of material that appears on the show (characterproducts.com, 2004; McMullin, 2001). McMullin argues that *Sesame Street* is the "single largest educator of young children in the world" (para. 2).

Despite the popularity and success of the program, we propose education as entertainment theory (EET), which suggests there is a dark side to educational programming such as *Sesame Street.* Specifically, the theory asserts that children exposed to television programming that seeks to blend education and entertainment are less likely to be motivated to learn when alternative instructional methods are used in an actual classroom setting. There are five key terms associated with this theory: *entertainment-education television programming*, *instructional style*, *expectations*, *motivation*, and *learning*.

Entertainment-education television programming. In 1990 the Children's Television Act (CTA) was approved by Congress (Federal Communications Commission, 2002). This act states that every broadcast television station in the United States must include educational programming, with at least 3 hours per week considered "core programming." Core programming, according to the FCC, is specifically designed to meet the educational needs of children under the age of 16, it must appear during the hours of 7:00 a.m. to 10:00 p.m., and it must be regularly scheduled. The CTA also limits the amount of commercial programming geared toward children. Research indicates that more children today are watching television at a younger age; a national survey found that 25% of children under the age of 2 have a television in their bedroom, and almost half watch television on a daily basis (Odland, 2004). This is partly because so much television is aimed at the preschool audience, with an educational bent. Yet "researchers are uncertain what the long-term implications will be of this media exposure; however, many studies have demonstrated that school performance improves when television viewing is limited," according to Odland (2004, p. 206B). EET argues that the reason school performance improves with limited television is an openness to instructional styles not focused on entertainment.

Instructional style. Instructional style refers to the techniques used in the education process. According to Forrest (2004), "A review of the research regarding learning processes suggests that instructors use a wide variety of teaching methods, believing that this affords all students an opportunity to gain the necessary knowledge, regardless of their learning styles" (p. 74).

The research makes a distinction between instructor-focused and student-focused teaching (Andersen, Nussbaum, Pecchioni, & Grant, 1999). Instructor-focused teaching is the traditional model, wherein the teacher is in charge of the pace and content of the class. Student-focused instruction encourages greater student participation, for example, cooperative learning (where students are put into groups or teams and teach and motivate each other) and class discussion (Andersen et al., 1999).

EET focuses on entertainment instructional style. This refers to efforts to make learning "fun." The entertainment instructional style relies on music, role playing, games, and visual stimulation, among other things. The goal is to increase interest and reduce boredom. Efforts are made to have students participate in the learning in an informal style (Handfield-Jones, Nasmith, Steinert, & Lawn, 1993).

Expectations. Expectations are what we anticipate will happen. In the case of EET, we are referring to expectations based on context, specifically, the learning context. According to Staton (1999), "Both instructors and students bring with them to the classroom certain expectations for the kind of speech that should and should not occur, for the kind of behavior that is and is not appropriate, for the roles that the instructor and students should and should not take, and for the nature of the social atmosphere that should and should not develop" (p. 35). In this case, we are specifically talking about expectations for entertaining instruction.

Motivation. Motivation refers to a student's desire for learning (Kerssen-Griep, Hess, & Trees, 2003). It is a drive for achievement in a particular course or content area. We presume that expectations influence motivation, such that when expectations are met, a student will be more motivated to learn. This is supported by research, which has found that instructional methods influence student motivation (Kerssen-Griep et al., 2003).

Learning. Learning is defined as "a process of progressive change from ignorance to knowledge, from inability to competence, and from indifference to understanding" (Fincher, 1994, as cited in Forrest, 2004, p. 74). According to Rubin (1999), learning is typically measured through assignments such as skills performance (e.g., a speech) or written assignments (exams, papers).

In summary, EET proposes that early childhood experiences with entertainment education programming (such as *Sesame Street*) increase an individual's expectations for an entertainment instructional style. If such expectations are met, the student will be more motivated and will learn more. If the expectations are not met, the student will be unmotivated, and will therefore learn less. This can be illustrated as follows.

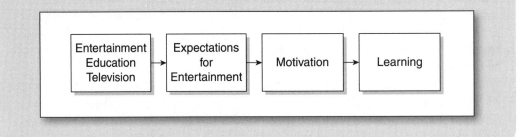

Questions for Consideration

1. The theorists associated with EET have not formally defined communication. Where do you think "communication" occurs in this theory (hint: consider the contexts listed in Table 1.2)? Provide evidence from the theory that might indicate how the theorists' views of communication might be classified using Dance's three ways definitions of communication vary.

2. Using the definition of communication competence provided in this chapter, what role might communication competence play in the EET process?

3. What are the concepts associated with EET? Why are these concepts (rather than theories or models)?

4. Which of the four types of models described in the chapter is used by the theory?

5. What do you think about EET? How do you think EET might fare if you evaluated its usefulness by using the criteria described in the chapter?

Theory Development

After reading this chapter, you will be able to...

1. Describe the differences between inductive theory and deductive theory, especially in terms of the theory development process.

2. Differentiate between primary and secondary research.

3. Explain the major research methods used by communication theorists, including what they reveal and what they conceal about the communication process.

4. Articulate why a particular research method is the appropriate method to answer a research question.

5. Recognize the differences between humanistic and social scientific approaches to communication study.

6. Summarize the ways theories change and grow.

In Chapter 1, we defined theory as "any systematic summary about the nature of the communication process." We further introduced the topic of scholarly theory, which is different from other forms of theory because it has been carefully researched. The focus of this chapter is on the methods by which scholarly theories are created, developed, and modified. Our first concern is the nature of how theory and research are related.

THEORY–RESEARCH LINK

As much as we would like to provide a simple answer to how theory and research are linked, we can't easily articulate the connection because of debate about the theory–research relationship akin to the classic question, "Which came first, the chicken or the egg?" In this case, scholars disagree as to what starts the process: theory or research.

Some scholars argue that research comes before theory. This approach is known as **inductive theory**. Scholars using inductive theory, also known as grounded theory, believe the best theories emerge from the results of systematic study (Glaser & Strauss, 1967). That is, these scholars study a particular topic, and, based on the results of their research, they develop a theory; the research comes *before* the theory. If someone wanted to develop a theory about how management style affects employee performance, then that person would study management style and employee performance in great depth before proposing a theory. Preliminary theories may be proposed, but the data continue to be collected and analyzed until adding new data brings little to the researcher's understanding of the phenomenon or situation.

On the other hand, some scholars believe in **deductive theory**. Deductive theory is generally associated with the scientific method (Reynolds, 1971). The deductive approach requires that a hypothesis, or working theory, be developed before any research is conducted. Once the theory has been developed, the theorist then collects data to test or refine the theory (i.e., to support or reject the hypothesis). What follows is a constant set of adjustments to the theory with additional research conducted until evidence in support of the theory is overwhelming. The resulting theory is known as a law (Reynolds, 1971). In short, deductive theory development starts with the theory and then looks at data. As an example, a researcher might start with the idea that supportive management styles lead to increased employee performances. The researcher would then seek to confirm his or her theory by collecting data about those variables.

As indicated earlier, these two approaches represent different starting points to what is in essence a "chicken or the egg" argument. But neither approach advocates a single cycle of theorizing or research. Instead, both approaches suggest theories are dynamic—they are modified as the data suggest, and data are reviewed to adjust the theory. Consider the model depicted in Figure 2.1. We believe this is the most accurate illustration of the link between theory and research. In this model, the starting points are different, but the reality of a repetitive loop between theory and research is identified.

Figure 2.1   The Theory–Research Link

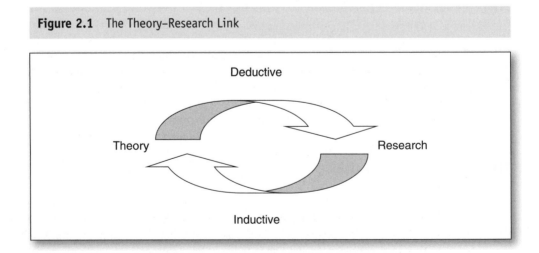

WHAT IS RESEARCH?

Because research is a fundamental part of theory development, we must turn our attention to the question of what counts as research. Frey, Botan, and Kreps (2002) described research as "disciplined inquiry that involves studying something in a planned manner and reporting it so that other inquirers can potentially replicate the process if they choose" (p. 13). Accordingly, we do not mean informal types of research, such as reflections on personal experience, off-the-cuff interviews with acquaintances, or casual viewing of communication media. When we refer to research, we mean the methodical gathering of data as well as the careful reporting of the results of the data analysis.

Note that *how* the research is reported differentiates two categories of research. **Primary research** is reported by the person who conducted it. It is typically published in peer-reviewed academic journals. **Secondary research** is reported by someone other than the person who conducted it. This is research reported in newspapers, popular or trade magazines, handbooks and textbooks, and, frequently, the Internet. Certainly, there is value to the dissemination of research through these media. Textbooks, for example, can summarize hundreds of pages of research in a compact and understandable fashion. The Internet can reach millions of people. Trade magazines can pinpoint the readers who may benefit most from the results of the research. Regardless of whether the source is popular or academic, however, primary research is typically valued more than secondary research as a source of information. With secondary research, readers risk the chance that the writers have misunderstood or inadvertently distorted the results of the research. Similar to the childhood game of "whisper down the lane," the message typically becomes more vague and less accurate as it gets passed from person to person.

RESEARCH METHODS IN COMMUNICATION

"The sheer volume of research we are exposed to in our daily lives is formidable and growing" (Crossen, 1994, p. 17). Even if you aren't an academic, and even if your job doesn't require you to conduct research, you are still inundated with research "facts" both at work and at home. Politicians cite polls and surveys to bolster their platforms. Advertisers cite research studies that indicate their product is superior. Organizations use research to make decisions for strategic planning. Even if you never conduct a research study in your life, understanding how research is performed will undoubtedly help you make more informed personal and professional decisions. This section focuses on the four research methods commonly used in the development of scholarly communication theory. When reading about these methods, pay particular attention to the types of information revealed and concealed by each method. This approach will allow you to be a better consumer of research.

Experiments

When people think of experiments, they often have flashbacks to high school chemistry classes. People are often surprised that communication scholars also use experiments, even though there isn't a Bunsen burner or beaker in sight. What makes something an experiment has nothing to do with the specific equipment or instruments involved; rather, experimentation is ultimately concerned with causation and control. It is important to emphasize that an **experiment** is the *only* research method that allows researchers to conclude that one thing causes another. For example, if you are interested in determining whether friendly customer service causes greater customer satisfaction, whether advertisers' use of bright colors produces higher sales, or whether sexuality in film leads to a more promiscuous society, the only way to determine these things is through experimental research.

Experimental research allows researchers to determine causality because experiments are so controlled. In experimental research, the researcher is concerned with two variables. A **variable** is simply any concept that has two or more values (Frey et al., 2002). Sex is a variable, because we have men and women. Note that just looking at maleness is not a variable because there is only one value associated with it; it doesn't *vary*, so it isn't a *variable*. Masculinity is considered a variable, however, because you can be highly masculine, moderately masculine, nonmasculine, and so on.

Returning to our discussion of experimental research, then, the research is concerned with two variables. One of the variables is the presumed cause. This is known as the **independent variable**. The other is the presumed effect. This is known as the **dependent variable**. If you are interested in knowing whether bright colors in advertisements cause increased sales, your independent variable is the color (bright versus dull), and the dependent variable is the amount of sales dollars (more, the same, or less). The way the researcher determines causality is by carefully controlling the study participants' exposure to the independent variable. This control is known as **manipulation**, a term that commonly conjures negative connotations but in the research world is imperative to establishing causality. In the study of advertisements just described, the researcher would expose some people to an advertisement that used bright colors and other people to an advertisement that used dull colors, and she or he would observe the effects on sales based on these manipulations.

Experiments take place in two settings. A **laboratory experiment** takes place in a controlled setting so the researcher might better control efforts at manipulation. In the communication field, laboratories often simulate living rooms or conference rooms. Typically, however, they have two-way mirrors and cameras mounted on the walls to record what happens. For example, John Gottman has a mini "apartment" at the University of Washington. He has married couples "move in" to the apartment during the course of a weekend, and he observes all of their interaction during that weekend.

Some experiments don't take place in the laboratory but in participants' natural surroundings; these are called **field experiments**. These experiments often take place in public places, such as shopping malls, libraries, or schools, but they might take place in private areas as well. In all cases, participants must agree to be a part of the experiment to comply with ethical standards set by educational and research institutions.

Surveys

The most common means of studying communication is through the use of surveys. Market research, audience analysis, and organizational audits all make use of surveys. Unlike experiments, the use of surveys does not allow researchers to claim one thing causes another. The strength of **survey research** is that it is the *only* way to find out how someone thinks, feels, or intends to behave. In other words, surveys capture people's perception. If you want to know what people think about your organization, how they feel about a social issue, or whether they intend to buy a product after viewing an advertising spot you created, you need to conduct a survey.

In general, there are two types of survey research. An **interview** asks participants to respond orally. It might take place face-to-face or over the phone. One special type of interview is a **focus group**, which is when the interviewer (called a facilitator) leads a small group of people in a discussion about a specific product or program (Frey et al., 2002). A **questionnaire** asks participants to respond in writing. It can be distributed by mail, via the Internet, or administered with the researcher present. Some research is more suited for interviews than questionnaires. Interviews allow the researcher to ask more complex questions because he or she can clarify misunderstandings through probing questions. Questionnaires, however, might be more appropriate for the collection of sensitive information because they provide more anonymity to the respondent (Salant & Dillman, 1994).

The key concepts associated with either type of survey research are questioning and sampling. First, the purpose of a survey is quite simple: to ask questions of a group of people to understand their thoughts, feelings, and behaviors. Questions might take two forms. **Open-ended questions** allow respondents to answer in their own words, giving as much (or as little) information as they would like. For example, a market researcher might ask study participants to describe what they like about a particular product. Or an interviewer might ask someone to respond to a hypothetical situation. **Closed-ended questions** require respondents to use set answers. In this case, a market researcher might say something like "Respond to the following statement: Product X is a useful product. Would you say you strongly agree, agree, neither agree nor disagree, disagree, or strongly disagree?" Neither method is better than the other; the two types of questions simply provide different kinds of data that are analyzed using different means.

The second key concept associated with survey research is **sampling**. Researchers are typically concerned with large groups of people when they conduct surveys. These groups are known as a **population**, which means all people who possess a particular characteristic (Frey et al., 2002). For example, marketing firms want to study all possible consumers of a product. Newspaper publishers want to gather information from all readers. Pharmaceutical industries want to study everyone with a particular ailment. The size of these groups makes it difficult to study everyone of interest. Even if every member of the population could be identified, which isn't always the case, studying all of them can be extremely expensive.

Instead, survey researchers study a sample, or a small number of people in the population of interest. According to a basic premise in statistics known as the law of large numbers (LLN), if a sample is well selected and of sufficient size, the survey's results are likely also to hold true for the entire group. A **random sample**, in which every member of the target group has an equal chance of being selected, is better than a **nonrandom sample**, such as volunteers, a convenience sample (college students), or a purposive sample (people who meet a particular requirement, such as age, sex, or race). Essentially, a random sample of consumers is more likely to give representative information about brand preferences than a convenience sample, such as stopping people at the mall on a particular day to answer a few questions.

Textual Analysis

The third method used frequently by communication scholars is textual analysis. A text is any written or recorded message (Frey et al., 2002). A website, a transcript of a medical encounter, and an employee newsletter can all be considered texts. **Textual analysis** is used to uncover the content, nature, or structure of messages. It can also be used to evaluate messages, focusing on their strengths, weaknesses, effectiveness, or even ethicality. So textual analysis can be used to study the amount of violence on television, how power dynamics play out during doctor–patient intake evaluations, or even the strategies used to communicate a corporate mission statement.

There are three distinct forms textual analyses take in the communication discipline. **Rhetorical criticism** refers to "a systematic method for describing, analyzing, interpreting, and evaluating the persuasive force of messages" (Frey et al., 2002, p. 229). There are numerous types of rhetorical criticism, including historical criticism (how history shapes messages), genre criticism (evaluating particular types of messages, such as political speeches or corporate image restoration practices), and feminist criticism (how beliefs about gender are produced and reproduced in messages).

Content analysis seeks to identify, classify, and analyze the occurrence of particular types of messages (Frey et al., 2002). It was developed primarily to study mass-mediated messages, although it is also used in numerous other areas of the discipline. For example, public relations professionals often seek to assess the type of coverage given to a client. Typically, content analysis involves four steps: the selection of a particular text (e.g., newspaper articles), the development of content categories (e.g., "favorable organizational coverage," "neutral organizational coverage," "negative organizational coverage"), placing the content into categories, and an analysis of the results. In our example, the results of this study would be able to identify whether a particular newspaper has a pronounced slant when covering the organization. One modern derivation of this type of research is **text mining**, also known as **data mining**. Data mining is the use of advanced "data analysis tools to discover previously unknown, valid patterns and relationships in large data sets" (Seifert, 2007, p. 2). Given the immense amount of information available on the Internet, organizations can use complex programs to sift through enormous amounts of data to uncover the frequency and uses of particular words or ideas.

The third type of textual analysis typically conducted by communication scholars is **interaction analysis** (also known as **conversation analysis**). These approaches typically focus on interpersonal or group communication interactions that have been recorded, with a specific emphasis on the nature or structure of interaction. The strength of this type of research is that it captures the natural give-and-take that is part of most communication experiences. The weakness of rhetorical criticism, content analysis, and interaction analysis is that *actual* effects on the audience can't be determined solely by focusing on texts.

Ethnography

Ethnography is the final research method used by scholars of communication. First used by anthropologists, **ethnography** typically involves the researcher immersing himself or herself into a particular culture or context to understand communication rules and meanings for that culture or context. For example, an ethnographer might study an organizational culture, such as Johnson & Johnson's corporate culture, or a particular context, such as communication in hospital emergency rooms. The key to this type of research is that it is naturalistic and emergent, which means it must take place in the natural environment for the group under study and the particular methods used adjusted on the basis of what is occurring in that environment.

Typically, those conducting ethnographies need to decide on the role they will play in the research. A **complete participant** is fully involved in the social setting, and the participants do not know the researcher is studying them (Frey et al., 2002). This approach, of course, requires the researcher to know enough about the environment to be able to fit in. Moreover, there are numerous ethical hurdles the researcher must overcome. Combined, these two challenges prevent much research from being conducted in this fashion. Instead, **participant–observer** roles are more frequently chosen. In this case, the researcher becomes fully involved with the culture or context, but he or she has admitted his or her research agenda before entering the environment. In this way, knowledge is gained firsthand by the researcher, but extensive knowledge about the culture is not necessarily a prerequisite (Frey et al., 2002). Researchers choosing this strategy may also elect which to emphasize more: participation or observation. Finally, a researcher may choose to be a **complete observer**. Complete observers do not interact with the members of the culture or context, which means they do not interview any of the members of the group under study. As such, this method allows for the greatest objectivity in recording data, while simultaneously limiting insight into participants' own meanings of the observed communication.

Communication scholars use four primary research methods: experiments, which focus on causation and control; surveys, which focus on questioning and sampling; textual analysis, which focuses on the content, nature, or structure of messages; and ethnography, which focuses on the communication rules and meanings in a particular culture or context. A summary of the strengths and weaknesses of each of the four methods is summarized in Table 2.1.

Table 2.1 Four Methods of Communication Research

Research Method	What It Reveals	What It Conceals
Experiments	Cause and effect	Whether the cause–effect relationship holds true in less controlled environments
Surveys	Respondents' thoughts, feelings, and intentions	Cannot establish causality; cannot determine what people actually do
Textual analysis	The content, nature, and structure of messages	The effect of the message on receivers
Ethnography	Rules and meanings of communication in a culture or context	May provide a highly subjective (and therefore biased) view of the culture or context

Because this textbook is oriented toward students who are likely to use theory and research in the professional realm, we wish to make clear that people who work in the professions also use research, although that research is not used to develop scholarly theory (although it might be used to develop or refine a working theory). Marketing and PR professionals, human resources executives, and managers in many industries conduct research as part of the creation and assessment of campaigns, for strategic planning, and for decision making. Like academics, professionals also use experiments (typically for product testing), surveys (especially focus groups), textual analysis (especially media monitoring), and ethnographies of a sort (typically observations of how customers use a product).

SOCIAL SCIENCE AND THE HUMANITIES

Thus far, we have talked about the central role research plays in the development of theories and how research comes either before creating the theory (in the case of inductive theory development) or after (in the case of deductive theory development). The reason for these differing approaches can be traced back to philosophical divisions within the field of communication. Communication has been described as both an art and a science (Dervin, 1993). On one hand, we respect the power of a beautifully crafted and creatively designed advertisement. On the other hand, we look to hard numbers to support decisions about the campaign featuring that advertisement. Although art and science are integrally related in the everyday practice of communication, in the more abstract realm of theory the two are often considered distinct pursuits. This concept can be traced to distinctions between the academic traditions of the humanities (which includes the arts) and the social sciences.

You might have some ideas about the terms *humanistic* and *social scientific* because most college students are required to take some courses in each of these areas. The distinctions between the humanities and social science are based on more than just tradition, however; they are based on very different philosophical beliefs. The interpretation of meaning is of central concern in the humanities (Littlejohn, 2002). Meaning is presumed to be subjective and unique to the individual, even though meaning is likely influenced by social processes. For individuals trained in the **humanistic approach**, **subjectivity** is a hallmark; one's own **interpretation** is of interest. Think about the study of English literature, a discipline at the heart of the humanities. English scholars study the interpretation of texts in an effort to understand the meaning of the object of study.

On the other hand, **objectivity** is a central feature of social science. Social scientists believe that through careful standardization (i.e., objectivity), researchers can observe patterns of communication that can hold true for all (or most) people, all (or most) of the time. These patterns that hold true across groups, time, and place are known as **generalizations**. To illustrate, psychology is a discipline rooted in the social sciences. As such, psychology scholars seek to explain general principles of how the human mind functions. These principles are intended to explain all people, all over the world, throughout history.

Because the humanities and social sciences have different areas of interest, they treat theory and research differently. Table 2.2 seeks to identify some of those distinctions. The first area of difference is the philosophical commitment to understanding the nature of human beings and the extent of their free will. Certainly, no one believes human beings are mere puppets who have no choice in how they behave. Communication theorists vary, however, in the extent to which they believe people *act* versus *react* to communication. For example, social scientists tend to follow **determinism**, which means they believe past experience, personality predispositions, and a number of other antecedent conditions *cause* people to behave in certain ways. Accordingly, deterministic approaches to human interaction propose that people in general tend to react to situations. Social scientists tend to look at the causes and effects of communication, such as what causes a marriage to fail or the effects of a particular marketing campaign.

Table 2.2 Differences Between Social Scientific and Humanistic Approaches to Communication

Issue	Social Science	Humanities
Belief about human nature	Determinism	Pragmatism
Goal of theory	Understand and predict	Understand only
Process of theory development	Deductive	Inductive
Focus of research	Particularism	Holism
Research methods	Experiments, quantitative survey, and textual analysis	Ethnography, qualitative survey, and textual analysis

Conversely, most humanists believe people have control over their behavior and make conscious choices to communicate to meet their goals. Theorists taking this stance are called pragmatists because they believe people are practical and plan their behavior. **Pragmatism** believes human beings are not passive reactors to situations but dynamic actors. Humanists, then, tend to focus on the choices people make, such as the choice of strategies used by major financial companies like Merrill Lynch to explain corporate bonuses after the financial bailout.

A second way to differentiate between humanistic and social scientific scholarship is through a focus on *why* theories are developed. For example, the goal of social scientific theory is to both understand and predict communication processes. Because social science is interested in generalizations, the ability to predict is paramount. If a theorist understands the general pattern at the heart of a social scientific theory, she or he should be able to predict how any one individual might communicate. Those in the humanities, however, believe interpretations are always subjective; they are unique to the individual. Accordingly, humanists believe theorists can never actually predict how a person will behave; all that can be done is to try to understand human communication.

Although not directly related to the distinction between social science and the humanities, we note that some theories strive to do more than simply predict or understand. A special group of theories, called critical approaches, seeks to improve the world through social change. The goal of critical theory is to empower people in their professional and personal lives. For more information on critical communication theory, see Craig (1999).

The third difference between social science and the humanities is the process of theory development. Recall our discussion of the theory–research link discussed earlier in the chapter. Deductive theory is based on the scientific method, so it should be no surprise that the **social scientific approach** to theory development is *deductive*. Those in the humanities, however, tend to start with data and subsequently develop theory. For example, scholars of English literature would start with reading Shakespeare's plays before developing a theory about them. Thus, those in the humanities tend to use inductive theory development.

Finally, the focus and methods of research also vary in the social scientific and humanistic approaches. The focus of research for the social scientific method is on standardization and control. Because of these objectives, social scientists incrementally study narrowly defined areas at a time, believing the whole picture will be uncovered eventually. This approach is known as particularism. Humanists, on the other hand, believe in looking at the big picture; they propose that all pieces of the puzzle contribute to an understanding of the problem. Accordingly, they use holism, looking at the situation in its entirety, as the focal point of research.

Given the different areas of focus, it's not a surprise that the final difference between social scientists and humanists is the research methods they use. Earlier in this chapter, we discussed the four research methods used by communication scholars. Of the four, one is clearly social scientific, and one is clearly humanistic. Experimental methods, with their concern for causation and control, are uniquely suited for the social sciences. Remember that social science seeks to make predictions, and the best way to do that is to have research that supports particular causes and effects. Similarly, ethnography is uniquely suited for humanistic research. Ethnography leans to the understanding of communication in contexts and cultures, which is appropriate for theory that uses holism in its quest for interpretation of communicative events.

The uses of survey research and textual analysis cannot be easily classified. Instead of the methods themselves being associated with either social science or the humanities, the specific way data are analyzed determines whether the method is social scientific or humanistic. The two methods of data analysis are quantitative and qualitative. Quantitative methods are adapted from those used in the hard sciences, such as chemistry and biology. Accordingly, quantitative methods are associated with social science. Qualitative methods are those that have historically been used by the humanities.

Quantitative methods typically rely on numbers or statistics as the data source (Reinard, 1998). These data and statistics are generally explanatory and comprehensive; they seek to predict what will happen for large groups of people. To accomplish this, researchers control the study by identifying the variables of interest before data collection takes place and trying to prevent extraneous influences from affecting the data. As described earlier, these commitments allow social scientists to make generalizations.

Qualitative methods reject the limitations on individual interpretation that control requires. Moreover, qualitative research eschews the use of numbers and uses verbal descriptions of communicative phenomena. Typically, the data are in the form of extended quotes or transcripts of communication. Finally, qualitative research typically centers on a description or critique of communication rather than on generalizations (Reinard, 1998).

Social scientists tend to use quantitative surveys or textual analyses. For example, they'll collect data about how many people prefer a new formulation of a product versus a previous formulation of a product or how frequently a manager uses a particular communication strategy in interaction. Humanists tend to use qualitative surveys and textual analyses. They ask participants to respond at length to questions in their own words about a particular product, or they identify various communication themes evident in a corporate brochure.

A final note should be made about the distinctions between social science and the humanities. The purpose of talking about these two academic traditions is because communication is *both* social scientific and humanistic. As such, you shouldn't view these distinctions as dichotomies but as continua. Individual theories may be more or less social scientific or humanistic (not either/or), with elements borrowed from both traditions.

HOW THEORIES CHANGE AND GROW

Our final concern in this chapter is to be clear that once developed, theories continue to change and grow. As we indicated in Figure 2.1, whether a researcher starts with the theory or starts with research, theory development continues the loop between research and theory, refining, modifying, and extending the theory. Specifically, Kaplan (1964) argues that theories can change by extension or by intention. Growth by **extension** means the theory adds more concepts and builds on what was already established. For example, in 1959 Thibaut and Kelley created interdependence theory, which is described in Chapter 5. One central aspect of the theory is the prediction that relationship dependence (otherwise known as commitment) can be determined by examining an individual's satisfaction with the relationship, as well as his or her perception of the availability and quality of alternatives to the relationship. Caryl Rusbult (1980), a student of John Thibaut, continued working on the theory and presented an expanded version of the theory, which she called the investment model. Her model argues that looking at satisfaction and alternatives is not enough to predict commitment; one also has to examine how much an individual has invested in the relationship. That is, people who are unhappy in their relationship, and who believe they can find a better partner, might stay in the relationship because they have invested a great deal of time, money, or even love, and they don't want to "lose" their investment. Thus, we can conclude that interdependence theory has grown through extension because a new concept—investment—was added to the theory to make its predictions more robust.

Conversely, growth by **intension** means scholars gain a deeper and more nuanced understanding of the original concepts presented in the theory. For example, communication accommodation theory, which is described in Chapter 6, was originally called speech accommodation theory, as the focus was purely on how our dialects and word choice varied based on to whom an individual was speaking. However, researchers quickly realized that accommodation occurs in other areas of verbal and nonverbal communication, such as speaking rate, politeness, and listening (see Gallois, Ogay, & Giles, 2005, for a review). The theory has grown by intension; the same principles of accommodation are still acknowledged by the theory, and no new concepts were added. Instead, additional research has allowed scholars to understand more fully the complex ways accommodation occurs, adding to the scope of the theory.

Summary

In this chapter, we looked at how theories are developed and changed. We looked at two ways to create theory: inductive and deductive theory development. We discussed the links between theory and research, and we differentiated between primary and secondary research. We also identified the four primary research methods used by communication scholars: experiments, surveys, textual analysis, and ethnography. In addition to describing the key elements of each of these methods, the chapter focused on what each reveals and conceals about communication. Next we turned our attention to the differences between social scientific and humanistic approaches to theory and research, centering our discussion on beliefs about human nature, the goal of theory, the development of theory, the focus of research, and the research methods used. Finally, we talked about how theories change through the processes of extension and intention.

Key Terms

Closed-ended questions   21
Complete observer   23
Complete participant   23
Content analysis   22
Deductive theory   18
Dependent variable   20
Determinism   25
Ethnography   22
Experiment   20
Extension   27
Field experiment   20
Focus group   21
Generalization   24
Humanistic approach   24
Independent variable   20
Inductive theory   18
Intension   27
Interaction analysis/conversation analysis   22
Interpretation   24
Interview   21
Laboratory experiment   20

Manipulation   20
Nonrandom sample   21
Objectivity   24
Open-ended questions   21
Participant-observer   23
Population   21
Pragmatism   25
Primary research   19
Qualitative   26
Quantitative   26
Questionnaire   21
Random sample   21
Rhetorical criticism   22
Sampling   21
Secondary research   19
Social scientific approach   26
Subjectivity   24
Survey research   21
Text/data mining   22
Textual analysis   22
Variable   20

Case Study 2: Education as Entertainment Reconsidered

In Chapter 1 you were introduced to a theory called EET. We want you to reconsider EET, relying on what you learned in this chapter, as well as the following additional information.

In order to test EET, we conducted a survey. We created a questionnaire, which asked about age, sex, the frequency of viewing *Sesame Street* and other educational programming, and expectations for instructional style, motivation, and perceived learning. For the expectations for instructional style, motivation, and perceived learning we asked survey respondents to respond to the four teaching styles using a 1-to-5 Likert-type scale, with 1 representing "not at all" and 5 indicating "always."

Survey

On average, how often did you watch educational television (for example, *Sesame Street*) when you were a child? (circle one)   *Not at All | Very Little | Occasionally | Every Week | Every Day*

To what extent do you *expect* college professors to use the following teaching styles (check one for each style)?

	Not at All	Very Little	Occasionally	Frequently	Always
Lecture					
Class discussion					
Group activities					
Entertainment (e.g., films, games)					

To what extent would each style *motivate* you to want to learn (check one for each style)?

	Not at All	Very Little	Occasionally	Frequently	Always
Lecture					
Class discussion					
Group activities					
Entertainment (e.g., films, games)					

To what extent do you think you *actually* learn using the following styles (check one for each style)?

	Not at All	Very Little	Occasionally	Frequently	Always
Lecture					
Class discussion					
Group activities					
Entertainment (e.g., films, games)					

We distributed the questionnaire to 75 current college students and 75 adults over the age of 50. We choose age 50 because those individuals would have been in school already when *Sesame Street* appeared. There were 58 female and 17 male college students. There were 51 female and 14 male adults.

Our results showed that the average amount of educational television viewing was 3.7 out of 5 for the college students, corresponding to viewing such programs every week. The average amount of educational viewing was 2.2 for the adults, corresponding to very little viewing. Accordingly, the college students viewed more educational programming than the adults did as children.

The remaining average answers are calculated in the following chart, with the instructional style listed in the far-left column and the mean expectation, motivation, and learning score for the two groups in the remaining columns.

Teaching Style	*Expect* College	*Expect* Adult	*Motivate* College	*Motivate* Adults	*Learn* College	*Learn* Adult
Lecture	4.7	4.8	2.4	3.2	4.1	4.2
Discussion	3.9	3.6	3.6	4.2	4.3	4.2
Group	3.4	3.2	2.9	3.2	2.6	3.2
Entertain	3.2	2.9	4.4	3.2	2.6	2.8

In looking at the chart, the only significant difference when considering entertainment education is in motivation, with college students reporting being motivated by entertainment education to a larger extent than adults. However, neither group seems to expect a whole lot of entertainment education, and neither group reports learning a lot from entertainment education. Thus, the predictions of EET are not fully supported.

Questions for Consideration

1. Based on what you read in Chapter 1 and the additional information just provided, was EET developed using an inductive or a deductive theory development process? Why?

2. What type of research (primary or secondary) was used in the development of EET? Was this a good choice?

3. Which research method was used to test the theory? Is this the appropriate method? Why or why not?

4. Is EET social scientific or humanistic? Provide details from the information in Chapter 1 and this chapter to support your case.

5. In what ways do you think EET should change or grow in the future? Be specific in detailing how it might change and why it should change in that manner.

Cognition and Intrapersonal Communication

After reading this chapter, you will be able to...

1. Explain the cognitive process and the importance of cognition in communicating and creating meaning with others.

2. Articulate how theories are developed and refined as shown in the development of attribution theory.

3. Explain and identify attribution biases that affect accurately determining intentionality of behavior.

4. Make predictions about the intentionality of behavior using Kelley's covariation model (consensus, consistency, distinctiveness, and locus of control).

5. Identify types of uncertainty and antecedent conditions for reducing uncertainty.

6. Explain, apply, and evaluate the axioms associated with uncertainty reduction theory.

7. Explain and apply strategies for reducing uncertainty in specific situations.

8. Predict the effectiveness of uncertainty reduction strategies in different contexts.

9. Describe how context, relationship, and a communicator's characteristics influence expectations in a given situation.

10. Explain and apply the concepts of expectancy, violation valence, and communicator reward valence so as to predict whether someone will reciprocate or compensate a violation.

11. Combine elements of uncertainty reduction theory with expectancy violation theory to explain how a violation can increase or decrease relational uncertainty.

12. Explain and identify the three possible relationships associated between beliefs and behaviors: irrelevance, consonance, and dissonance.

(Continued)

(Continued)

13. Articulate the four perceptual processes associated with minimizing dissonance: selective exposure, attention, interpretation, and retention.

14. Explain how, by increasing or decreasing the magnitude of dissonance between beliefs and behaviors, one can influence or prevent change.

15. Illustrate how cognitive dissonance theory is a postdecision theory.

16. Compare and contrast major theoretical approaches to intrapersonal communication.

Regardless of whether you take a source or receiver orientation to communication, messages have no meaning without an individual's interpretation. Everyone has to process every message internally while considering how best to make sense of these messages. In other words, meaning is derived only after an individual perceives a message and gives it meaning; meaning resides in our *interpretations* of words or actions, not in the words or behaviors themselves. Consequently, communication is also an intrapersonal process.

COGNITIVE PROCESS

The roots of communication as an intrapersonal process can be traced to one of the major debates in psychology in the 20th century. At the beginning of the 1900s, American psychology was dominated by a focus on **behaviorism** (Runes, 1984). Most of us are familiar with Pavlov and his studies of salivary production in dogs. By associating the ringing of a bell with food, Pavlov was able to experimentally cause dogs to salivate when hearing a bell, even if the food was not present. Such is a description of a behavioral approach—a focus on external cause and behavioral effect. Major psychological figures such as J. B. Watson and B. F. Skinner argued that because we cannot observe mental processes, we should focus only on these causes and effects (Runes, 1984).

However, in the middle part of the 1900s, psychologists began arguing for a **cognitive** approach to understanding human behavior. Rather than focusing solely on external causes (or stimuli) and behavioral effects, these scholars argued we should be concerned with the mental processes used to process stimuli and generate particular effects (Runes, 1984). A major proponent of this approach was Noam Chomsky, who spearheaded a significant critique of behaviorism. **Cognition**, then, includes the processes of reducing, elaborating, transforming, and storing stimuli (Neisser, 1967). It refers to what happens in the mind that causes us to behave in particular ways.

In this chapter, we explain four theories that examine the cognitive and intrapersonal aspects of communication. First, attribution theory explains the process by which individuals assign causation or motivation to their own and others' behavior. The second theory presented in this chapter, uncertainty reduction theory, strives to explain and predict initial encounters with people. In other words, what drives you to initiate communication, and how do you go about reducing your uncertainty in a new situation? Third, expectancy violations theory seeks to predict and explain people's behavior when their expectations about what will happen are breached. The fourth theory presented, cognitive dissonance theory, explains and predicts how persuasion may be understood as a self-induced, intrapersonal event.

Altogether these theories emphasize the internal processes that serve as antecedents to the highly personalized creation of meaning, and each perspective applies to numerous communication contexts. From making judgments about a co-worker based on her behavior as compared to others (i.e., attribution theory) to determining how best to reduce one's uncertainty during a job transfer (i.e., uncertainty reduction theory), each of the theories presented illustrates the internally driven process necessary to bring individual meaning to various messages.

ATTRIBUTION THEORY

According to attribution theorists, human beings often work like naïve detectives, continually trying to understand and make sense of what inspired various events, personal mannerisms, and individuals' conduct. Just as a crime scene investigator pieces together clues in an effort to determine a suspect's motive, you, too, go through life picking up clues and making judgments about what you believe influenced your own and others' behavior. These judgments and conclusions that provide reasons for behavior are called **attributions**. Attribution theory, then, explains the cognitive process one uses when trying to make causal explanations for behavior.

Attributions as Naïve Psychology

Attribution theory is not a new concept; researchers have long studied the ways in which people process events and then derive explanations for them. In the mid-1950s, however, Heider (1958) focused his attention on the process of drawing inferences—the assumptions individuals make regarding the causes of behavior as well as the judgments made about who is responsible for that behavior. According to Heider, individuals act as "naïve psychologists." When you see a person act, you immediately make judgments about the causal nature of the conduct. Specifically, Heider found that individuals try to determine whether a behavior in question was caused by dispositional or situational factors. Dispositional factors refer to internal or personal features, such as one's personality, character, or biological traits. These factors are relatively stable and unique to each individual. Conversely, situational factors refer to external dynamics that are relatively uncontrollable and determined by the environment or circumstance at hand. External factors obviously vary to a much greater extent than do internal factors because they are inherently based on the context of a given situation, not on more stable personality traits.

For example, if, at your monthly staff meeting, Ron's presentation of current sales figures appears disjointed and jumbled, you might attribute his awkwardness to the fact that his PowerPoint slides failed to upload properly onto the laptop. Here, the inference made suggests that because of the situation (i.e., defective software), Ron was forced to give the presentation from memory and without visual aids. Thus, you might attribute Ron's bumbled speech to a technological glitch, thereby making a situational attribution for his behavior. On the other hand, you might attribute Ron's poor presentation to his lack of preparation (i.e., a character flaw). Surely by now everyone knows not to rely solely on PowerPoint; Ron should have come prepared with a backup plan ready in case of technical difficulties. Looking at the situation this way, you might blame Ron's failed presentation on his lazy preparation—something within his personal control, thereby making an internal attribution.

Correspondent Inference Theory

Expanding Heider's work, Jones and Davis (1965) were concerned with the intentionality of dispositional (internally driven) behavior. They argued that when a perceiver attributes the cause of a behavior to dispositional factors, the perceiver also makes judgments about the actor's intentions. Jones and Davis referred to these judgments of intention as correspondent inferences.

As Texter (1995) noted, "Before we can draw correspondent inferences from observing a person's behavior, we must make a determination about the person's intention: Did the person intentionally act in a certain way, knowing the effects the behavior would have?" (p. 55). When a dispositional inference mirrors an action and the perceiver labels the disposition and the action similarly (e.g., lazy), these inferences are said to "correspond." For instance, you might infer the disposition of laziness or apathy from Ron's seemingly lazy preparation for the meeting.

Determining the intentionality of an act is not easy; however, there are several factors one can consider when determining the purpose of another's behavior: choice, assumed desirability, social role, prior expectations, hedonic relevance, and personalism (Jones & Davis, 1965). Beginning with choice, individuals can assess an actor's intention by examining whether the actor in question had any alternatives. If you perceive alternative courses of action, you are also likely to assume the "selected" behavior was deliberate. Second, you can assess intentions by focusing on the assumed **social desirability** of the actor's actions. That is, if a person behaves in a manner contrary to social conventions, you are more likely to infer that the behavior reflects the person's true character and not merely an attempt at social correctness. Similarly, an actor's social role, or public position, can help determine the intentionality of a behavior, particularly when this person behaves in a manner contrary to the prescribed role.

Just as one's position affects expectations and assumptions of intentionality, so do prior expectations of that individual. Thus, your previous encounters with an actor, or knowledge about the person's background, may influence your assessments about the actor's intentions. **Hedonic relevance**, or the degree to which you believe an actor's behavior directly affects you (either positively through rewards or negatively through punishment), also shapes your assessment of the actor's intentions. The greater you perceive the hedonic relevance, the more likely you are to view the actor's behavior as deliberate. Last, **personalism** refers to the belief that an actor specifically and intentionally behaves in ways to hurt or help you. Thus, if you assume a person's behavior changes when you are not present, you may imagine the actions are intentional. Notably, although each of these six factors can aid in assessing an actor's intentions, relying on any of these reasons may lead to biased judgments of an actor's disposition.

Kelley's Covariation Model

Perhaps a more holistic approach to attribution theory, Kelley's (1967, 1973) covariation model explains the causal nature of the complete attribution process. Specifically, this model has a greater scope than does Jones and Davis's correspondent inference theory because Kelley seeks to explain attributions overall, whereas Jones and Davis focused only on the intentionality of dispositional inferences.

According to Kelley (1967, 1973), individuals judge the causality of another's behavior by examining four factors: consensus, consistency, distinctiveness, and controllability. When the first three of these features are combined (i.e., consensus, consistency, distinctiveness), a perceiver can judge whether the actions were internally controlled (i.e., disposition) or externally controlled (i.e., situational). That is, you assign meaning based on perceived controllability—how much command an individual had over the behavior in question.

First, the perceiver determines if an actor's behavior demonstrates **consensus**, that is, would other people react similarly if placed in the same situation? The more you observe people behaving similarly, the greater the perception of consensus. If Rebecca storms out of the quarterly sales meeting in a huff and snarls at everyone in her path while the other members of the sales team leave the meeting with smiles and small talk, low consensus has occurred. If, however, everyone on the sales team heads out of the meeting sporting a grimace and a foul mood, then you have observed high consensus.

Second, the perceiver must determine whether the actor's behavior demonstrates consistency. **Consistency** refers to whether the person in question engages in similar behaviors over time. Comparable to consensus, the more you observe an actor engaging in the same behavior, the greater your perception of consistency. If Rebecca always seems to be angry and rude to colleagues, then you would say that her ill-tempered behavior after the sales meeting is highly consistent with her previous behavior. Conversely, if you typically view Rebecca as pleasant and enthusiastic, you would conclude that her sudden change of behavior has low consistency.

Third, a perceiver judges an actor's **distinctiveness**, that is, whether the person acts differently depending on the situation. Unlike consensus and consistency, which increase with others' conformity and number of observances over time, distinctiveness decreases when the actor behaves similarly across many situations. That is, a behavior is only labeled distinctive if it is "markedly different in one situation or task from others" (Texter, 1995, p. 60). Continuing with our example, if Rebecca speaks rudely and demonstrates hostility toward everyone in the company, to her friends, to her children, and to her neighbors, then Rebecca's offensive mannerisms have low distinctiveness because her rudeness is not unique. On the other hand, if Rebecca's anger and disrespectful tone occurred only after this one meeting and in no other meetings or situations, then you would conclude this behavior is highly distinctive because it appears contrary to the other circumstances in her life.

As mentioned earlier, by combining these judgments of consensus, consistency, and distinctiveness, the perceiver can determine the controllability of the actor's behavior. For example, you suppose an **interior locus of control** when you believe the actor could have controlled the behavior. Alternatively, you assume an **exterior locus of control** when the behavior appears to have been unavoidable.

Considered individually, predications made using any single variable (i.e., consensus, consistency, or distinctiveness) may provide and incomplete picture. However, by combining the judgments of consensus, consistency, and distinctiveness, eight possible combinations result. It is the combination of variables that allow the perceiver to predict with greater accuracy the controllability of the actor's behavior as either internally or externally motivated (Kelley, 1973).

Specifically, an external (or situational) attribution is made about the individual when consensus is high, consistency is low, and distinctiveness is high. For example, if Rebecca and her entire team leave the sales meeting angry (high consensus), and Rebecca doesn't usually leave meetings in a huff (low consistency), and Rebecca is usually pleasant around the office, not bad-tempered (high distinctiveness), we will assume that something happened at the meeting (the situation) to cause the unpleasant mood. Conversely, an internal (or dispositional) attribution is made about another person when consensus is low, consistency is high, and distinctiveness is low. Returning to the previous example, if only Rebecca leaves the sales meeting angry while the rest of the team is jovial (low consensus), and Rebecca often leaves the sales meetings in a huff (high consistency), and Rebecca snaps at people at work, at home, and at church (low distinctiveness), we can assume that it's Rebecca's disposition influencing her behavior. A summary of the predictions of Kelley's covariation model are in Table 3.1.

To review, attribution theorists have emphasized various explanations for the attributions you make in assigning the causes and motivations of your own and others' behavior. Whereas Heider examined the causal location of dispositional and situational sources of behavior, Jones and Davis focused more narrowly on determining the perceived intent that drives dispositional behavior. Kelley broadened the scope of attribution theory by examining the interplay of consensus, consistency, and distinctiveness.

Table 3.1 Types of Attributions Based on Kelley's Predictions

Consensus	"Do other people act this way?"
	If **yes**, an external attribution is likely. If **no**, an internal attribution is likely.
Consistency	"Has this person behaved similarly **many times** before?"
	If **yes**, an internal attribution is likely. If **no**, an external attribution is likely.
Distinctiveness	"Has this person behaved similarly in other **types of situations**?"
	If **yes**, an internal attribution is likely. If **no**, an external attribution is likely.

UNCERTAINTY REDUCTION THEORY

The second intrapersonal theory discussed here is uncertainty reduction theory (URT). Berger and Calabrese's (1975) URT holds that social life is filled with ambiguities. Not knowing what to wear on the first day at a new job (Should I wear a suit or go with business casual?), uncertainty as to how to greet a new boss (Should I call her Megan? Ms. Smith? Mrs. Smith? Dr. Smith?), and wondering whether you will get along with the new office mate who just transferred from another location (Will she bother me with questions? Will he gossip about team members?) are just a few typical concerns during an average workday. Guided by several assumptions and **axioms** of human behavior, URT seeks to explain and predict when, why, and how individuals use communication to minimize their doubts when interacting with others.

Three assumptions guide the uncertainty reduction framework. First, Berger and Calabrese (1975) maintained that the primary goal of communication is to minimize uncertainties humans have about the world and the people therein. Second, they proposed that individuals experience uncertainty on a regular basis and that the experience of uncertainty is an unpleasant one. Third, Berger and Calabrese assumed that communication is the primary vehicle for reducing uncertainty. Importantly, with so many uncertainties presented to you within a given 24-hour period, Berger (1979) admitted individuals couldn't possibly reduce uncertainty about all of these new people or situations. Instead, he argued there are three possible preceding conditions that influence whether people have the motivation necessary to reduce their uncertainty.

Reducing Uncertainty

Antecedent Conditions

Berger (1979) argued that individuals are motivated to reduce uncertainty only under one of three specific antecedent conditions. First, anticipation of future interaction suggests you are more motivated to reduce uncertainty about someone you are likely to see again. Thus, you are more inclined to use uncertainty reduction behaviors when a new office mate joins the team because you know you will be working with this person on a daily basis. The second condition, **incentive** value, includes the notion that you are prompted to learn more about someone when the individual in question has the potential to provide you with rewards or even punishments. In other words, what can this person do for you or to you? The third antecedent condition is **deviance**. If a person is odd, eccentric, bizarre, or unusual in some way that counters your expectations, URT suggests individuals will be more likely to reduce their uncertainty about the individual.

Types of Uncertainty

Beyond the antecedent conditions that prompt people to want to reduce uncertainty, Berger and Bradac (1982) argued there are two distinct variations, or types, of uncertainty. The first type, **behavioral uncertainty**, takes into account your insecurity about which actions are appropriate in a given situation. For example, when starting a job at a new company, there is often some ambiguity about the hours "required." Do employees of my position begin promptly at 9:00 a.m. and leave right at 5:00 p.m.? Or am I expected to arrive early and stay late? Should I work through lunch, eating at my desk, or do colleagues expect me to go out to lunch with them and socialize? These are all examples of typical behavioral uncertainty for a new employee not yet sure as to how to act within the new corporation.

The second type of uncertainty is **cognitive uncertainty**. Whereas individuals experiencing behavioral uncertainty question how they should act in a given situation, those who experience cognitive uncertainty are unsure as to what to think about someone or something. In other words, cognitive uncertainty emphasizes the doubts in your ability to pinpoint the attitudes and beliefs of others. When a colleague makes a comment about how "comfortable" you look on a casual Friday, you may wonder, was this a compliment? Or was the remark a subtle hint that you may be dressed in a manner that is too casual for the office? Should you even care what the person thinks of your attire? All of these questions emphasize cognitive uncertainty.

Axioms Explaining the Uncertainty Reduction Process

URT seeks to explain and predict the ways in which individuals use communication to reduce ambiguity. Specifically, the process of reducing uncertainty is predicated on eight axioms, or self-evident truths, established and supported in previous research (Berger & Calabrese, 1975). These axioms are summarized in Table 3.2.

As you can see, these axioms make sense; they are, after all, "self-evident truths." Unlike a commonsense theory, however, URT's axioms have been classified, paired together to create theorems, and tested systematically over time, thereby providing URT with scholarly credence. Moreover, the axioms presented in Table 3.2 supply only the backbone of the theory. In other words, to say that using friendly nonverbal behaviors reduces uncertainty

Table 3.2   Axioms of Uncertainty Reduction Theory

Axiom 1	As your verbal communication with a communication partner increases, your level of uncertainty about that person decreases; as a result, verbal communication continues to increase.
Axiom 2	As welcoming nonverbal expressions increase, uncertainty decreases and vice versa.
Axiom 3	The greater your uncertainty, the more information-seeking behaviors you use. Conversely, as your uncertainty lessens, you seek less information.
Axiom 4	When uncertainty in a relationship is high, the intimacy level of communication content will be low. On the other hand, the reduction of uncertainty leads to greater intimacy.
Axiom 5	The more uncertain you are, the more you will use reciprocal communication strategies and vice versa.
Axiom 6	The more similarities you perceive to share with the target person(s), the more your uncertainty is reduced. Alternatively, perceiving dissimilarities leads to increased uncertainty.
Axiom 7	As uncertainty decreases, liking increases. Conversely, if your uncertainty rises, your liking of the person will decrease.
Axiom 8	Shared communication networks, or shared ties, lessen your uncertainty. On the other hand, if you share no common relations, your uncertainty intensifies.

Source: Axioms 1 through 7 are adapted from Berger and Calabrese, 1975. Axiom 8 is adapted from Parks and Adelman, 1983.

is not enough to warrant a scholarly theory. Discussed next, communication strategies to reduce uncertainty provide additional substance to URT's axioms.

Uncertainty Reduction Strategies

When examining communication strategies for reducing uncertainty, it is important to remember Berger and Calabrese's (1975) original premise: Uncertainty reduction is central to all social relations. Likewise, Berger (1995, 1997) noted that much of social interaction is goal driven. In other words, you communicate for a reason, and you create cognitive plans that guide individuals' social interaction.

URT is related to Berger's (1995, 1997) notion of plan-based messages. Specifically, when seeking information about social realities, individuals create and use plans that vary in complexity. Individuals may vary widely in their relational goals and have a range of specific tactics available to cope with uncertainty. Despite these differences in goals, however, three overarching strategies typify most uncertainty-reduction communication: passive, active, and interactive.

Indicative of the passive strategy, individuals observe their surroundings and surreptitiously gather clues about which behaviors are appropriate as well as which attitudes and beliefs others hold. The passive approach is much like playing detective. The active strategy to uncertainty reduction involves seeking information from a third party. Rather than playing detective yourself, you go to someone else who may know more about the person or situation in question. Last, the **interactive strategy** is when you go straight to the source in question and ask for as much information as possible.

For example, imagine yourself in a new position at a new company. As the December holiday season approaches, you begin to wonder whether you should give a gift to your boss. You could wait to see if others give gifts (passive strategy), you could ask several peers what they do for their supervisors (active strategy), or you could directly ask your boss what the company culture is like and what he or she expects (interactive strategy). Clearly, there are many possible goals that would influence which plan to enact. If the overarching goal is to appear appropriate, effective, and appreciative, the active strategy is probably the best choice. By asking others in your position what they do, you can get a good sense of what your supervisor expects without offending or embarrassing him or her.

Beyond Initial Interactions

Uncertainty reduction theory was originally concerned with explaining and predicting the ambiguity associated with initial interactions (Berger, 1979; Berger & Calabrese, 1975). That is, research using URT emphasized when, why, and how individuals minimize doubt when in new situations or when meeting new people. Berger (1997) has since expanded his position on URT, however, noting that uncertainty exists in new and developing relationships as well as in long-term, ongoing relationships. For example, when Allen is suddenly laid off, Dan and Davida become (understandably) uncertain about their own job security. Even in the face of positive change, uncertainty is inevitable. Imagine you are promoted and will now manage some of your closest friends at work. This change in power—from peer to superior—will likely increase your uncertainty. All relationships are characterized by change and growth—both of which promote the rise of uncertainty. Furthermore, as discussed in Chapter 5, some researchers believe a little bit of uncertainty is actually necessary for maintaining a healthy relationship.

To review, URT focuses on when and why individuals use communication to reduce uncertainty about others. Uncertainty predictably decreases when nonverbal immediacy, verbal messages, self-disclosure, shared similarities, and shared social networks increase. People routinely use passive, active, and interactive information-seeking strategies to reduce their uncertainty when encountering others.

EXPECTANCY VIOLATIONS THEORY

Developed by Judee Burgoon (1978, 1994), expectancy violations theory (EVT) explains the meanings people attribute to the violation, or infringement, of their personal space. Importantly, whereas much of Burgoon's work emphasizes nonverbal violations of physical space (known as the study of proxemics), personal space can also refer to psychological or emotional space. Similar to URT, EVT is derived from a series of assumptions and axioms.

Assumptions

EVT builds on a number of communication axioms; most central to the understanding of EVT, however, is the assumption that humans have competing needs for personal space and for affiliation (Burgoon, 1978). Specifically, humans all need a certain amount of personal space, also thought of as distance or privacy; people also desire a certain amount of closeness with others, or affiliation. When you perceive that one of your needs has been compromised, EVT predicts you will try to do something about it. Thus, Burgoon's initial work focused on the realm of physical space—what happens when someone violates your expectations for appropriate physical distance or closeness.

Beyond explaining individuals' physical space and privacy needs, EVT also makes specific predictions as to how individuals will react to a given violation. Will you **reciprocate**, or match, someone's unexpected behavior, perhaps moving closer or turning toward the individual? Or will you **compensate**, or counteract, by doing the opposite of your partner's behavior? Before making a prediction about reciprocation or compensation, however, you must evaluate EVT's three core concepts: expectancy, violation valence, and communicator reward valence.

Core Concepts of Expectancy Violations Theory

First, **expectancy** refers to what an individual anticipates will happen in a given situation. Expectancy is similar to the idea of social norms and is based on three primary factors. The first factor associated with expectancy emphasizes the context of the behavior. In a formal business meeting, for example, hugging a colleague to show support may be inappropriate and may raise some eyebrows. If, however, you hug the same colleague while attending his mother's funeral, the gesture may be perfectly acceptable. A second factor, the relationship one has with the person in question, must be examined. If attending the funeral of your boss's mother, a hug may still be perceived as inappropriate, whereas if the funeral is for the mother of a colleague who is also a personal friend, a hug would likely be more suitable. The third factor, the communicator's characteristics, also fuels your expectations; you have expectations for the way people of both sexes and of certain ages, ethnicities, socioeconomic status, and the like will communicate.

By examining the context, relationship, and communicator's characteristics, individuals arrive at a certain expectation for how a given person should and will likely behave. Changing even one of these expectancy variables might lead to a different expectation. Once you have determined, however, that someone's behavior was, in fact, a breach of expectation, you then judge the behavior in question. This breach is known as the **violation valence**—the positive or negative evaluation you make about a behavior you did not anticipate. Importantly, not all violations are evaluated negatively. Very often a person behaves in a way you might not have expected, but this surprising behavior is viewed positively. For example, a normally bad-tempered colleague brings coffee and bagels to the

Monday morning staff meeting or the habitually shy intern actually makes eye contact with you and asks for your opinion on a new project.

Notably, others' behavior can be confusing and hard to interpret. Therefore, the third element that must be addressed before predicting reciprocation or compensation involves assessing the person whose behavior is in question. Similar to the violation valence, the **communicator reward valence** (also called the rewardingness of partner) is an evaluation you make about the person who committed the violation. Specifically, how rewarding or interpersonally attractive do you perceive this person to be? If you view the person engaging in the violation to be likeable, charismatic, nice looking, and smart, then you will likely believe the person has a positive reward valence. Conversely, if you perceive the violator to be rude, stingy, unattractive, or conceited, you will likely judge this person as having a negative reward valence. Importantly, the same behavior can be interpreted positively if committed by someone with a positive communicator reward valence and negatively by someone with a negative reward valence. For example, let's say you make a flawless presentation to a difficult client. Afterward, a respected colleague congratulates you and gives an unexpected pat on the shoulder. You will likely judge this act positively and as a gesture of support. On the other hand, let's say it's a different colleague who gives the unexpected pat on the shoulder, one who is always grandstanding and trying to make the focus of attention all about him. In this second case, you will probably view the pat on the back as negative and patronizing. Thus, assessing the behavior itself is insufficient to make a reasonable prediction of how one will react to the violation. You need to take into account your relationship and view of the person performing the violation.

Predicting Reactions When Expectations Are Violated

After assessing expectancy, violation valence, and communicator reward valence of a given situation, it becomes possible to make rather specific predictions about whether the individual who perceived the violation will reciprocate or compensate for the behavior in question. These predictions are described in Figure 3.1.

Guerrero and Burgoon (1996; Guerrero, Jones, & Burgoon, 2000) noticed that predictable patterns develop when considering reward valence and violation valence together. Specifically, if the violation valence is perceived as positive and the communicator reward valence is also perceived as positive, the theory predicts you will reciprocate the positive behavior. For example, your boss gives you a big smile after you've given a presentation. Guerrero and Burgoon would predict that you smile in return. Similarly, if you perceive the violation valence as negative and perceive the communicator reward valence as negative, the theory again predicts you reciprocate the negative behavior. Thus, if a disliked co-worker is grouchy and unpleasant to you, you will likely reciprocate and be unpleasant in return.

Conversely, if you perceive a negative violation valence but view the communicator reward valence as positive, it is likely you will compensate for your partner's negative behavior. For example, one day your boss appears sullen and throws a stack of papers in front of you. Rather than grunt back, EVT predicts you will compensate for your boss's negativity, perhaps by asking if everything is okay (Guerrero & Burgoon, 1996). More difficult to predict, however, is the situation in which someone you view as having a negative reward valence violates you with a positive behavior. In this situation, you may reciprocate, giving the person the "benefit of the doubt." Alternatively, you may view the communicator

Figure 3.1   Predictions of Expectancy Violations Theory

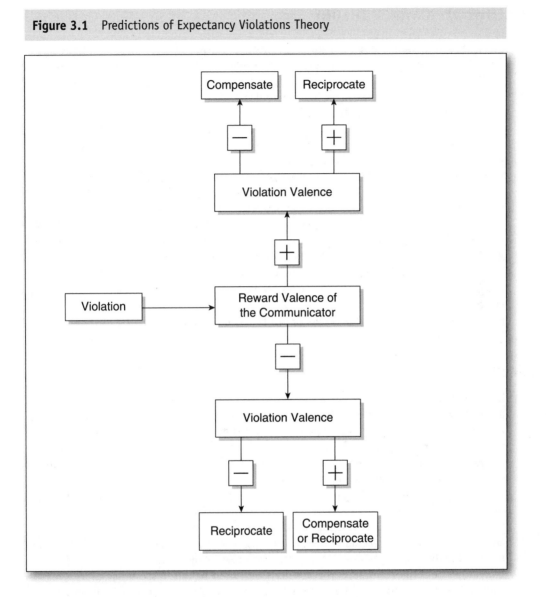

as having suspicious motives, thereby compensating. For example, if the disliked co-worker comes in one day and is very pleasant, you might be pleasant in return, but you also might treat the person with suspicion.

As evidenced, EVT focuses broadly on the infringement of one's expectations for "normal" behavior. Burgoon's research has chiefly emphasized the violation of nonverbal space; however, other expectations, such as behavioral norms, can also be violated. Notably, violations are not necessarily negative. One must evaluate the anticipated behavior, the communicator's characteristics, and the violation itself.

COGNITIVE DISSONANCE THEORY

The final intrapersonal theory featured in this chapter is cognitive dissonance theory—a way of understanding how persuasion may be understood as a cognitive event whereby an individual is motivated to create balance between one's own beliefs and behavior. Discussed in Chapter 7 along with other theories of persuasion, it is often assumed an outside source simply has to provide enough ammunition to change another's attitudes or beliefs. For example, public health campaigns often presume the best way to get a smoker to quit is to infuse the smoker with information about mortality rates, health problems, and the social stigma associated with smoking in order to change the person's attitude about cigarettes. If the smoker's attitude changes, surely he or she will stop smoking, right? After all, it doesn't make sense to engage in a habit known to cause premature aging and cancer and banned in many public places.

According to cognitive dissonance theory, however, this line of thinking may seem logical but is potentially incorrect, possibly explaining why there are so many smokers who acknowledge the health and social risks yet continue to indulge in the behavior. Cognitive dissonance theory (CDT) explains that persuasion is not simply the result of injecting new or refined beliefs into others. Instead, CDT predicts that influence is often an intrapersonal event, occurring when incongruence between our attitudes and behavior creates a tension resolved by altering either our beliefs or our behaviors, thereby effecting a change.

Schemata: Creating Familiarity or Discomfort

According to Festinger (1957, 1962), when presented with a new or unfamiliar stimulus, individuals use **schemata**—that is, cognitive structures for organizing new information. Essentially, for new information to be understood or useful, we must find schemata with which to link the new stimulus to previously understood experiences. For example, when trying frog legs for the first time, many people claim the dish tastes "just like chicken"; in this case, the previous experience of being familiar with the taste of chicken serves as schemata for relating the taste of frog legs.

Importantly, however, when newly presented information is inconsistent with our previously established beliefs (i.e., schemata), we experience an imbalance or dissonance (Festinger, 1957). It is this dissonance that becomes a highly persuasive tool because, according to Festinger, humans feel so uneasy with holding contradictory beliefs and actions that they will make every attempt to minimize the discomfort. In other words, when individuals behave in a manner incongruent with their beliefs, dissonance is created; dissonance creates discomfort. Because humans do not like to feel unnerved, individuals actively seek to change the situation to restore a balance between thought and action.

Relationship Between Beliefs and Behaviors

Three possible relationships between beliefs and behaviors exist: irrelevance, consonance, and dissonance (Festinger, 1957). Briefly stated, **irrelevance** simply refers to beliefs and behaviors that have nothing to do with each other. For example, Cory's beliefs about preserving the environment and his position on gun control are completely unrelated. Thus, irrelevance is the absence of both consonance and dissonance. Second, **consonance** occurs when two stimuli or pieces of information are in balance or achieve congruence. For example, if Cory believes recycling is an important way to maintain the environment, and he recycles everything from plastic bottles, to Styrofoam peanuts, to junk mail, it could be said Cory has consonance between his beliefs (recycling benefits the environment) and his actions (he avidly recycles household waste). According to Festinger (1957), individuals prefer consonant relationships; that is, we strive to feel consistency between actions and beliefs.

Conversely, **dissonance** occurs when two stimuli or pieces of information contradict each other (Festinger, 1957). Continuing the previous example, if Cory believes the environment is a precious commodity that deserves protection yet he drives an SUV for his 40-mile commute each day, he has created dissonance. Cory's beliefs (preserving the environment) and his actions (driving a gas-guzzling SUV) are incongruent. CDT predicts this dissonance will give Cory discomfort, at least until he can rationalize or augment the dissonance—either by shifting his belief (sure, the environment is important, but driving a car won't harm anyone) or by changing his behavior (trading in the SUV for an electric hybrid car).

Importantly, not all dissonance is created equally. That is, a magnitude of dissonance exists whereby some forms of incongruence produce greater discomfort than others (Zimbardo, Ebbesen, & Maslach, 1977). This magnitude of dissonance can be measured by three variables. First, the amount of dissonance one experiences is affected by the perceived importance of an issue. Recycling soda cans may not be as important an issue when compared with driving while intoxicated. Similarly, spending $5,000 on a beach rental that turns out to be a dilapidated shack is far more devastating than spending $100 to watch your favorite football team lose. Second, the **dissonance ratio** affects the amount of discomfort one feels. The dissonance ratio is simply the proportion of incongruent beliefs held in relation to the number of consonant beliefs. If you hold a greater number of incongruent beliefs and behaviors compared with consistent thoughts and actions, you will experience more discomfort. Third, one's ability to **rationalize**, or justify, the dissonance also affects the amount of discomfort experienced when faced with conflicting beliefs and behaviors. The more you can justify these contrasting attitudes and actions, the less discomfort you endure.

A related issue is perception. Specifically, the perceptual processes of selective exposure, attention, interpretation, and retention can help minimize dissonance. CDT argues that an individual selectively perceives various stimuli so as to minimize dissonance. For example, with **selective exposure**, a person actively avoids information inconsistent with previously established beliefs or behaviors. Thus, a pro-choice supporter will likely avoid pro-life demonstrations and vice versa. Similarly, **selective attention** suggests that if you have to expose yourself to a situation incongruent with your beliefs, you will only attend to information that reaffirms your beliefs, disregarding any information that fails to support your views. Thus, if pro-choice supporters happen to come face-to-face with a pro-life demonstration, they will likely only attend to those details that support their previously held beliefs, for example, that pro-life supporters are religious "fanatics."

With regard to **selective interpretation**, CDT predicts individuals will carefully decipher ambiguous information so it is perceived to be consistent with their established beliefs. To illustrate, consider *Zero Dark Thirty*, a film that includes the explicit depiction of "enhanced interrogation techniques" used in the pursuit and killing of Osama Bin Laden. Individuals who support the use of torture in warfare are likely to have interpreted the film as providing evidence of the efficacy of the technique; those who do not support the use of torture may very well have interpreted the film as a condemnation of these techniques (Bruni, 2012).

Finally, CDT maintains individuals use selective retention to uphold their viewpoints while more easily dismissing or forgetting information that creates dissonance. Accordingly, we might remember all the good times we had in college and conveniently forget how stressful we found trying to balance the demands of schoolwork with the need to work to pay for college.

Persuasion Through Dissonance

By now it should be understood that CDT assumes humans prefer congruency between beliefs and behaviors. When we engage in an action that opposes our attitudes, we experience distress known as dissonance. Depending on the importance of the issue and the degree of our discomfort, we are motivated to change our beliefs or behaviors (i.e., be persuaded). CDT is often considered a **postdecision theory**, meaning individuals attempt to persuade themselves after a decision has been made or course of action has been enacted that the decision or behavior was okay (Gass & Seiter, 2003). The notion of buyer's remorse is an obvious example. After spending more than you feel comfortable with on a new home, car, vacation, or some other luxury item, you probably had to rationalize, or convince yourself, that the purchase was "worth" it. Thus, you try to reduce the dissonance created after making a decision to buy. Yet the question remains: How can communicators use CDT as a tool to persuade others?

Recall that, according to CDT, motivation results from an individual's internal struggle to change beliefs or behaviors to restore consonance (Festinger, 1957). Consequently, if a persuader can create or exploit dissonance while also offering a solution to minimize the disparity, it is likely the receiver will adopt these suggested new behaviors (or change beliefs).

In the case of buyer's remorse, sellers and real estate agents can capitalize on principles of CDT by reinforcing the wisdom of making certain choices. Realtors often encourage buyers to make a list of pros and cons before even looking for that new home with breathtaking views, a gourmet kitchen, or a sunken Jacuzzi tub (Light, 2002). This way, buyers can reduce dissonance that typically occurs after their bid is accepted by reinforcing their decision to purchase with the list of advantages. Home inspections and contingency clauses in the agreement of sale also help prospective buyers feel better about their decision to purchase.

Advertisers have also been using principles of CDT for decades, convincing consumers to buy their clients' products. For instance, the diet industry has made billions of dollars by preying on the average person's insecurities about his or her appearance and body image. Most adults know they should engage in exercise or physical activity on a daily basis, yet the majority of them don't. And although we may not be motivated enough to get off the couch and onto the treadmill, we are motivated to relieve the dissonance by purchasing so-called miracle products such as fat blockers, diet supplements, cellulite creams, and even cocktails formulated for skinny women. Thus, by presenting an easy alternative, these manufacturers help consumers to minimize their discomfort by realigning their beliefs and behaviors, if only on a temporary basis.

Within an organizational context, CDT predicts that by increasing employee commitments and loyalties, employee turnover could be reduced and satisfaction improved. That is, "once we've invested our time and energy or poured our hearts and souls into a cause, a person, an idea, a project, or a group we find it too difficult to let go" (Gass & Seiter, 2003, p. 69). If you have already invested years, overcome financial burdens, or forged meaningful relationships with co-workers, you are much less likely to leave an organization—regardless of pay or other adverse circumstances. Instead, you suppress second thoughts about other career opportunities, rationalize our corporate loyalty, and may even intensify your efforts to prove to yourself and others that the job is worth it.

We would like to offer a few words of caution, however. Take care when trying to capitalize on others' inconsistencies as a persuasive strategy for changing receivers' beliefs or behaviors. As Gass and Seiter (2003) noted, if you create too much dissonance, the receivers may simply create balance by changing their attitudes so as not to like you. Likewise, ethical issues abound when individuals plot to exploit consumers' or employees' dissonance for material gain. We believe competent persuaders must think of each consumer or employee as an individual worthy of respect. If creating or magnifying another's dissonance strips that individual of self-worth, then such techniques should be avoided.

CDT focuses primarily on an individual's psychological response to inconsistencies in beliefs and actions. Because dissonance produces distress, human beings seek to maintain consonance or the appearance of consonance whenever possible. This adverse effect may mean changing one's behaviors or realigning one's beliefs through some type of rationalization or selective perception. Although often a postreactive approach, communicators can use this knowledge of CDT to better target their persuasive messages. By offering a solution, product, or course of action that bridges the gap between receivers' incongruent beliefs and behaviors, communicators may influence receivers to use these methods to create cognitive harmony.

Summary and Research Applications

This chapter focused on cognition and communication, which refers to the way individuals assess others' behavior, attitudes, and messages to assign meaning. First, attribution theory focuses on how and why individuals assign causes to other peoples' behavior. Related to workplace communication, attribution theory has been applied to understanding how recipients of e-mail messages are interpreted by the sender when a response is not returned, as well as how recipients interpret their own behavior when a reply is not provided (Easton & Bommelje, 2011). Related to public relations and crisis communication, attribution theory has also been applied to understanding public reactions to a petroleum corporation that caused an oil spill (Jeong, 2009). Second, URT states that when individuals encounter someone or something new, they experience uncertainty; uncertainty is uncomfortable, so people use communication strategies to reduce it. One application of URT is its usefulness in explaining how employees experience uncertainty and use uncertainty reduction strategies to manage both temporary (Rhodes, 2008) and long-term organizational change, such as job transfers (Kramer, 1993, 1994) and reactions to management decisions such as promotions (Kramer, 1999). Next, EVT predicts whether people will reciprocate or compensate when their conversational partner violates their expectations. Within organizational contexts, EVT has been used to explain negative perceptions of organizations' responses to consumer complaints (Bolkan & Daly, 2009) as well as how unexpected touch between opposite-sex workers, either managers or subordinates, can lead to perceptions of inappropriateness and harassment for both men and women (Guerrero & Smith, 2009). Finally, cognitive dissonance theory explains persuasion as a cognitive response to inconsistencies in beliefs and actions, whereby individuals prefer to maintain consistency between their beliefs and behaviors. Again related to crisis communication, Waters's (2009) research on individuals' motivations to donate to the American Red Cross after a disaster found that donors were more likely "to experience feelings of cognitive dissonance than non-donors, and their donations resulted in a consonance restoration" (p. 139). Nonprofit organizations, particularly those dealing with disaster relief, might be able to improve fund-raising efforts by highlighting dissonance among nonresidents and then publicizing how nonresident donations to the victims can restore consonance.

Key Terms

Attribution   35
Axiom   39
Behavioral uncertainty   40
Behaviorism   34
Cognition   34
Cognitive   34
Cognitive uncertainty   40
Communicator reward valence   44
Compensate   43
Consensus   37
Consistency   37
Consonance   47
Deviance   40
Dissonance   47
Dissonance ratio   47
Distinctiveness   38
Expectancy   43

Exterior locus of control   38
Hedonic relevance   36
Incentive   40
Interactive strategy   42
Interior locus of control   38
Irrelevance   46
Personalism   37
Postdecision theory   48
Rationalize   47
Reciprocate   43
Schemata   46
Selective attention   47
Selective exposure   47
Selective interpretation   47
Selective retention   53
Social desirability   36
Violation valence   43

Case Study 3: Caught in Between

Julie Miller had recently joined the internal audit department of a large pharmaceutical company as an analyst. As a team, these analysts conducted thousands of inspections to ensure the sales representatives complied with federal regulatory guidelines. It was a Monday afternoon, and Julie grabbed a seat at the weekly staff meeting. Her boss, Pat, sat at the head of the large conference room table, notebook open, looking ready to begin. Over the next hour, Pat previewed a new plan that he and a senior analyst, Erin, would create to standardize the team's daily logging process.

Pat started the meeting by saying, "I done some checkin', and I can tell that yooz are not doin' the same amount of inspeckin. Uhbeaht heahf of yooz are checkin awwl da voided cards to look for blanks. The udder heahf of yooz aren't looking at no more 'an a hanful. We godda get this more together, ya know?"

He continued in his heavy Philly accent, saying that this type of inconsistency could leave the department open to liability issues and might be a problem in the department's yearly internal audit.

"I jus' wanna make sure ever'bod's on da same page uhbeaht awl dis," Pat explained. "If any of yooz got any ideas 'bout what should be include' in da process, gimme a kawl on the phowen. Me enn Erin are gawn head up this projeck."

With that, as he did at each meeting, Pat asked each person around the table for any questions or issues they wished to discuss.

As soon as Julie got back to her desk after the meeting, the woman from the next cubicle rushed into her space, visibly angry. "What was *that* all about? Are we trained monkeys? Can you even believe him?" Marissa sputtered.

Julie felt a twinge of discomfort; she had been one of the people who recognized a large discrepancy in the analysts' process. She actually looked forward to having more definite guidelines.

Before Julie could respond, Marissa went on, "Why do we even need a standardized process? Is he really so sure I don't know how to do my own job? I've been in this department for 12 years! I think I know how to do an audit by now. Every day, I speak to senior directors who are so far above his head, he couldn't even see them! Of course, with him being so short and bald, that's not that difficult! I can't believe this!"

Here we go again, Julie thought silently to herself. Although only a few months into the job, Julie had witnessed enough of Marissa's complaints to know that if left unchecked, she would go on and on.

Julie again attempted to speak but was interrupted by Marissa's rant: "And when will the man learn how to speak? Who talks like that in management? I can't believe they hired this man to be *my* manager. He's absolutely stupid! I'm supposed to respect him? I can't. I won't. And why did he pick Erin? I have more seniority than she does—even if my title doesn't reflect it! Please! It's a shame you weren't here before Pat got here, Julie. The old boss knew we were doing a good job and left us alone."

Julie didn't know how to respond. She shared a cubicle wall with Marissa and didn't want to get on the woman's bad side. At the same time, Julie and Pat had gotten along well since he hired her a few months ago. Although she agreed he was rough around the edges, she liked his straightforward manner. Pat had been a captain in the Philadelphia Police Department, until two years ago when he was injured in the line of duty and relegated to a desk job. He came to this company after being recruited by Mary, the senior director and a former Philadelphia detective herself who had worked for Pat. Julie had spoken privately with Pat a few times about his difficult transition from being a manager at the police department, which used a managerial style that was very confrontational, aggressive, and structured, to this company, which encouraged a managerial style that sometimes seemed to him to be more about *how* the job got done than actually getting it done. Sometimes, even now, Julie could tell that Pat had to stop and think about the "right" way to respond to a situation, instead of responding in his natural style.

Complicating matters, Julie had learned from a co-worker that Marissa had applied for Pat's job but wasn't chosen. Knowing Mary's history with Pat, Julie assumed Mary had an interest in bringing in people with a background in criminal justice to round out the investigative skills on the team. Marissa, on the other hand, had chalked it up to plain old nepotism.

Julie could not imagine Marissa as a manager. An attractive woman in her mid-50s, Marissa was always meticulously put together. Twice divorced, Marissa had a sarcastic, if caustic, sense of humor that had initially turned Julie off. Marissa rarely held back from sharing her opinion as if it were the only correct one.

Over the past few weeks, however, Julie's initial opinion had softened. From chatting with Marissa, Julie learned she had endured a lot early in life and, as a result, wasn't able to finish college. Starting as a secretary years before, Marissa had slowly worked her way up the ranks, even without a degree. Although she really was good at her job, Julie noticed Marissa was rarely commended. Still, Julie was learning to take Marissa's tirades about Pat with a grain of salt. Everyone else did as well.

Julie whispered quietly, so as not to be overheard, "Well, why didn't you raise any of your objections to the process in the meeting when Pat asked for feedback? He said he wanted to hear people's concerns."

"Are you kidding me?" Marissa replied, in her regular speaking voice. "He only *says* he wants feedback because that's what he learned in some managerial class."

At that moment, Pat walked by Julie's cube on his way to Erin's desk. Marissa stopped and looked a little guilty. Julie sensed the tension, but knowing she had done nothing wrong she just smiled and greeted Pat as she usually did. She assumed Pat would smile and make a friendly joke as he typically did when he saw Julie. Instead, he curtly nodded his head in their direction and barked, "Yo Marissa, why don' I got those refurr'l ledders back? I gave 'em to you two-tree days ago. If you can't hannel your work, lemme know. I'll get summon else a do it."

Marissa's face reddened, but she coolly replied, "I'll have them to you within the hour." Pat turned to Julie, smiled, and continued on his way.

Julie was taken aback; Pat had never spoken to her in this way. She had recently turned in some requested referrals a day late herself and had been reassured by Pat that they were "no big deal, just more paperwork."

Julie plopped down at her desk and sighed. *I'm staying out of this*, she thought. *I'll just be nice to both of them and do my work.*

Questions for Consideration

1. What attributions has Julie made about Marissa's complaints? Make sure to include information about consensus, consistency, distinctiveness, and controllability.

2. Julie is fairly new to the organization. What strategies has she used to reduce her uncertainty about Pat? Marissa?

3. Using examples for each of EVT's core components (expectancy, violation valence, and communicator reward valence), what does EVT explain about Julie's reaction to Pat? Then, think about it from Pat's perspective. What does EVT explain about Pat's reaction to Julie "gossiping" with Marissa?

4. Do you believe Julie experiences any cognitive dissonance about Marissa's complaints? Why or why not? What about Marissa? Do you see any evidence that either has engaged in selective attention, selective exposure, selective interpretation, or selective retention?

5. Which theory alone seems to provide the "best" explanation for the situation? Why do you believe this to be the case? What situations might surface that would make a different theory or theories better at explaining the situation? How could you combine several theories to make for an even "better" explanation of the encounter?

CHAPTER 4

Individual and Social Approaches to Communication

After reading this chapter, you will be able to...

1. Describe some of the characteristics of a nature and a nurture approach to communication.
2. Articulate what a standpoint is and how it influences communication.
3. Summarize a communibiological approach to communication.
4. Explain the differences between sex and gender.
5. Compare and contrast communal qualities and agentic qualities and ascertain how these qualities are associated with social roles.
6. Describe descriptive and prescriptive prejudices.
7. Explain the double bind facing women who are leaders.
8. Summarize research investigating the perceptions and realities of sex differences in communication.
9. Identify the components of emotional intelligence.
10. Differentiate between transactional and transformational leadership.
11. Distinguish the three message design logics.
12. Use the axioms of the interactional perspective to analyze a communication interaction.
13. Summarize the differences between the values and behaviors of the five U.S. generations.
14. Apply the axioms of the interactional perspective to generational conflicts in the workplace.
15. Summarize major theoretical approaches to individual and social approaches to communication.
16. Compare and contrast major theoretical approaches to individual and social approaches to communication.

US NURTURE

sus nurture? One of the fundamental questions of philosophy is the extent to ian beings are shaped by their biology versus the environment in which they are example, are some people born liars, or is it the way people are raised and the social conditions in which they live that foster a tendency to engage in deceptive practices? The perception about whether a communication theory places an emphasis on nature or nurture has much to do with one's own view of the debate. Scholars on the nature side of the debate suggest the communication discipline historically has been focused on the nurture side of the debate. That is, they argue that much of communication scholarship has focused on how social rules and roles impact the communication process (Hickson & Neiva, 2002; Sherry, 2004). Conversely, those that firmly believe in the role of the environment tend to argue that the communication discipline suffers from placing too much emphasis on the individual rather than on the way interaction creates a social world (Leeds-Hurwitz, 1992).

On the nurture side of the debate, social approaches to communication focus on how lived experiences influence the individual. For example, a standpoint approach argues that expectations for communication are socially constructed. Developed first within philosophy to explain master–slave relationships (Hegel, 1807/1966) and later used in feminist scholarship (Hartsock, 1983), standpoint approaches build on the notion that you cannot understand others unless you walk a mile in their shoes. A **standpoint** is a position from which you view and understand the world; the point in time, the location, and the experiences you bring to an observation influence your standpoint. Groups of individuals who share similar viewpoints and understandings also share standpoints. Standpoint theory argues that the differences in people's lives stem from imbalances in social, economic, and symbolic power (Wood, 1993). That is, many men and women have different standpoints because the two groups have different social, economic, and symbolic experiences as a result of gender expectations. Because boys and girls are socialized differently (Maccoby, 1990), they have different sets of rules, norms, goals, and meanings for their social experiences.

On the other hand, more and more communication scholars are recognizing the power evolutionary mechanisms, and especially genetics, play in communication practices. Beatty and McCroskey's (2001) **communibiological approach**, for example, is grounded in neuroscience. The approach argues that neurobiological structures create different temperaments or traits; that these temperaments and traits are genetic; and that temperament and traits are what cause variations in communication behavior. To illustrate, research suggests characteristics such as assertiveness, empathy, aggressiveness, and nurturing are inherited qualities passed on through genetics (McCroskey, 2006). However, McCroskey suggests that even though there is a genetic basis for these behaviors, our social environment does play some role. "Children do not learn to be aggressive or empathic. These and a large number of other trait orientations are what they are born with. How they respond to the genetically based temperamental demands, however, depends on a large number of other things. . . . Children learn culturally appropriate means of expressing (or not expressing) their genetically driven temperaments" (McCroskey, 2006, p. 34).

The theories in this chapter focus on the interplay of individual traits and social expectations in predicting or explaining communication activity. First, we consider social role theory, which argues that perceptions of men and women's behavior are always filtered through our stereotypes of how men and women should behave. We specifically apply this theory to research investigating women and leadership. Next, we describe emotional intelligence (EI), which suggests that personal and professional success might not be explained by an individual's intelligence quotient (IQ) but, rather, by the extent to which the individual is attuned to emotional experiences. We link EI to transformational leadership. The third theory we consider is message design logics, which proposes that variations in beliefs about communication explain problematic communication encounters. Finally, we describe the interactional perspective formulated by the Palo Alto Group. The tenets of this approach are used to explain why there is so much focus on the communication difficulties among members of different generations in the workplace.

SOCIAL ROLE THEORY OF GENDER

Examining sex and gender differences in communication is perhaps one of the most controversial and widely debated areas of communication research in recent decades (see Canary & Hause, 1993; Wood & Dindia, 1998). Despite the number of popular self-help books proclaiming the idea that men inhabit one planet while women occupy another (see Gray, 1992) or alleging men and women "just don't understand" each other (see Tannen, 1990), there is actually very little communication theory—or research—to support these stereotypical claims of widespread sex differences (Canary, Emmers-Sommer, & Faulker, 1997; Canary & Hause, 1993).

Yet there has to be a reason why these books are bestsellers. According to social role theory, perhaps one of the reasons we find it so tempting to believe men and women are fundamentally different is because sex is the single easiest characteristic we can use to classify people into categories; it is easier, even, than using race, age, or other easily observable groupings (Eagly & Karau, 2002). Not only that, but stereotypes based on sex can be activated at very low levels of consciousness. Much like expectancy violations theory described in Chapter 3, social role theory focuses on our expectations for behavior and how we respond when our expectations are violated. Unlike EVT, however, social role theory suggests that violations of our expectations almost always lead to negative responses.

Sex and Gender: What's the Difference?

"Not biology, but gender prescriptions for women and men account for most differences in priorities, behaviors, attitudes, feelings, and self-concepts of the sexes" (Julia Wood in a dialogue with Kathryn Dindia, see Wood & Dindia, 1998, p. 30).

How many times have you filled out a survey or questionnaire that asks for your gender and then has boxes for "male" or "female"? Really what the survey is probably trying to determine is your sex. You may scratch your head and wonder, "What's the difference?" The difference could be drastic or insignificant, depending on the context. When discussing messages and communication patterns between women and men, it is helpful to understand there is a substantial difference between sex and gender.

Social role theory assumes **sex** is genetically determined; it is your biological makeup as either a male (with XY chromosomes) or a female (with XX chromosomes). Barring rare genetic abnormalities, sex is a dichotomous variable; you are one or the other, not both or neither. Whereas sex is a biological categorization determined at conception, gender is far more fluid. **Gender** is "the consensual beliefs about the attributes of women and men" (Eagly & Karau, 2002, p. 574). Importantly, all societies assign certain behaviors to each sex; in this way, gender is related to, but not equated with, sex. In Western culture, for instance, girls typically receive baby dolls and kitchen sets and are told to be "sugar and spice and everything nice," while their brothers typically receive trucks and toy guns and are told not to "cry like a girl." As adults, women are still expected to be primary caregivers, while men are expected to be primary breadwinners. When boys and girls and men and women behave outside of these prescriptions, eyebrows raise, a person's sexuality may be questioned (e.g., assuming male dancers are gay), and boundaries are pushed.

One of the central ways people stereotype women and men is in terms of communal and agentic qualities (Eagly, 1987). **Communal qualities** are stereotypical female attributes. They demonstrate a concern for other people through the expression of affection and exhibiting sympathy, helpfulness, sensitivity, nurturance, and gentility. **Agentic qualities**, on the other hand, are stereotypically associated with men. These qualities include being assertive, controlling, confident, ambitious, and forceful. Social role theory suggests people assume a connection between gender roles and individual dispositions; even when faced with evidence to the contrary (e.g., a very dominant woman or a very nurturing man) people cling to social role expectations.

Role Congruity Theory and Leadership

Because leadership is most often described in masculine terms (i.e., leaders are supposed to be ambitious, assertive, and direct) social role theory has been extended to focus on sex differences in the realm of organizational leadership. Called role congruity theory, the theory suggests women in leadership positions are likely to experience two types of prejudice (Eagly & Karau, 2002). **Descriptive prejudice** refers to stereotypes that women have less leadership potential than men because they lack agentic qualities. **Prescriptive prejudice** (also called injunctive prejudice) refers to actual evaluations of women as less effective than men. Combined, these prejudices leave women in a **double bind**. "If they conform to their traditional gender role, women are not seen as having the potential for leadership; if they adopt the agentic characteristics associated with successful leaders, then they are evaluated negatively for behaving in an unfeminine manner" (Elsesser & Lever, 2011, p. 1557).

Eagly and Karau (2002) predict that because of this role incongruity women are actually less likely to emerge as a leader in professional settings than will men. Of course, some might question whether the stereotypes might be based on reality. Research suggests this is not the case, however; even when women possess agentic qualities they are less likely to emerge as a leader in a mixed-sex group than are men (Ritter & Yoder, 2004). Unfortunately, these negative stereotypes can be exacerbated by the context of the workplace. Garcia-Retamero and López-Zafra (2006) found that people showed stronger prejudice against female leaders who worked in a stereotypically male industry (e.g., the auto industry as compared to the clothing industry) and that older individuals reported more prejudice against female leaders than did younger individuals.

Research has found some support for the predictions made by role congruity theory. Surveying over 60,000 workers, a recent study found evidence for a strong descriptive prejudice against female leaders (Elsesser & Lever, 2011). The good news is that competence ratings for actual male and female bosses were similar, and respondents did not view leaders who behaved in a counterstereotypical style (e.g., a sensitive male manager or a direct female manager) as less competent than those who behaved in a stereotypical fashion. However, although it appears prescriptive prejudices may be fading, the results suggested that a cross-sex preference might exist such that women reported having better relationships with male managers and vice versa.

What About Actual Differences in Communication?

Beyond the stereotypes we hold about men and women, and our evaluations of actual men and women because of these stereotypes, communication research shows little support for the notion that men and women differ with regard to their actual communication behavior simply because of their biological sex. In fact, research suggests we are more similar to the opposite sex than we are different. For example, Canary and Hause (1993) used a statistical procedure known as meta-analysis to compare more than 1,200 studies looking at sex differences in communication. When combined, they found that one's biological sex accounts for less than 1% of differences in communication behavior! This means that 99% of differences in communication behavior are likely created by something other than simply having XX or XY chromosomes.

On the other hand, there is support for the idea that gender roles influence communication styles. Regardless of biological sex, having a relationship partner who exhibits a feminine (i.e., communal) style of communication is positively related to romantic relationship satisfaction (Lamke, Sollie, Durbin, & Fitzpatrick, 1994), the use of positive and collaborative strategies for dealing with romantic relationship jealousy (Aylor & Dainton, 2001), and decreased loneliness among long-distance friends (Dainton, Aylor, & Zelley, 2002). Masculinity (i.e., engaging in agentic behavior) has been associated with more effective political campaign ads (Wadsworth et al., 1987), and more strategic uses of communication (Aylor & Dainton, 2004).

Despite little evidence of actual sex differences in communication, social role theory provides a way to understand how social expectations for behavior result in stereotypes. Although these stereotypes affect both men and women, they have a particularly insidious effect on women leaders, placing them in a double bind of being judged negatively regardless of the leadership style they adopt.

EMOTIONAL INTELLIGENCE AND TRANSFORMATIONAL LEADERSHIP

A second theory that focuses on the interplay of individual and social qualities is **emotional intelligence** (EI). In 1995 Daniel Goleman wrote a best-selling book on the topic that revolutionized the way people thought about career success. Building on the work of Salovey and Mayer (1989), Goleman wrote that emotional intelligence—the ability to monitor one's own and others' emotions—was more powerful than IQ and that "nearly 90% of the difference between star performers at work and average ones was due to EI" (Goleman, 1998, as cited in Mayer, Salovey & Caruso, 2008, p. 504). As the public face for emotional intelligence, Goleman himself has certainly provided support for the connection between the ability to recognize others' needs and public and financial recognition.

Aside from the popular culture version of EI, however, Salovey and Mayer have continued to carefully develop and refine their theory of emotional intelligence. They argue emotional intelligence is an ability that explains differences in individuals' problem solving and relationship maintenance. Specifically, they suggest EI is associated with the ability to monitor one's own and others' emotions, being able to carefully discriminate between emotions, and use emotional information strategically to make decisions and achieve goals. Despite other scholars' view that EI is a trait (see Bar-On, 2006), Salovey and Mayer assert that emotional intelligence is not based on personality types and claim that like other types of intelligence, EI changes and develops with age and experience (Caruso, Mayer, & Salovey, 2002; Mayer, Caruso & Salovey, 1999).

Mayer and Salovey's (1997) theory suggests emotional intelligence is comprised of four branches arranged in a hierarchy from most basic to most complex. Further, within each branch abilities range from the very basic to the most intricate. Table 4.1 describes each branch from the least to most complex.

Although Salovey and Mayer are careful to distance themselves from Goleman's claim that high EI is a strong predictor of organizational success, research does support the notion that EI plays a role in the way an individual performs in an organizational setting (Mayer et al., 2008; Salovey, Caruso, & Mayer, 2004). One particularly intriguing connection links emotional intelligence to the use of a transformational leadership style (Gardner & Stough, 2002; Palmer, Walls, Burgess, & Stough, 2001; Sivanathan & Fekken, 2002; Wang & Huang, 2009). First described by Bass (1997), transformational leadership is the ability to change (i.e., "transform") employees and the organization through communication. Bass differentiates between two leadership styles—transactional and transformational—arguing that, although both can assist organizations in achieving goals, transformational leadership is superior in a contemporary business climate.

Transactional leadership seeks to achieve solid, consistent performance from subordinates through a process of bilateral exchange (Bass, 1985). Specifically, leaders fulfill the needs of the employee in exchange for the employee meeting performance expectations. To illustrate, there are three primary characteristics of transactional leaders. First, transactional leaders work with subordinates to develop clear and specific objectives. For example, a manager might meet with an employee to create performance standards jointly for an upcoming year. Second, transactional leaders exchange rewards and promises of rewards

Table 4.1 The Four-Branch Model of Emotional Intelligence

Component	Definition
Perceiving emotions	Ranges from the ability to accurately recognize one's own and others' emotions to the ability to discriminate between sincere and insincere expressions of feelings
Using emotions to assist thinking	Ranges from the ability to use emotions to direct attention to important information to the ability to use emotions to facilitate creativity or engage in inductive reasoning
Understanding and analyzing emotions	Ranges from the ability to recognize connections between emotions (e.g., envy and jealousy) to the ability to recognize emotional blends (e.g., fear and surprise) and transitions between emotions
Regulation of emotions	Ranges from the ability to be open to all feelings, including pleasant and unpleasant emotions, to the ability to manage one's own or others' emotional displays

for employee effort. Accordingly, a leader might reward an employee on completion of a difficult task with an "Employee Excellence Award" or a financial bonus. Third, transactional leaders are responsive to the self-interests of workers, particularly if the workers' needs can be met while also getting the job done (Bass, 1985). For example, consider a single parent who receives a phone call that her child is sick. A transactional leader would be supportive of the employee going home to care for the sick child if acceptable arrangements can be made to ensure that the work would still be accomplished, for instance, working late another day or negotiating with a co-worker to cover the required tasks. Transactional leadership is responsive to employees and offers clear and structured expectations. It is a natural result of bureaucratic systems. This leadership style focuses on meeting immediate needs as quickly and effectively as possible (Bass, 1985). Subordinates are respected and encouraged to participate in planning and decision making.

Transformational leadership, on the other hand, is founded on particular attitudes and behaviors that support organizational change (Bass, 1985). Whereas transactional leadership seeks to achieve reliable and stable functioning, transformational leadership seeks to inspire exceptional performance (S. E. Bryant, 2003). At the center of transformational leadership is the ability to use subordinates' ideas and actions as a catalyst for transformation—moving ideas and actions toward the greater good of the organization.

Bass (1985) identified four facets of transformational leadership. First, **idealized influence** refers to the fact that transformational leaders serve as role models for employees. Associated with charisma, idealized influence involves establishing trust, pride, and respect among all members of the organization. In so doing, the leader models ideal behavior for employees.

Second, **inspirational motivation** requires transformational leaders to present employees with a clear vision and desirable future. Followers are motivated by the attainment of this vision and receive encouragement and support for doing so. As such, employees' self-interest is subsumed to the interest of the greater good.

Third, transformational leaders provide **intellectual stimulation**. The status quo is not taken for granted; transformational leaders challenge their own assumptions and encourage new approaches. Differences of opinion are addressed openly and without fear; leaders willingly acknowledge their own mistakes and recognize the superior ideas of others. Followers are encouraged to reject tradition as a means for operating and to challenge their own thinking.

Fourth, **individualized consideration** is considered the hallmark of transformational leadership. The transformational leader considers each individual's needs and abilities, while supporting development and mentoring efforts. In this way, the confidence of followers is enhanced, and subordinates can turn their attention from simple existence (i.e., keeping the job) to achievement and growth. Effectiveness is preferred to efficiency, and equity (considering outputs relative to inputs) is preferred to equal exchange (i.e., everyone receiving the same rewards).

Both transactional and transformational leadership are associated with achievement of organizational goals (Bass, 1985). Moreover, any given leader can be both transactional and transformative. Research has consistently shown, however, that transformational leadership is associated with greater individual and organizational outcomes (Bass, 1998). Research linking transformational leadership to EI suggests a leader's emotional intelligence predicts his or her use of transformational leadership, which in turn predicts employee satisfaction (Lam & O'Higgins, 2012).

Individuals high in EI have the ability to succeed in the workplace because they are able to recognize, manage, and use their own and others' emotions strategically. One important way individuals high in EI have an impact on organizations is through transformational leadership. As we will see shortly, other important qualities might explain positive (and problematic) interactions. Our third theory is message design logics.

MESSAGE DESIGN LOGICS

Everyone has been faced with the challenge of having to confront a co-worker or subordinate who isn't pulling his or her weight. The dilemmas communicators confront when dealing with these sorts of situations can be understood by the theory of message design logics. According to O'Keefe (1988, 1997), because people think about communication differently, they also construct very different types of messages. A **message design logic (MDL)**, then, is your belief about communication that, in turn, links thoughts to the construction of messages. Stated differently, people's views about the nature and function of communication affect their messages. Variation in message type is particularly evident when a person is faced with communication challenges such as dealing with a difficult co-worker. According to O'Keefe (1997), there are three types of design logics from which people operate.

Three Message Design Logics

Using an inductive approach, O'Keefe (1988) developed her theory after studying the techniques people used to try to persuade others. Despite a plethora of strategies that might be used, she found that people tended to use "fairly uniform" techniques (1997, p. 87). Through this work, O'Keefe uncovered three distinct MDLs: expressive, conventional, and rhetorical.

Expressive logic is a sender-focused pattern (O'Keefe, 1988). That is, a person using this pattern is concerned primarily with self-expression. Communication is viewed as a means for conveying the sender's thoughts and feelings. People who use the expressive MDL have a very difficult time holding back their thoughts; if it's in their head, it's out their mouth. They value openness, honesty, and clarity in communication and are mistrustful of anyone who seems overly strategic in his or her communication. Such communicators pay little attention to context and what may be appropriate behavior. They can't help themselves— they feel a genuine pressure to say what is on their mind right there and then. When the situation calls for them to protect someone else's self-esteem, they typically accomplish this by editing their comments (e.g., replacing profanity with a euphemism) rather than through genuine efforts at politeness (see Chapter 5 for a discussion of politeness theory). For example, when faced with potential sexual harassment, a person using an expressive MDL might respond in this way: "You are the most rude and disgusting man I have ever met. You're nothing but a dirty old man. Where do you get off thinking you could force me to have an affair with you? You make me sick!" (Bingham & Burleson, 1989, p. 192).

Note that the content of this message is focused entirely on what the sender is feeling at the time. The sender might have made an effort to temper his or her anger by editing his or her language, but other than that, little effort is made to modify the expression of thoughts and feelings.

Second, **conventional logic** views communication as a rule-based game played cooperatively (O'Keefe, 1988). As such, those using a conventional MDL are primarily concerned with appropriateness; these individuals view communication contexts, roles, and relationships as having particular guidelines for behavior (O'Keefe, 1997). They are concerned about saying and doing the "right" thing in any given situation. To do the right thing, they follow the rules of politeness (see Chapter 5 for more on politeness theory). Keeping our example of dealing with potential sexual harassment, a person using a conventional MDL might respond like this: "There's absolutely no chance I will have an affair with you, and if you try to fire me over this I won't keep quiet about it. That kind of behavior is not appropriate in the workplace. Besides that, you're married. Don't approach me again" (Bingham & Burleson, 1989, p. 192).

In this case, the message sender makes several allusions to communication rules; not only does she or he point out that this behavior is "not appropriate in the workplace," but the speaker also refers to an implicit rule by saying "you're married," which is a social relationship constrained by certain behavioral guidelines.

The third MDL is **rhetorical logic**. Individuals using a rhetorical MDL view communication as a powerful tool used to create situations and negotiate multiple goals (O'Keefe, 1988). Instead of emphasizing self-expression (expressive logic) or social appropriateness (conventional logic), "those acting on the basis of a rhetorical design logic focus on the effect of messages on the recipient" (Bonito & Wolski, 2002, p. 256). This approach is noted for flexibility, as well as for its sophistication and depth of communication skill. Those using a rhetorical MDL pay close attention to other people's communication in an effort to figure out others' points of view. They try to anticipate and prevent problems by redefining situations to benefit all parties involved in the interaction. Unlike the expressive MDL, which is reactive, the rhetorical MDL is proactive (O'Keefe, 1988). An example of a rhetorical MDL in the potential sexual harassment situation is as follows:

> We've got a great working relationship now, and I'd like us to work well together in the future. So I think it's important for us to talk this out. You're a smart and clear-thinking guy and I consider you to be my friend as well as my boss. That's why I have to think you must be under a lot of unusual stress lately to have said something like this. I know what it's like to be under pressure. Too much stress can really make you crazy. You probably just need a break. (Bingham & Burleson, 1989, p. 193)

In this case, the sender seeks to balance his or her own goal of stopping the harassment with the target's goal of protecting against embarrassment. At the same time, the sender strives to maintain a good working relationship with the person in the future. This is accomplished by redefining the situation from one of sexual harassment to one of excessive stress. By reframing the message, the rhetorical communicator has found "a common drama in which to play" (O'Keefe, 1988, p. 88).

Message Design Logics Preferences

Reading the three examples presented might give you insight into the MDL under which you tend to operate. More than likely, one of those messages is similar to something you might say in a situation you perceive as harassing, and the other message types might reflect something you would never say in a million years. Indeed, one of the challenges highlighted by this theory is the difficulty individuals have when dealing with others who use a different MDL. O'Keefe, Lambert, and Lambert (1997) argued that when two people use the same MDL, these individuals recognize that the problems are communication problems. When two parties use different MDLs, however, these individuals often do not realize they have communication problems; instead, they blame the difficulties on perceived bad intentions, mistaken beliefs, or undesirable personality characteristics (see attribution theory presented in Chapter 3). For example, a person who uses an expressive MDL tends to view those using a rhetorical MDL as dishonest because they "manipulate" their perception of the situation. Table 4.2 presents some forms of miscommunication due to differing MDLs.

Although individuals tend to prefer using one MDL to another, O'Keefe and colleagues have cautioned that MDLs are not the same as personality traits. Similar to EI, MDLs are not considered to be stable personality traits; instead, they can change and develop over an individual's life span. In fact, O'Keefe and Delia (1988) found that the three MDLs reflect a developmental process, with the expressive MDL the least developed and the rhetorical MDL the most developed pattern. However, O'Keefe et al. (1997) warned that this developmental trajectory should not imply that the rhetorical strategy is superior to others: "Every

Table 4.2   Forms of Miscommunication Due to Message Design Logics

Message Producer	Message Recipient		
	Expressive MDL	**Conventional MDL**	**Rhetorical MDL**
Expressive MDL	Genuine differences in opinion prevent communicators from achieving any connection.	Expressive remarks perceived as embarrassing or crude due to inappropriateness.	Expressive person perceived as inconsiderate and uncooperative.
Conventional MDL	Ritualistic messages are taken literally by the expressive person (such as "Let's get together soon").	Differing views of appropriateness of the situation lead to perceived inappropriate behavior.	Conformity to appropriateness viewed as rigidity, overly conservative approach to interaction.
Rhetorical MDL	Messages viewed as unnecessarily elaborate and indirect; sender viewed as dishonest.	Failure to see coherence of complex messages because of focus on "correct" context.	Incompatible assumptions about goals can lead to misunderstanding of others' intent.

Source: O'Keefe, B. J., Lambert, B. L., & Lambert, C. A. (1997). Conflict and communication in a research and development unit. In B. D. Sypher (Ed.), *Case studies in organizational communication 2*, p. 42. New York: Guilford Press.

design logic provides a logically consistent and potentially satisfactory way for an individual to use language" (p. 49). They believe all communicators should recognize and accommodate diversity in MDLs. Knowing the variation is half the battle.

Again, O'Keefe's (1988, 1997) theory suggests that individuals tend to operate using one of three MDLs. Users of expressive MDLs view communication primarily as a means of sharing their unique feelings, beliefs, and ideas. Those who rely on conventional MDLs perceive communication as a rules-based game; to play the "game" one must operate using social conventions for appropriateness. Last, a rhetorical MDL emphasizes a highly flexible approach to communication in which the speaker adapts to the situation, using self-expression or relying on social conventions as appropriate.

INTERACTIONAL PERSPECTIVE ON WORKPLACE GENERATIONS

In 1967, a group of psychiatrists at the Mental Research Institute in Palo Alto, California, published a book called *Pragmatics of Human Communication*. Their focus was to uncover the reasons for schizophrenia, which they hypothesized had an environmental basis (we have since learned schizophrenia is much more on the "nature" than the "nurture" end of the continuum). However, Watzlawick, Bavelas, and Jackson (1967) presented a model for human communication grounded in a number of axioms, or assumptions, about the communication process. Called the interactional perspective, Watzlawick et al.'s view profoundly influenced our assumptions about communication and has been applied to everything from understanding foreign policy problems (Calhoun, 2008) to understanding brand relationships in advertising (Heath, Brandt, & Nairn, 2006).

According to the Palo Alto Group, there are five axioms of communication (Watzlawick et al., 1967). The first axiom is on the impossibility of not communicating. Widely misinterpreted and debated, the axiom suggests all behavior has the potential to be communicative, regardless of whether the sender intended the behavior to be interpreted as a message. For example, according to this axiom the "silent treatment" is indeed communicative because the recipient of the silent treatment is clearly receiving the message "I'm angry with you." Within a work setting, the person who is chronically tardy might be perceived as communicating his or her disinterest in the work activities. The group member who answers a cell phone in the middle of a meeting might be perceived as sending the message to his or her teammates that "I'm more important than you are." Intentionality is a complex issue in the field of communication, with scholars on both sides of the debate passionate about the role of intent (see Chapter 1). Regarding this debate, the Palo Alto Group is firmly committed to the belief that communication need not be intentional.

The second axiom is that all communication has both content and relationship levels. When people interact with each other, they are sending particular messages, which are considered the **content level**. These messages may be verbal or nonverbal. At the same time they are sending content, they are also sending additional information. The **relationship level** is characterized as how the content should be understood, particularly in terms of the relationship between the communicators. To illustrate, consider the following statements: "Peter, can you work on getting that brochure copy done?" and "Peter, get the brochure copy done." The content is virtually the same; however, the relationship level gives us quite different information in the two scenarios. The first statement can be understood as a request, whereas the second can be understood as a command. More than that, in the first situation you understand that the two people are on equal footing and that their relationship is respectful. In the second situation, the speaker either has a legitimate superior status over the listener or the speaker is trying to exert dominance over a status equal. The implications of this information are likely to affect the patterns of communication among everyone in the system.

The third axiom focuses on the tendency of communicators to punctuate sequences of behavior. The grammatical definition of the term **punctuation** refers to the use of marks to separate sentences, clauses, and so forth. For example, the previous sentence has a capital *T* to indicate the beginning of the sentence, two commas to indicate pauses between a series, and a period to indicate the end of the sentence. Watzlawick et al.'s notion of punctuation is similar. They believe interaction is understood by the people involved in it as a series of beginnings and endings, of causes and effects. For example, in the example used for content and relationship levels, Peter might respond to the command by sarcastically responding, "Why yes, ma'am, right away ma'am, whatever you say, ma'am." Peter would likely view the perceived inappropriate command as the cause of his sarcasm, whereas the person who gave the command might view his flippant attitude as the reason why she had to give a command rather than a request in the first place. The point of this axiom is that although communicators tend to assign causes and effects to interactions, it is likely that interactants will view the same interaction as having different causes and effects; punctuation is always a matter of individual perception, with no perception being wholly correct or incorrect. Moreover, Watzlawick et al. argue that differences in punctuation frequently lead to conflict among system members.

The fourth axiom is that communication entails both digital and analogic codes. Analogic codes are those in which the symbol actually resembles the object it represents. For example, holding two fingers up to indicate the number *2* is an analogue. Another analogue is crying to represent sadness; the tears are a physical representation of the emotion. Most nonverbals are analogues, although this is not entirely the case. Many emblems, such as giving someone the middle finger or using the OK sign, are not analogues. On the other hand, few verbal messages are analogues, but there are exceptions. Onomatopoeia, in which the word sounds like what it means (words such as *buzz* or *click*), can be considered examples of **analogic communication**. The point is that analogic communication is rarely misunderstood because of the direct connection between the symbol and its meaning; even people from vastly different cultures can likely understand each other's analogic communication.

Digital communication is that in which the symbol and its meaning are arbitrarily linked. For example, there is nothing inherently catlike about the word *cat*, nor is there anything particularly democratic about the word *democracy*. The symbol H_2O does not in any way resemble water. Instead, the meanings of these symbols are culturally determined. Most digital communication is verbal, but some nonverbals, particularly emblems (which have dictionary-type definitions), can be considered digital. The OK symbol, wherein you make a circle with your thumb and forefinger, is an example of digital communication (which is why it has different meanings in different cultures). The problem with digital communication is that two people operating from different digital codes (e.g., different language systems or different rules for nonverbal expression) likely don't understand that misunderstandings might be due to the nuances inherent in the use of digital codes.

The fifth and final axiom proposes that communication can be symmetrical or complementary. When communicators behave in the same manner, they are using a **symmetrical pattern**. For example, Mike is sarcastic to you, and you are sarcastic to Mike. Mike defers to you, and you defer to Mike. When the communicators behave in different ways, they are using a **complementary pattern**. For example, Mike commands, and you defer. Mike is sarcastic, and you whine. Notice that behaving in a complementary fashion does not mean interactants are behaving in an *opposite* fashion, just that the patterns of behavior are different. This axiom has most frequently been used to study control behaviors (Millar & Rogers, 1976).

Combined, these axioms explain the basis for a number of potential reasons for miscommunication. One increasingly popular context for investigating miscommunication in the workplace centers on differences in the values, beliefs, and behaviors of members of different generations. How many times have you heard an older person grouse about a younger person that "hasn't paid her dues?" How many times have you heard a younger person grumble that an older person is "completely rigid" when it comes to change? Popular books such as Lancaster and Stillman's (2003) *When Generations Collide*, Tulgan's (2003) *Managing Generation* X, and Alsop's (2008) *The Trophy Kids Grow Up: How the Millennial Generation Is Shaking up the Workplace* highlight potential age-based variations in professional settings. As of yet, no theories explain generational variations in communication behaviors at work, but we believe the interactional perspective can explain why miscommunication might occur.

What Are the Generations?

Twenge and Campbell (2008) argued that each generation is influenced by specific events. Do you remember where you were when you heard JFK was shot? When the *Challenger* exploded? When the events of 9/11 unfolded? When the Boston Marathon suspects were captured? These cultural touchstones have influenced each generation in subtle ways.

> Just as people raised in Japan have different personality traits and attitudes (on average) from people raised in the USA, there are true differences among generations. Growing up in the 1990s was a fundamentally different experience from growing up in the 1970s or especially the 1950s. (Twenge & Campbell, 2008, p. 863)

Before addressing how an interactional perspective can explain intergenerational conflict, we need to identify generational differences in the United States. Most authors identify four generations in the contemporary workplace: Veterans (meaning WWII veterans), Baby Boomers, Generation X, and Millennials (also called Generation Y). Table 4.3 identifies the major characteristics associated with each of the groups.

Perhaps the strongest evidence to date comes from a cross-temporal meta-analysis. Twenge and Campbell's (2008) research reviewed hundreds of studies examining personality traits of college students over the span of 80 years and included more than 1.4 million people in their sample. Their results showed the current generation (Millennials) varies from previous generations in five ways that affect the workplace. First, they discovered a decreased need for social approval. That is, Millennials are less likely to follow rules simply because the rules exist. For organizations, implications include more informality in dress and communication styles. Second, Twenge and Campbell noted a simultaneous increase in both self-esteem and narcissism. Together, these personality characteristics translate into higher expectations for the workplace as well as an increased demand for employers to meet individual employee needs. For the Millennial generation, according to Twenge and Campbell, "it's all about me" (p. 864). Third, the meta-analysis determined that the current generation has an external locus of control (Twenge & Campbell, 2008). *Locus of control* refers to the tendency to explain the causes of events to either one's own effort (internal) or to the environment or outside forces (external). Millennials tend not to take responsibility for their own successes or failures, requiring their managers to push them harder in order to produce. Interestingly, although the current generation does not feel as much individual responsibility as do previous generations, the fourth discovery made by Twenge and Campbell revealed that Millennials have higher levels of anxiety and depression than preceding generations, requiring organizations to provide more mental health services than ever before. Finally, the study found that women in the Millennial generation are more assertive. Twenge and Campbell concluded that this assertiveness will require organizations to provide more work–life balance, as female employees will simply demand it.

Table 4.4 seeks to blend the axioms proposed by the interactional perspective with some of the implications for generational variations. Of course, thus far we have only sought to uncover potential areas of disagreement. The interactional perspective also

Table 4.3 Generational Characteristics

Characteristics	Veterans	Baby Boomers	Generation X	Millennials or Generation Y
Date of birth	1922 to 1945	1946 to 1964	1965 to 1980	1980 to 2000
Core values	Respect, discipline	Optimism, involvement	Cynicism, informality	Clarity, flexibility
View of work	An obligation	Self-fulfillment	Entrepreneurship	A mechanism for success
Satisfaction comes from	A job well done	Making a difference	Changing the rules	Lots of recognition
Preferred rewards	Delayed and intrinsic (did their duty, private praise)	Primarily intrinsic (feeling good about self)	Extrinsic (recognition through time, money, and freedom)	Very extrinsic (recognition through immediate praise, opportunity, and status)
Communication style	Formal; letters and memos	Face-to-face discussion, meetings	Direct; comfortable with technology	Constant connection; heavy reliance on technology
Leadership style	Autocratic	Consensual	Confrontational	Passive-aggressive
Loyalty	High	High	Low	Low

Sources: Information synthesized from Busch, Venkitachalam, and Richards, 2008; McGuire, Todnem By, and Hutchings, 2007; Smola and Sutton, 2002; Tomkiewicz and Bass, 2008; Twenge and Campbell, 2008; Twenge, Campbell, Hoffman, & Lance, 2010; Westermann and Yamamura, 2007.

provides possible solutions. Watzlawick, Weakland, and Fisch (1974) argue there are two types of change. **First-order change** refers to changing the behaviors of individuals in the system. In the case of patterns of behavior among those from different generations, first-order change would likely involve training and development, mentoring, or coaching efforts aimed at modifying communication styles. However, Watzlawick et al. (1974) caution that first-order change is analogous to treating the symptoms without curing the disease: Although communication between the generations might sound more polite and supportive, the underlying values and beliefs would still be at odds. Instead, they would recommend **second-order change**. Second-order change seeks to resolve underlying differences in perspective, most often through the process of reframing. Reframing is a process of intentionally seeking alternative perspectives to a problem. Interestingly, one way reframing might occur in the case of intergenerational conflict in the workplace might be to have members of each generation seek to understand each other's standpoint.

Table 4.4 Interactional Perspective Axioms and Implications for Generational Conflict

Axiom	Implication for Interpersonal Communication
The impossibility of not communicating	Members of different generations might not intend for their behaviors to cause workplace conflict, but those from different generations might interpret others' behavior as disrespectful or inappropriate.
Content and relationship levels	The content of communication might not be problematic, but the relationship dimension of messages might highlight disagreements about how workplace communication should be handled.
The problem of punctuation	Members of different generations are likely to see the cause of the perceived disrespect/inappropriateness as starting from the other generation.
Digital and analogic codes	The same word (e.g., *respect*) might be understood very differently by members of different generations.
Complementary and symmetrical communication	Within the workplace, complementary patterns are likely to emerge when members of different generations work together.

There is early evidence of generational differences in values and ways of behaving. However, scholars have only started to document these differences. As yet, we do not have a specific theory that can explain and predict why they occur, what they mean, and what might happen in the future, but the interactional view highlights some issues likely to emerge as well as some ways to manage those differences.

Summary and Research Applications

In this chapter we highlighted theories that seek to uncover how individual and social variations influence the communication process. First, we described the social role theory of gender, which highlights how assumptions of appropriate behavior for men and women influence our judgments about individual men and women in the workplace. We specifically discussed how role incongruity causes a double bind for female leaders. Second, we focused on emotional intelligence and how individuals high in EI are more likely to engage in transformational leadership. Interestingly, Lopez-Zafra, Garcia-Retamero, and Martos (2012) recently investigated connections between role congruity theory, emotional intelligence, and transformational leadership. They found the communal approach associated with the female social role combined with emotional intelligence predicted transformational leadership better than did emotional intelligence alone. The third theory explained was message design logics, which argues that because people have different beliefs about communication they communicate in notably different ways. To illustrate, Barbour, Jacocks, and Wesner (2012) studied message design logics and the organizational change process. Among other things, they found people were likely to use more sophisticated messages (i.e., a rhetorical style) when seeking to persuade someone at a higher level in the hierarchy than themselves. Finally, we used the interactional perspective to analyze generational differences in the workplace. The axioms of communication highlight how and why miscommunication might occur, and the approach provides a mechanism to overcome potential conflict.

Key Terms

Agentic qualities   58

Analogic communication   67

Communal qualities   58

Communibiological approach   56

Complementary pattern   67

Content level   66

Conventional logic   63

Descriptive prejudice   58

Digital communication   67

Double bind   58

Emotional intelligence   60

Expressive logic   63

First-order change   70

Gender   58

Idealized influence   61

Individualized consideration   62

Inspirational motivation   62

Intellectual stimulation   62

Message design logic   62

Prescriptive prejudice   58

Punctuation   66

Relationship level   66

Rhetorical logic   63

Second-order change   70

Sex   58

Standpoint   56

Symmetrical pattern   67

Transactional leadership   60

Transformational leadership   61

Case Study 4: Military Misunderstanding

Much like a large corporation that divides its employees into departments based on tasks and expertise, the U.S. Air Force organizes its tasks and personnel into divisions called squadrons. Each squadron has a specific job to do; for example, the 705th AGS performs air ground support, and the 714th handles maintenance. Although ultimately all working for the air force, each squadron operates relatively independently from the others; as a result, there is a high degree of loyalty to one's squad. Despite intrasquad allegiance, however, a person's rank supersedes this loyalty. For example, if a major were to approach an enlisted or lower-ranking individual from a different squadron, let's say a sergeant, the sergeant would have to defer to the major. Obviously, then, one's squad and rank mean a great deal, particularly when sending and receiving messages.

A civilian employee, Suzanne Miller, worked as an administrative assistant at an air force base. Although she worked for the 714th MXS squadron that handles maintenance, her unit was required to share half of its hangar with another squadron, and for reasons unknown to Suzanne, the two units didn't get along to say the least. Sure, she knew intrasquad loyalty was important; however, the constant bickering between members of the two squadrons seemed adolescent.

As a civilian, Suzanne wasn't required to defer to anyone other than her direct supervisors—Master Sergeant (MSGT) Robinson and Staff Sergeant (SSGT) Lakey. Even if a high-ranking officer from another squadron asked her to make some copies or run an errand, Suzanne couldn't comply; only MSGT Robinson and SSGT Lakey had the authority to make requests or require specific duties.

Usually Suzanne's days consisted of filing paperwork, answering phones, and helping to manage the squadron's snack bar. Conveniently located in the main hall of the hangar, the snack bar was common ground for members of both squadrons to mill around. For a civilian just out of college, Suzanne found her job to be an interesting experience, if a bit mundane.

One day, however, her military experience became a bit more remarkable. Suzanne had recently discovered that an old friend, Rebecca Truman, was working as a civilian for the other squadron occupying the hangar. On this particular day, Suzanne decided to use her midmorning break to catch up with Rebecca. She walked over to Rebecca's work area, and the two women began chatting. A few minutes into their conversation an unfamiliar man stormed over. Standing directly in front of Suzanne with his hands on his hips, he angrily stated, "I don't know who you are, but I do know you shouldn't be here. Get the hell out of this squadron, you are causing a disturbance!"

Shocked, Suzanne stared blankly at him. Usually she could distinguish rank and squadron immediately by looking at a person's uniform, complete with pins of rank and commendation and nametag. This man was not wearing his uniform or a nametag, however. Not recognizing him from her own squadron, Suzanne was unsure of who he was or why he was there barking at her. Irritated, she retorted, "Well, I don't know who you are, but I know you aren't my boss, and I know that I will not be talked to that way. For your information, I'm allowed to be here talking to my friend because we are both civilians and we are on our break." The strange man took another step closer, and with closed fists and a bright-red face he screamed: "I *said* get out of here! I have work to do!" He abruptly turned and marched away.

Suzanne was furious. The guy was a jerk! Rather than stay and cause any difficulties for her friend, however, Suzanne left Rebecca's work space and went back to her squadron's office, trying to forget the incident.

Unfortunately, the episode didn't go away. Later that afternoon, SSGT Lakey called Suzanne into her office. The sergeant explained that the enraged man who had confronted Suzanne was Lieutenant Meyers. Suzanne's face went white because she realized the lieutenant was an officer—and thus higher ranking than any sergeant. Moreover, Suzanne had heard rumors that Lt. Meyers made trouble for those he didn't like.

SSGT Lakey told Suzanne the lieutenant had approached Suzanne's chief supervisor, MGST Robinson, and had filed a formal complaint against her. Apparently, the lieutenant had a radically different perception of his encounter with Suzanne, thus casting her in a poor light. His complaint indicated that Suzanne was disruptive, unprofessional, and noncompliant. He wanted her disciplined for incompetence and insubordination. His report concluded by saying, "The air force can't afford to have sloppy and defiant employees, even if they are civilians!"

Hearing the report, Suzanne protested, "But that's not what happened!" She gave her account of the situation to SSGT Lakey. Familiar with Lt. Meyers's hotheaded temper and "jump-the-gun" conclusions, SSGT Lakey was inclined to believe Suzanne. After conferring with MGST Robinson, however, the two sergeants agreed they didn't want to approach the lieutenant to clarify the situation.

The next day, Suzanne was still bothered by the incident. She wanted to protect her reputation and her record. She asked to meet with MGST Robinson and explained to him that she was still concerned. In fact, Suzanne thought the lieutenant could be accused of defamation of character for some of the things he had claimed in the report against her. She wanted the report dismissed from her records. MGST Robinson replied, "Well, I think that both sides have been explained and now we can all move on. Just try to stay away from the lieutenant, and if he says anything to you, just look down and walk away."

MGST Robinson thought he had diffused the situation until Lt. Meyers approached him, demanding to know what actions had been taken against Suzanne. Suzanne overheard MGST Robinson saying, "I think everything's fine. I spoke with her and there's no need for everyone to be upset. Why don't we just forget this whole thing?"

Questions for Consideration

1. How might social role stereotypes explain the interaction? Is there any evidence of descriptive or prescriptive prejudices?

2. Discuss Lt. Meyers, Suzanne, and SSGT Lakey in terms of emotional intelligence. How do they fare on each of the four branches?

3. What message design logic does Lt. Meyers appear to rely on? What about Suzanne? How about MSGT Robinson? Using Table 4.2 identifying forms of miscommunication due to MDL, analyze what might have happened.

4. Assess the extent to which the axioms are present in the case. Do you believe generational variations might have played a role in the misunderstanding? Why or why not?

5. Which theory seems to explain the situation "better" than the others? Why do you believe this to be the case? Are there other theories or a combination of theories that might explain what happened more fully?

CHAPTER 5

Interpersonal Communication

(Continued)

17. Compare and contrast the central *internal* and *external* dialectics Baxter believes are inherent in close relationships.

18. Apply and evaluate the effectiveness of the four primary strategies used to manage internal and external dialectics.

19. Describe the possible tensions between privacy and disclosure.

20. Articulate the complexities associated with information management using Petronio's six principles of privacy management.

21. Explain and apply privacy rule criteria so as to evaluate decisions about whether or not to reveal private information.

22. Compare and contrast and apply major theoretical approaches to interpersonal communication.

It's difficult to imagine a profession that doesn't require you to interact with other people. You likely use interpersonal communication every day—to handle complaints from a demanding client, to persuade your boss to give you some time off, or to comfort a friend dealing with a difficult relationship. This chapter explains a variety of interpersonal communication theories, including those that explain how relationships are initiated and developed, theories of how relationships are maintained over time, and theories that explain why and what to do when people behave in unexpected ways.

INTERPERSONAL COMMUNICATION DEFINED

Interpersonal communication (IPC) has been defined in many ways. Some scholars define IPC based on the situation and number of participants involved (see Miller, 1978). Using Miller's definition, IPC occurs between two individuals when they are in proximity, are able to provide immediate feedback, and use multiple senses. Others define IPC based on the degree of "personalness," or perceived quality, of a given interaction (see Peters, 1974). In Peters's view, IPC includes communication that is personal and occurring between people who are more than acquaintances. Another view of IPC is a goals approach; that is, IPC includes communication used to define or achieve personal goals through interaction with others (see Canary, Cody, & Manusov, 2003).

For the purpose of examining IPC theory, we argue that IPC encompasses a number of these definitions. IPC includes those messages between two interdependent persons, with a particular focus on how IPC messages are offered to initiate, define, maintain, or further a relationship. IPC is more than just saying a polite hello to the salesclerk in our favorite department store and then scurrying away never to be seen again. Instead, it refers both to the *content* and *quality* of messages relayed and the possibility of further relationship development. We present four theories in this chapter critical to current understandings of IPC and the relationships that develop from these communications. First, politeness theory clarifies the strategies individuals use to maintain their "face," or sense of desired public image. Second, social exchange theory (SET) evaluates relationships on the basis of rewards and costs; this ratio of benefits to drawbacks explains whether a relationship will continue as well as whether partners will feel satisfied. Third, the dialectical perspective describes the contradictions individuals inevitably face within their personal relationships and explains how management of these contradictions can predict a relationship's success or failure. Finally, communication privacy management theory builds on these earlier theories and focuses on the decisions we make to reveal or conceal information.

POLITENESS THEORY

Mentioned in Chapter 3, expectancy violations theory (EVT) presents an explanation and specific predictions about what individuals do when others behave in ways that contradict their assumptions—particularly assumptions and preferences for personal space. In a somewhat related vein, politeness theory (PT) explains how and why individuals try to promote, protect, or "save face," especially when embarrassing or shameful situations arise unexpectedly.

Developed by Brown and Levinson (1978, 1987), PT clarifies how we manage our own and others' identities through interaction, in particular, through the use of politeness strategies. Building on Goffman's (1967) notion of identity and facework, Brown and Levinson (1978, 1987) determined when, why, and how interpersonal interaction is constructed through (or in the absence of) politeness.

Assumptions of Politeness Theory

Three primary assumptions guide PT. First, PT assumes all individuals are concerned with maintaining face (Brown & Levinson, 1978, 1987). Simply put, **face** refers to your desired self-image, the identity you wish to present to others. Erving Goffman (1959) first proposed a dramaturgical approach to understand face, arguing that human interaction is akin to the theatre. In different "scenes" and with different "actors," we often wear different "masks" either to highlight or deemphasize different aspects of our personality. Goffman wasn't suggesting we're all narcissistic phonies but rather that individuals are selective in revealing different aspects of themselves, in different contexts, and to different audiences. At the law office where she works, for example, Marta might want to project her image as intelligent, competent, and fair. With her young nieces and nephews, however, Marta might want to project the image of a caring and silly aunt who does cartwheels down the sidewalk. And with her new boyfriend, Marta might want to be viewed as fun-loving, spontaneous, and romantic. All of these qualities are part of Marta's identity, but she is thoughtful about what part of her image is highlighted and with whom.

Not only does face refer to the image you want others to have for you, it also includes the recognition that your interactional partners have face needs of their own. Thus, Marta must recognize that her colleagues, family members, and significant other also each have self-images they want to maintain while at work, at home, and at play. Much like a dance, each party must help the other to uphold his or her desired image for face to work. If Marta's colleague, Rich, views her attempts to be seen as intelligent as pretentious and unsubstantiated, then Marta hasn't achieved the face she desires.

There are two dimensions to the concept of face: positive face and negative face (Brown & Levinson, 1978, 1987). **Positive face** includes a person's need to be liked, appreciated, and admired by select persons. Thus, maintaining positive face includes using behaviors to ensure these significant others continue to view you in an affirming fashion. **Negative face** assumes a person's desire to act freely, without constraints or imposition from others. It is difficult to achieve positive and negative face simultaneously—that is, acting in a way so that you gain others' approval often interferes with autonomous and unrestricted behavior.

Second, PT assumes human beings are rational and goal oriented, at least with respect to achieving face needs (Brown & Levinson, 1978, 1987). In other words, you have choices and make communicative decisions to achieve your relational and task-oriented goals within the context of maintaining face. Notably, Brown and Levinson posited that face management works best when everyone involved helps maintain the face of others. In other words, because "everyone's face depends on everyone else's [face] being maintained" (Brown & Levinson, 1987, p. 61), it is in your own best interest to make decisions that uphold this mutual, and rather vulnerable, construction of face.

The final assumption, despite the understanding of face as mutually constructed and maintained, is that some behaviors are fundamentally face threatening (Brown & Levinson, 1978, 1987). Inevitably, you will threaten someone else's face, just as another person will, at some point, threaten yours. These **face-threatening acts** (FTAs) include common behaviors such as apologies, compliments, criticisms, requests, and threats (Craig, Tracy, & Spisak, 1993).

PT, then, ties together these assumptions to explain and predict how, when, and where FTAs occur, as well as what individuals can do to restore face once endangered. Discussed next, we clarify strategies used to uphold and reclaim one's own face and present strategies that pertain to maintaining or threatening the face of others.

Preserving Face

As stated earlier, face is the self-image individuals desire to present to others as well as the acknowledgment that others have face needs of their own. To create and maintain this desired self-image, individuals must use **facework**—specific messages that thwart or minimize FTAs (Goffman, 1967). Preventive facework strategies include communications people use to help themselves or others avert FTAs (Cupach & Metts, 1994). For example, avoiding certain topics, changing the subject, or pretending not to notice an FTA are all preventive facework strategies.

Similar to preventive facework, **corrective facework** consists of messages people use to restore their own face or to help others restore face after an FTA (Cupach & Metts, 1994). Corrective facework includes the use of strategies such as avoidance, humor, apologies, accounts or explanations of inappropriate actions, and physical remediation wherein one attempts to repair any physical damage from the FTA.

As noted earlier, your own face needs may conflict with your partner's face needs. How you manage this discrepancy between self and others' needs may instigate your use of an FTA. As you might imagine, behaving so as to gain others' approval (positive face) can obviously interfere with acting so as to appear self-sufficient and unrestricted (negative face). Sometimes, then, individuals need to choose between positive and negative face needs. Especially when your desire to appear unencumbered outweighs your desire to be liked, you may need to engage in an FTA.

According to PT, individuals can choose one of five suprastrategies when communicating in a manner that could potentially threaten the face of another (Brown & Levinson, 1978). Moving from most polite (and least direct) to least polite (and most direct), these suprastrategies include avoidance, going off-record, negative politeness, positive politeness, and bald-on-record. A speaker who uses **avoidance** simply chooses not to communicate in a way that would create embarrassment or a loss of face for another, whereas when a speaker is going **off-record**, he or she subtly hints of or indirectly mentions the face-threatening topic. Hinting or making indirect suggestions leaves the message open to interpretation, thereby minimizing any face threat. For example, Josephine works as a technician in a veterinary hospital where every fourth weekend she is expected to be on call for emergencies and to make daily rounds, checking in on the animals. If something comes up and Josephine wants to switch her weekend shift with a colleague, she can hint that "it really stinks that I have to work this weekend because my friends invited me to go to the beach for one of those last-minute weekend getaway specials." If Josephine's co-worker picks up the hint, he may offer to cover her weekend shift. If the colleague doesn't pick up on her subtlety or doesn't want to work the weekend, he can simply take her disclosure at face value—Josephine wishes she were spending the weekend at a beach resort with friends.

A somewhat more direct approach, **negative politeness** occurs when the speaker makes an effort to recognize the other's negative face needs—that is, the receiver's need of freedom and lack of restraint. With negative politeness, you appeal to the receiver's negative face needs through apologies and self-effacement to make yourself appear vulnerable to the other, while also acknowledging that the FTA is impolite and inhibits the other's independence. For example, when Josephine attempts to get a co-worker to cover her weekend shift, she might say, "I am so sorry to ask, but I need a huge favor. I know this is last-minute, and I really hate to be such a pain, but could you cover my shift this weekend? I know this is really inconvenient, and I wouldn't ask if it weren't really important." By expressing such regret and making oneself appear self-conscious about committing an FTA, the speaker directly acknowledges the other person's discomfort and potential restriction, while still managing to engage in the FTA for which she claims to be so embarrassed.

An even more direct yet less polite strategy is that of **positive politeness**. Using positive politeness, the speaker emphasizes the receiver's need for positive face—that is, the need to be liked. By ingratiating the receiver with flattery and compliments, you hope to camouflage your face-threatening behavior. For example, Josephine might attempt to "butter up" her colleague with praises before asking him to cover her weekend shift, saying, "Bill, you are such a reliable colleague and are so well respected. I feel like I can really count on you. Would you cover my weekend shift?" Finally, the most direct and least polite strategy is **bald-on-record**. Using this strategy, the communicator makes no attempt to protect the other's face and simply commits the FTA. Continuing Josephine's predicament, then, she might simply demand Bill cover for her, saying, "Bill, cover my shift this weekend."

According to PT, people choose to engage in FTAs rather tactically. Specifically, there are a number of factors people use to decide how polite to be. These factors are described in Table 5.1. For example, when considering how polite to be, communicators determine whether the person has more or less **prestige** than they do, whether the communicator has **power** over them at the time, and whether what is going to be said runs the **risk** of hurting the other person (Brown & Levinson, 1987).

Table 5.1 Factors Influencing Politeness Strategies

Consideration	Prediction
Prestige	If someone has more prestige than you (someone with an impressive title or a great deal of money), you will be more polite. If someone holds little or no prestige over you, you need not be so polite.
Power	If someone has power over you (your boss or even your auto mechanic if your car is not running), you will be more polite. If it is someone with little power over you, you need not be so polite.
Risk	If what you are going to say has a high chance of hurting someone (you are going to fire them or you are going to report that a spouse is cheating), you will be more polite. If it is not likely to hurt, you need not be so polite.

Each of the strategies for engaging in an FTA has positive and negative consequences. Going off-record to make a request, for example, leaves much room for ambiguity and a high chance the hint will be ignored. Conversely, using the bald-on-record approach will likely get you what you want but may cost you your own positive face in the process. Furthermore, PT predicts that because humans typically commit FTAs to achieve a desired goal (e.g., to obtain weekend shift coverage), individuals will not use strategies that are more polite than necessary because the cost of ambiguity is too great (Brown & Levinson, 1978).

We should also underscore that the very understanding of face, both positive and negative, varies across cultures, within specific relationships, and even among individuals, to some degree. Thus, a person must carefully weigh each decision to commit an FTA, considering the anticipated payoff in relation to the context, culture, and individual communicator characteristics of a potential FTA target.

In brief, PT emphasizes the notion of face. Particularly in embarrassing or inappropriate situations, individuals typically try to balance their own positive and negative face while also attending to the other's face needs. When deliberately committing an FTA, individuals can save face using a variety of strategies.

SOCIAL EXCHANGE THEORY

Social exchange theory (SET) is a broad approach used to explain and predict relationship maintenance. Developed by Thibaut and Kelley (1959), SET clarifies when and why individuals continue and develop some personal relationships while ending others. Additionally, the theory takes into account how satisfied you will be with the relationships you choose to maintain.

As the name of the theory suggests, an exchange approach to social relationships is much like an economic theory based on the comparison of rewards and costs. Thibaut and Kelley's (1959) theory therefore looks at personal relationships in terms of costs versus benefits. What rewards do you receive from a given relationship, and what does it cost you to obtain those rewards? Before making specific predictions, however, certain assumptions must be understood.

Assumptions of SET

Three assumptions guide SET. First, Thibaut and Kelley (1959) argued that personal relationships are a function of comparing benefits gained versus costs to attain those benefits. Second, and intrinsically tied to the first assumption, people want to make the most of the benefits while lessening the costs. This is known as the **minimax principle**. Last, Thibaut and Kelley maintained that, by nature, humans are selfish. Thus, as a human being, you tend to look out for yourself first and foremost. Although these assumptions are sometimes difficult for students and the general public to accept, they become easier to recognize when explained more clearly within the frame of SET's three core components: outcome value, comparison level, and comparison level of alternatives.

Core Components of SET

Three core components make up SET. First, and prefaced in the previous paragraphs, to understand SET, we must acknowledge that social relationships bring both rewards and costs. The outcome of a relationship, therefore, is the ratio of rewards to costs in a given relationship; this can be represented by a simple mathematical equation: Rewards – Costs = Outcome (Thibaut & Kelley, 1959). Relational **rewards** include any benefits you perceive as enjoyable or that help you achieve specific aspirations. For example, rewards between spouses might include companionship, affection, and sharing a joint savings account. Rewards between colleagues might be social support or task-related assistance. Relational **costs** are those drawbacks we perceive as unpleasant or that prevent us from pursuing or achieving an objective. For example, negotiating holiday visits with the in-laws, losing social independence, and having to put grad school on hold because of family obligations all could be potential costs for a married couple. In a professional setting, putting up with a colleague's endless complaining, having to share space with an untidy office mate, or coping with a perpetual text messenger might be viewed as costly.

What an individual perceives as a reward or cost in a given relationship will, of course, vary. The general idea is that people make mental notes of the rewards and costs associated with their relationships. One hopes the rewards outweigh the costs, resulting in a positive **outcome value**. If an individual perceives the relationship to yield more drawbacks than benefits, however, a negative outcome value will result. But the outcome value itself is not enough to predict whether a person will choose to stay in or leave a relationship. Rather, the outcome value becomes a benchmark used to help measure our relational rewards in comparison to our expectations and alternatives. Once the outcome value of a relationship is determined, individuals can begin to determine satisfaction with and stability of that relationship, as well as the likelihood of its continuing.

The second core element of SET is the **comparison level** (CL). The CL represents the rewards a person expects to receive in a particular relationship (Thibaut & Kelley, 1959). Expectations may be based on models for relationships (e.g., parents, friends), one's own experiences with relationships, television and other media representations of relationships, and the like. The importance of understanding what you expect in a relationship is this: SET maintains that individuals compare their current outcome value with their CL. In other words, if you perceive more rewards than costs in your relationship and this matches or exceeds your expectations for the relationship, SET predicts your satisfaction (Outcome > CL). Conversely, if you perceive more rewards than costs in a current relationship but expected to receive even more rewards than you currently have, a sense of dissatisfaction is predicted (CL > Outcome). Thus, predicting one's satisfaction with a relationship is based on a positive outcome value that also meets or exceeds one's expectations (CL).

The third and final component to SET is the **comparison level of alternatives** (CL_{alt}). Thibaut and Kelley (1959) recognized that simply determining one's satisfaction, or dissatisfaction, with a relationship is still not enough to predict whether the relationship will continue or end. Everyone knows a handful of individuals who are dissatisfied with any one of their personal relationships—whether it is a friendship, marriage, or work partnership—and yet, despite their unhappiness, these individuals remain in that relationship. Why?

SET holds that for any relationship to continue or end, individuals must also examine their CL_{alt} (Thibaut & Kelley, 1959). That is, what are your alternatives to staying in the relationship? Is ending it better or worse than the current situation? Only when you perceive the alternatives to be greater than your outcome and greater than your CL will you end a relationship. Even if satisfied with a current relationship (i.e., Outcome > CL), you may perceive that your alternatives are even better, in which case SET predicts you will terminate the relationship (represented mathematically by CL_{alt} > Outcome > CL).

It should be obvious, then, that many scenarios are possible, depending on the perceptions of CL_{alt}—*Outcome*—*CL*. Only when individuals have knowledge of all three elements is it possible to make predictions about the state and status of a relationship. An overview of the specific predictions made is shown in Figure 5.1.

Figure 5.1 Predictions Made by Social Exchange Theory

Outcome > Comparison Level (CL) = Satisfied

Outcome < CL = Dissatisfied

Outcome > Comparison Level of Alternatives (CL_{alt}) = Stay

Outcome < CL_{alt} = Terminate

To review, SET explains and predicts an individual's decision to maintain or deescalate a particular relationship. Specifically, people evaluate the rewards and costs associated with remaining in their relationships while also considering their expectations and other alternatives.

DIALECTICAL PERSPECTIVE

The dialectical perspective is also useful for explaining and understanding how individuals sustain interpersonal relationships. Specifically, Baxter and Montgomery (1996; Baxter, 1988) argued that relationships are dynamic; these researchers believe it is impossible for a relationship to maintain a certain level of satisfaction or reach a constant status quo. Much like a spiralling trajectory, people continue to develop their relationships by managing a series of opposing, yet necessary, tensions or contradictions.

Assumptions of the Dialectical Perspective

Four primary assumptions guide a dialectical approach to relationship maintenance: praxis, change, contradiction, and totality (Baxter & Montgomery, 1996). First, **praxis** suggests the development of a relationship is neither linear (always moving forward) nor repetitive (cycling through the same things again and again). Instead, a dialectical perspective assumes relationships can become more intimate or less intimate over time (Canary & Zelley, 2000). Thus, relational partners act and react while their relationship's trajectory spirals—moving forward in time and therefore transforming reality.

Change, or motion, is the second assumption (Baxter, 1988; Baxter & Montgomery, 1996). A dialectical approach presumes the only guarantee in a relationship is that it will change. Viewed this way, it is virtually impossible to "maintain" a relationship because maintenance implies a steady state. Instead, Montgomery (1993) argued that relationships are "sustained," not maintained.

Third, a dialectical approach assumes relationships are grounded in interdependent, yet mutually negating, **contradictions** (Baxter, 1988; Baxter & Montgomery, 1996). Stated differently, within every relationship, both partners have essential, yet opposing, needs. Because these needs counteract each other such that you can't achieve both needs at the same time, ongoing tensions result. For example, spouses need to spend time together to sustain their marriage; on the other hand, both partners need to have some time to themselves, away from their partner and relational obligations. Both togetherness and independence are needed, but you can't have both at the same time. The dialectical perspective maintains that relationships are sustained based on partners' communication used to manage these ever-present contradictions.

The fourth and last assumption, **totality**, emphasizes interdependence between relationship partners (Baxter, 1988; Baxter & Montgomery, 1996). Dialectical approaches recognize that without interdependence a relationship cannot exist. Accordingly, a tension you feel will ultimately affect your relationship partner and vice versa, even if that person didn't initially feel the tension.

When these four assumptions are brought together, we reach a rather complex understanding of relationships. To sustain a relationship, therefore, means the relationship will constantly fluctuate, spiralling forward in time, while relational partners experience and try to satisfy **dialectical tensions**, or interdependent, yet opposing, needs.

Between any two relationship partners (e.g., husband/wife, boss/subordinate, friend/friend, parent/child), three central tensions are thought to exist: autonomy–connection, openness–closedness, and predictability–novelty (Baxter, 1988). These tensions are known as **internal dialectics** because they exist within a dyad. With each pairing of internal tensions, you can see that each individual in a given relationship needs both elements, yet it is impossible to fulfill both needs simultaneously. The **autonomy–connection** dialectic refers to the tension between the desire to feel connected to one's partner versus the desire to maintain a sense of independence. Similarly, the **openness–closedness** dialectic includes the pull between wanting to open up and self-disclose while also wanting to maintain one's privacy. Finally, the **predictability–novelty** dialectic is the tension between wanting stability or steadiness while also wanting opportunities for spontaneity. According to the dialectical perspective, then, relational partners continually vacillate between each of these three poles.

For example, Will and Vanessa have been married for 8 years. Both have demanding careers and are raising twin boys. To feel satisfied within this marriage while balancing two careers and a family, Will and Vanessa must make time to spend together. This might mean hiring a babysitter and going to dinner occasionally or making a point of staying up after the boys go to bed to discuss their day. In each case, however, the couple is trying to feel connected. At the same time, Will and Vanessa need to maintain a certain amount of independence, some time to pursue their own hobbies or just some quiet time to meditate or read a book.

It should be obvious that it is difficult, if not impossible, to have togetherness and independence simultaneously, hence the dialectical tension. Furthermore, these tensions become magnified when one partner desires connection while the other needs some autonomy. It is this constant struggle and balancing act that propels a relationship forward.

Just as internal tensions exist between two individuals in a relationship (e.g., between husband and wife), three tensions arise externally between the dyad and other people in their lives (e.g., between a couple and their children). These tensions, or **external dialects**, mirror the internal dialectical tensions: inclusion–seclusion, revelation–concealment, and conventionality–uniqueness (Baxter, 1988). The key difference between internal and external tensions is that internal dialectics only involve the competing needs of the two people in the relationship. External dialectics appear when the pair interacts with other people in their lives (e.g., co-workers, friends, other family members). Figure 5.2 provides an illustration.

Again, note that it is both necessary and difficult to satisfy both poles of each contradiction simultaneously. The **inclusion–seclusion** dialectic emphasizes the tension partners as a unit experience when they want to spend time with friends, family, or co-workers versus wanting to spend their time alone together as a couple. The **revelation–concealment** dialectic involves the tension between relationship partners who want to reveal aspects of their relationship to the outside world while also wanting to keep some aspects of their relationship private. Last, the dialectic of **conventionality–uniqueness** emphasizes the tension partners feel between wanting to behave in ways considered normative or traditional versus wanting to emphasize their relationship's uniqueness by doing something differently. Table 5.2 presents an overview of internal and external dialectics.

Figure 5.2   Comparison of Internal and External Dialectics

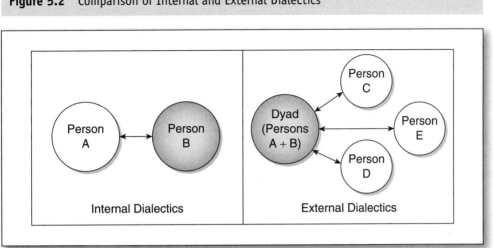

Table 5.2   Comparison of Internal and External Dialectics

Internal Dialectics	Corresponding External Dialectics
Autonomy–Connection. Desiring some independence but also desiring a union with your partner.	*Inclusion–Seclusion*. Desiring to have strong friendship and family networks but also desiring alone time with your partner.
Openness–Closedness. Desiring to be completely open and honest but also desiring to have some private thoughts and feelings.	*Revelation–Concealment*. Desiring to tell your family and friends relational information but also desiring to have some private information.
Predictability–Novelty. Desiring a stable relationship but also desiring some excitement and spontaneity.	*Conventionality–Uniqueness*. Desiring to have a traditional relationship but also desiring a unique relationship.

Returning to Will and Vanessa, they learn they are pregnant with their third child. Elated but also worried about the complications involved in the early stages of pregnancy, they aren't sure whether they should reveal their good news to their family or if they should wait until the first trimester passes. The struggle between deciding whether to disclose their news to friends and family (revelation) or to keep the pregnancy secret (concealment) until the second trimester is difficult, particularly if one partner wants to reveal and the other wants to conceal.

To manage or sustain a relationship, then, these tensions must be managed. Baxter and Montgomery (1996) identified four primary strategies used to handle the internal and external tensions: selection, cyclic or spiraling alteration, segmentation, and integration. The **selection** strategy involves favoring one pole or need at the expense of the other. For example, a couple who dates over long distance may eventually choose autonomy and break up because the tension between living an independent life versus making time to visit the other partner proves too difficult. Much like children playing on a seesaw, partners who use **cyclic alteration** (sometimes referred to as spiraling alteration) fulfill one pole or need now and shift to fulfill the other pole at a later time, creating a back-and-forth, back-and-forth strategy of coping.

The third strategy, **segmentation**, compartmentalizes the relationship such that certain issues coincide with one pole or need, and other issues are appropriate for the opposite pole. For example, if two close friends agree on mostly everything except for their bitter arguments about politics, a segmentation strategy would allow the friends to choose the closedness pole for politics but the openness pole for everything else. The fourth strategy, **integration**, includes several variations and is predicated on incorporating aspects of both poles so as to create a more fulfilling experience. For example, a couple who wants to integrate novelty and predictability might agree that Friday is date night—every Friday (predictability) they will get a babysitter and try a new restaurant (novelty). Obviously a more sophisticated way of managing relational tensions, integration implies relationship partners have an awareness of the tensions and can talk about them so as to find ways to creatively integrate and manage relational tensions.

All told, dialectics presents a rather complicated view of close relationships. This unwieldy depiction is also why it is a "perspective" and not a more precise theory. Nonetheless, dialectics' emphasis of the changing nature of relationships as well as its understanding of the various contradictions and tensions individuals experience makes it a logical approach to which many can easily relate.

COMMUNICATION PRIVACY MANAGEMENT THEORY

In many ways, Petronio's (2002) communication privacy management theory (CPM) builds upon each of the three previous theories. Like PT, CPM is concerned with the dilemma of how and what a communicator should say. Like SET, CPM recognizes the power of maximizing rewards and minimizing costs in making decisions. And, like dialectics, CPM recognizes that managing tensions is the central way relationships are sustained. The basic premise of the theory is that people create decision-making rules to help them determine when to reveal and when to conceal private information.

Sandra Petronio developed the theory after 25 years of researching the process of self-disclosure. Although we discuss this theory in the context of interpersonal communication, Petronio views CPM as a macrotheory, as it also can be applied in group and organizational settings. Her theory moves beyond a focus of just self-disclosure to a focus on disclosure in general. Moreover, she argues that disclosure can only be understood in terms of privacy; the two concepts are interdependent.

Principles of CPM

Petronio and Durham (2008) outlined six principles of CPM. The first is the **public–private** dialectical tension. As we just discussed, a dialectical tension refers to competing demands in a relationship. In the case of CPM, the major tension is between revealing and concealing private information. When on a job interview, for example, should you tell the interviewer you had a challenging relationship with your previous employer? That might be the honest answer to the question about why you are leaving your present position. But if you reveal the rocky relationship with your boss, will it make the potential employer wary of hiring you?

The second major principle concerns the nature of **private information** (Petronio & Durham, 2008). Because CPM derives from research into self-disclosure, the theory defines private information as information inaccessible to others. It may be about you, but the information can also be about a team member, a friend, or even about an entire organization. For example, you might have information about a new product under development at your workplace that the company does not want known to competitors. According to Petronio (2002), the central feature of private information is possession. That is, private information is something you own, and because you own it, you have the right to control it. The theory suggests that individuals with private information make decisions about with whom to share information, as well as what they share, when they share it, where they share it, and how they share it.

Next, CPM suggests these decisions about sharing private information are regulated by particular **privacy rules** (Petronio & Durham, 2008). Our decisions about sharing private information are informed by five decision criteria, outlined in Table 5.3. First, privacy rules are developed based on cultural criteria. As we discuss in Chapter 6, cultures have varying values, beliefs, and ways of communicating. As such, an individual's culture is likely to influence decisions about what should or should not be revealed. Second, **gender criteria** plays a role in privacy rules. Petronio suggests men and women have been socialized to have differing understandings of disclosure; thus, they may make different decisions when confronted with the tension of whether to share private information. Third, personal variations in **motivational criteria** are used in developing privacy rules. In Chapter 4, we described message design logics (MDLs), individual beliefs about the function of communication. Using MDLs as an example, a person with an expressive MDL is likely to be motivated to share more information than would a person with a conventional MDL, simply because of their individual beliefs about the purpose of communication. Of course, **contextual criteria** also influence privacy rules. Team members attending an off-site retreat at a resort might feel more inclined to share private information than would the same team members at a weekly department meeting. Finally, individuals weigh the **risk–benefit criteria** when considering whether they should disclose private information. Much like what was explained by SET, individuals assess potential rewards and costs of disclosure. For example, knowing that, like yourself, a co-worker is also an adult child of an alcoholic, you might decide that sharing your own family history with the co-worker might have benefits in terms of cohesion and increased understanding that might overshadow any possible risks.

Table 5.3   Privacy Rule Criteria

Criteria	Example
Cultural	Many African Americans value assertiveness and openness in sharing information.
Gender	In the United States, women are socialized to disclose more than men.
Motivational	Introverts may be less likely to share information than extroverts.
Contextual	Working in a cubicle might make an individual less likely to share information than working in a private office.
Risk–benefit	In an environment of "don't ask, don't tell," being ambiguous about your sexual orientation might minimize risks.

Much like a fence around your home or even that little plastic bar you use to separate your groceries while in the grocery store checkout lane, the fourth principle focuses on **boundaries** (Petronio & Durham, 2008). The metaphor of a boundary is meant to provide a visual representation of two sides; on one side people keep information to themselves, and on the other side people share private information. Personal boundaries are those that contain individual information (e.g., Bob is the only one who knows he was fired from his last job), and collective boundaries are those that contain shared information (e.g., Bob and Carol both know Bob was fired from his last job). Once an individual shares information, the ownership of the information changes, as do the decision rules about privacy. The boundary has shifted, and managing the information becomes more complex.

Building on the notion that multiple people might have to maintain a boundary, the fifth principle of CPM is **boundary coordination**, which refers to the ways collective boundaries are maintained (Petronio & Durham, 2008). Petronio (2002) explains that boundary coordination takes place through boundary linkages, boundary ownership, and boundary permeability. First, **boundary linkages** refer to alliances between the owners of the information. Such alliances might be intentional, as when an individual accused of a crime shares incriminating information with a lawyer. That link is easily maintained because of attorney–client privilege. However, boundary linkages might also be unintentional. Imagine that another individual overhears this confession. The person who has overheard the information is now a part of the alliance. In this case, coordination is likely difficult, as the people in the alliance might have competing risk–benefit rules for disclosure.

Boundary ownership refers to the rights and responsibilities borne by the owners of the information (Petronio, 2002). The clearer the privacy rules are to the shared owners of the information, the more likely the information will be managed consonantly. Thus, when an individual intentionally creates a boundary linkage, she or he is also likely to indicate the rules for disclosure ("Don't tell Harry I forgot to order the supplies!"). Not surprisingly, the rights and responsibilities are more problematic with unintentional linkages, especially if the individual who shared the information is unaware of the unintended recipient. How many times have you gossiped about someone and realized that someone else may have overheard you? Do you approach the person and say "please don't repeat this," or do you take the risk that he or she didn't hear what you said?

Boundary permeability refers to how much information is easily passed through the boundary (Petronio, 2002). Some boundaries are permeable (easy to cross), and others may be impregnable (difficult, if not impossible, to cross). In the popular parlance of the television series *Seinfeld*, impregnable boundaries are "in the vault." To illustrate, an individual might feel fairly comfortable in disclosing to colleagues what she had for dinner the night before, and other colleagues are likely to reciprocate. This represents a permeable boundary. However, that same individual might be much less comfortable sharing information with colleagues about a disastrous dinner date with another colleague that turned into a romantic fiasco. Of course, when the information is located within a collective boundary the notion of permeability may be more problematic. This leads to the final principle of CPM.

Petronio (2002) recognized that the management of boundaries is not always a smooth process. Accordingly, she developed the notion of **boundary turbulence**, which occurs when the rules for privacy management are not clear. Refer back to Table 5.3 on privacy rules. Imagine Lance tells Maggie about a forthcoming merger at work. Lance is a white male who believes information is power, and so his privacy rules dictate keeping this information private. Maggie, on the other hand, is an African American female who believes people have the right to know about issues that might affect them. Her cultural, gender, and individual motivation criteria lead to a privacy rule that would suggest this information should be shared. In this case, differing privacy rules might cause problems with managing the information. Other causes of boundary turbulence are privacy violations, ethical dilemmas, differing expectations, and misconceptions about ownership.

Taken together, these six principles articulate the complexities associated with information management. The theory "allows us to better understand what individuals disclose, what they keep private, and how private information is handled among people" (Petronio & Durham, 2008, p. 320). CPM provides a detailed analysis of a universal problem: What should (or shouldn't) I say?

Summary and Research Applications

This chapter provided an overview of four theories of interpersonal communication. PT explains and predicts strategies individuals use to maintain "face," or sense of desired public image. Useful in personal as well as business and educational contexts, PT has explored dilemmas managers experience when providing criticism to subordinates (Rogers & Lee-Wong, 2003), how employees handle unethical requests from colleagues (Bisel, Kelley, Ploeger, & Messersmith, 2011), and competitive behavior of adult female friends (Dunleavy & Zelley, 2013). SET predicts individuals initiate and maintain relationships so as to maximize personal outcomes; at the same time, however, expectations and alternatives play a role in individuals' ultimate satisfaction and whether they stay in the relationship. Examples of SET include research explaining the donation habits of university alumni (O'Neil & Schenke, 2007) and supervisor-directed organizational citizenship behaviors

(Moideenkutty, 2006). The dialectical perspective suggests that sustaining interpersonal relationships requires communication to manage the necessary but contradictory tensions inherent in all relationships. It has been particularly useful in exploring challenges faced by blended families (see Braithwaite, Toller, Daas, Durham, & Jones, 2008; L. E. Bryant, 2003). When combined with PT, dialectics has also shed light on organizational conflict management (Jameson, 2004). Finally, CPM articulates a way of understanding the reasons for and the challenges associated with the decision to reveal or conceal private information. Valuable in health care contexts (see Petronio, Sargent, Andea, Reganis, & Cichocki, 2004), CPM also has explored employee perceptions of workplace surveillance (Allen, Coopman, Hart, & Walker, 2007) and documented consumers' decision rules for determining how much information to provide Internet retailers (Metzger, 2007).

Key Terms

Autonomy–connection   84
Avoidance   79
Bald-on-record   80
Boundaries   88
Boundary coordination   88
Boundary linkages   88
Boundary ownership   88
Boundary permeability   89
Boundary turbulence   89
Change   83
Comparison level   82
Comparison level of alternatives   82
Contextual criteria   87
Contradictions   83
Conventionality–uniqueness   84
Corrective facework   78
Costs   81
Cyclic alteration (spiraling alteration)   86
Dialectical tension   84
External dialectic   84
Face   77
Face-threatening act   78
Facework   78
Gender criteria   87
Inclusion–seclusion   84

Integration   86
Internal dialectic   84
Minimax principle   81
Motivational criteria   87
Negative face   78
Negative politeness   79
Off-record   79
Openness–closedness   84
Outcome value   81
Positive face   78
Positive politeness   79
Power   80
Praxis   83
Predictability–novelty   84
Prestige   80
Privacy rules   87
Private information   87
Public–private   87
Revelation–concealment   84
Rewards   81
Risk   80
Risk–benefit criteria   87
Segmentation   86
Selection   86
Totality   83

Case Study 5: With a Friend Like This

A global financial institution serving five business sectors, Arden Financial Services (AFS) employed nearly 1,500 employees at its Wilmington, Delaware, headquarters. Mia and Lily started at AFS at the same time and went through orientation together. Although they worked in different business sectors, their departments were on the same floor, so they routinely ran into each other. The two quickly became good friends, meeting frequently for lunch, chatting at each other's cubicles, and going out to Friday happy hours together. Both single at the time, they easily bonded over the frustrations of dating as well as sharing general workplace gossip.

Having more education, experience, and ambition than Mia, Lily had advanced more quickly. Most recently, she was promoted to senior sector manager. Mia was genuinely happy for Lily, and the title shift didn't hinder their friendship, especially since they continued to work in different divisions. The two still met in the cafeteria for lunch almost every day, regularly convened at The Pub on Fridays, and now that both women were married, they occasionally socialized as couples for dinner or a round of golf.

With her elevated position, Lily now had more insight into company politics and information. She thought nothing of telling Mia the latest gossip from a "higher" corporate view; after all, the two had agreed that nothing would change with Lily's latest position, and she wanted to keep her word. Plus, it was fun to have extra gossip to share. Lily told Mia which VPs really were tyrants and who was having interoffice affairs. Mia knew who Lily was going to promote, reprimand, or fire before they did. It wasn't just gossip; Lily also went to Mia for support. When Lily had to fire a subordinate for the first time, she met with Mia for advice.

Mia had always kept these talks to herself, whether just rumors or professional details; working in different sectors, there was no real conflict of interest.

Last week, however, Mia was temporarily transferred to Lily's business sector to help cover for two employees who were working at AFS's European office for 6 months; things suddenly got tricky. Lily was now Mia's direct superior. Lily now had more responsibility. She immediately started to worry that the other subordinates would complain that Lily favored Mia. She knew her friendship with Mia was very visible and might give other employees the wrong idea.

Unsure how to handle the situation, Lily wanted to keep her friendship with Mia, but she also wanted to keep her professionalism with her team. At first, she cancelled their daily lunches, claiming she simply had too much work. After a week of missed meals, though, Mia knew something was up and confronted her friend in the hallway.

"Hey, Lily. Are you okay? I feel like you've been acting kind of strange lately."

Lily tried to brush it off, saying, "Oh, you know. It's the month's end, and it's just crazy around here! I guess I'm just stressed out with all of the work." Trying to give Mia a hint, she added, "And on top of it, I have to attend leadership training next week. I guess I need to learn how to communicate more professionally with my team."

"Really?" Mia remarked. "I think you're already pretty professional. That's why they keep promoting you, right?" Mia clearly hadn't picked up the clue. "Well, it sounds like a lot of corporate nonsense if you ask me. How 'bout we catch up tonight at The Pub instead?"

Lily paused. No one could complain if she went to a public place with a friend, right? "Okay, sounds good! I'll meet you there around 6 o'clock." Once back at her desk Lily thought more about it. Mia really was a good friend. She would just tell her the truth over a beer and wings. They'd probably even get a good laugh over it!

That evening at The Pub, Lily revealed her fears about appearing biased to the other employees. "You know, I think some of them are worried not only because we're friends but also because you might know gossip about them," Lily confided.

"Well, they'd have a point, because I do know an awful lot about your team," Mia replied. The two sat for a moment in uncomfortable silence. "Look, Lily, this is just going to be temporary until Kim and Rich get back. Why don't we just agree that during these few weeks, we won't talk shop?"

Lily immediately felt relieved. "Are you sure you're okay with that, Mia? I feel like I'm being a terrible friend and like I don't want to be seen with you!" They laughed and Mia reassured her friend. "Look, if it's going to cause problems for you, we don't have to meet for lunch or anything. You do your thing, and when Kim and Rich return from Amsterdam, we'll go back to normal."

The plan worked well. No one seemed bothered by Mia's presence in the sector. The two friends kept some distance while at work and socialized privately instead.

Five weeks went by. Lily attended the annual managers' retreat to review the company's financial situation. This year, the news was grim. Sales were down, business was down, and revenue was down. The vice president of AFS, Ben Patina, announced his plan for company-wide layoffs. Each senior sector manager would have to reduce his or her workforce by 20% by week's end. Lily was shocked! She had heard through the grapevine that Ben was cutthroat, but she hadn't expected this type of news. She was going to have to select four employees to let go. In the past, she would have gone to Mia with her problem and sought advice. This time, however, it was clear she couldn't.

To complicate matters, Ben requested a meeting with Lily the following morning. Upon entering her office, he closed the door. *Uh oh*, Lily thought to herself.

"Look, Lily, there's no easy way to say this, so I'm just going to be blunt. I want you to lay off Mia." Lily stared blankly at him. "Her old sector's managing without her. I talked with Robin about it, and she's on board," Ben continued. "I mean, she's a great worker—don't get me wrong. But if we have to let someone go, and they're already dealing without her, it just makes sense."

Lily felt a burst of emotion bubble up inside of her. Not only couldn't she sacrifice an employee as competent as Mia but she also wanted to protect her friend. "Ben, how can you possibly ask me to let go of Mia? She's doing the work of two people for me right now!"

"Remember, Lily, I'm your boss, so you don't really have a say in this. If you fire Mia, you can keep the rest of your team intact. That saves three other employees. Be grateful you don't have to make the decision. You just have to execute mine."

Lily was fuming inside but bit her tongue. It would be professional suicide to argue with the vice president.

Ben started to walk out of Lily's office but stopped and turned. "I know you and Mia are friends and all, Lily, but be a professional, damn it. And if you can't do it, I will."

Ben left, and Lily slumped into her chair. What was she going to do?

Questions for Consideration

1. Explain Lily's face needs and how they have shifted throughout the case. Did she follow PT's predictions when initially confronted by Mia? Use PT to explain Lily's interaction with Ben.

2. Use SET to assess the rewards and costs associated with the friendship. Then predict whether or not Mia and Lily will remain good friends if Mia is terminated. What conditions, if any, would change your prediction?

3. Identify the internal and external dialectics that appear in the story. What strategies were used to manage these tensions? What strategies might have been better?

4. What private information and privacy rules exist in this story? How did Lily and Mia develop boundary coordination to separate their work and personal lives? What boundary turbulence does Lily experience?

5. Which theory alone seems to provide the "best" explanation for the situation? Why do you believe this to be the case? What situations might surface that would make a different theory or theories better at explaining the situation? How could you combine several theories to make for an even "better" explanation of the relationships?

Culture

LEARNING OBJECTIVES

After reading this chapter, you will be able to...

1. Define culture, cross-cultural communication, and intercultural communication.

2. Explain and identify examples for each of Hofstede's five primary cultural dimensions.

3. Describe how each continuum relates to communication differences.

4. Compare and contrast select countries' cultural preferences, based on Hofstede's dimensions.

5. Articulate the difference between cultural generalizations and individual variations within a culture, recognizing that culture is dynamic, not monolithic.

6. Explain how individuals communicate social identity through in-groups and out-groups.

7. Discuss the process of accommodation through convergence or divergence.

8. Analyze the positive and negative consequences associated with accommodation.

9. Predict whether a communicator should converge or diverge her or his speech by considering risk versus reward.

10. Describe the connections between communication accommodation theory and leader–member exchange theory.

11. Describe the role of anxiety and uncertainty in intercultural and intergroup communication.

12. Explain how the threshold for anxiety and uncertainty can either impair or motivate communication effectiveness.

13. Discuss how mindful communication affects anxiety and uncertainty reduction while simultaneously contributing to the positive outcomes of communication effectiveness and intercultural adjustment.

14. Compare and contrast uncertainty reduction theory (see Chapter 3) with anxiety/uncertainty management theory.

(Continued)

(Continued)

15. Discuss the importance of face in intercultural communication, particularly within the context of conflict management.

16. Define conflict and intercultural conflict.

17. Describe the process of developing face negotiation theory by combining elements of politeness theory and Hofstede's cultural dimensions.

18. Compare and contrast the Western, individualistic conflict styles with the Eastern, collectivistic conflict styles.

19. Predict intercultural conflict due to cultural differences in conflict management.

20. Compare and contrast and apply major theoretical approaches to intercultural communication.

Although a beloved icon in the United States, the Walt Disney Company opened Euro Disney in 1992 (later renamed Disneyland Paris) to widespread criticism. The company was taken to task for cultural imperialism; the French press, in particular, accused the company of mass producing American values and replacing European customs and traditions with American consumer culture (Forman, 1998). For the first several years, the park was considered a flop. Yet by 2008, there were over 50 million visitors annually, and in 2013, the resort was listed as France's number-one tourist attraction, surpassing the Eiffel Tower and the Louvre (Frommer's, 2013). What explains the turnaround? Jay Rasulo, former Euro Disney CEO and current chairman of Walt Disney Parks and Resorts, asserted that the newfound success required intercultural awareness: "When we first launched, there was the belief that it was enough to be Disney. Now we realize that our guests need to be welcomed on the basis of their own culture and travel habits" (Prada & Orwall, 2002, p. A12). Retail giant Walmart faced similar difficulties when it tried expanding to Germany, South Korea, and Japan. Failure to pay attention to German culture and local business practices, for example, wound up costing the company hundreds of millions of dollars before it pulled out of Germany altogether (Landler & Barbaro, 2006).

Understanding the dynamics of cross-cultural and intercultural communication is critical in today's multicultural society and global economy (Ting-Toomey, 1992). Within the United States, multicultural communities continue to expand and flourish. Privately, international travel is relatively easy and common; in the corporate sector, global competition and cooperation is the norm. Although the proliferation of cross- cultural and intercultural communication is probably not new to you, the implications of, difficulties with, and strategies for improving these exchanges is profound, particularly considering the high failure rate of such interaction.

CULTURE DEFINED

Recognizing the diversity of today's personal and professional landscape is one thing, but what exactly is culture? We embrace Collier's (1989) notion of **culture** as one's identification with and acceptance into a group that shares symbols, meanings, experiences, and behavior. Cross-cultural communication and intercultural communication expand on this notion. **Cross-cultural communication** is the comparison of two or more cultural communities (Ting-Toomey, 1991a); for example, comparing conflict styles of U.S. managers with those of Korean managers. Somewhat differently, **intercultural communication** involves the actual interaction between members of different cultures; for instance, examining what happens when a German executive reprimands a Chinese subordinate.

Using these definitions, we have selected four theories that examine broadly defined notions of culture and emphasize how culture shapes and is shaped by communication. First, Hofstede's cultural dimensions provide a typology useful for assessing cultural differences across social contexts. Next, we look at communication accommodation theory as a way of predicting when individuals will or should adapt to or diverge from another cultural group. Third, we consider anxiety/uncertainty management theory. Finally, face-negotiation theory addresses how cultural differences with face influence conflict management.

HOFSTEDE'S CULTURAL DIMENSIONS

Geert Hofstede is a Dutch management researcher who developed an inductive theory of culture. Specifically, he gathered statistical data from 100,000 employees of IBM around the world to determine the values on which cultures vary (Hofstede, 1980). In the process, he surveyed workers from 50 countries and three regions. His analysis resulted in five dimensions with which to differentiate and rank cultures (Hofstede, 1980; Hofstede & Bond, 1984). Each dimension is described as a continuum, with distinct cultures classified somewhere along the continuum.

Individualism–Collectivism

Hofstede's (1980) first dimension is individualism–collectivism. This dimension addresses how people define themselves and their relationships with others. Cultures that fall on the **individualism** side of the continuum share four characteristics (Triandis, 1995). First, such cultures consider the individual to be the most important entity in any social setting. Think about some common phrases you have heard in the United States (a highly individualistic culture). When asked to do something beyond one's responsibilities, an American is likely to ask, "What's in it for me?" In explaining why an individual is ending a romantic relationship, the person might say, "I was putting more into it than I was getting out of it." In short, in individualistic cultures the focus is on the self before all other relationships.

Second, individualistic cultures stress independence rather than dependence (Triandis, 1995). Recall the description of face needs in Chapter 5. Positive face is the desire to be appreciated and liked. Negative face is the desire to be free from impositions. Ting-Toomey (1988) argued that people from individualistic cultures tend to place relatively more emphasis on negative face needs compared with individuals from collectivistic cultures; there is a cultural preference to be free from imposition, which is in essence a desire to be independent.

Third, individualistic cultures reward individual achievement (Triandis, 1995). To illustrate, U.S. organizations frequently use merit pay and employee recognition programs. These programs focus on recognizing particular individuals and their performance, raising them above other employees in the organization. Likewise, individual achievement tends to accompany the value of competition. In individualistic cultures, competition is viewed as a good thing. This is not always the case in collectivistic cultures.

Finally, individualistic cultures value each individual's uniqueness (Triandis, 1995). In such cultures, standing out from the crowd is highly valued, whereas in collectivistic cultures, standing out from others is a source of embarrassment. Consider the variations in two cultural proverbs (Mieder, 1986). The American proverb "the squeaky wheel gets the grease" implies you will receive rewards by distinguishing yourself from others; you ought to speak up and be noticed. The Japanese proverb "the tallest nail gets hammered down" implies punishment is associated with being different—you are better off being the same as others.

Thus far we have talked at length about individualism but have not addressed collectivism in detail. **Collectivism** refers to a social system based on in-groups and out-groups. In collectivistic cultures, groups (relatives, clans, organizations) are the central way of understanding relations between people; identity is understood solely through group membership.

There are also four characteristics associated with collectivism (Triandis, 1995). First, in collectivistic cultures the views, needs, and goals of the group are more important than any individual views, needs, or goals. For many Americans, the idea of kamikaze pilots or suicide bombers makes no sense. Yet in collectivistic cultures, the needs of the group supersede the needs of the individual. In these sorts of systems, dying for the good of a group makes sense.

Second, obligation to the group is the norm in collectivistic cultures; behavior is guided by duty, not by individual pleasure or rewards (Triandis, 1995). This focus on duty over pleasure is apparent in mate selection. In individualistic cultures, people are "free" to marry the mate of their choice. In collectivistic cultures, acceptance of the potential mate by the family is of central importance (Dion & Dion, 1993).

Third, in collectivistic cultures, the self is defined in relation to others, not as distinct from others (Triandis, 1995). Jandt's (2004) example best illustrates this point. Imagine a person from Colombia (a more collectivistic culture) coming to the United States. In the United States, a common question for the visitor would be "What do you do for a living?" because Americans are understood by their individual accomplishments. In Colombia, however, the first question asked of this same person would likely be "Who are you related to?" Knowing a person's "connections" enables strangers to place that person into particular groups; knowing where a person comes from is the same as knowing who that person is.

Fourth and finally, those from collectivistic cultures focus on cooperation rather than competition (Triandis, 1995). This characteristic manifests in particular communication patterns in collectivistic cultures. Collectivistic cultures tend to use a **high-context communication** style (Hall, 1976). A high-context message privileges relational harmony over clarity or directness; messages tend to be indirect, circular, or unspoken so as not to offend. It is assumed the receiver will actively seek to understand what is really meant. By contrast, a **low-context communication** style, characteristic of individualistic cultures, values direct, explicit expression of ideas. In low-context communication, the meaning is in the message, and sometimes "the truth hurts."

We have presented a number of details unique to individualism and collectivism, but individualism and collectivism exist together in all cultures—they are, in essence, two sides of the same coin. Certain cultures, however, tend to operate at one end of the continuum or the other. We turn next to the second dimension of culture as described by Hofstede (1980), uncertainty avoidance.

Uncertainty Avoidance

We talked about the concept of **uncertainty** in Chapter 3. As a cultural dimension, uncertainty **avoidance** refers to the extent to which "people within a culture are made nervous by situations which they perceive as unstructured, unclear, or unpredictable" (Hofstede, 1986, p. 308). Those cultures that seek to avoid ambiguity are known as high-uncertainty-avoidance cultures. Typically, cultures high in uncertainty avoidance maintain strict codes of behavior and support a belief in absolute truths. For instance, in high-uncertainty-avoidance cultures, the workplace is typified by rules, precision, and punctuality (Jandt, 2004). The preference for a business meeting would be a structured agenda, which would be rigidly followed (Lewis, 2000).

Cultures low in uncertainty avoidance tend to accept ambiguity and lack of structure more easily (Hofstede, 1986). Individuals in low-uncertainty-avoidance cultures are more inclined to take risks, innovate, and value "thinking outside of the box." Clearly, American culture is a low-uncertainty-avoidance culture. In the workplace, individuals from low-uncertainty-avoidance cultures tend to work hard only when needed (Jandt, 2004). Rules are often rejected or ignored, and punctuality has to be taught and reinforced.

Power Distance

The third dimension uncovered by Hofstede (1980) is power distance, or the extent to which people with little power in society consider inequity normal and acceptable. Cultures with **high power distance** accept power as a scarce resource; power differences are natural and inevitable. In these sorts of cultures there is greater centralization of power and a great importance placed on status and rank. In the workplace, high-power-distance cultures tend to have a large number of supervisors, a rigid system that classifies each job along a hierarchy, and decision making only among those at the high end of the hierarchy (Adler, 1997). There also tends to be a wide salary gap between those high and low in the hierarchy (Jandt, 2004).

Cultures with **low power distance** value the minimization of power differences (Hofstede, 1980). Although hierarchy might exist, people higher in the hierarchy are not assumed to be superior to people lower in the hierarchy; people at all levels reach out to people at all other levels. Moreover, people lower in power believe that through motivation and hard work they can achieve power (Hofstede, 1980). In the workplace, low-power-distance cultures view shared decision making with subordinates as empowering (Jandt, 2004).

The United States falls on the lower end of this power distance spectrum but is not extremely low. A pervasive management style in the United States is that of "status–achievement," meaning status can be earned "via hard work, personal ambition, and competitiveness . . . and displayed effectively and proudly (e.g., by driving expensive cars or having the spacious corner office)" (Ting-Toomey, 2005, p. 75). And when you consider the following statistics, it appears the United States is becoming increasingly higher in power distance. According to Bloomberg financial data, CEO salary for Fortune 500 CEOs has increased 1,000% since 1950 (Smith & Kuntz, 2013). In 1980, the average salary of a CEO was 42 times that of the average worker. In 2000, the average CEO made 120 times as much as the average worker. After the "great recession" and stock market collapse of 2008–2009, CEO salaries took a dive but quickly bounced back. According to the Standard & Poor's 500 Index of companies, executive salaries continued to climb to 204 times the average worker's salary in 2013. These figures mirror statistics indicating the difference between the "haves" and "have-nots" is growing in the United States; the rich are growing richer, and the poor are not sharing the wealth. The extent to which American citizens believe this power differential is acceptable and normative demonstrates an acceptance of increasingly higher power distance.

Masculinity–Femininity

Hofstede's (1980) fourth dimension focuses on the relationship between biological sex and what is considered sex-appropriate behavior. **Masculine cultures** use the reality of biological sex in the creation of distinct roles for men and women. In masculine cultures, men are expected to be assertive, ambitious, and competitive; women are expected to be supportive, nurturing, and deferent. Translating these values to the workplace, countries with a masculine orientation believe managers are supposed to be decisive and assertive (Jandt, 2004). More important, women have a difficult time achieving workplace equality; they are given lower wages, less stable work, and few opportunities to advance (Kim, 2001).

The United States is a masculine country. Although women are making inroads in organizational life, there is still a significant wage gap (U.S. Bureau of Labor Statistics, 2008), and the glass ceiling remains a reality ("The Conundrum," 2005). Moreover, women are often expected to conform to masculine norms if they hope to succeed at work (Ragins, Townsend, & Mattis, 1998).

By contrast, **feminine cultures** have fewer rigid roles for behavior based on biological sex (Hofstede, 1980). Men and women are equally permitted to be assertive or deferent, competitive or nurturing. Instead of rigid sex roles, the focus in feminine cultures tends to be on the facilitation of interpersonal relationships and concern for the weak (Jandt, 2004). In the workplace, feminine cultures manifest consensus seeking and a preference for quality of life over material success. To illustrate, consider Sweden, a highly feminine culture. In Sweden, the law allows both men and women to balance parenthood and employment. At the birth or adoption of a child, parents are jointly eligible for 480 days of paid, child-rearing leave ("Gender Equality in Sweden, 2013).

Long-Term and Short-Term Orientation

Hofstede's (1980) original research stopped after the first four dimensions. Responding to accusations of a Western bias to his work, Hofstede collected additional data with the assistance of Chinese scholars and ultimately added a fifth cultural dimension. Grounded in Confucian thinking, Hofstede (2001) called this dimension the orientation toward long term versus short term. A **long-term orientation** is associated with thrift, savings, perseverance, and the willingness to subordinate one's self to achieve a goal. In cultures with a long-term orientation, employees typically have a strong work ethic and keep their eyes toward the achievement of distant goals (Hofstede, 2001). A **short-term orientation** centers on a desire for immediate gratification. Individuals in these cultures tend to spend money to "keep up with the Joneses" and prefer quick results to long-term gain (Hofstede, 2001). Employees seek immediate pay and benefits and are less willing to sacrifice in the short run to achieve in the long run.

Dimensions Combined

Table 6.1 plots eight countries or regions on each of the five dimensions (Hofstede, 2001). Note that just because two countries are similar in one dimension does not mean they will be similar in another. Moreover, recognize that the rankings described are generalizations about each culture; it should come as no surprise that individual variations exist within each culture. Finally, in many countries, including the United States, different groups in the same culture might rank quite differently within a given dimension. For example, although the dominant U.S. culture is individualistic, researchers believe that African Americans and Hispanics tend more toward collectivism (e.g., Hecht, Collier, & Ribeau, 1993).

Table 6.1 Rankings of Select Countries or Regions on Hofstede's Dimensions

	Individualism–Collectivism	Uncertainty Avoidance	Power Distance	Masculinity–Femininity	Long-Term and Short-Term
Arab countries	Both	Moderate	High	Moderate masculinity	Not available
Italy	High individualism	Moderate	Moderate	Extreme masculinity	Short term
Japan	Both	Extremely high	Moderate	Extreme masculinity	Long term
Mexico	Moderate collectivism	High	High	Extreme masculinity	Not available
South Korea	High collectivism	High	Moderate	Moderate femininity	Long term
Sweden	Moderate individualism	Extremely low	Very low	Extreme femininity	Both
United States	Extreme individualism	Low	Moderate	High masculinity	Short term
Venezuela	Extreme collectivism	Moderate	High	Extreme masculinity	Not available

COMMUNICATION ACCOMMODATION THEORY

Have you ever caught yourself slipping into a southern drawl or using *y'all* while speaking to a native Texan? Maybe you have found yourself speaking in fast, clipped tones when talking with a New Yorker, or upon returning from a European vacation, friends point out that you suddenly sound more like Kate Middleton than Kate Hudson. Do you speed up while talking with some colleagues but slow your speech when speaking with others? Communication accommodation theory (CAT) can explain many of the changes in your speech and language use.

Originally conceived as speech accommodation theory (Giles, Mulac, Bradac, & Johnson, 1987) and later refined as communication accommodation theory (Giles & Coupland, 1991), CAT provides an informative platform from which to understand how we adapt our communication when we interact with others. Essentially, Giles and colleagues argued that when interacting with others, individuals will accommodate their speech and language patterns, either by matching their partners' speech or by differentiating their speech and language use. In this section, we explain Giles and colleagues' notion of accommodation through both convergence and divergence.

Communicating Social Identity Through In-Groups and Out-Groups

Giles and Coupland (1991) assumed individuals belong to a wide variety of social groups based on ethnicity, race, gender, and religion. Moreover, they maintained that these groups shape each person's collective identity. For example, "most ethnic minority groups in the United States have tended to form communities, however small, where they have other people of similar heritage to sustain their ethnic values, socialization practices, and culture" (Vivero & Jenkins, 1999, p. 9). Similarly, your marital status (e.g., married), your political alignment (e.g., Republican), your career (e.g., public relations director), and your ethnicity (e.g., Irish American) all represent social groups that influence the way you perceive yourself and others perceive you.

Like it or not, human beings categorize information to simplify and create understanding. One way in which we commonly categorize others and ourselves is through these social identity groups; these clusters are divided into in-groups and out-groups. **In-groups** are social affiliations to which an individual feels he or she belongs (Giles & Coupland, 1991). **Out-groups** are those social affiliations to which a person feels he or she does not belong. In the workplace, for example, you may go to happy hour with members from your team or department but would feel out of place socializing with members of another department. Similarly, if you play on a company softball league, your teammates may become an in-group, even if you had not interacted previously.

In-groups and out-groups are important for understanding CAT. According to Giles and Coupland (1991), language, speech, and nonverbal messages all communicate one's in-group and out-group status. For example, if you have been around a group of teenagers recently, you may feel very much part of the out-group because your poor command of slang (language) and lack of body piercings (nonverbal artifacts) clearly differentiate you from them. When your teenage son mumbles, "NONYA", in response to your simple question of "Where are you taking your date tonight?" he has differentiated himself (a hip teen) from you (a stodgy middle-aged parent). Instead of simply saying, "It's none of your business," his use of Twitter slang leaves you wondering what the heck he is talking about, thereby creating a gap between his generation and yours.

The use of slang to create in-group and out-group status applies to the workplace as well. Each profession has its own set of jargon, or specialized language, that not only gives precision to words and meanings but also helps create and maintain a distinct in-group. Thus, jargon includes those individuals who have similar training and experience and excludes everyone else. A member of your company's information technology (IT) department may use computer jargon that intimidates the nontechnology minded. For instance, when Karen calls her company's IT department with a question about a problem she is having with a website password, the help desk manager asks her, "What's your ISP?" Karen has no idea what an ISP is, much less which one she is using. In this instance, the help desk manager may use the jargon unintentionally when communicating with out-group members such as Karen and employees from other departments simply out of habit. Conversely, the manager may intentionally rely on jargon so as to intimidate the out-group members or to promote one's own credibility. Because she doesn't know what her ISP is, Karen may feel inferior, or she may perceive the help desk manager as possessing complex and invaluable information. Karen may even feel frustrated or annoyed because members of the help desk can't seem to explain things in plain English. Importantly, then, jargon is both inclusive and exclusive and should be used cautiously with out-group members.

Accommodation Through Convergence or Divergence

Individuals adjust their speech and conversational patterns either in an effort to assimilate with or to deviate from others (Giles & Coupland, 1991). When a person wants to be viewed as part of an in-group, CAT predicts this person will accommodate by **convergence**. That is, you will alter your speech and behavior so that it matches that of your conversational partner. Speech includes word choice, pronunciation, pitch, rate, and even gestures such as smiling and gaze. For instance, elementary school teachers often converge their speech, using more expressive registers, slower speaking rates, and shorter words or phrases to accommodate their young pupils. When individuals match their speech, they convey acceptance and understanding. Interpersonal attraction also leads to convergence (Giles et al., 1987). That is, the more a person is likable, charismatic, and socially skilled, the more likely you are to try to match his or her communication patterns.

Conversely, there are times when individuals don't want to be associated with a certain group or do not find a person interpersonally attractive; sometimes you want to differentiate yourself from a particular crowd. In this instance, you will alter your speech through **divergence**. Rather than match your partner's communication patterns, you will seek to make your speech different. Deliberately diverging from the speech of your partner signals disagreement or rejection. A kindergarten teacher may use a more stern tone when disciplining the class for misbehavior. Similarly, you may overhear your 16-year-old neighbor conversing in strings of expletives with her friends simply as a way of countering adult authority. In addition to expressing disagreement or rejection of a speaker, divergence also illustrates one's cultural identity (e.g., maintaining a Scottish accent despite living in the United States) or differences in one's status (e.g., a physician's use of elaborate medical terminology when talking with a patient).

Who Accommodates to Whom?

It is worthy to note differences in accommodation across groups because these differences say a great deal about the importance of perceived status, authority, and cultural and social identity within our multicultural society. In her review of research, Larkey (1996) reported that when looking at race, ethnicity, and sex in the workplace, Euro American male employees typically diverge; that is, they maintain their communicative style regardless of conversational partner because it is commonly defined as the "standard" in both the United States and much of Europe.

Conversely, minority employees (including women and members of racial and ethnic minorities) typically must converge to this "standard" to achieve status within the organization. Persistent convergence may create cognitive dissonance for minority members by placing them in a dilemma; maintaining their cultural and social identity is sacrificed when using the mainstream speech patterns that are expected and rewarded.

Pitfalls of Accommodation

Accommodation is not always appropriate or effective (Giles & Coupland, 1991). When in doubt, individuals rely on social norms to inform their decision to accommodate or not. Norms are implicit expectations that guide social behavior; thus, we must rely on our perceptions of social appropriateness when determining whether to converge or diverge. Table 6.2 provides some consequences of accommodation. Note both positive and negative consequences for both types of accommodation.

Accommodation and Leader-Member Exchange

The notion of accommodation has many practical implications. One particular link might be made between the notion of accommodation and a theory called leader–member

Table 6.2   Consequences of Accommodation

	Positive Effects	Negative Effects
Convergence	Increased attraction; social approval; increased persuasion	Incorrect stereotypes of out-group; perceived condescension; loss of personal identity
Divergence	Protects cultural identity; asserts power differences; increased sympathy	Perceived disdain for out-group; perceived lack of effort; increased psychological distance

exchange (LMX). Developed by Graen and associates (Dansereau, Graen, & Haga, 1975; Graen & Uhl-Bien, 1995), LMX theory recognizes that leadership consists of an interpersonal relationship between a superior and a subordinate and that not all relationships are created equally; within organizations there are also in-groups and out-groups. Because of limited time and resources, supervisors cannot exert the same amount of energy with every employee. Accordingly, relationships between superiors and subordinates can be placed on a continuum. At one end are **leader–member exchange** relationships. LMX relationships, considered to be in-group relationships, are characterized by mutual trust, social support, and liking. There is much more interaction between organizational members in an LMX relationship than in other types.

At the other end of the continuum are **supervisory exchange** relationships (SX relationships). Interaction between the supervisor and subordinate is defined entirely by the roles they perform and the contractual obligations provided by the organization. In short, SX relationships are out-group relationships; they are impersonal, with little superior–subordinate interaction taking place.

At the midpoint of the continuum are middle-group relationships. Not surprisingly, these relationships involve elements of both LMX and SX relationships. Interaction is often impersonal, but there are occasional provisions of social support. Moderate amounts of trust and liking occur between the supervisor and the subordinate. Individuals in the middle-group are often aware they are not in the in-group, however.

The practical implications of these varying types of relationships are profound in terms of organizational outcomes. LMX relationships are associated with higher employee job satisfaction, greater satisfaction with the manager, and higher organizational commitment (Nystrom, 1990; Vecchio, Griffeth, & Hom, 1986). Subordinates in these types of relationships also evidence more innovative behaviors and greater organizational citizenship (e.g., helping others with heavy workloads, providing assistance without being asked, listening to the problems of others, and going out of their way to assist new employees). The converse is also true (Manzoni & Barsoux, 2002). Those who have an SX relationship with their supervisor report lower job satisfaction, less satisfaction with the manager, and decreased organizational commitment, and they engage in more nonconforming behaviors (e.g., taking undeserved breaks, being absent without notifying others, spending time on personal conversations, violating company rules, and complaining).

Obviously, LMX relationships are beneficial to an organization. What determines the type of relationship that will develop between any given manager and employee? Research points consistently to two factors. First, simple **liking** tends to have an impact. Dockery and Steiner (1990) found that liking was most associated with perceived similarity; the more perceived similarity between the manager and the employee, the more likely an LMX relationship. Accordingly, perceived similarity in terms of attitudes about family, money, career, strategies, goals, and education is beneficial to LMX relationships. Such attitudinal similarity is more important than demographic similarity (e.g., age, sex, race). Linking CAT to the development of an LMX relationship, one simple way an employee can develop an LMX relationship with his or her supervisor is to converge with him or her.

Second, performance has an impact. But the causal route on performance isn't clear; does high employee performance lead to an LMX relationship, or does an LMX relationship lead to high employee performance? Both explanations make sense; it is likely that high-performing individuals will receive more trust and respect from their supervisor, but it is also true that people given trust and respect might perform at higher levels. Nevertheless, it seems that when a supervisor perceives an employee as highly skilled, the supervisor is more likely to develop a leader–member exchange relationship. Unfortunately, the link between LMX relationships and performance is not as clean as researchers might like. One study found that poorly performing in-group employees were given high-performance ratings regardless of their actual performance, whereas the ratings of out-group employees were more consistent with actual performance (Duarte, Goodson, & Klich, 1993).

All told, CAT explains and predicts the experience of convergence and divergence in interpersonal communication. The more we like a person or perceive ourselves as part of an in-group, the more likely we are to adapt and match our speech patterns. The more we want to communicate our difference, status, or unique cultural identity, the more likely we are to differentiate our speech from our partner's. Communicators must be aware, however, that accommodation is not always effective or well received and can have implications for workplace relationships.

ANXIETY/UNCERTAINTY MANAGEMENT THEORY

The third culture-based theory featured in this chapter is anxiety/uncertainty management theory (AUM). Developed and refined by William Gudykunst (1985, 1993, 1995, 2005) and clearly influenced by uncertainty reduction theory (see Chapter 3), AUM predicts that communication effectiveness and intercultural adjustment is a combined result of reducing intercultural anxiety and uncertainty. The key difference between uncertainty reduction theory and anxiety/uncertainty management theory is context. Whereas URT focuses on interpersonal encounters, AUM focuses on intercultural (or intergroup) encounters wherein people from different cultural backgrounds interact. Specifically, AUM posits that mindful awareness of intercultural anxiety and uncertainty motivates intergroup participants to manage the reduction of this apprehension. Developed over nearly two decades and still a work in progress, the theory employs 47 axioms and numerous theorems. In this section, we present AUM's key principles and predictions, while recognizing that our summary is a simplified version of Gudykunst's theory.

Although AUM has undergone many refinements over the last three decades, one central assumption is that at least one person in an intercultural encounter is a **stranger** (Gudykunst, 2005). Similar to the notion of in-groups and out-groups as discussed with communication accommodation theory, AUM theory views cultural strangers as out-group members, while the cultural natives are in-group members. You don't have to be in a foreign country to experience feeling like a stranger. Moving from a suburban subdivision to an urban neighborhood, shopping for specialty meats or herbs in an ethnic market, leaving the military to join a civilian lifestyle, or ordering custom furniture from an Amish carpenter might all be examples of feeling like a stranger in a strange land.

A second assumption of AUM theory is that when a stranger interacts with a cultural in-group member, uncertainty and anxiety abound. Although related, uncertainty and anxiety are distinct concepts according to AUM. Congruent with uncertainty reduction theory, AUM theory maintains that cognitive uncertainty leaves individuals unable to explain or predict their own or their partners' behavior in intercultural situations (Gudykunst, 1993). Gudykunst assumed strangers and in-group members always feel some degree of uncertainty when faced with a new interpersonal, intergroup situation. Different from uncertainty reduction theory, however, AUM argues that when the exchange is between people of different groups or cultures, individuals become hypersensitive to cultural differences.

Not all uncertainty is damaging. Gudykunst (1993) reported that individuals vary in their minimum and maximum thresholds for uncertainty. Too much uncertainty will leave you unable to make useful predictions about your partner's behavior, while too little uncertainty leads to overconfidence and opens the door for misinterpretations. If you can appropriately discern and reduce your uncertainty about your interaction partner's behavior, however, you've successfully achieved **attributional confidence** (Gudykunst & Hammer, 1988). Think of an uncertainty threshold like job stress; too much stress leaves the employee feeling overwhelmed and powerless, while too little stress leads to a lack of effort and boredom. However, the right amount of stress (termed *eustress*) motivates the employee to perform to his or capability.

In addition to uncertainty about why and how intergroup partners will act, **anxiety** is also present in intercultural encounters. Related to but distinct from uncertainty, anxiety refers to an emotional state of apprehension, worry, or fear of negative consequences (Gudykunst & Hammer, 1988). For example, anxiety may become magnified in an intercultural interaction because in-group members don't want to appear to be biased or prejudiced against cultural strangers. As with uncertainty, anxiety also operates with a threshold of minimum and maximum limits. Too much apprehension about interactions with cultural strangers leads to a reliance on stereotypes; in other words, too much anxiety shuts down people's ability to think critically about the situation, forcing them to use simplistic schema. Conversely, having too little anxiety is associated with a lack of motivation to communicate. Stated differently, if you don't have any reservations about the consequences of your actions, you may not be motivated to interact at all. Griffin (2006) provides the classic example of the "ugly American" tourist. Travelers who don't take the time to consider how they will be perceived by locals are likely to come across as rude and insensitive, whereas tourists concerned with appearing incompetent are more likely to make efforts to blend in with the natives.

Presented in Table 6.3, AUM's 47 axioms can be more easily described by categorizing them as seven general factors that predict the extent to which a person will experience anxiety and uncertainty in predicting a cultural stranger's behavior in intergroup communication (Gudykunst, 2005). Subsumed within each factor are numerous predictions that forecast the increase or decrease in anxiety and uncertainty during intergroup interactions.

AUM predicts it is only when this anxiety and uncertainty are appropriately discerned and reduced that effective communication can occur. According to Gudykunst (1995), all messages must be interpreted for meaning to be conveyed. **Effective communication** occurs when "the person interpreting the message attaches a meaning to the message that is relatively similar to what was intended by the person transmitting it" (p. 15). In other words, when misunderstandings are minimized, the person receiving the message interprets the meaning in a way congruent with the meaning intended by the sender.

Table 6.3 Predictors of Anxiety and Uncertainty in Intercultural and Intergroup Interactions

Self-concept	An individual's self-concept (including self-esteem, personal identity, and social identity) affects anxiety and uncertainty. More specifically, AUM predicts that when an individual's self-concept is threatened, his or her intercultural anxiety increases and he or she is less likely to make accurate predictions about the cultural stranger. AUM posits the opposite when intercultural interactions uphold an individual's self-concept. That is, the more one's intergroup dealings support one's view of self, the less anxiety and uncertainty, thereby increasing the individual's ability to predict strangers' behavior.
Motivation to interact with strangers	A person's need for predictability, group inclusion, and identity sustainability influences anxiety and uncertainty. In other words, AUM proposes that as an individual's ability to predict a cultural stranger's behavior increases, anxiety and uncertainty are reduced. Conversely, AUM suggests that the greater a person's need for group inclusion, the greater one's anxiety and uncertainty, thereby making accurate predictions about behavior less likely.
Reactions to strangers	Empathy, tolerance for ambiguity, and rigidity of intergroup attitudes influence anxiety and uncertainty. Specifically, AUM predicts that empathy and the ability to tolerate ambiguity lessen anxiety and improve the ability to make accurate predictions about behavior. Conversely, AUM predicts that the more rigid one's attitudes about strangers, the greater one's anxiety and uncertainty, thereby making accurate predictions about a stranger's behavior improbable.
Social categorization of strangers	Positive expectations, perceived similarities, and intergroup knowledge reduce anxiety and uncertainty, increasing one's ability to predict strangers' behavior accurately. In particular, AUM forecasts that positive expectations, perceived similarities, and an increase in intergroup knowledge will reduce anxiety, thereby increasing the ability to make accurate predictions of actions. Conversely, AUM predicts that anxiety will increase when one expects negative behavior, perceives few similarities, and has little intergroup understanding.
Situational processes	Perceived in-group power and the cooperative–competitive nature of tasks influence anxiety and uncertainty, making it more likely to predict strangers' behavior accurately. Specifically, AUM predicts that as in-group members increase in number or perceive they have power, anxiety about the cultural stranger lessens. Likewise, when intergroup interactions focus on cooperative tasks, anxiety lessens.
Connections with strangers	Attraction, interdependence, and the quantity and quality of contacts with strangers lessen individuals' anxiety and reduce uncertainty, making it more likely to predict strangers' behavior accurately. In other words, AUM predicts that as one's social attraction to and interdependence with strangers increase, anxiety and uncertainty decrease. Likewise, AUM proposes that spending more time with strangers reduces anxiety and uncertainty.
Ethical interactions	AUM predicts that showing respect and dignity for others, as well as engaging in moral inclusiveness with strangers, reduces anxiety and minimizes uncertainty, making it more likely to predict strangers' actions with accuracy.

Imagine the following intercultural business exchange adapted from Becker (2012). Alexandra, an American businesswoman, meets with Karthik, a potential business partner in Singapore, to discuss developing a new product for use in Southeast Asia. After a lengthy meeting, they agree to research the feasibility of the new product and then go into production. Assuming they're on the same page, the pair never discusses what they mean by "research." To Alexandra, research means contracting a market research firm to conduct phone surveys over a 4-week period, analyzing the data, and making adjustments to the proposal before going to production. To Karthik, research means asking some friends for their opinion. They leave the meeting believing they're in agreement, but clearly effective communication has not occurred.

According to AUM, the key to communication effectiveness is **mindfulness** (Gudykunst, 2005; Miller & Samp, 2007). Mindful communication suggests thoughtful, conscious behavior rather than relying on stereotypes or knee-jerk reactions to a situation. Being mindful allows us to engage in anxiety and uncertainty management because we are discerning the situation, reflecting on our communication, and striving to increase our effectiveness. Recall the predictors of anxiety and uncertainty listed in Table 6.3. Engaging in mindfulness for each of these predictors helps reduce anxiety and uncertainty, "which in turn brings out positive communication outcomes such as communication effectiveness and intercultural adjustment" (Ni & Wang, 2011, p. 272). **Intercultural adjustment**, therefore, is a secondary outcome of positively reducing anxiety and uncertainty, whereby the cultural out-group member feels emotionally secure, socially appropriate, and communicatively competent (Gudykunst, 2005).

Although anxiety/uncertainty management theory may appear overwhelming, at least with regard to the impressive volume of axioms and predictions about intercultural communication effectiveness, remember that intercultural communication itself is a complicated, dynamic process. With a clear focus on using mindfulness to help individuals reduce anxiety and uncertainty when interacting with cultural strangers, AUM makes a concerted effort to capture this phenomenon in a way that is both comprehensive and readily applicable.

FACE NEGOTIATION THEORY

In Chapter 5, we discussed the importance of "face" with regard to interpersonal communication (IPC) and politeness theory (PT). That is, individuals typically try to balance their own positive and negative face needs while also attending to their partner's face needs. Within the context of intercultural communication, the concept of face emerges again. This time, however, Ting-Toomey (1988, 1991b, 2005) uses face to explain and predict the cultural differences associated with conflict management. Specifically, Ting-Toomey's research has illustrated differences between individualistic and collectivistic cultures' face concerns and face needs. Predictably, differing face needs influence one's approach to conflict. Face negotiation theory (FNT) explains cultural differences in conflict as the result of combining differing face needs and conflict styles.

Combining Face With Cultural Orientation

FNT begins with an understanding of face. As presented in Chapter 5, **face** is the desired self-image an individual wants to present to others (Brown & Levinson, 1978, 1987;

Goffman, 1967). Recall that face includes two dimensions: positive and negative. **Positive face** includes the need to be liked, appreciated, and admired; **negative face** emphasizes the desire to act freely without constraints or imposition from others. Face is not a one-way concept; face also includes the recognition that those around us have their own face needs. Awareness of others' face needs (both positive and negative) is known as having face concern. (See Chapter 5 for a complete discussion of face.)

Discussed earlier in this chapter, Hofstede's (1980) research categorized cultures along several dimensions. Central to FNT are the dimensions of individualism–collectivism and power distance described earlier in this chapter. FNT posits that members of individualistic cultures primarily focus on negative face—that is, they prefer to present themselves as confident, self-directed, and independent (Ting-Toomey, 1988). Conversely, members of collectivistic cultures primarily emphasize positive face, presenting themselves as likable, cooperative, and interested in building relationships. Similarly, members of low-power-distance cultures prefer to view individuals as equals, whereas members of high-power-distance cultures accept and rely on hierarchies and status differences (Ting-Toomey, 2005).

Together, Ting-Toomey (2005) predicts these cultural differences affect face management, and differences in face management lead to different communication patterns. Moreover, these communication differences can lead to misinterpretation and disagreement. Consider the example of an American executive who compliments a Japanese business partner's fluency in English in front of other Japanese co-workers (Cupach & Imahori, 1993). The American believes his or her actions to be face enhancing—that is, giving someone a compliment is viewed as boosting one's face. To the Japanese, however, such a compliment is actually face threatening—by singling out one individual, the cooperative emphasis is damaged. Even the best-intended messages, then, can lead to misunderstanding and intercultural conflict.

Toward a Global Understanding of Conflict Management

As you might imagine, conflict is of great interest to communication scholars and is a widely studied phenomenon. With regard to FNT, conflict is defined as either the perceived or actual incompatibility of values, expectations, processes, or outcomes between two or more individuals (Ting-Toomey, 1994). Among North American relationships, five conflict styles commonly emerge: avoiding, accommodating, competing, compromising, and collaborating (Kilmann & Thomas, 1977; Rahim, 1986; Thomas & Kilmann, 1974). These researchers likely did not think about the conflict styles in terms of being particular to "North Americans" (where they are most often tested) or cultural exclusion. As will become clear, however, these five approaches to conflict appear to exclude significant components of a collectivistic orientation.

According to Kilmann and Thomas (1977), these five conflict styles vary on two dimensions: assertiveness (concern for self) and cooperation (concern for other). Those practicing **avoidance** lack assertiveness and cooperation; they withdraw from or seek to evade conflict altogether. As such, there is little concern for self or others. Individuals with an **accommodating** style cooperate with others but demonstrate little assertiveness—typically conceding to their partner's requests. Conversely, those **competing** in a conflict situation are highly assertive but lack cooperation; they push their viewpoints on others, sometimes to the extent of sacrificing the relationship altogether. A person with a **compromising** style has moderate concern for self and others; this individual is somewhat assertive and fairly cooperative. Compromising typically involves a willingness to give up some demands to gain others. Finally, individuals with a **collaborating** style have a high regard for self and others, making the person very assertive and also very cooperative. Collaboration occurs when one actively seeks to create new solutions that meet both partners' interests without having to make the sacrifices involved with compromise. Note that conflict style is not a fixed trait; instead, it is a person's preferred response to conflict in a given situation. You can alter your conflict style depending on the partner involved and the circumstances at hand (Cupach & Canary, 1997).

Although Ting-Toomey (1988, 1991b) acknowledged the body of North American research showing support for the five previously mentioned conflict styles, she also maintained these styles represent primarily a Western view of conflict. Ting-Toomey proposed that a global understanding of conflict management is remiss without examining issues of face. Consequently, her research extends the Western understanding of conflict management by viewing conflict styles on dual dimensions of **self-face concern** and **other-face concern**. Simply put, this means individuals must consider their own positive and negative face needs (self-face concern) as well as their partner's positive and negative face needs (other-face concern). **Mutual-face concern**, then, is the recognition of both self- and other-face needs. FNT predicts a causal relationship between culture, face, and conflict style. Conflict is particularly salient for intercultural communication because, during conflict, both parties can easily lose both positive and negative face through face-threatening acts (see Chapter 5).

Indeed, research using FNT not only shows links between culture and face management but also illustrates that when culture and face are combined, individuals can predict another's conflict management style (see Oetzel & Ting-Toomey, 2003; Ting-Toomey, 1988, 1991b). After studying students' conflict responses in China, Japan, South Korea, Taiwan, and the United States, eight responses to conflict emerged (Ting-Toomey & Oetzel, 2002; see Figure 6.1). Although the terminology varies slightly, the first five conflict responses mirror those identified previously (see Kilmann & Thomas, 1977): avoid, oblige (accommodate), dominate (compete), compromise, and integrate (collaborate). When considering self-face concern and other-face concern, three additional styles emerged: emotional expression, passive aggression, and third-party help.

The **emotionally expressive** style refers to an affective response to conflict as opposed to a cognitive response. That is, emotional expression emphasizes a person's desire to react to his or her feelings or "gut reaction." A person who relies on a **passive-aggressive** style surreptitiously attempts to make his or her partner feel guilty. Passive aggression is more active than avoiding the situation altogether but less active than openly addressing the conflict; the passive-aggressive individual only drops blameful hints of the problem. Finally, the tendency to rely on **third-party help** means the person is more comfortable asking a person outside of the relationship to help manage the conflict. For example, within the context of business communication, Asians often use such intermediaries to help preserve face (Ting-Toomey, 1992).

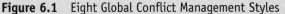

Figure 6.1 Eight Global Conflict Management Styles

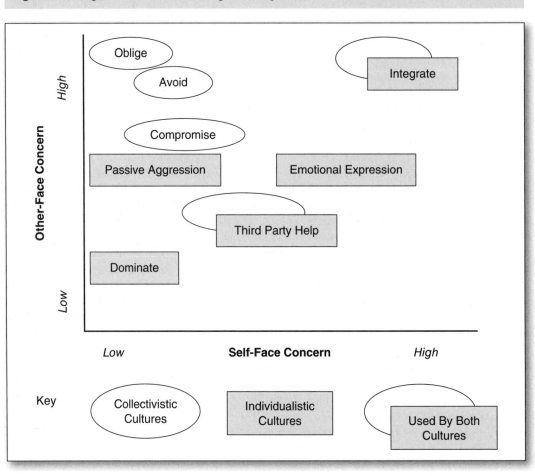

Source: From "Cross-Cultural Face Concerns and Conflict Styles: Current Status and Future Directions," by S. Ting-Toomey and J. Oetzel. In W. B. Gudykunst and B. Mody (Eds.), *Handbook of International and Intercultural Communication* (2nd ed., pp. 143–164), © 2002 by SAGE. Reprinted by permission of SAGE.

Americans typically use confrontational and dominating conflict strategies with a stronger win–lose orientation to preserve self-face (Ting-Toomey, 1992). Conversely, Asians prefer conflict avoidance in an effort to maintain mutual face. More precisely, Taiwanese and Chinese rely more heavily on a compromising conflict style; when working with in-group (Japanese) members, the Japanese also rely on conflict avoidance. Notably, however, the Japanese mirror Americans' more dominating conflict style when dealing with out-group (non-Japanese) associates. This ability to switch between styles depending on in-group/out-group affiliations may help explain Japanese competence when communicating in global business relationships.

All told, Ting-Toomey's (1988, 1991b, 2005) FNT offers a more holistic view of conflict, particularly within the context of cultural communication. According to her causal model, one's cultural orientation (individualism–collectivism and power distance) coupled with self- and other-face concerns predict one's likely repertoire of conflict responses. Intercultural conflict—that is, perceived disagreement between members of different cultures—may arise as a direct result of these cultural differences.

Summary and Research Applications

We discussed four ways of examining culture and communication in the workplace. Hofstede's five dimensions help create understanding of variations across cultures. Avery, Baradwaj, and Singer (2008) used Hofstede's framework to analyze Citibank's country-specific websites, finding the cultural dimensions of power distance, individualism, masculinity, and uncertainty avoidance influence the design of the bank's various online facades. Their study suggests organizations with international clients would be wise to pay attention to these cultural differences in order to attract and retain clients. Second, we took a look at communication accommodation theory. Giles and Coupland's (1991) theory predicts an individual's desire to join the in-group will lead to convergence, while one's wish to remain an out-group member will result in divergence. In a study examining accommodation and text messaging, Riordan, Markman, and Stewart (2013) found that relational and conversational contexts affect convergence. In a different vein, researchers used communication accommodation theory to analyze police interactions during traffic stops with both Latino and non-Latino drivers, finding that ethnicity and driver accent predicted the degree to which convergent or divergent strategies were used (Giles, Linz, Bonilla, & Gomez, 2012). Third, we reviewed anxiety/uncertainty management theory. Gudykunst (1985, 2005) sought to provide a comprehensive understanding of how communication effectiveness can be increased by mindfully reducing intercultural anxiety and uncertainty. Within the context of organizational and public relationships, Ni and Wang (2011) used AUM to study outcomes associated with building intercultural relations within a multicultural university setting. And in the wake of an increasing number of pandemic health crises, Johnson Avery and Kim (2008) used AUM to frame their analysis of national and international press releases on a flu pandemic to gauge the effectiveness of their anxiety-inducing and uncertainty-reducing messages. Finally, FNT offers a transcultural approach to conflict management. By incorporating cultural variations of facework, FNT demonstrates that conflict strategies are a by-product of one's culture and face concerns. One way to manage these seemingly inevitable cultural differences might include technology. Gunawardena, Walsh, Gregory, Lake, and Reddinger (2005) studied cultural differences in an online learning environment and found mixed support for FNT's predictions. They concluded that although negotiation of face in an online learning environment does differ by culture, most participants were concerned with presenting a positive image online.

Key Terms

Accommodating 110
Accommodation 104

Anxiety 107
Attributional confidence 107

Case Study 6: The Trouble With Tourists

Historic Philadelphia is booming as a travel destination. Among the many sites tourists visit while in Philadelphia is the Granovetter Church*, a partially restored building nearly 300 years old noted for being a secret meeting place of the early founders of the United States. In 2013 nearly 1.5 million people visited the political and religious landmark, with an estimated one in five hailing from a foreign country. The sheer number of tourists visiting the site, as well as the number who spoke languages other than English, combined to create significant challenges for the volunteers who provide guidance and interpretation to visitors. Unlike the nearby Independence National Park, which is run by the National Park Service, the Granovetter Church is still a congregation of the Presbyterian Church of the United States of America. All touring is done in coordination with a group of volunteers, who are managed by an oversight committee of the Philadelphia Presbytery.

During a general meeting of volunteers, it became apparent the volunteers were having increasing trouble with meeting the needs of international visitors, particularly with Japanese visitors to the park. Volunteers had difficulty with explaining the general concerns and rules for behavior in what was in essence a place of worship. Further conversation among the volunteers implied that aggressive tour leaders were often the root of the problem. Such was the case with many tour leaders from an organization called Marzu Tours.

Marzu Tours frequently burst into the church with bullhorn in hand, talking in Japanese while an English-speaking interpretive presentation was in progress. The group would push and shove to remain together throughout the presentation, interrupting and interfering with existing tour groups. Moreover, the Marzu Tour leaders would wander through the building on their own, often requiring a volunteer to run to prevent the tour from entering a sacrosanct area. Other tour operators and visitors frequently complained about these groups.

After years of avoiding the problem, Mark Hastings, the chair of the oversight committee, determined direct confrontation of the problem was inevitable. He began the process of trying to contact the director of Marzu Tours. His efforts led him to Yushiko Sato, a female employee of the company. Mark decided the best approach would be to present his complaint in a straightforward manner, even though he was actually quite frustrated and angry after wasting so much time with bureaucracy and red tape while trying to find the right person to talk with.

"Ms. Sato, we at Granovetter Church are having trouble with some of your tour guides," Mark began. "They do not wait their turn for admittance, they do not follow our rules for where they can go, and they seem to push their groups in front of other groups during the tours."

"I am so sorry," Yushiko replied with a great deal of sincerity. "I will bring this to the attention of our director."

Mark hung up the phone, satisfied that the problem would be resolved and impressed with the service he had received from Yushiko. However, several months later he was still receiving complaints about the company from the volunteers. He retraced his steps and called Yushiko Sato again. This time, he asked to speak to her director.

"That is a little difficult," Yushiko replied.

Mark was frustrated by the stonewalling. "This is a problem with a fairly simple solution!" he shouted.

"Mr. Hastings, you cannot change the Japanese. The Japanese are different," Yushiko calmly explained, with just a touch of condescension.

Mark refused to take the bait. "All of our visitors are important to us; the Japanese are not more important than others, I just want to level the playing field," Mark responded with what he thought was great patience. "Can we perhaps set up a meeting to discuss this in person?"

"I will see what we can do," Yushiko replied.

Two weeks later, Mark still had not heard back from Yushiko so he called her yet again. He was as clear and firm as he could be. She agreed to have an in-person meeting the next week. Mark was a little bit late for the meeting because a rainstorm had flooded some of the roads leading out of the city to the Marzu Tours office in the suburbs. He was shocked when he actually met Yushiko, who appeared to be very young and immature. The contrast between her innocent appearance and her clear distaste for his late arrival was intriguing. It was also very obvious she was a low-level employee. He realized the issue wasn't that she *would* not address the problem of her company's tour guides but that she *could* not do so; she didn't have the authority.

Mark concluded the meeting by thanking Yushiko for her concern. He had given up on working with the company and decided his volunteers would simply need better training to deal with Japanese tourists. To his bewilderment, Yushiko suggested Mark meet the local director of the company. "Finally!" he thought. "Maybe now we'll get somewhere!"

Questions for Consideration

1. How might the troubles with the tourism company be explained by Hofstede's dimensions of culture? Make sure to look at both Japanese and American cultures.

2. Did either Yushiko or Mark ever accommodate? How? With what effect?

3. Relate AUM's seven predictors of anxiety and uncertainty to the case. Which predictors seem to be the greatest contributors to the problem at Granovetter Church? How might Gudykunst advise both Mark and Yushiko so they can engage in more mindful communication?

4. To what extent did Mark and Yushiko recognize the other's face needs during the conflict? What conflict strategies did they use? Were the strategies consistent with the predictions of face negotiation theory?

5. Do any of the theories emerge as "better" than the others? Why do you believe this to be the case? What situations might surface that would make a different theory or theories better at explaining the situation?

*The location, history, and events of this story are entirely fictional. The Granovetter Church does not exist and is not based on any real building.

CHAPTER 7

Persuasion

After reading this chapter, you will be able to...

1. Define persuasion.
2. Describe the relationship between attitudes and influence.
3. Explain the importance of audience analysis prior to creating a persuasive message.
4. Describe the central and peripheral routes to persuasion and discuss when a communicator should use each route.
5. Differentiate between types of elaborated arguments: strong, neutral, and weak.
6. Differentiate between types of peripheral cues: strong, neutral, and weak.
7. Give examples for each of the seven peripheral cues.
8. Analyze the effectiveness of persuasive messages by determining which route, arguments, or peripheral cues were used.
9. Discuss the importance of behavioral intention and its relationship to influencing behavior.
10. Explain why changing a target's attitude is not enough to influence behavioral change.
11. Articulate how the theory of reasoned action was extended to form the theory of planned behavior.
12. Describe how the interplay of attitudes, normative beliefs, and perceived behavioral control is critical in persuading people to change their behavior.
13. Discuss how individuals might resist being persuaded using an inoculation approach.
14. Identify an inoculation threat.
15. Explain refutational preemption and identify examples of counterpersuasion efforts.
16. Explain the assumptions of the narrative paradigm.
17. Compare and contrast the narrative paradigm with the rational-world paradigm.
18. Discuss how narrative coherence and narrative fidelity work together to create narrative rationality.
19. Analyze persuasive narratives to assess the logic of good reasons.

Since the mid-1930s when Dale Carnegie first published his best-selling book *How to Win Friends and Influence People*, the notion of how to persuade others has been both a popular and profitable subject. Concurrently, with the rise of mass media and the pervasiveness of propaganda used in both World Wars, the study and understanding of mass-mediated persuasive messages became critical to understanding political and social change. Today, the importance of understanding the power of persuasive messages is greater than ever. According to marketing experts, the average American has "gone from being exposed to about 500 ads a day back in the 1970s to as many as 5,000 a day today" (Walker-Smith, quoted in Johnson, 2009, para. 15). Plastered on bus windows, revolving on your favorite sports team's stadium marquis, popping up on your "free" Spotify app, and even visible on New York's subway turnstiles, advertisements are everywhere. Clearly, we are inundated with messages of persuasion and influence in all aspects of our lives—relational, social, political, and economic. Accordingly, we believe having an understanding of how persuasive messages work (or don't work!) is central for surviving in today's advertising and media-blitzed society.

PERSUASION DEFINED

Persuasion is typically defined as "human communication that is designed to influence others by modifying their beliefs, values, or attitudes" (Simons, 1976, p. 21). O'Keefe (1990) argued there are requirements for the sender, the means, and the recipient to consider something persuasive. First, persuasion involves the intent to achieve a goal on the part of the message sender. Second, communication is the means to achieve that goal. Third, the message recipient must have free will (i.e., threatening physical harm if the recipient doesn't comply is usually considered force, not persuasion). Accordingly, persuasion is not accidental—nor is it coercive. It is inherently communicational.

Many theories in this chapter are concerned with shifts in attitude, so it is important to make clear what we mean by that term. An **attitude** is a "relatively enduring predisposition to respond favorably or unfavorably" toward something (Simons, 1976, p. 80). We have attitudes toward people, places, events, products, policies, ideas, and so forth (O'Keefe, 1990). Because attitudes are enduring, they are neither fleeting nor based on whims. Yet at the same time, attitudes are *learned* evaluations; they are not something people are born with. As such, attitudes are changeable. Finally, and perhaps most importantly, attitudes are presumed to influence behavior; although, as we will see later, this influence is not as strong as we might presume.

In this chapter, we present four theories of persuasive communication. Although portrayed as theories of persuasion, each of these viewpoints can be applied to a wide variety of communication contexts. From well-crafted public relations campaigns designed to foster positive attitudes about a company to strategically forewarning a partner he is about to hear something that might upset him, the theories presented highlight the varied ways to develop persuasive messages. The four theories we discuss in this chapter are the elaboration likelihood model, the theory of planned behavior, inoculation theory, and the narrative paradigm.

ELABORATION LIKELIHOOD MODEL

Turning to our first theory of persuasion, the elaboration likelihood model (ELM) views persuasion primarily as a cognitive event, meaning the targets of persuasive messages use mental processes of motivation and reasoning (or a lack thereof) to accept or reject persuasive messages. Developed by Petty and Cacioppo (1986), ELM posits two possible routes, or methods, of influence: centrally routed messages and peripherally routed messages. Each route targets a widely different audience. Accordingly, ELM emphasizes the importance of understanding audience members before creating a persuasive message.

Slow and Steady: The Central Route to Persuasion

Petty and Cacioppo's (1986) model depicts persuasion as a process in which the success of influence depends largely on the way the receivers make sense of the message. As mentioned earlier, ELM presents two divergent pathways one can use when trying to influence others. The more complex of the two paths is known as the **central route**, also referred to as the elaborated route. Centrally routed messages include a wealth of information, rational arguments, and evidence to support a particular conclusion. For example, during each election season, political hopefuls engage in speeches, debates, and roundtable discussions; each message is filled with elaborated and presumably rational information regarding the candidate's viewpoints, platform, and political history.

Centrally routed messages are much more likely to create long-term change for the recipient than are peripheral messages (discussed later); however, not all individuals are capable of receiving centrally routed messages. ELM argues that centrally routed messages succeed in long-term change only when two factors are met: the target must be highly motivated to process all the information given, and the target must be able to process the message cognitively. For example, if you are not willing to sit through a 2-hour televised debate between presidential candidates, then ELM suggests you do not have the motivation required to process an elaborated message in this instance. Alternatively, imagine you are motivated to watch the candidates debate, but the politicians' messages are so filled with complex issues of international policy that you do not understand them. In this case, ELM suggests that despite your motivation, the ability to understand the highly specific and intricate messages offered is not present. The theory states that without *both* motivation and ability, an elaborated message is of little value.

Types of Elaborated Arguments

It should be apparent that understanding one's audience is critical when choosing the appropriate route; it is also imperative to understand the audience when constructing an **elaborated argument** (Petty & Cacioppo, 1986). In other words, it isn't enough to view your audience as motivated and able when considering the central route of persuasion. You must also consider how the audience members will likely react to the quality and arrangement of the arguments presented. Elaborated arguments can be measured as strong, neutral, or weak.

Strong arguments create a positive cognitive response in the minds of receivers while also positively aligning receivers' beliefs with those views of the persuader (Petty & Cacioppo, 1986). Strong arguments inoculate the audience against counterpersuasion and are most likely to create long-term attitude change that leads to predictable behavior. Repetition is thought to enhance the persuasive effect of strong arguments; conversely, interruptions will diminish their effectiveness. Neutral arguments generate a noncommittal cognitive response from the receiver. In other words, no attitude change occurs, and the ambivalent receiver may instead turn to peripheral cues, or shortcuts, to persuasion. Finally, weak arguments produce a negative cognitive response to the persuasive message. This negative response will not only prevent attitude change but may, in fact, have a reverse or boomerang effect, thereby reinforcing the opposing point of view.

Taking a Shortcut: The Peripheral Route to Persuasion

Noted earlier, elaborated messages are ineffective when targeted participants are neither capable nor interested in the information (Petty & Cacioppo, 1986). Although the persuader might prefer an involved audience so as to produce enduring change, it is unreasonable to expect every persuasive target to be motivated or skilled enough to understand the barrage of influential messages put forth each day. As a result, when motivation or ability is missing from the target audience, the persuader can use the **peripheral route** to persuasion. Peripheral messages rely on a receiver's emotional involvement and persuade through more superficial means. Returning to our political campaign example, it is common for presidential candidates to air 30-second commercials that focus on portraying feel-good images of their "family values," patriotism, character, and likability. As well, some candidates use celebrity endorsements, such as having a famous person or group give public support. For example, Oprah Winfrey publicly supported Barack Obama during his 2008 run for the presidency. Thus, ELM predicts that when the audience is unmotivated or unable to process an elaborated message, persuaders should focus on quick and easy ways to produce change. One significant drawback is that the peripheral route leads only to short-term change, if any change at all.

Types of Peripheral Cues

Cialdini (1993, 1994) identified seven common cues of a peripheral message: authority, commitment, contrast, liking, reciprocity, scarcity, and social proof.

With the first peripheral cue, the persuader uses the perception of **authority** to convince the audience to accept the beliefs or behaviors presented. Parents often use this peripheral cue with their children: "Clean up your room because I said so!" This message may influence children to straighten the covers and hide the toys in the closet before Grandma's visit, but it probably won't create long-term neatness.

Peripheral messages that rely on **commitment** emphasize a person's dedication to a product, social cause, group affiliation, political party, and so on (Cialdini, 1993, 1994). For example, some people publicly announce their commitment to a certain group or cause. They attend rallies; run for office; or wear pins, hats, and other logos that symbolize the affiliation (Canary, Cody, & Manusov, 2003). Similarly, wearing a polo shirt that displays your company's corporate logo demonstrates some amount of dedication to the organization. Other people demonstrate their commitment more privately, for example, by sending anonymous donations to political campaigns or charitable organizations. However, "people usually feel greater commitment to a cause if they are publicly committed to it" (Canary et al., p. 369).

One very common sequential procedure that underscores the commitment principle is the foot-in-the-door tactic (Cialdini, 1994). Here, a persuader convinces you to do something small first, like wear a campaign button. Then the persuader asks to put a campaign sign in your yard. Next, the persuader may ask you to make a donation or to host a reception. The strategy is to convince you to agree to a small, seemingly innocuous request first. Once you agree and commit yourself to the campaign, it becomes harder to refuse larger requests because there is a threat of appearing inconsistent with your commitment.

Persuading through **contrast**, or using contrast effects, requires the communicator to set up uneven points of comparison (Cialdini, 1993, 1994). For example, asking a co-worker if she could do you a "giant favor" and then contrasting the statement with a simple request ("Would you page me if FedEx drops off a package while I am in a client meeting?") sets up a disparity. By inflating the co-worker's expectations for the "giant favor" requested and then contrasting it with a simple favor, it is more likely to result in compliance. Retail salespeople also use this contrast principle by "reducing" prices or by showing customers the most expensive item first (because anything else will seem cheaper in comparison).

Liking messages stress affinity toward a person, place, or object (Cialdini, 1993, 1994). That is, if we like you, we will like your ideas. Many companies often rely on such messages of liking in their advertisements. By using soccer sensation David Beckham to sell Adidas or pop star Taylor Swift to sell CoverGirl cosmetics and Diet Coke, these companies expect that if you like Beckham or Swift, you will also like their product (and will—they hope—buy it).

Messages of **reciprocity** try to influence by emphasizing a give-and-take relationship (Cialdini, 1993, 1994). For example, it is easier to persuade your sister-in-law to babysit your children if you have done something similar for her. Advertisers also use reciprocity: "Buy these steak knives in the next 10 minutes, and we'll throw in a free cutting board!" Here, the advertiser tries to influence the receiver by throwing in some extras. If you do this for us, we'll give you a freebie. Similarly, **scarcity** is a peripheral message that preys on people's worry of missing out on something. This "Quick! Get it before they're all gone!" approach creates a sense of urgency for receivers. Home shopping channels, department stores, car dealers, and furniture stores all rely on this strategy by imposing time limits on the sale of items; presumably, you won't be able to purchase the deluxe salad spinner after the sales event expires. Realtors also use this approach; alerting prospective buyers that an offer has been placed on a property creates a sense of urgency and may start a bidding war. A house that was "of interest" now seems that much more appealing when it may disappear from the market.

Finally, the peripheral cue of **social proof** relies on the age-old notion of peer pressure (Cialdini, 1993, 1994). Although you might mistakenly believe only teenagers succumb to the "everyone's doing it" mentality, adults are also swayed by messages of social proof. Within the workplace, for instance, many corporations participate in charity drives such as with the Red Cross or the United Way. Here, employees who participate in blood drives or fund-raising are given pins to wear or balloons to display, thereby gaining influence by putting subtle pressure on other employees to "get on board."

If unaware of these techniques in the past, you should now be able to identify these seven peripheral cues—they are everywhere! Again, however, it is important to stress that these peripheral messages emphasize fleeting emotional responses and are not likely to create long-lasting change.

Types of Peripheral Messages

As with centrally routed arguments, peripheral messages can be evaluated as positive, neutral, or negative (Petty & Cacioppo, 1986). Positive peripheral messages are those perceived favorably by the audience and create a positive affective state. Positive peripheral messages have a chance at yielding weak, positive changes in attitude. For example, if you are a fan of *The Daily Show* and Jon Stewart publicly endorses Candidate X over Candidate Y, you may feel more positively about Candidate X. However, a change in attitude does not necessarily predict a change in behavior. For instance, you may believe voting is an essential civic duty for American citizens, yet you may not vote in your local primary election because you don't think you are knowledgeable of the candidates. Here, we see incongruence between a belief (voting is important) and behavior (failing to vote).

Neutral peripheral messages leave receivers feeling emotionally ambivalent; they really don't know or care about the cue used to capture their interest (Petty & Cacioppo, 1986). If you don't know who Jon Stewart is or don't really care about his political views, then his endorsement of Candidate X will not create any attitude change—nor is it likely to influence your voting behavior. Finally, negative peripheral messages produce negative or disapproving emotional responses within the receiver. If you can't stand *The Daily Show*, then Jon Stewart's ad endorsing Candidate X will likely irritate you. Thus, you are now left with a negative impression of Candidate X because of this person's "association" with an actor or TV show you find objectionable.

ELM makes very clear predictions, summarized in Figure 7.1. The theory predicts that if listeners are motivated and able to consider an elaborated message, persuaders should rely on strong, factually based arguments. Arguments can backfire if they are weak or poorly presented, however. Conversely, persuaders should focus on emotionally based peripheral messages if receivers cannot or will not consider an elaborated message. Persuaders must recognize that using a peripheral route guarantees no long-term change. Instead, effects, if any, will be minimal and fleeting.

THEORY OF PLANNED BEHAVIOR

ELM gives clear advice if you are trying to persuade someone to think or feel a particular way about an organization, a person, an idea, or a product. But what if your goal is to move beyond attitude change to actually changing someone's behavior? What if you want someone to buy your product, act on your proposal, or comply with instructions? Our second theory, the theory of planned behavior, may provide a template for how to persuade people to change their behavior.

Figure 7.1   Elaboration Likelihood Model

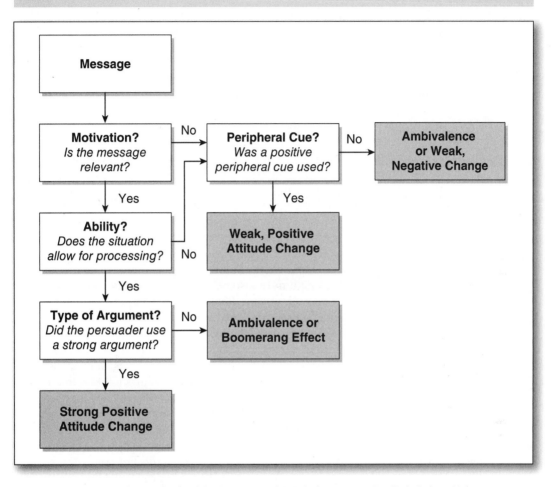

Source: Communication and Persuasion (p. 4) by R. E. Petty and J. T. Cacioppo, 1986, New York: Springer-Verlag.

Theory of Reasoned Action

The roots of the theory of planned behavior can be traced to an earlier theory, the theory of reasoned action, developed by Martin Fishbein and Icek Ajzen in the 1960s (Fishbein & Ajzen, 1975). Fishbein was frustrated by the body of persuasion research at the time; although the notion of an attitude had been well developed, studies could not provide evidence linking attitudes and behavior. Simply being *in favor* of a particular political candidate doesn't guarantee votes for him or her, and supporting the notion of environmental conservation does not necessarily prevent people from taking 30-minute showers. Fishbein, who later worked with Ajzen, recognized that something likely mediates the relationship between an attitude and behavior.

First, Fishbein and Ajzen (1975) assumed all behavior is intentional: We don't accidentally behave in a particular manner; we have reasons for doing so. The idiot who cut you off on your drive to work this morning likely did so because he was in a hurry. The co-worker who leaves work early may be doing so to care for a sick child. The assumption that there are reasons for all of our actions led Fishbein and Ajzen to develop the notion of **behavioral intention**, which simply means your plan to act a particular way.

The next step for these authors was to determine what creates behavioral intention. Fishbein and Ajzen (1975) believed there are two predictors of behavioral intention: attitudes and normative beliefs. We have discussed attitudes already; *attitude* is defined as the sum of beliefs about something. The theory of reasoned action states that our attitudes are made up of two components: our evaluation of the object and our belief strength. Take, for example, your attitude toward technology. Would you be lost without your cell phone? Are you the type of person who needs to get the newest gadget as soon as it is released? Or are you a late adopter, someone who only uses technology after it has been established and there is no getting around using it? Different people evaluate technology differently. Some absolutely love technology, others hate it, and still more think technology is great when it helps you and horrible when it malfunctions. These variations reference your evaluation of the object, but your belief strength must also be taken into account. Do you feel very strongly that your life is better because of your iPhone, or are your positive feelings fairly weak? Your attitudes provide one indication of your behavioral intent.

According to the theory of reasoned action, the second predictor of behavioral intention is **normative beliefs**, which are your perceptions about what others in your social network expect you to do. Notably, behavioral intention is not formed by beliefs about all others in our social network but only our valued others. A disliked associate is unlikely to persuade us to behave in a particular way, but a respected colleague is likely to have that power. In addition to the value you place on others in your network, the theory suggests you must also consider the motivation to comply with these others. Some people are conformists and likely to succumb to peer pressure because of their people-pleasing ways. Others rebel, intentionally doing the opposite of what even valued others expect of them. Returning to our example of technology, if your boss wants you to keep your cell on 24 hours a day "just in case," your intention to do so will be influenced by how much you value your boss (and your job!) and how motivated you are to comply.

The determination of behavioral intention is achieved by looking at the relative weights of the two predictors. In some cases, attitudes might be weighted more strongly, and in others normative beliefs will be weighted more strongly. In order to persuade someone to act a particular way, then, the persuader has to send a message to affect the proper predictor. Consider trying to convince a technophobe to buy a smartphone. If attitudes are very strong and normative beliefs are not, then a message should be sent to address attitudes ("It's hard to find a pay phone anymore; shouldn't you have one in case of an emergency?"). If the opposite is true, you should focus your message on complying with valued others ("What would family members think if your child was at risk just because you don't like cell phones?"). Finally, the persuader can try to change the relative weights of the attitudinal and normative components. If, for example, normative beliefs are weighted more than an attitude, you can try to reduce the strength of the normative beliefs ("It's your life; you need to decide what's important for you").

Adding to the Theory

Although research has provided some strong support for the tenets of the theory of reasoned action, Ajzen (1988, 1991) extended the theory by adding a third major predictor, changing the name to the theory of planned behavior. Ajzen recognized that sometimes we might intend to behave a certain way, but our plans are not carried through because we don't have control over the situation. Like attitudes and normative beliefs, **perceived behavioral control** is also comprised of two elements: self-efficacy and controllability. **Self-efficacy** refers to an individual's belief that she or he can actually perform the behavior. Many adults over the age of 50 consider the speed and frequency of teenagers' text messaging abilities something they couldn't duplicate even if they wanted to! People often "talk themselves out" of doing something because they fear they won't be successful. In short, you need to believe you can truly do something in order to develop the intention to do so. The second component, **controllability**, recognizes that sometimes things are simply out of our control—or are at least perceived that way. You might intend to purchase a new cell phone, but a power outage might shut down the store, or demand for the new phone might exceed supply. Figure 7.2 pulls all of these components together.

Figure 7.2 Theory of Planned Behavior

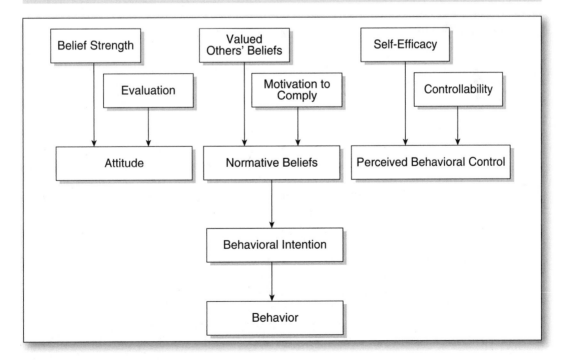

The theory of planned behavior provides an explanation for why campaigns that focus only on providing information are unlikely to have any behavioral effect. Simply changing someone's attitude is not enough. If your goal as a persuader is to convince someone to act in a particular way (e.g., buy your product, donate blood, or engage in fewer arguments), you need to provide attitudinal, social norm, and controllability incentives.

INOCULATION THEORY

Thus far, we have discussed theories that give advice about how to persuade someone. But what if your goal is to persuade someone *not* to be persuaded? Given the plethora of persuasive attempts that surround us on a daily basis, knowing how to resist persuasion is also a useful tool. McGuire's inoculation theory (1961) presents a way to understand how resistance to persuasion might be achieved. Using a medical metaphor, McGuire argued that like a vaccine that prevents you from getting a disease, particular messages might "inoculate" you from attacks on your beliefs. Specifically, an **inoculation** message presents a weaker form (i.e., a "small dose") of a contrary argument, much like a vaccine includes a weakened form of a virus. Once exposed to this weaker argument, people are less likely to change their attitudes when presented with a stronger form of the argument; they have, in essence, developed a formidable defense system. Research has supported this assertion, indicating people are more resistant to persuasion when an inoculation process takes place than when original beliefs were simply bolstered by stronger evidence (Banas & Rains, 2008; McGuire & Papageorgis, 1961).

Developing the Concept

McGuire's original theory focused solely on what he called "cultural truisms" (McGuire, 1962), such as "you should brush your teeth after every meal" and "mental illness is not contagious." Critics challenged this focus, suggesting these noncontroversial issues did not provide an adequate test of how well people will resist persuasive efforts about controversial subjects (Ullman & Bodaken, 1975, as cited in Banas & Rains, 2008). In recent years, a communication scholar named Michael Pfau and his colleagues have examined how inoculation theory might work in broader persuasive contexts, particularly in terms of health communication (Godbold & Pfau, 2000), political communication (An & Pfau, 2004), employees' organizational commitment (Haigh & Pfau, 2006), and corporate advocacy (Burgoon, Pfau, & Birk, 1995). The result is that inoculation theory has "almost limitless application" (Banas & Rains, 2008, p. 1).

Pfau (1997) suggests there are two major components to an inoculation message: threat and refutational preemption. First, **threat** is a necessary component of any inoculation effort. Note that threat is not the same as fear appeal. Instead, threat simply involves a forewarning of a potential persuasive attack on beliefs, making sure the target of the persuasive effort is aware of his or her susceptibility to the attack. According to Pfau, making you aware of a threat should motivate you to defend your attitudes or beliefs. For example, Compton and Pfau (2004) studied the marketing of credit cards to college students. They created a fake credit card company and developed a campaign designed to convince students to sign up with the company. Then some of the students received an inoculation message with a threat in advance, forewarning of the lengths to which credit card companies will pursue them. Part of the inoculation said, "Some of their [credit card companies'] claims are so persuasive that they may cause you to question your current cautious attitude toward credit cards" (Compton & Pfau, 2004, p. 362). Others received no forewarning. After being exposed to the fake campaign, results indicated that individuals who received the threat message reported healthier attitudes toward credit card debt and were less likely to say they would sign up with the fictitious credit card company than was the control group. The threat need not be a strong warning; Banas and Rains (2008) found that even low levels of threat provided inoculation.

The second component of an inoculation effort is **refutational preemption**. Not only should targets receive information about potential threats, but the inoculation message should also anticipate the counterpersuasive effort by raising specific challenges and then contesting them. In the study by Compton and Pfau (2004) described previously, the researchers determined that marketing by credit card companies typically centers on increasing financial independence, providing a safety net of available credit, and building a strong credit history. Thus, the inoculation message they developed provided statistics and stories to combat these arguments.

Research consistently shows that "matching" the content of refutations exactly to what actually occurs in the counterargument is unnecessary; any preemptive refutation seems to bolster the inoculation effect (Banas & Rains, 2008). The bigger question appears to be how strong the preemptive arguments need to be. Using the vaccine analogy, how much "disease" in the vaccine protects the recipient, and how much is too much? McGuire (1964) argued that inoculation efforts should be "threatening enough to be defense-stimulating, but not so strong as to overwhelm" (p. 202). In testing this issue, Compton and Pfau (2004) concluded that even weak refutations provide protection.

Inoculation theory provides clear advice for professional communicators challenged (or who think they may be challenged) by "bad press." Consider the efforts of the soda industry. In the last several years over 30 municipalities have proposed increasing taxes on the sale of sugary drinks (Yudell, 2012). The goals of such efforts are twofold: to address the rising obesity epidemic in the United States and to provide a means to reduce budget shortfalls in an uncertain economy. The industry leaders (Coca-Cola and PespsiCo) have partnered with the American Beverage Association (ABA) to make sure the public is not persuaded to vote in favor of these tax increases, however. It's estimated the ABA has spent nearly $100 million in efforts to prevent the public from being persuaded to tax soft drinks. Table 7.1 depicts the argument presented in one advertisement called "Your Cart Your Choice," which clearly demonstrates an inoculation effort.

NARRATIVE PARADIGM

Whereas ELM emphasizes the importance of strong, logical arguments for persuading a motivated and able audience, the narrative paradigm stresses the effectiveness of influence

Table 7.1   Inoculation Campaign Against Proposed Food Taxes

	Example
Threat	"Some politicians still don't think we can choose what's best for our families without new laws, regulations, or taxes telling us what to buy."
Refutational preemption	"Getting serious about obesity starts with education, not laws and regulations." "Look around your grocery store lately? There are more choices and more information than ever before. New kinds of beverages. Different portion sizes. Calories right up front."
Conclusion	"The fact is, it's not the government's job to grocery shop for my family. It's mine."

through narration—that is, persuasion through storytelling (Fisher, 1984, 1987). Using a more subjective theoretical orientation, Fisher argues that human beings are fundamentally storytelling creatures; therefore, the most persuasive or influential message is not that of rational fact but instead a narrative that convinces us of "good reasons" for engaging in a particular action or belief.

Consider television advertising. Are the most memorable ads those that inundate the audience with facts about the products, or are they those that craft a memorable story? Budweiser has relied on the "Bud Bowl" saga for more than 25 years to sell its beer during the Super Bowl. Likewise, Subaru's advertising has increasingly focused on narratives after recognizing the transformational power of stories (Randazzo, 2006). Their love story narratives emphasize the brand's four themes—longevity, safety, versatility, and adventure. According to Nudd (2013), "The automaker is particularly adept at father-daughter tales—like 'Baby Driver,' the Emmy-nominated spot from 2010, and now 'Cut the Cord,' about a girl's first day of school" (para. 1). These story-focused ad campaigns have yielded impressive results. In the United States, Subaru sales doubled from 2008 to 2013, and in May 2013, the manufacturer had its best sales in company history.

Not all narrative advertisements are long-term campaigns, however. One of the most memorable commercials during the 2013 Super Bowl was Tide's "Miracle Stain" ad. The humorous vignette focused on a 49ers fan who spills salsa on his jersey only to notice that the stain resembles the almighty Joe Montana. This "miracle" stain goes viral, leading to 15 minutes of fame for the lucky 49ers fan. Unfortunately for him, however, his wife, a Ravens fan, removes the stain with Tide. The 60-second story capitalized on that year's Super Bowl rivalry—the 49ers versus the Ravens—while also humorously poking fun at sports fans and their superstitions. Current marketing experts understand that "the real power of strategic storied advertising is in its ability to build strong, enduring brands" (Randazzo, 2006, p. 13). It is these stories that "give brands their unique identity and personality, which in turn create an emotional bond between the consumer and the brand" (p. 13).

As we explain subsequently, Fisher's (1984, 1987) view of communication contrasts much of a Western emphasis on rational decision making. Yet by juxtaposing a narrative worldview with a rational worldview, we hope you will give some thought to this strikingly different way of considering communication and influence.

Fisher's Narrative Assumptions

Five assumptions drive Fisher's (1987) explanation of the narrative paradigm. First and foremost, Fisher proposed that what makes humans unique and distinct from other creatures is our ability and drive to tell stories. Narration does not refer to "fictive composition whose propositions may be true or false" (p. 58); instead, a **narrative** includes the symbolic words and actions people use to assign meaning. Fisher evoked the Greek term **mythos** to explain human communication primarily as a collection of stories expressing "ideas that cannot be verified or proved in any absolute way. Such ideas arise in metaphor, values, gestures, and so on" (p. 19). According to this view, not even the keenest expert knows everything about his or her area of specialization; there is an element of subjectivity in even the most "logical" of messages. Instead, your values, emotions, and aesthetic preferences shape your beliefs and actions. As such, individuals relay messages and experiences through stories in an attempt to capture these subjective experiences.

Second, the narrative paradigm suggests that because individuals' lives and understanding of reality are centered on these subjective narratives, people need a way to judge which stories are believable and which are not (Fisher, 1987). Here, Fisher argued that individuals use **narrative rationality**—a logical method of reasoning by which a person can determine how believable another's narrative is. Narrative rationality relies on **good reasons** as the basis for most decision making. As opposed to relying solely on argumentative logic, good reasons allow us to validate and accept (or reject) another's narrative based on the perceived truthfulness and **consistency**. Thus, coherence and fidelity are two ways to make this narrative judgment of "good reasons." When the narrative used appears to flow smoothly, makes sense, and is believable, we say there is **narrative coherence**. Similarly, when the narrative appears truthful and congruent with our own experiences, we say there is **narrative fidelity**. To accept a narrative, an individual must perceive the narrative's fidelity first; without fidelity, coherence is irrelevant.

A related third assumption is that what a person accepts as a good reason is based on that individual's culture, character, history, values, experience, and the like (Fisher, 1984, 1987). In other words, what appears to have coherence and fidelity to one person may not appeal to another who comes to the narrative relationship with a different set of values and experiences.

Fourth, the narrative paradigm proposes that "rationality is determined by the nature of persons as narrative beings" (Fisher, 1987, p. 5). Rather than conceiving of reason as rooted only in fact and logical argument, Fisher argued that rationality—and therefore persuasion—stems from humans' ability to create a coherent story. Thus, piling on the facts about a political candidate's legislative record isn't what is persuasive for voters; what will influence constituents is a candidate's ability to share his or her experiences via narrative.

Finally, the narrative paradigm presumes the world as humans know it is based primarily on sets of both cooperative and competing stories (Fisher, 1987). Individuals must use the logic of good reasons to choose among these narratives, thereby creating and re-creating their social reality. Because "human communication . . . is imbued with mythos—ideas that cannot be verified or proved in any absolute way" (p. 19), Fisher believed individuals must rely on narratives as the creation and re-creation of a common understanding. The narratives we choose can fundamentally affect our life.

Table 7.2   Comparing the Narrative and Rational-World Paradigms

Narrative Paradigm	Rational-World Paradigm
1. Human beings are storytellers.	1. Human beings are rational.
2. Communication, persuasion, and decision making are based on the logic of good reasons.	2. Communication, persuasion, and decision making are based on sound arguments.
3. What one accepts as "good reasons" is determined individually by a person's culture, character, experiences, and values.	3. Strong arguments adhere to specific criteria for soundness and logic (e.g., using the premise-inference-conclusion model).
4. Rationality is based on one's awareness of how consistent and truthful a story appears when compared with one's own (and others') lived experiences.	4. Rationality is based on the accuracy of information presented and on the reliability of the reasoning processes used.
5. People experience the world as a series of stories from which to choose. As we make these choices, we create and re-create reality.	5. The world and reality can be viewed as a series of logical relationships revealed through reasoned argument.

Study in Contrasts: Comparing Narrative and Rational Paradigms

Mentioned earlier, the narrative paradigm contrasts with much of Western thought, including the emphasis on the rational paradigm. Table 7.2 presents the contrast between the narrative paradigm and the rational paradigm. Specifically, Fisher (1987) argued that **logos**, or purely rational argument, has been unfairly privileged as the ultimate measure of rationality. For example, he cited Aristotle's preference for persuasion and intellectual arguments grounded first and foremost in logos. As previously discussed, the narrative paradigm assumes little in our social worlds can be understood as purely fact; everything around us is shaded with the subjectivity of individual values and experiences. As such, "rationality is grounded in the narrative structure of life and the natural capacity people have to recognize coherence and fidelity in the stories they experience and tell to one another" (p. 137). Consequently, Fisher posited that mythos (narratives) and pathos (emotional appeals) are more meaningful to humans and, therefore, more persuasive.

Importantly, the narrative paradigm does not exclude logic (Fisher, 1987). Instead, Fisher argued no rhetorical proof (credibility, emotion, or reason) should be regarded as superior to other forms of rhetorical proof. Fisher also maintained humans should move away from dualistic approaches (i.e., that we are either rational or narrative) and embrace more integrated perspectives (i.e., that we are both rational and narrative).

According to the narrative paradigm, then, human communication and our understanding of "reality" relies heavily on narration. What's more, Fisher (1987) believed narrative is a more effective means of influence than traditional forms of logic based on reasoning. However, only when a narrative exhibits good reasons and narrative coherence will it be convincing enough to permeate a receiver's consciousness and become translated into a change in action.

Organizational Storytelling

Lest the narrative paradigm seem too intangible for practical use, consider the influence of organizational storytelling. Barker and Gower (2010) argue that integrating good storytelling in diverse, multicultural work environments has tremendous benefit to the organization and its workforce. They contend that "stories serve a persuasive communication function for organizations by representing personal, interpersonal, and corporate perspectives" (p. 304). Online retailer Zappos has shown great success with organizational storytelling, both internally by using narratives to communicate organizational values to employees and externally with customers (Greenberg, 2013). In their extensive review of literature on organizational storytelling, Barker and Gower (2010) cite numerous examples of the power of organizational narratives. From using narratives to convey organizational culture (Barker, Rimler, Moreno, & Kaplan, 2004), to encouraging organizational learning (Lämsä & Sintonen, 2006), to promoting employee expertise (McLellan, 2006), to conveying authenticity in organizational leadership (Driscoll & McKee, 2007), the narrative paradigm has numerous applications for leaders of organizational development.

Summary and Research Applications

This chapter examined four theories of persuasion. ELM argues that persuaders must carefully consider their audience before crafting a message. Receivers must be motivated and able to process objective, elaborated messages. When audience members are unmotivated or unable to process such messages (or both), peripheral cues should be used. ELM has been successful in explaining a variety of management and marketing topics, including consumer perception of shopping websites. Chen and Lee (2008) concluded that online marketers need to include peripheral messages for consumers who primarily "shop for fun" and seek an emotional and sensory experience, while centrally routed messages work better for task-related shoppers. In our second approach, the theory of planned behavior takes persuasion a step further, stating three concepts can predict an individual's behavior: attitude, normative beliefs, and controllability. This theory has been used extensively in health care contexts, where health care providers often attempt to convince patients or the public to adopt specific behaviors, such as becoming organ donors (Park & Smith, 2007) or practicing safe sex (Cha, Kim, & Patrick, 2008). The theory of planned behavior also has use in marketing, for example, to study intended consumer behavior when new technologies become available (Pederson, 2005).

Third, inoculation theory provides a means to argue proactively in support of a position by sending preemptive messages that include forewarning of the threat and refutations to anticipated arguments. The theory's application has wide reach, including public relations' research demonstrating that inoculation messages are a viable proactive strategy in crisis communication (Wan & Pfau, 2004). Inoculation theory has also been used to craft resistance messages applicable to public health communication professionals. From trying to prevent youth from excessive gambling (Lemarié & Chebat, 2013), to studying antibullying messages in schools (Rosenberg, 2004), to creating the HIV "Prevention Is Care" campaign aimed at health care providers to share prevention and resistance messages with HIV patients (Etheridge, 2012), inoculation theory is frequently employed as a means of discouraging behaviors that negatively affect public health. Our fourth and final theory, the narrative paradigm, looks at persuasive messages through a descriptive lens. That is, persuasion isn't so much a rational process as it is an emotional one based on storytelling. Narratives must have coherence and the logic of good reasons to be influential. In addition to the benefits of organizational narratives discussed earlier, the narrative paradigm has been used to analyze storytelling in news media reports of notable crises (Caldiero, 2007), in health crisis reporting (Boudes & Laroche, 2009), and in legal reporting (Johnston & Breit, 2010).

Key Terms

Attitude   118
Authority   120
Behavioral intention   124
Central route   119
Commitment   120
Consistency   129
Contrast   121
Controllability   125
Elaborated argument   119
Good reasons   129
Inoculation   126
Liking   121
Logos   130
Mythos   129
Narrative   129

Narrative coherence   129
Narrative fidelity   129
Narrative rationality   129
Normative beliefs   124
Pathos   130
Perceived behavioral control   125
Peripheral route   120
Persuasion   118
Reciprocity   121
Refutational preemption   127
Scarcity   121
Self-efficacy   125
Social proof   121
Threat   126

Case Study 7: A Lack of CONNECTion?

CONNECT is an up-and-coming company that specializes in entertainment via websites, social media, and smartphone apps. A small business, CONNECT employs roughly 60 people and offers three products: bActive, a social media site for outdoor enthusiasts, Rendezvous, a dating service, and Clash, an online gaming community. Three separate product directors manage each of these three services. Ultimately, these directors are held accountable for their product as well as their staff.

Because of the company's small size, as well as the open attitude of upper management, CONNECT has created a unique environment where individual opinions, ideas, and criticisms are not only heard but encouraged. Employees value one another and the work they do because they realize their own success relies on the company's success.

A collaborative work environment such as this has its downsides, however. For example, one drawback is the sheer abundance of new ideas (some good, some bad). Every idea and suggestion gets attention and needs to be researched—a time-consuming and often frustrating processes because many ideas lack the resources, practicality, and efficiency to be used.

As manager of the Digital Marketing Department, Bryan Hopkins has worked for 2 years at CONNECT and supervises four employees. Bryan's chief responsibility is digital marketing for both online and print sources. Specifically, he oversees the selection and placement of web-based and print advertising. To an untrained eye, ad placement may seem simple; however, for its advertising to be effective, CONNECT relies on a fairly detailed procedure. First, the Digital Marketing Department purchases advertising space, usually on a commercial website, social media site, or in print media. The Digital Marketing Department then contacts the Graphics Department with an ad request, basically letting the graphics manager know what needs to be created (e.g., ad type, size, color, format) and when it needs to be completed. After completing the ad, Graphics sends the copy back to the Digital Marketing Department for approval. Bryan checks each ad; only after he gives final approval is the ad sent to the particular website or print source for publication. Although it seems tedious, Bryan designed this procedure himself and keeps it as streamlined as possible. The marketing world runs on deadlines, so efficiency is critical.

Jim Martsky is the product director for Rendezvous, CONNECT's dating services site, and he's extremely enthusiastic about his service. In Bryan's view, Jim is a perfectionist who tends to complicate, micromanage, and overanalyze things. Recently, Jim mentioned to Bryan that CONNECT might be changing its ad procedure. He wanted to schedule a meeting in the next few days to discuss the proposed changes. Jim also casually mentioned that he would like to be a part of the ad procedure process; for example, maybe the Digital Marketing Department could show him each ad before giving final approval. As digital and print media manager, it was up to Bryan to determine the ad procedure, not Jim. What's more, Bryan didn't want to have someone peering over his shoulder and questioning his department's decisions.

No way am I going to show this guy every ad that comes along! Bryan thought to himself, *Jim will want to haggle over each graphic, font selection, and comma use; it'll take months to get an ad published!*

Not wanting to appear difficult, however, Bryan decided not to say anything. He figured he would wait until the next management meeting when he and the other directors could properly discuss Jim's ideas in more depth. Although he really didn't have the time for such busywork, Bryan planned to create a detailed slide presentation, knowing that overanalytical Jim would appreciate research showing timetables, magazine commitment deadlines, and revenue charts to show how effective their ad placement has been since he took over a few years back.

Later that same afternoon, Bryan passed by the graphics department's studio and spotted Jim talking with Jamila, the graphics manager. Jim caught Bryan's eye and waved Bryan into the room.

"Hey, Bryan! Come here—just for a minute. I've worked everything out." A bit perplexed, Bryan poked his head into the graphics studio. "Hey, Jim. I'm on my way to meet with the ad buyer for *DigitalNews Magazine*. What's up?"

"I'm glad we ran into you! It's all set up. From now on, your department will show all ads to me before giving final approval," Jim declared, not defiantly but rather as if he had just solved a major world problem.

"Jim, I thought we were going to have a management meeting to discuss this. In fact, I'm not even sure there *is* a problem," Bryan replied.

"Well, Bryan, you know we are always on deadline here. I wanted to get things in place before our next series of ads is due. You know what they say, 'Time is of the essence'!"

Bryan didn't know what to say. Keeping in mind Jim's overzealous approach and recognizing his own stress level was high, Bryan answered with a quick "Uh . . . hmmm. Okay, well, I'll get back to you," and headed back out the door. Although Bryan firmly believed Jim's proposal wasn't a good idea, he also knew discussing it while on his way to meet with an ad buyer wasn't the proper time or place to resolve it.

Later that afternoon, Bryan e-mailed Jim a meeting request to discuss the newly proposed ad procedure. It looked like there wasn't going to be a group discussion with the other project directors, so Bryan would have to use his knowledge of the ad placement procedure to convince Jim on his own that the Digital Marketing Department's current method was a good one and that it worked. At the very least, Bryan figured they could come up with a modified ad procedure that would not inconvenience anyone involved.

The next day, the two men met in an unoccupied office with the door closed. Bryan started the meeting, "Hi, Jim, thanks for meeting with me today to discuss your new ad placement idea. Although I think your intentions are good, as the person responsible for ad placement procedure, I have some serious concerns about the plan you suggested." Bryan went on to say that Jim's idea simply was not practical for their fast-paced, deadline-driven industry. "Media places too many ads for CONNECT's services; we can't run around and chase down all of the project directors for their approval when ad deadlines need to be met." Bryan expressed that Jim's new procedure created unnecessary steps, making it inefficient.

"I have an alternative solution," Bryan suggested, "one that combines your idea of having extra eyes look over the ads along with my belief that we shouldn't put up additional barriers in the approval process." Jim nodded slowly, "Okay, I'm game—what's your idea?"

Bryan went on to explain his proposal. Graphics could show each ad to the respective project director for his or her approval prior to sending it back to Media for final approval. Bryan explained, "This way, the Digital Marketing Department's flow wouldn't be disrupted as much, and it would allow for the graphic artists and the project directors to work together on getting everything just right. And, when Media does receive the ad, we could just do our normal checking routine before Graphics sends the ad out."

Jim indicated he originally had suggested this idea to Jamila in the Graphics Department but that she had expressed the same concerns about this second proposal that Bryan had about the first proposal. "Essentially," Jim said, "Jamila told me it's simply inefficient; Graphics doesn't have time to chase down project directors for each ad's approval either."

As Jim began to feel as though a solution to the situation was hopeless, Bryan started asking some questions aimed at finding out exactly what the "problem" was. According to Jim, he had noticed some ads going out for his product that did not meet his approval. Bryan pressed Jim for more details; it turned out that "some ads" was really just two ads—one was a personal preference regarding layout, and the other was due to Jim's own forgetfulness about an ad he had previously approved.

When pressed even further, it turned out the real issue was a communication problem between Jim and Sean, the graphic artist who typically worked on Rendezvous' ads. According to Jim, they didn't get along well. Despite CONNECT's open communication culture, Sean didn't seem to take criticism or direction well. Although Sean was clearly a talented designer, Jim recounted several times in which he requested meetings with Sean just to be brushed off or have Sean cancel the meeting at the last minute. Just recently, Jim noticed a published ad where an adjustment he had requested Sean make was ignored. Jim had lost trust in the ad procedure, fearing these errors would continue to happen unless he was involved in some way.

Based on Jim's story, Bryan quickly recognized Jim's problem was not with the ad procedure but between Jim and Sean. Bryan also knew changing the ad procedure was not going to fix a communication problem between the two men.

By listening to Jim's difficulties with working with Sean, Bryan realized a slight change to the ad procedure, if done correctly, could benefit everyone. Together, Bryan, Jim, and Jamila came up with a joint proposal. They would set up an electronic in-box in each project director's office and in the Digital Marketing Department. Once Graphics finished an ad, they would simply e-mail the ad to the project director's in-box. The project directors would check their in-boxes on a daily basis. If they agreed with the look of the ad and were satisfied with everything, they would sign off on the ad and send it to the Media in-box. Media would then check the ad as usual, give final approval, and then give Graphics the okay to send the ad. If, for some reason, a project director was not happy with an ad left in the in-box, he or she would go directly to Graphics to work out the problems. Once satisfied, the project director would sign off on the ad and then place it in the Media in-box for final approval.

This solution left the final approval in the hands of Media while also allowing all project directors to have a say in the ads, and it avoided any inefficiency in getting approvals because ads could now just be left in various in-boxes. Amazingly, all staff members involved agreed to this joint solution. A month later, all were satisfied with the new procedure.

Questions for Consideration

1. What peripheral strategies did Jim use to try to convince Bryan there was a problem with the current ad approval method? Why didn't these strategies work? Would an elaborated message produce a different result? Explain.

2. How do Bryan's attitudes and normative beliefs affect his behavioral intention when initially interacting with Jim? How does perceived behavioral control come into play as Bryan tries to convince Jim his own plan is the better one?

3. If given more time or opportunity to discuss Jim's proposal with the other managers, such as Jamila, how could Bryan have engaged in inoculation techniques? Specifically, discuss how Bryan could have used the concepts of threat and refutational preemption to create an inoculation message.

4. It is only after Jim opens up and shares his personal experiences with the ad process that Bryan begins to understand and accept Jim's frustrations. Although not fully elaborated in the case study itself, imagine a narrative Jim could have used to convey to Bryan his frustrations with the ad process and Sean, the graphic designer. Construct a narrative that demonstrates coherence and the logic of good reasons while convincing Bryan there was, in fact, a problem with the current ad approval method. Likewise, construct a competing narrative from Sean's point of view, again demonstrating coherence and the logic of good reasons while convincing Bryan management shouldn't interfere with the creative process.

5. Which persuasion theory seems to explain the situation better than the others? Why do you believe this to be the case? What situations might surface to make a different theory or theories better at explaining the situation? What theories could you combine to make for an even better explanation of the encounter?

CHAPTER 8

Group Communication

LEARNING OBJECTIVES

After reading this chapter, you will be able to...

1. Differentiate between a group and an aggregate.
2. Describe the differences between a group and an organization.
3. Summarize the nature of task-oriented, maintenance-oriented, and disruptive group roles.
4. Explain what a communication function is.
5. Articulate the four functions identified in the functional approach to decision making.
6. Identify the three types of communication identified in the functional approach to decision making.
7. Describe the meaning of groupthink.
8. Recognize the antecedent conditions of groupthink.
9. Distinguish the symptoms of groupthink.
10. Recommend strategies to prevent groupthink.
11. Explain the meaning of structure.
12. Describe how structures are produced and reproduced.
13. Explain how adaptive structuration theory uses the concepts of agency, rules, and resources.
14. Summarize the elements of social interaction in adaptive structuration theory.
15. Articulate how adaptive structuration theory illuminates the group decision-making process.
16. Apply the principles of adaptive structuration theory to understand virtual teams.
17. Define the following concepts from symbolic convergence theory: dramatizing message, fantasy, fantasy theme, fantasy chaining, symbolic convergence, and rhetorical vision.
18. Explain the development of a rhetorical vision.
19. Summarize major theoretical approaches to group communication.
20. Compare and contrast major theoretical approaches to group communication.

Whether you work for a publishing company, a retail organization, or a Fortune 500 corporation, U.S. businesses are increasingly adopting a "team" structure. To succeed as a communication professional, an understanding of how groups work, as well as the principles and pitfalls of group decision making, is crucial to your career. In this chapter, we explain a broad range of group theories—from those that focus specifically on group decision making to those that focus on the ways group communication creates the norms for group behavior.

GROUP COMMUNICATION DEFINED

Popular understanding implies a group is simply a collection of people. Scholars studying group communication are more precise when using the term *group*, however. According to scholars, a **group** refers to a system of three or more individuals who are focused on achieving a common purpose and who influence and are influenced by each other (Rothwell, 1998). A group is different from an **aggregate**, which is simply a set number of individuals— say, the people standing at a bus stop or the people on an elevator. Moreover, a group is distinct from an organization. Organizations typically involve formal hierarchies (e.g., CEO, director, manager) and structured channels of communication (e.g., annual performance reviews, employee newsletters). In contrast, a group's structure and patterns of communication typically emerge through interaction (Rothwell, 1998).

Because of the increased use of team-based structures in organizations, it is also of interest to articulate the nature of a **team**. In an organizational setting, a team is an ongoing, coordinated group of people working together (Dyer, 1987). Teams are typically self-directed and self-regulating, meaning typical chains of organizational command are suspended; teams are empowered to complete a task from start to finish. Not all groups are teams (if control is primarily external, for example), but all teams meet the qualification of being a group.

Group communication is distinct from other types of communication because all groups must balance **task communication** (communication focused on achieving the instrumental goal the group is trying to achieve) with **socioemotional communication** (communication focused on developing, maintaining, and repairing the relationships between group members). Put simply, the more time the group spends on the task, the less their focus on relationship needs, and vice versa. Because group members likely have different orientations toward the importance of these two activities, balancing task communication and socioemotional communication is often quite challenging and typically leads to group members enacting group roles. **Group role** refers to a pattern of communicative behaviors performed by one individual in light of expectations held by other group members. Typically, group roles are classified as task-oriented roles, maintenance-oriented roles, and disruptive roles, which are roles that meet individual versus group needs. For example, the isolate is someone who withdraws from participating in the group, the zealot is someone who tries to convert all group members to his or her belief system, and the stagehog monopolizes the conversational floor and prevents others from expressing their thoughts and opinions (Rothwell, 1998).

This chapter emphasizes understanding the communication that takes place within groups and teams. The four theories we present vary in focus. First, functional group decision making centers on the tasks communication achieves in the decision-making process. Continuing with a focus on decision making, the second theory, groupthink, provides a mechanism for explaining poor or ineffective group decision making. Adaptive structuration theory also considers decision making, but it offers a broader perspective on group communication, focusing on how the communication process itself creates the norms for interaction. Finally, symbolic convergence theory explains the development of a group consciousness, including shared emotions, motives, and meanings.

FUNCTIONAL GROUP DECISION MAKING

Although groups have a number of purposes, one of the central purposes is decision making. Gouran and Hirokawa (1983, 1986, 1996) are the key researchers associated with the functional approach to group communication. A **function** refers to what communication does. For example, an apology serves the function of relationship repair, and a joke can serve the function of tension release. As such, the functional approach to decision making focuses less on what is actually said and more on what the communication in groups does; how does it function?

Gouran and Hirokawa began theory development by asking the basic question, "Why do some groups make good decisions while others make bad ones?" (Hirokawa; see Miller, 2002, p. 219). Their model argues that the answer to this question has to do with whether the group has successfully accomplished four functions, which they call *requisite functions* (Gouran & Hirokawa, 1983). These functions are highlighted in Table 8.1.

The first function is **problem analysis**. This means the group must take a realistic look at the nature, extent, and likely causes of the problem. A thorough analysis often involves information gathering. As an example, let's consider a group convened to address the larger organization's continued budget shortfall. The functional group decision-making theory

Table 8.1   Four Functions of Decision Making

Function	Means of Achievement
Problem analysis	Focus on the nature, extent, and likely causes of the problem. Be careful to differentiate between problems and symptoms of problems.
Goal setting	Identify what an ideal solution would "look like." What are the necessary elements, and what would be ideal but not necessary?
Identify alternatives	Generate a large number of possible solutions: Quantity matters more than quality at this point.
Evaluate and select	Evaluate each alternative using the established goals.

suggests the group should spend a significant amount of time analyzing the actual gap between essential and realized revenues, the implications of the budget shortfall, and the possible causes for the shortfall. Were there too many expenditures? Slow growth in sales? Or is it just a normal downturn in the economy, which might bounce back? The answers to these questions are important because recognizing the root cause and implications of the problem determines the form the solution should take.

The second function is **goal setting**. It necessitates all members are clear about what they are trying to accomplish (Gouran & Hirokawa, 1983). Returning to our example, the group members studying the budget shortfall need to be clear about their goals (e.g., are they an advisory group that can only make recommendations, or are they an actual decision-making group?). Typically, this goal-setting function also requires group members to develop criteria; these criteria, or standards, will be used to evaluate possible solutions. Thus, our example group should also determine the requirements for a solution. Some sample criteria might include the following: budget cuts shouldn't exceed more than 5%, the implementation of the solution must be achievable within 6 months, and the solution must support the organization's mission.

The third function is to **identify alternatives**. Here, group members brainstorm to generate many possible solutions, maximizing the likelihood that a good solution is ultimately chosen (Gouran & Hirokawa, 1983). **Brainstorming** requires group members to come up with as many solutions as possible while following these rules: don't evaluate ideas; don't clarify ideas; encourage zany ideas; expand on others' ideas; record all ideas with no reference as to who contributed; and encourage participation from everyone (Putnam & Paulus, 2009).

Fourth, the group must **evaluate and select** the solution (Gouran & Hirokawa, 1983). To accomplish this, group members must evaluate the possible solutions generated in the previous function; specifically, the members must compare the possible solutions with the criteria they developed in the second function. Both positive and negative characteristics of the proposed solutions should be considered before selecting the solution that best meets the group's goals (Gouran & Hirokawa, 1983). Returning to our example decision-making group, the chosen solution will likely be altered if the group determined the problem was slow sales growth rather than overexpenditure.

Functional group decision-making theory states that all four functions need to be accomplished to maximize the likelihood of an effective decision and that no one function is more important than another. Hirokawa (1994) acknowledged, however, that a specific problem might make a particular function less challenging to accomplish. For example, because some problems are particularly obvious, problem analysis is relatively easy. Other problems might naturally have few possible solutions; again, generating alternatives might not be a time-consuming task. On the other hand, some problems are more challenging and can impede the effective accomplishment of the four functions. Impeding factors include ignorance of the issue, relying on faulty facts, operating under misguided assumptions, failing to evaluate the alternatives adequately, making illogical inferences, disregarding group procedures, or suffering from undue influence by one of the group members (Griffin, 2003).

Despite appearance of a logical order to the requisite functions, research suggests it doesn't matter whether they are completed in a particular order; it only matters that the functions are completed (Hirokawa, 1994). Nevertheless, Hirokawa found that groups tackling complex problems tend to follow a similar path. Specifically, the pattern suggests that an analysis of the problem tends to happen first but that the group then cycles back and forth between goal setting and identifying alternatives. Once criteria are established and the group is satisfied with the proposed alternatives, they move on to evaluation and selection.

Finally, functional group decision-making theory makes particular claims about communication in groups. The theory argues that "communication is a social tool used to accomplish effective decision-making" (Hirokawa & Salazar, 1999, p. 169). As such, it proposes that human beings actively construct group experience based on their communication. Gouran and Hirokawa (1986) specifically delineated three types of communication in small groups. **Promotive communication** is geared toward one of the requisite functions. **Disruptive communication** diverts, retards, or frustrates the ability of the group to achieve the requisite functions. Disruptive communication might include social communication. Finally, **counteractive communication**, or messages that return a disrupted group back to the requisite functions, is likely to be most important for group decision making.

Relatively narrow in scope, the functional perspective focuses solely on task communication associated with group decision making. It is the promise of improved group success that makes this theory a significant practical application for communication, business, and other professions.

Groupthink

Whether or not you know the details of the theory, it's likely you've heard the term *groupthink*. Developed by Janis (1972), the notion of groupthink has bridged the gap from the realm of academics into popular culture. We performed a LexisNexis search of the term and found literally hundreds of hits during the past year, with the term referenced in major newspapers, magazines, and even newsletters. Clearly the concept is being used—but is it being used the way Janis intended?

Groupthink is a dysfunctional "way of deliberating that group members use when their desire for unanimity overrides their motivation to assess all available plans of action" (Janis, see Miller, 2002, p. 193). As such, groupthink was designed to explain and predict how bad decisions are made by groups. At its core, the notion of groupthink represents a failure of the group to demonstrate critical thinking. When groups "go along to get along" the end result of the decision-making process is likely to be less effective than if group members question the information at hand, being careful to look at the problem from a variety of perspectives.

Janis (1982) articulated three **antecedent conditions** to groupthink. According to Janis, these preexisting conditions make groupthink more likely. Note that the existence of the antecedent conditions does not guarantee groupthink. Instead, Janis calls these "necessary but not sufficient" conditions. The antecedent conditions are high cohesion, structural flaws, and situational characteristics.

First, **cohesion** refers to the degree of connection, or sense of solidarity, between group members (Janis, 1982). Because groupthink emphasizes the preservation of group harmony, a high degree of cohesion is necessary for groupthink to occur. Yet Janis's notion that cohesion might engender bad decision making is novel. Think about your own workplace; in how many "team-building" activities have you taken part? If you are a full-time student, how many of your classes have started with "icebreakers" so the class might feel more connected to each other? Typically, workplace cohesion is viewed positively, but Janis warns cohesion might make people reluctant to "rock the boat"; yet rocking the boat might be necessary to make the best possible decision.

The second antecedent condition, **structural flaws**, refers to problems with the way the group is organized (Janis, 1982). Janis identified four specific structural flaws, any one of which might lead to groupthink. First, *group insulation* means the group is somehow isolated from the larger world. Perhaps they meet so frequently with each other and so infrequently with others outside the group that they are disconnected from the larger system. Perhaps the group hasn't had direct experience with the problem at hand. This insulation might lead to an inability to process adequately all of the information necessary to make an effective decision. The second structural flaw is *biased leadership*. If the leader already has his or her mind made up or has a personal stake in the decision, group members might defer to the leader simply because of the power differential, regardless of whether the leader's solution is good. Third, *a lack of procedural norms* can lead to groupthink. Not having a process in place for how to make a decision can happen either because the group has not taken the time to create the process or because the group fails to follow the process. In either case, following a standard process can prevent the group from inadvertently missing a key component of the decision-making process. Last, too much *homogeneity* is problematic. Homogeneity refers to similarity; group members who are very similar—in background, values, or beliefs—are less likely to challenge each other's ideas.

The third and final antecedent condition is **situational characteristics** (Janis, 1982). In short, groupthink is more likely to occur in times of high stress. This high stress might come from pressures outside the group. Groups that work in the pharmaceutical industry experience stress from Federal Drug Administration requirements. Television network executives experience pressure from advertisers. Sometimes external forces place undue pressure on the group through operating constraints, threats, or legal requirements. High stress might also come in the form of time pressures; the more rapidly a decision has to be made, the less likely all possible solutions have been adequately studied.

Stressors don't always come from outside the group, however (Janis, 1982). Groups that have experienced recent failures may lose confidence in their decision-making ability, and the loss of confidence might create a self-fulfilling prophecy. The final category of situational characteristics is moral dilemmas; if a group feels the viable alternatives represent ethical challenges, they are more likely to fall prey to groupthink. Consider a situation where a group can come up with only three solutions to a problem, but two of the three are deemed ethically inappropriate—the group is likely to pursue the third option, regardless of how good it might be.

Again, these three antecedent conditions are necessary, but not sufficient, for groupthink. In other words, all three conditions must be present to some degree for groupthink to occur; however, these circumstances alone don't guarantee groupthink. Instead, Janis (1982) argued you have to examine how the group operates to observe symptoms of the groupthink process. He identified eight symptoms grouped into three categories: overestimation, closed-mindedness, and pressure toward uniformity.

The first classification of symptoms falls into the category known as **overestimation of the group** (Janis, 1982). Overestimation occurs when group members have an inflated view of the group's abilities. Two specific symptoms to look for are an illusion of invulnerability (a belief that the group won't or can't fail) and a belief in the inherent morality of the group (because the group is good, the decisions the group makes have to be good). Note that both of these symptoms are representative of unwavering confidence in the group and its abilities. As such, group members might not feel it necessary to analyze critically the decisions being made.

Janis (1982) labeled the second category of groupthink symptoms **closed-mindedness**. These symptoms demonstrate polarized thinking, which means viewing the world in extremes. Things are perceived either as good or bad, right or wrong. If they are good, they are wholly good; if they are bad, they are wholly bad. If a decision is right, it must be completely right. Two specific instances of this category are stereotyping out-groups, and collective rationalization. First, *stereotyping* out-groups refers to the process of demonizing other groups and their leaders. Frequently, images of good and evil are invoked, such as former President Ronald Reagan's designation of the Soviet Union as the "Empire of Evil." When other groups are portrayed as uncompromisingly bad, it is easier to justify decisions that might put those groups in jeopardy. *Collective rationalization* means that the group members tend to justify their decisions by talking themselves into it. As an example, consider a group that spends only 5 minutes coming up with a solution, and 25 minutes discussing why they are right in making the decision. Rather than critically analyze the decision, group members come up with a litany of reasons to defend why it's a good decision.

The third and final symptom of groupthink is organized around the notion of **pressure toward uniformity** (Janis, 1982). When groupthink occurs, it is not only because the group has an inflated view of themselves or because they demonstrate polarized thinking; it is also because individual group members actively suppress critical thinking. Self-censorship means group members tend to keep their mouths shut when experiencing doubts. Often they feel as though everyone else is "on board" with the decision, so they are afraid to go out on a limb with their concerns. This tendency also highlights the illusion of unanimity, which means group members perceive a consensus, even if one hasn't been reached. As such, silence tends to be interpreted as consent. In fact, self-appointed mindguards are careful not to present any contrary information, even if they know it exists; in other words, a self-appointed mindguard engages in self-censorship. If someone actually does question the decision, a group experiencing groupthink will often place pressure on dissenters; challenges to the group are squashed.

To prevent groupthink, Janis (1982) recommends group members take the following steps: encourage critical evaluation; avoid having the leader state a preference; set up several independent subgroups to study the problem and propose solutions; discuss what is happening in the group with people outside of the group; invite outsiders into the group; assign someone to be a devil's advocate; monitor the group for the symptoms; and take time between the initial decision and the confirmation of the decision to analyze the decision critically.

Table 8.2 presents an overview of the antecedents and symptoms of groupthink. As you can see, Janis (1982) identified a large number of factors present before the group begins deliberating, as well as factors recognizable while the group is deliberating. Groupthink itself—the tendency to avoid critical thinking so cohesion can be maintained—occurs somewhere in between antecedent conditions and the symptoms.

Table 8.2 Antecedents and Symptoms of Groupthink

Antecedents		Symptoms
Cohesion		*Overestimation of group* • Illusion of invulnerability • Belief in morality
Structural flaws • Insulation • Biased leadership • No procedural norms • Homogeneity	*Groupthink*	*Closed-mindedness* • Stereotypes • Collective rationalizations
Situational characteristics • High stress • Time pressure • Recent failures • Moral dilemmas		*Uniformity pressures* • Self-censorship • Illusion of unanimity • Self-appointed mindguards • Direct pressure on dissenters

STRUCTURATION THEORY

Originally proposed as a general theory of social interaction (Giddens, 1979), structuration theory served as a springboard for Poole and McPhee (McPhee, 1985; Poole, 1985, 1988; Poole & McPhee, 1983) to explain group and organizational communication processes. At the core of structuration theory is the notion of structure. Structures are not physical entities but, in essence, patterns of relationships and patterns of interaction; they provide guidelines for behavior. Poole (1988) argued that structures are featured characteristics of organizations: "Division of labor, organization of workflow, arrangement of people into hierarchical positions, the use of budgets all are the hallmarks of the organization, and all involve the imposition of structure" (p. 1).

According to Poole (1988), structures serve five primary functions in groups and organizations: they provide a means for coordination and control, they assist members in defining their identities in the organization, they provide a means to monitor member performance, they help the organization to relate to its environment, and they serve a symbolic function, indicating to group members and outsiders the nature of the organization. Despite the importance of structures in groups and organizations, Poole's theory contends that structures are not as permanent as you might think; they require constant maintenance and repair. Specifically, communication is the means by which structures are developed, maintained, and changed. This process is known as structuration.

Assumptions of Structuration Theory

There are two major assumptions of structuration theory. First, the theory assumes humans are actors who make choices (Giddens, 1979). This assumption, also called **agency**, means people have free will in terms of their communicative behavior. The second assumption is that groups and organizations are produced and reproduced through structures in interaction (Giddens, 1979). This assumption requires people to understand what Giddens means by the terms **structure**, **production**, and **reproduction**.

As indicated earlier, structure is not a physical entity but a set of rules and resources used by a group in order to meet its goals. **Rules** are *how* the group should accomplish its goals. Think of rules as either formal or informal prescriptions for how to do things. A formal rule might be a company policy that everyone must show up by 8:00 a.m., and an informal rule might be that group members believe decisions are made by consensus. Resources are the properties organizational members rely on to get things done. Two types of resources are available to members. **Allocative resources** are material forms of assistance, such as time and money. **Authoritative resources** are interpersonal characteristics of group members, such as cohesion, experience, and status.

With the understanding that structures (rules and resources) are central to group life, we turn to the second premise of the theory, that groups are produced and reproduced through structures in interaction. Through their behavioral choices, group members create (produce) structures. To illustrate, group members who act as though time is more important than money will create a structure (i.e., a rule) that making rapid decisions is more important than making cost-effective decisions. The effect of this structure lives on, however. Future group members can refer back to this rule and then prioritize their decision making so that time efficiency is more important than fiscal conservation. As such, they have reinforced (or reproduced) the rule initially created. Through interaction, the structure is produced and reproduced; individuals have created it, but they are also constrained by it.

This notion that group members' action (agency) both creates and constrains interaction is known as the **duality of structure**. Note that the theory is firmly committed to pragmatism; human beings have complete free will with regard to their behavior. However, structuration theory suggests the notion of structure is intertwined with human action, providing a subtle force or influence. Ellis (1999) characterized agency and structure as "braided social entities" (p. 127). Throughout the process of structuration, human beings have the choice to change the rules or adjust the resources available to them in their interaction, but they feel pressured by the constraints of previous actions. Moreover, these activities often occur at low levels of consciousness. Group members are not always aware of structures, nor are they aware of their ability to change structures.

Adaptive Structuration Theory

Recall that Poole, Seibold, and McPhee used Giddens' structuration theory as a basis for their theory, which they called adaptive structuration theory (AST). AST builds on the original theory by adding two concepts that make it applicable specifically to group communication. First, they believed structures are often borrowed from larger groups (Poole, Seibold, & McPhee, 1985, 1986). For example, a work group may appropriate, or borrow from, the structures of the larger corporation, such as the organizational culture. As such, the group is not starting from scratch but relying on the structures already available to them prior to interaction. Similarly, organizations can appropriate larger societal structures, such as individualism, patriotism, or capitalism. This behavior would be considered appropriation from society.

Second, AST assumes all social interactions include elements of communication, morality, and power (Poole et al., 1985, 1986). The communication element dictates organizational members operate within a given set of meanings or understandings. As such, their language choices are important. A worker might use particular words such as *competitive* or *innovative* as symbolic reflections of the rules of the group. The idea of morality means group norms about what is and is not acceptable behavior affect the agency, or actions, of group members. Finally, *power* refers to implicit power structures (e.g., equality, or hierarchy, or authority) that affect the interactional choices made by group members.

Structuration and Group Decision Making

The first two theories of this chapter focus on decision making in groups, and adaptive structuration theory also discusses the decision-making process. An adaptive structuration approach to decision making centers on the extent to which given structures influence the process groups use to problem solve and make a determination for action. For example, Poole and Roth (1989) investigated the paths groups took in their decision-making efforts. They identified three distinct paths. The **unitary path** is taken when a group uses the same process to generate solutions, regardless of the type of problem. For example, group members might use functional group decision making not only when deciding how to address a financial crisis but also when deciding what to order for lunch or determining the quarterly meeting schedule. As such, the single way to make decisions has become a rule for action.

In the **complex cyclic path** group members cycle through the types of activities identified by functional group decision making, but they do so in a circular fashion (Poole & Roth, 1989). For example, the group might first seek to identify the problem, might talk about solutions, and then might go back and reinterpret the problem. This path involves a lot of discussion, and it often requires revisiting the rules and resources available to the group.

The final path is the **solution-orientation path** (Poole & Roth, 1989). In this pattern, group members make little or no effort to investigate the problem. Rather, group members assume they understand the problem and immediately seek a solution that will satisfy group members. The focus in this pattern is not on process but on resolution. As such, the rules and resources center on efficiency and results.

Structuration and Virtual Teams

Beyond its ability to explain the development of group norms and decision-making structures, adaptive structuration theory has also emerged as one of the most frequently used explanations for what happens in virtual teams (Schiller & Mandviwalla, 2007). AST allows scholars to understand how multiple outcomes can result from the implementation of technology in the decision-making process. According to DeSanctis and Poole (1994), advanced information technologies themselves influence the production and reproduction of structure. That is, the features of the technology used by virtual teams influence the types of rules and resources available to the group members. For example, imagine a virtual team is using a particular group decision support system (GDSS) that allows for anonymous comments. Because of this feature, team members feel free to post "honest" feedback to ideas, rather than needing to concern themselves with the politics of organizational hierarchy or coalitions. As such, the social structure that emerges would be quite different from the social structure produced by a virtual team that did not have that technological option.

The major way AST contributes to our understanding of virtual groups is by providing a mechanism to understand how and why the technology necessary for geographically dispersed groups influences the way the group functions. DeSanctis and Poole (1994) identify five group interaction dimensions influenced by communication technologies. These dimensions are described in Table 8.3.

Table 8.3 Dimensions of Technology's Structures

Dimension	Description
Decision process	The way a decision is made; examples include consensus, simple majority, and authority rule
Leadership	Whether a leader (or leaders) is appointed or emerges and the type of leadership that develops (e.g., authoritative, democratic)
Efficiency	The way time is handled, including whether group interaction is shorter or longer than it would be if technology were not being used
Conflict management	The extent to which interaction is orderly or chaotic; the extent to which group members seek to resolve conflict and if so, which conflict resolution strategies they select
Atmosphere	The formality of the interaction and the extent to which interaction is structured or unstructured

AST states that group members have the power to create the nature of their own group through the rules they create and modify in their interaction. This theory also recognizes, however, that previous rules become structures that impinge on the group's communication in the future, such that members feel pressure to abide by the rules and resources they have already created.

SYMBOLIC CONVERGENCE THEORY

The final group theory we discuss is symbolic convergence theory (SCT). Although considered a general theory of communication, SCT was developed within the traditions of group communication and has been applied most frequently to this context (Bormann, 1982). Like adaptive structuration theory, SCT is based on the notion that group members cooperatively create and sustain a shared consciousness, including shared meaning, through interaction. Specifically, SCT focuses on two aspects of group communication: the creation of a group identity and the ways group identity influences norms for behavior.

Central Concepts of SCT

As with many theories, a number of concepts are critical for understanding the explanation of group communication provided by SCT. The most important concept is a fantasy theme. The term **fantasy** can be misleading. According to SCT, *fantasy* does not refer to something desired or something fictional; rather, it refers to a creative understanding of events that fulfills a psychological or rhetorical need (Bormann, 1982).

A fantasy theme starts with a **dramatizing message**—a joke, pun, figure of speech, anecdote, double entendre, or metaphor, among other things (Bormann, 1996). These messages do not refer to present happenings; instead they reference events that have happened in the past or that are anticipated for the future. Moreover, dramatizing messages always include some level of emotional revelation, typically including both a surface level and a deeper level (Bales, 1970). For example, imagine Missy has recently solved a problem for her work team. When walking into her next team meeting, Jim starts singing the theme from *Mighty Mouse* ("Here she comes to save the day!"). This message serves the surface function of tension release but also serves the deeper function of recognizing the value of the work Missy did. Sometimes these messages are sent and immediately dropped, but if the rest of the group responds to the dramatizing message, a **fantasy theme** has emerged.

Continued embellishment of the fantasy theme can result in a **fantasy chain** when the fantasy theme is developed through group interaction and enters group consciousness (Bormann, 1982). If, for example, the "superhero" theme develops and is built on by other group members, a fantasy chain has emerged. At a later meeting, group members might name a difficult supervisor after a comic book villain or might joke about the superpowers needed to accomplish a project on time.

According to symbolic convergence theory, building fantasy chains results in group cohesion, a process termed **symbolic convergence** (Bormann, 1982). In other words, the emergence of a fantasy chain transforms the group from a collection of individuals to an identifiable group with a group consciousness. Consider the superhero fantasy chain. Imagine a subsequent meeting that includes the original work team as well as other organizational members not part of that team. Again, Jim whistles the *Mighty Mouse* theme, and all of the original team members laugh—they understand the reference. The individuals who were not a part of the original team may feel left out, however, because they don't understand the joke. Bormann, Cragan, and Shields (1994) argued that when people have a shared fantasy theme, they have come to share a consciousness that can be set off by a commonly agreed upon symbolic cue. Only those that have shared the fantasy theme to which the inside joke refers will respond in an appropriate fashion.

Any given group might have numerous fantasy chains. That is, the same group that chains the superhero fantasy theme might also use sports metaphors when referring to business situations ("You really hit that one out of the park, Jane" or "It's third and long, and we have to go for it if we're gonna win"). In addition, the group might have a stock story about a team member who failed to follow procedure and lost his job. New members might be told the story as a cautionary tale, and current members might be sanctioned by being told, "Don't be a Don!" The ways fantasy chains combine within a group leads to a **rhetorical vision**. A rhetorical vision is a unified way of viewing the world. Consider the three fantasy chains just described: superheroes, sports, and sanctions against violating rules. All three fantasy chains share a common way of viewing the world. All three suggest the world is clearly divided: right and wrong, good and evil, winners and losers. If you are on the side of good you play hard and win; if you are on the side of evil you will lose. This rhetorical vision provides a set of implicit norms for group behavior.

In addition, the process of symbolic convergence affects decision making (Bormann, 1996). For instance, building a sense of common identity and shared meaning fosters group members' creativity in decision making. Moreover, group consciousness and shared motivation also influence assumptions and preferred processes by which decisions are made. In fact, Bormann contended that group members might create fantasy themes about the decision-making process itself.

Figure 8.1 provides a visual representation of the process of symbolic convergence. Starting at the upper left-hand side of the diagram, a group member sends a dramatizing message. If others in the group interact as a result of that message, a fantasy theme has emerged. If and when group members embellish that fantasy theme, a fantasy chain results. When studying a group, observers can examine the fantasy chains to uncover the underlying rhetorical vision that provides the group with a sense of cohesion and implicit norms for behavior.

Figure 8.1   The Symbolic Convergence Process

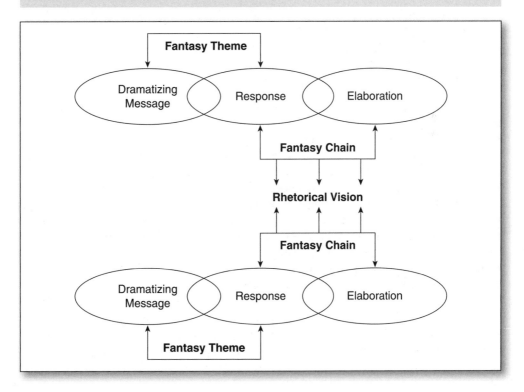

The discussion of SCT thus far implies the theory is concerned only with events internal to a group. One of the strengths of the theory, however, is that it links groups to other social systems, such as a larger organization or social movement (Poole, 1999). For example, a rhetorical vision might start in a group and spread to other parts of an organization. Conversely, the rhetorical vision of a larger organization might restrict the types of fantasy themes generated within a group.

Summary and Research Applications

In this chapter, we discussed four distinct theories of group communication. Functional group decision-making theory delineates specific tasks group members need to complete to make an effective decision. When studying the decision making of corporate work groups, researchers have found that effective groups, compared to ineffective groups, communicated significantly more when establishing decision criteria and when evaluating alternatives (Graham, Papa, & McPherson, 1997). Groupthink provides a means to understanding why group members make poor decisions through a particular focus on cohesion, structural faults, and situational constraints. Matusitz and Breen (2007) recently used the approach to illustrate why "pack journalism" (i.e., groups of reporters from diverse media outlets who collaborate to cover the same story) leads to

> journalistic laziness, short-term and long-term misguidance and paranoia to readers and viewers (due to sensationalizations and the redundant reporting styles), an increased invasion into the privacy of famous and regular people, a reduction of independence in news reporting, the potential hazard of lost credibility in the content of news reported by packs, and economic and fiscal mismanagement. (p. 4)

Our third approach, adaptive structuration theory, focuses on how structures, or enduring patterns of relationships, develop based on group interaction and how these structures in turn constrain group interaction. Zhang and Poole (2007) used AST to examine a cross-functional project management team's change management efforts. They found that a shifting organizational culture combined with an ambiguous task created a structure that led to a preference for e-mail use so information could be permanently recorded and accessed by all group members. Finally, SCT suggests that particular types of messages called fantasy themes contribute to a sense of group identity or consciousness. An examination of these fantasy themes and how they might combine provides a rhetorical vision that provides the principles by which the group operates. To illustrate, Broom and Avanzino (2010) used SCT to investigate the rhetorical visions of a community coalition focused on crime and blight. They found that two competing visions had emerged, which threatened the long-term sustainability of the group.

Key Terms

Agency   145
Aggregate   138
Allocative resources   145
Antecedent conditions   141
Authoritative resources   145
Brainstorming   140
Closed-mindedness   143
Cohesion   141
Complex cyclic path   146
Counteractive communication   141
Disruptive communication   141
Dramatizing message   148
Duality of structure   145
Evaluate and select   140
Fantasy   148
Fantasy chain   148
Fantasy theme   148
Function   139
Goal setting   140
Group   138

Group role   138
Groupthink   141
Identify alternatives   140
Overestimation of the group   142
Pressure toward uniformity   143
Problem analysis   139
Production   145
Promotive communication   141
Reproduction   145
Rhetorical vision   149
Rules   145
Situational characteristics   142
Socioemotional communication   138
Solution-orientation path   146
Structural flaws   142
Structure   138
Symbolic convergence   148
Task communication   138
Team   138
Unitary path   146

Case Study 8: The Gifted Group

A new leader brought renewed enthusiasm to the Brunswick County Conference & Visitors Bureau (BCCVB), the official tourism promotion agency for Brunswick County, Pennsylvania. Under her leadership, the bureau underwent both programmatic and physical expansion. Shortly after the BCCVB relocated its offices and visitor center to a newly constructed building, the executive director decided to create a gift center committee. The purpose of the committee was to devise a plan for a visitor gift center shop—something the BCCVB had never had—in which a variety of merchandise bearing the Brunswick County logo could be sold to visitors.

The committee consisted of the following five BCCVB staff members: John Maher, communication assistant; Laura Doherty, office manager; Nannette Kearny, membership director; Lisa Berman, assistant director; and Donald Johnson, corporate sales manager. The newly formed group was highly cohesive; they had worked together for more than 5 years, and they were all committed to the vision of the visitor's bureau developed by the executive director. The committee was given 3 weeks, meeting as often as they deemed necessary to devise a plan detailing how the BCCVB would establish a visitor center gift shop. The time frame was difficult to achieve given that the group members still had to perform the duties of their regular jobs, but all of the members were committed to doing so.

The first meeting turned out to be a "meeting of the minds" to establish a consensus as to how the group would move forward. Because of their cohesion, committee members were sociable, gregarious, and comfortable working with one another. As a result, members spent a good 15 minutes at the onset of the meeting catching up with one another. Donald, the group clown, decided that an important first step was to come up with a name for the committee, and he decided the group members should be known as the "gifted group." This name led to much laughter and joking that it would be the first time Donald had ever been called "gifted" in his life.

Lisa Berman also participated in this social interaction but took naturally to a leader-type role when it came time to discuss business matters. She made an effort to focus the committee's attention to the matter at hand—the gift shop—and enabled the group to transition from social-related to more task-related communication. At that point, the committee began discussing the overall idea of a gift shop and how to devise a plan to initiate such a venture. The group quickly came to a rather dramatic realization following this discussion: Nobody on the committee had any retail or gift shop experience. Committee members, undoubtedly discouraged by this realization, became reluctant to move forward. The meeting closed, however, with John recommending that each member research visitor center gift shops before the next gathering. Donald and Nanette initially disagreed with the proposal, saying they didn't have time to do so. Nannette asked Laura if she would be willing to do the research, and Laura quickly complied. However, Lisa pointed out that if each person did a little research, no one person would be overburdened. She persuaded the group members to take on the task as a whole.

At the second meeting, each committee member arrived with an impressive arsenal of visitor center gift shop research. Again, the first 10 or 15 minutes were devoted to socializing. And again, Lisa had to work to get people back on task. At first, Donald fought with Lisa for control of the meeting. He continued joking around, calling one of the organizational members not on the committee "special Ned." When Lisa tried to get the group back on task again, Nanette responded, "Hey, not everyone can be considered gifted," and the group continued laughing. Lisa tried to remain lighthearted because she wasn't the official leader, but she was frustrated that others were wasting time. She remarked, "We won't continue to be considered gifted if we don't get this done." Donald responded, "Uh oh, teacher is mad. Are you gonna keep us after school if we don't hit the books?" At this, everyone laughed, including Lisa.

Finally turning to the job at hand, the meeting entailed a thorough investigation of each member's materials and a lengthy discussion about how the group would use the research to proceed. The committee decided to compile the research that related most directly to the BCCVB and to set a calendar indicating how, armed with such information, they would move forward with subsequent meetings. Collectively, the committee established a heavy meeting schedule, with a meeting scheduled every day for the remainder of the 2-week time frame.

Each meeting flowed in a manner very similar to that of the first and second meetings. The first 10 or 15 minutes of every meeting, even as the deadline drew near, were set aside for social interaction. Donald would joke around and the others would follow his lead. Then, the committee would either progress naturally toward the task at hand, or Lisa Berman would comment about moving forward or getting down to business and eventually the group would do so.

Toward the end of the second week, group energy was sagging. Everyone had been devoting a significant amount of time not only to the meetings but to "homework" each tackled in between the meetings. At this point, John's role shifted from group member to group cheerleader. He encouraged others when they became frustrated or tired. He reminded everyone that although the short time frame meant they weren't running a marathon, the work they were doing wasn't a sprint either. Donald responded, "What, we're doing the 800 meter?" Nanette retorted, "Well, hell, that's my problem, I'm out of shape!" John joined in, saying, "Actually, the hurdles were always my specialty! But yes, it is an 800-meter race; we need to keep a rapid pace, but we can't all-out sprint the whole time."

After the 3 weeks were over, the group presented their final proposal to the executive director. Following the meeting, Laura presented all of the members a track jersey with the words "The Gifted Group" written across the chest.

Questions for Consideration

1. Using the functional model, was the decision on how to establish the gift shop likely to be effective? Why or why not? Describe how and when each function emerged.

2. What is the likelihood that groupthink occurred? What antecedents are present? Do you see any symptoms of groupthink?

3. Using adaptive structuration theory, what structures did the group create? Make sure to consider both rules and resources. Also, consider how the rules and resources might have been different if the group had used more technology in their group decision-making process.

4. Discuss the elements of symbolic convergence as related to the group. How do you think symbolic convergence might have affected the decision-making process?

5. Do any of the theories emerge as "better" than the others? Why do you believe this to be the case? What situations might surface that would make a different theory or theories better at explaining the situation?

Organizational Communication

After reading this chapter, you will be able to...

1. Compare and contrast the management approach to organizational culture with a communication approach to organizational culture.

2. Articulate the four elements used by Deal and Kennedy to understand organizational culture.

3. Apply Deal and Kennedy's four cultures to classify an organization's culture.

4. Explain Schein's three levels of organizational culture.

5. Describe the four stages of organizational assimilation.

6. Recognize the differences in the four levels of control highlighted by OIC theory.

7. Use the concept of a double interact to understand the communication process in an organization.

8. Illustrate the sociocultural evolutionary process by applying the process to a real-life organizational scenario.

9. Summarize major theoretical approaches to organizational communication.

10. Compare and contrast major theoretical approaches to organizational communication.

> "The single biggest problem with communication is the illusion that it has taken place."
>
> —George Bernard Shaw

One of the most intriguing paradoxes of corporate life is how often organizational members stress the importance of communication yet how few of these members exhibit effective organizational communication. In Chapter 1, we argue that popular culture tends to oversimplify the communication process. Nowhere is this more evident than in the organizational setting.

ORGANIZATIONAL COMMUNICATION DEFINED

According to Feldner and D'Urso (2010), modern approaches to organizational communication center on the extent to which meaning is created between individuals in an organizational setting, between individuals and organizations, and between organizations and societies. Rejecting the oversimplified idea that an organization exists as a "container" in which communication occurs, organizational communication scholars instead focus on communication as a process rather than an event. Specific communication processes of interest to organizational communication scholars include the development and maintenance of workplace relationships, the socialization of new organizational members, the development of organizational cultures, the ways organizations and organizational members exert and resist power, the ways communication processes create organizational structures, and the ways organizational structures alter communication processes.

SYSTEMS METAPHOR

Much of organizational communication relies on a systems metaphor. The core of the systems metaphor is a focus on the interdependence that develops whenever people interact with each other. A **system** is a group of individuals who interrelate to form a whole (Hall & Fagen, 1968). Examples of systems are a family, a work group, and a sports team. Any time that a group of people has repeated interaction with each other, they represent a system. Systems are embedded in a hierarchy, with systems existing within other systems (Pattee, 1973). Accordingly, a subsystem is a smaller part of the group as a whole: the defensive line of a football team or the accounting department of an organization. A suprasystem is the larger system within which the system operates: The National Football League (NFL) is a suprasystem for an individual football team, and the industry of an organization is a suprasystem for that organization.

Systems approaches involve more than simply focusing on these sorts of interrelationships, however. Systems theories hinge on **nonsummativity**, or the idea that the whole is greater than the sum of its parts (Fisher, 1978). Think of your favorite sports team. Some sports teams have few superstars, but when they work together, they win a lot of games. On the other hand, some teams have "big-name" athletes, but as systems, these teams are not successful. From a systems perspective, individuals in and of themselves don't make or break the system. Instead, the system as a whole might work together to create more than what might be accomplished by those individuals alone. This ability to achieve more through group effort than individual effort is positive **synergy** (Salazar, 1995). Of course, occasionally negative synergy occurs, meaning the group achieves less than the individual parts would suggest. Nevertheless, the point of nonsummativity is that you cannot understand a system by looking only at its components, as a system is more than just its individual parts.

A major reason nonsummativity takes place is because of **interdependence** (Rapoport, 1968). Interdependence means all system members are dependent on all other system members; if one group member drops the ball—literally or figuratively—the organization as a whole is unlikely to achieve its goals. Many of you probably have had this experience at work, because there are few professional positions in which an individual operates completely independently. In the example of a newspaper, the failure of an advertising sales rep to meet his or her deadline means the editor can't determine how many pages an issue will have, which means a writer doesn't know whether his or her story will run in that issue and also that the production people can't do preproduction. Every member of a system is dependent on every other member.

Another principle central to systems approaches is **homeostasis** (Ashby, 1962). Homeostasis refers to the natural balance or equilibrium within the system. From a systems perspective, homeostasis is not meant to imply change doesn't happen. Instead, it is the tendency for a given system to maintain stability in the face of change. This effort at stability can be either functional or dysfunctional for the system. On the one hand, a successful system that achieves homeostasis is likely to continue to be successful. However, imagine a system that has a great deal of conflict, which impedes the system's ability to achieve its goals. Homeostasis would suggest that efforts to reduce the conflict might only engender more conflict, because conflict is the "natural" balance of that group. Thus, a systems approach recognizes that when a system experiences a novel situation, whether positive or negative, its members will somehow adjust to maintain stability, whether that stability is positive or negative.

A final systems concept of interest in the study of organizational communication is **equifinality**. Equifinality suggests multiple ways to achieve the same goal (von Bertalanffy, 1968). Let's say a production group is challenged with the goal of increasing revenue by 10%. They can do so by selling more product, increasing the price of the old product, reducing manufacturing costs of the old product, developing a new product, or reducing the workforce needed to make the product, among other things. In short, there are multiple paths the organization might take to achieve its goals. In addition, at any given time, there are multiple goals the organization can address. If the organization is not only trying to increase revenue but also trying to increase employee morale, it might choose to develop new products, which would simultaneously increase revenue and morale. The organization might decide morale is more important than revenue, however, and focus on that rather than revenue.

Organizational communication theories tend to rely on a systems metaphor (and its associated concepts) to describe the activities of organizations. Still, perhaps because organizational communication scholars are interested in both micro issues (such as interpersonal communication in organizations) and macro issues (such as how organizational communication shapes society), a broad range of philosophical and methodological commitments are evident in organizational communication theory. Some scholars use a social scientific approach to try to make predictions regarding workplace satisfaction or productivity. Others take an interpretive approach, with a focus on organizational storytelling or narratives. Still others take a critical approach, looking to uncover the extent to which organizational communication practices empower or marginalize organizational members or publics.

This chapter focuses on four theories of organizational communication: organizational culture, organizational assimilation, organizational identification and control, and Weick's organizing theory. The first, organizational culture, provides a language for understanding how and why organizations develop values, beliefs, behavioral norms, and ways of communicating. The second, organizational assimilation, focuses on how individuals become socialized into an organization, with a recognition of the role of organizational culture. The third, organizational identification and control, also builds on the notion of culture and assimilation, with a particular focus on how power is enacted in organizations. Finally, Weick's organizing theory puts communication processes at the heart of the ultimate success or failure of an organization.

ORGANIZATIONAL CULTURE

Few of the concepts covered in this book are more popular than the notion of **organizational culture**. Bookshelves are overflowing with tomes like *The Corporate Culture Survival Guide* and *Diagnosing and Changing Organizational Culture*. Before discussing any specific approaches to organizational culture, however, it is important to note there are at least two competing perspectives on organizational culture: approaches that view culture as something an organization *has* and approaches that view culture as something an organization *is* (Smircich, 1983).

The first approach is exemplified by Deal and Kennedy (1982), who argued that organizations become high performing when they have a strong organizational culture. These authors identified four central elements to culture: values, heroes, rites and rituals, and the cultural network. **Values** underscore the organization's core beliefs, for example, how the organization treats clients, suppliers, stakeholders, and employees. Heroes are the people who best represent or personify these values, such as the late countercultural visionary Steve Jobs of Apple or the ostentatious real estate mogul Donald Trump. Rites and rituals are public performances that demonstrate the organizational values. The most obvious of these rituals are entry rituals, such as an academic convocation to welcome incoming students or a dinner for new employees. Finally, the cultural network is the informal communication processes within the organization, including stories, jokes, and gossip.

Given these components, Deal and Kennedy (1982) identify four organizational cultures based on the degree of risk the organization is willing to take (low versus high) and the type of feedback and reward system it has (rapid versus slow). Table 9.1 identifies how these qualities interact to form the four cultures.

The *work hard–play hard culture* is characterized by fun and action (Deal & Kennedy, 1982). Organizations of this type encourage lots of activity, but the activity has high levels of certainty. Stress comes from the rate at which one works and not from the work itself. This type of culture is typical among sales organizations. *The tough-guy macho culture* is one of quickly taking gambles, with the potential of high rewards or huge losses. People who thrive in this type of culture need constant feedback and are often temperamental in their demands. In fact, this type of culture values superstars rather than team players. Not surprisingly, the tough-guy macho culture is often found among advertising agencies and

Table 9.1   The Four Organizational Cultures

		Risk	
		Low	**High**
Feedback and Reward	**Rapid**	Work hard–play hard culture	Tough-guy macho culture
	Slow	Process culture	Bet-the-company culture

the entertainment industries. Employees in *a process culture* typically can't measure what they do but focus instead on how it is done. The work is stable and consistent. Highly regulated industries often fall into this realm, such as banking, insurance, and pharmaceuticals. Finally, the *bet-the-company* culture is exemplified by high-stakes gambles that take years to pay off. Unlike the work hard–play hard culture, stress here is a low-level constant, and being deliberate is the name of the game. Oil companies, who invest billions of dollars on a drilling operation, and capital goods manufacturers, who spend years researching and developing new products, are examples of this type of culture.

As should be evident, Deal and Kennedy's (1982) approach focuses on qualities of an organization that a manager can develop or change. The second approach to organizational culture, described by Smircich (1983), instead focuses on the processes of communication that create, sustain, and constrain interaction within the organization. To illustrate this perspective, we focus on the work of Schein. Schein (1985, 1992) described the elements that comprise an organizational culture and how organizational cultures assist individuals in making sense of their experiences. According to Schein (1992), *culture* refers to a pattern of shared assumptions that have been invented, discovered, or developed by a given group and are taught to new members as the correct way to perceive, think, and behave. Although this definition seems to imply organizational members are consciously aware of organizational cultures, Schein argued this is not always the case; frequently organizational members are not aware of the cultural assumptions they hold. Moreover, culture emerges from interaction and continuously develops, although it is resistant to change.

Schein's (1992) model includes three levels of culture: artifacts, values, and assumptions. Although all three make up a culture, he believed the third level, assumptions, is at the crux of organizational culture and that the first two levels, artifacts and values, may simply reflect the more abstract and subconscious assumptions shared by organizational members.

Level 1: Artifacts

Similar to Deal and Kennedy's components of a strong culture, *artifacts* refers to the observable evidence of culture (Schein, 1992). Artifacts may take the form of physical entities, such as architecture, dress, and documents, but they also consist of patterns of behavior. These patterns of behavior can take the form of rituals, acronyms, forms of address, approaches to decision making, and management style. Table 9.2 lists some examples of artifacts.

Table 9.2   Cultural Artifacts and Behaviors

Artifact/Behavior	Examples
Architecture	Open floor plan, cubicles; offices with windows; size of offices; rented suites versus owned campus
Technology	Up-to-date versus archaic computer systems; availability/type of Internet connection, e-mail, tablets, smartphones
Dress	Business attire versus casual attire; casual Fridays; dress codes
Forms of address	Titles used versus first names; differences in address by hierarchical level
Decision-making style	Autocratic versus participatory; rapid versus slow; conservative versus risk taking
Communication patterns	Formal versus informal; friendly versus distant; use of acronyms, unique terms, myths, stories; rituals

Source: Miller, *Organizational Communication*, 3rd ed. © 2003 Wadsworth.

Although artifacts are, by definition, observable, interpreting what they mean may not always be obvious (Schein, 1992). For example, imagine an organization that develops a pattern of using formal titles among organizational members. According to Miller (2003), such a behavioral artifact might mean the organization is very formal. On the other hand, it might simply mean organizational members hold each other in high esteem and wish to show each other respect. Or it might be an indication that organizational members dislike each other and seek to maintain distance. Thus, while this level of culture is readily apparent, it does not provide much substance to an understanding of organizational culture. Attention must be turned to higher levels for such understanding.

Level 2: Values

The second level of culture is organizational members' values, defined as preferences about how situations should be handled (Schein, 1992). These preferences represent shared beliefs about how things ought to happen. By nature, values are intangible, but organizational members are typically able to articulate them. Organizational leaders are frequently the source of values; for instance, research shows the values held by the founder of a company strongly influence the values described by other employees (Morley & Shockley-Zalabak, 1991). Certainly, literature suggests leadership is, by definition, the ability to shape members' perceptions of the task and the mission of the organization (Barge, 1994). Accordingly, it's not surprising organizational members are persuaded to adopt the values of organizational leaders.

Still, simply because a leader articulates a value system does not make it so. Championed values are not always authentic values, as evident when the ideals expressed do not match behavior (Schein, 1992). Consider, for instance, two organizations that claim to value innovation. When scrutinizing the artifacts of the first organization, observers notice the company encourages risk and gives employees time to experiment. Failures are not punished; in fact, the company encourages employees to talk about failures, because one person's failure might be the solution to another person's problem. A significant portion of the annual budget is earmarked for research and development. In this case, the artifacts seem to support the value of innovation. At the second company, however, failure is not an option; people who fail are punished. The organization is resistant to change and has very rigid systems to implement even the smallest change. Little of the budget is slated for research and development, and employees are kept so busy maintaining the current product line that they have virtually no time to develop any new ideas. In fact, employees have facetiously created the following company slogan: "We don't innovate; we duplicate." Clearly, these artifacts do not seem to suggest innovation is actually practiced. The point is that espoused values are not always identical to the actual values of the organization; just because it appears in the mission statement does not mean it reaches the level of everyday practice.

Level 3: Assumptions

The final level of culture is the most difficult to identify because it is often taken for granted by organizational members. *Assumptions* refers to the viewpoints organizational members hold about the world, including perceptions, thoughts, feelings, and beliefs. These assumptions are subconscious because they have been reinforced over and over again as the organization faces challenges. Assumptions lie at the heart of organizational culture because such presumptions are made uniformly throughout the organization (Schein, 1992).

Specifically, organizations develop assumptions about the nature of reality, time, space, human nature, and human relationships, among other things (Schein, 1992). These concepts are profound philosophical commitments, such as the "right" way for people to interact with each other, whether human beings are by nature good or evil, and whether truth is singular (i.e., there is one absolute "truth") or conditional (e.g., some things are true at some times in some places for some people).

Although this notion sounds complex, such assumptions have a substantial effect on organizational life. Morton (1999) illustrated this effect through an analysis of assumptions in child welfare agencies. Specifically, a fundamental assumption of one child welfare agency might be that people are capable of changing. Such an assumption will affect the everyday decisions made because organizational members will spend energy seeking to develop and reward individuals rather than punish them for past infractions. Yet a different organization might assume the best predictor of future behavior is past behavior. In this case, organizational members are likely to view individuals who have made mistakes as risky prospects likely to repeat those mistakes.

According to Schein's (1992) model of organizational culture, an analysis of assumptions could assist organizational members in generating a coherent blueprint for how the organization should operate. This prediction is not always the case. Some organizations might simultaneously hold seemingly conflicting assumptions. For example, employees of a Catholic institution of higher learning may be challenged by incompatible assumptions. For instance, assumptions the Catholic Church makes about "truth" may contrast the assumptions some of the university's academic disciplines hold about "truth." Such contradictory assumptions might cause problems for members seeking to behave in concert with organizational assumptions. How the organization reconciles these inconsistent assumptions determines the overarching organizational culture.

Schein (1985, 1992) proposed three levels of culture: artifacts, values, and assumptions. Although there may be surface inconsistencies within and across these levels, a careful analysis of the patterns that emerge will give observers an understanding of the organizational culture. These cultures are created by employees, with particular emphasis placed on the influence of those at the highest levels in the organization. Organizational cultures both aid and constrain organizational communication.

ORGANIZATIONAL ASSIMILATION

Many of us have learned very quickly that we don't "fit" with a particular organization. You might find, for example, you are a blue jeans kind of person in a three-piece-suit kind of world. Or you might find an organization's values (e.g., slow and steady wins the race) don't mesh with your personality (e.g., Type A). We've just finished discussing what organizational cultures are and how we might identify a particular organization's culture. Taking this a step further, Jablin (1987, 2001) created **organizational assimilation** theory as a way to explain how individuals become integrated into the culture of an organization.

Jablin (2001) argued the process of being socialized into an organization is complex and takes place over years. Moreover, the process of assimilation can be planned, for example, through a potential employee's active researching of a company or formal training procedures. But assimilation is often unplanned. Co-workers' interaction styles might not be intended to send messages about the organizational culture, but the new organizational member might perceive these messages regardless.

The theory identifies four stages organizational newcomers go through before becoming full members of an organization. These stages are summarized in Table 9.3.

Vocational Anticipatory Socialization

Before we ever get our first job, we learn about the nature of work. We watch our parents leave us in the morning and return to us in the evening, oftentimes frazzled and grumpy. We listen to our teachers tell us that we've done a good job or that we have not worked hard enough. We have laughed at the incompetence of Michael Scott on *The Office* or cringed at the cruelty of the bosses in the movie *Horrible Bosses*. We've had part-time jobs and even full-time jobs, and we have listened as our professors tell us what it's really like to be a

Table 9.3   Stages of Assimilation

Stage	Description
Vocational anticipatory socialization	Developing a set of expectations and beliefs about the nature of work and work settings. Example: The people I work with will be my close friends.
Anticipatory socialization	Learning about a particular vocation, position, and organization. Example: DanCo provides networking services to nongovernment organizations
Encounter	Making sense of the organizational culture. Example: Unlike my last job, people at DanCo come to work late and stay late.
Metamorphosis	Transitioning from outsider to insider. Example: We work hard and play hard—it's just what we do here at DanCo.

journalist, or a PR rep, or a manager. In short, we spend years collecting information about the nature of work, yet much of what we learn is distorted, biased, or just plain wrong. Jablin (2001) describes a host of studies indicating the media overrepresent managerial and professional work and underrepresent low-prestige jobs. People are often stereotyped by race and sex. Moreover, the nature of communication in the workplace is distorted, with much of the conversation focused on socializing, giving orders, or giving advice. All these notions of work are brought together in **vocational anticipatory socialization**, or the expectations and beliefs about work we bring with us as we begin to assimilate into an organization.

Anticipatory Socialization

The second stage of organizational assimilation theory is **anticipatory socialization**. Here, individuals gather information about a specific vocation, position, or organization. This stage includes the process of choosing an organization, interviewing, and preparing to enter the organization. Jablin (2001) argued that in many cases individuals retain unrealistic and inflated notions of the organization because organizations typically communicate only their positive aspects. These unrealistic expectations are often problematic, as organizational members find it difficult to meet these expectations once on the job. Clearly, during this phase the organizational newcomer starts to become socialized into the organization before he or she ever works in the organization.

Encounter

The third phase is one of uncertainty and anxiety. In the **encounter** phase, the organizational newcomer enters the workplace and begins to learn the normal work patterns and expectations of the organization. As described in Chapter 3, there are many ways people reduce uncertainty, including observation and asking questions. Typically, the organizational newcomer relies on co-workers and his or her supervisor for uncertainty reduction. The individual in this stage frequently undergoes a "culture shock" as she or he compares expectations with the reality of the new workplace and disillusionment as she or he lets go of old values and behaviors.

Metamorphosis

The final stage of assimilation, **metamorphosis**, reflects the movement of the individual from an outsider to an insider. During this stage, the newcomer and the organization exert mutual influence in the process of developing a "fit" between the organization and the employee. Here, the newcomer internalizes values and behaviors in order to fulfill organizational expectations (known as socialization) while at the same time seeks to have an impact on his or her role and work environment (known as individualization). Imagine you have begun working at an organization that rigidly follows the rules of the employee handbook. You have reached metamorphosis if you still allow the handbook to guide your behavior, but you also use inconsistencies and missing areas of the handbook to achieve your goals. In this case, you have been socialized to rely on the handbook, as is the organizational culture, but you have adapted the culture to your own needs by taking advantage of the handbook's limitations to get what you think you need to accomplish your job.

The next theory, organizational identification and control, takes this notion of organizational assimilation a step further by articulating the hidden aspects of becoming a member of an organizational culture.

ORGANIZATIONAL IDENTIFICATION AND CONTROL

As indicated in Chapter 8, organizations are increasing their use of team-based structures to improve quality, engender creativity, and increase employee involvement (Deetz, Tracy, & Simpson, 2000). Although these are the *stated* goals of work teams, research suggests team-based structures also serve another purpose: control over employees (Barker, 1999). Consequently, organizational identification and control (OIC) theory centers on the way an individual's connection to the organization influences behavior and decision making in team-based structures (Barker, 1999). Three main concepts tie the theory together: identification, control, and discipline.

Identification

OIC's first major concept, **identification**, refers to the sense of oneness with or belongingness to an organization; when individuals experience identification, they define themselves in terms of the organization (Mael & Ashforth, 1992). Identification happens most frequently in the metamorphosis stage of organizational assimilation, as described earlier in the chapter. Evidence of identification happens when you listen to organizational members speak. Often they will say things such as, "We don't operate that way here" or "We launched a new product today." In these cases, the organizational member is adopting the persona of the organization—she or he may have had little to do with the new product, but there is a sense of pride in and ownership of the product because of identification. This process of identification plays a central, yet subtle, role in how organizations control their employees.

Control

Quite simply, "an organization needs control to get things done" (Miller, 2003, p. 210). OIC suggests there are, however, several forms of control an organization might use. Based on Edwards's (1981) delineation, an organization may exert control through three traditional methods. **Simple control** involves direct, authoritarian control. If a manager makes threats (e.g., "do this or you'll get fired") or places conditions on an employee (e.g., "you can leave early if you finish the Kegway project"), she or he is using a classic way of controlling employees by simply directing the employee as to what can or should be done.

The second method of control is slightly more subtle. **Technological control** involves the use of technology to manage what can and can't be done in the workplace (Edwards, 1981). A factory assembly line is a perfect example; employees must go exactly as fast as the assembly line is moving—no faster and no slower (as the classic episode of *I Love Lucy* in the candy factory illustrated). Employees on an assembly line can only take prescribed breaks, as well, because the whole line must be shut down if one person takes a break. A more contemporary example of this type of control is the limitation of computer technology. How often have you been told by someone, "The computer program won't let us do that"? The technology you have access to and the ways technology works serve as a means of organizational control.

The third kind of control is **bureaucratic control** (Edwards, 1981). Undoubtedly, you are familiar with the term *bureaucracy*, and it is usually associated with negative perceptions. Edwards, however, was referring to the vision of bureaucracy first articulated by Max Weber, a German sociologist. Writing at the turn of the 20th century, Weber argued that modern organizations are served best by a hierarchical system of rules, with rewards and punishments drawn from those rules. That hierarchy is evident in contemporary organizations through company policies and formal procedures. Employee handbooks and other such formalized rule systems are the clearest example of bureaucratic control.

These three forms of control are the ways power has typically been exerted in organizations. In developing OIC, however, Tompkins and Cheney (1985) suggested changes in organizations during the latter part of the 20th century have shifted the way control is wielded. With the growing use of team-based organizations and organizations grounded in participation and empowerment, Tompkins and Cheney identified two additional types of control: unobtrusive and concertive.

First, **unobtrusive control** is based on shared values within the organization. Put simply, in the modern organization, management's job is to create a vision and mission for the organization. When organizational members make decisions based on the vision or credo of the organization, they are not making those decisions because they are forced to but because they believe in the mission of the organization—they identify with the organization. Thus, the commitment to organizational values controls employees.

Similarly, the second type of control is based on interpersonal relationships and teamwork (Tompkins & Cheney, 1985). More obvious than unobtrusive control, **concertive control** happens when co-workers develop mechanisms to reward and control behavior that influences the team. For example, Barker (1999) suggested group members can discipline nonconforming co-workers through criticizing directly, monitoring, being silent, and exerting social pressure, among other things. As with simple control, concertive control is obvious and direct. It is not, however, a managerial function in this system but happens among hierarchical equals. Because of this, it is often described as a hidden form of control. Table 9.4 provides an overview of the types of control.

Table 9.4 Organizational Identification and Control

Type of Control	Examples
Simple	• Commands • Threats
Technological	• Assembly lines • Removing computer games from workplace machines
Bureaucratic	• Employee handbooks • Employment contracts
Unobtrusive	• Identification with organizational values • Decision making based on organizational mission
Concertive	• Monitoring of other team members' performance • Co-worker pressure on nonconforming members

Discipline

Pulling together the concepts of identification and control, Barker (1999) and colleagues (see also Tompkins & Cheney, 1985) suggested **discipline** is achieved through a sense of responsibility to the work group because members identify with their organization and because they share common values and a vision for the organization. When individuals are faced with a decision, they will rely on organizational values to make that decision—there is no need for top-down management directives. If an individual is not behaving in concert with organizational values, work group members tend to censure that individual.

Notably, according to OIC theory, superiors need not do the disciplining themselves; the norms for behavior generated by the organizational mission and values coupled with the identification of organizational members work together to maintain organizational control. Thus, the creation of organizational missions and visions might have the explicit function of driving the organization's business, and work teams might provide a mechanism for employee empowerment, but these initiatives also serve the implicit function of controlling employees.

ORGANIZING THEORY

The previous theories in this chapter have linked communication processes to organizational processes. The fourth and final perspective, Weick's (1969) organizing theory, takes this link one step further by stating that communication *is* the organization. Instead of viewing organizations as containers in which communication occurs, Weick argued communication is what constitutes an organization. Instead of examining an organization (a noun), Weick examined the process of **organizing** (a verb).

With roots in Darwin's theory of evolution, information theory, and systems theory, organizing theory assumes organizations exist in an **information environment** (Weick, 1969). Rather than focusing on the physical environment, Weick's theory is concerned with the massive amounts of information organizations have available to them, from internal and external sources. Organizations depend on information to accomplish their goals, and the challenge of processing it all is a Herculean task.

In addition to issues of quantity, managing the information environment is difficult because much of the information organizations deal with is unpredictable. The term **equivocality** references the ambiguity of information available to organizations (Weick, 1969). Messages are equivocal to the extent there may be multiple understandings of the information. Equivocality is different from the concept of uncertainty. When individuals are uncertain about a message, they can gather more information to reduce uncertainty. However, when individuals find a message to be equivocal, they do not need additional information; instead, they must decide which of multiple interpretations is the best fit. Consider the example of an individual who has to decide how to invest her money. The state of the economy is equivocal; some financial planners argue the stock market will pick up, and so she should invest in the stock market, whereas others suggest that because the market is poor and looks like it will continue to perform poorly, she should invest in real estate. Gathering more information is likely only to add to the equivocality. In the end, she has to interpret the state of the economy for herself, but her interpretation is only one of many.

According to Weick (1969), one way to reduce equivocality is to rely on **rules** (also called recipes). The term *rule* most often refers to guidelines for behavior, and Weick's use of the term is consistent with this conceptualization. Typically, organizations have rules, or guidelines, for analyzing both the equivocality of a message and how to respond to it. These rules are developed to make a process more efficient and are generally based on past successes. There are many obvious examples of rules, such as rules for whom to contact to accomplish certain tasks, rules about specific forms to be used, and rules about processes to be followed. Rules can also be less formalized. For example, an organization might have had past success with increasing profits by reducing packaging costs for its products. Accordingly, the next time corporate earnings are in question, the stock response is to seek to reduce packaging costs: Cost reduction has become a rule.

Rules don't always work, and there isn't always a rule for every situation. Organizing theory suggests a second way to reduce equivocality is for organizational members to engage in communication cycles known as double interacts (Weick, 1969). Double interacts are suited for instances of high equivocality because they require organizational members to develop interdependent relationships in the process of communicating. Recall the concept of nonsummativity discussed earlier: The whole is greater than the sum of its parts. Weick's theory is grounded in systems principles, and so he argued greater involvement among organizational members can produce greater results in reducing equivocality.

A **double interact** consists of an act, a response, and an adjustment (Weick, 1969). An act is a communication behavior initiated by one person or group of people. The receivers of the message communicate in return, which is considered a response. This two-way exchange of messages is most typically used to understand the communication process. Weick proposed genuine communication requires a third step, an adjustment to the information originally received. This adjustment can take several forms. It might be a confirmation that the information has been understood. If the information is still equivocal, the adjustment might be additional information gathering.

To illustrate, the marketing department of a major manufacturing company has created a new product configuration to be sold only at Walmart. They approach production with the new idea, but members of the production team respond by telling marketing the configuration they have sold cannot be produced on the current assembly lines. Marketing amends the proposal so the customer receives the specialty product and the production department can use existing equipment and materials: act, response, adjustment.

At the beginning of this section, we stated Weick (1969) was more concerned with the process of organizing than with the entity of an organization. Double interacts are the process of organizing; according to Weick, they are the links that hold an organization together. Weick also believed, however, that organizing is an evolutionary process. Much like Darwin's theory of evolution, which suggests organisms become extinct if they can't adapt to their environment, organizing theory maintains organizations that don't adapt to their environment will collapse. Accordingly, Weick (1969) proposed a three-stage process of **sociocultural evolution** for organizations.

The first stage of sociocultural evolution is **enactment**. Enactment occurs when members of an organization take note of equivocal information in their information environment. Recall that equivocal information can be interpreted in multiple ways. Recognizing multiple interpretations and putting into practice a mechanism for making sense of the information are at the heart of enactment.

The second stage is **selection**. In seeking to reduce equivocality, organizational members must choose how to respond. As described earlier, organizational members can choose between rules, or standard guidelines for how to respond, and a double interact, or communication process that allows members to adapt solutions to the problem.

The third stage is **retention**. Retention is a form of organizational memory. What was done and how it was done is stored, formally or informally, so organizational members can refer to it again. Notice what is happening here; even if organizational members go through a double interact to reduce equivocality, in this stage the double interact is retained as a new rule or guideline for behavior in the future. Accordingly, retention should be used sparingly. Figure 9.1 provides a visual illustration of sociocultural evolution.

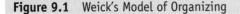

Figure 9.1 Weick's Model of Organizing

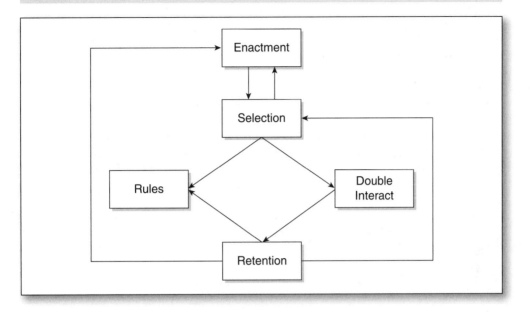

To complete the analogy with Darwin's theory of evolution, Weick's (1969) theory of organizing posits that organizations exist in a complex information environment. This environment is complex because organizations have to deal with equivocal information. Organizations that don't adapt to equivocality, whose members don't use double interacts to resolve new forms of ambiguity, will not survive and flourish. In short, change is the key to organizational success, and change occurs through the process of communicating.

Summary and Research Applications

This chapter introduced four theories of organizational communication. We first looked at organizational culture, using two distinct theories to illustrate this concept: Deal and Kennedy's strong culture approach, which identifies four types of organizational cultures, and Schein's model of organizational culture, which suggests three levels of culture: artifacts, values, and assumptions. His model proposes that assumptions are at the heart of organizational culture, and his model has been applied to a new paradigm of business development called corporate sustainability (see Baumgartner, 2009). Specifically, an organization can only become socially, environmentally, and economically viable with a strong organizational culture that supports these sustainable values. Schein's model has been used to investigate the organizational culture of a 100-year-old family business (Armenakis, Brown, & Mehta, 2011). Second, organizational assimilation theory details three stages of socialization into a new organization, for example, explaining how disabled people adjust to their workplace (Cohen & Avanzino, 2010). As another example, when studying interactions of teachers and administrators, Gómez (2009) found when time was perceived as scarce, newcomers had less chance to socialize with existing organizational members, thereby inhibiting the assimilation process.

Next, organizational identification and control proposes that when organizational members identify with the values of an organization, they can be controlled through self-discipline and peer pressure. Kiyomiya (2006) used this theory to explain how Mitsubishi Motors was able to engage in corporate misconduct during the early part of the century because of identification with the organization and concertive control. Finally, Weick's theory of organizing argues organizations and their members must process equivocal information in order to succeed. Hermann (2007) used this approach to study online discussions of financial experts, finding participants frequently used the double interact to better understand contradictory financial messages. Such application extends Weick's theory beyond brick-and-mortar organizations, suggesting today's businesses must work even harder to create a uniform and unambiguous message.

Key Terms

Anticipatory socialization   163
Bureaucratic control   165
Concertive control   166
Discipline   166
Double interact   168
Enactment   168
Encounter   163
Equifinality   157
Equivocality   167
Homeostasis   157
Identification   164
Information environment   167
Interdependence   157
Metamorphosis   164
Nonsummativity   156

Organizational assimilation   162
Organizational culture   158, 159
Organizing   167
Retention   168
Rules   167
Selection   168
Simple control   165
Sociocultural evolution   168
Synergy   156
System   156
Technological control   165
Unobtrusive control   165
Values   158
Vocational anticipatory socialization   163

Case Study 9: Losing Hope

For more than 80 years, Hope Medical Center had serviced its local residents as a privately run, not-for-profit community hospital. However, with the rapidly escalating cost of medical care, last year, Hope's board of directors agreed that, for the hospital to survive, it was in their best interest to partner with the Greater Valley Hospital Alliance (GVHA)—a for-profit hospital management group. Under GVHA's management, resources could be used more efficiently, the hospital would have more financial security, and patients and doctors alike would have access to other facilities in GVHA's network of hospitals. GVHA had promised that Hope's daily operations would remain untouched after the merger. When announced in the local newspaper, nearby residents and the hospital staff enthusiastically supported the partnership.

Stella Brindle had worked for Hope for the last 8 years in its community relations department. She helped publicize the hospital's services, success stories, and awards. She also helped the hospital raise money, and she was particularly proud of her work directing the most recent fund-raising campaign that helped finance the hospital's pediatric unit renovations. Stella was excited by the merger; by sharing resources, she believed the partnership would free her from some of the more tedious job duties and allow her team to focus more on fund-raising and developing the hospital's services.

Additionally, Stella's team had spearheaded an initiative called the Beacon of Hope, a mission statement and motto for all employees. Called the Beacon for short, its purpose was to "inspire all members of the Hope community to realize what it means to be truly exceptional caregivers." The Beacon had emerged after the American Medical Association named Hope as "the nation's most compassionate hospital." The director of community relations, Mathilde Auberge, wanted to formalize this standard of care and assigned Stella to lead the Beacon initiative.

With support from the entire hospital community, the Beacon was to serve as a code of conduct for all physicians, nurses, staff members, and volunteers. Stella ran a number of focus groups and sought input from various stakeholders. As a result, Hope employees were quite proud of the Beacon and what it stood for. The mission statement appeared prominently on all of the hospital's promotional materials, and a framed copy hung in each patient's room. The hospital gift shop even sold a variety of items with the Beacon's logo. Hope's physicians were invited to use the Beacon in their patient office areas, and the Beacon logo was stitched on all hospital lab coats and scrubs.

Despite the Beacon initiative's success and the initial community support for merging with GVHA, however, tough times were on the horizon for Hope. Six months into the merger, Stella and many other employees had serious regrets about joining the GVHA network. When initially proposed by the board, Hope employees were led to believe that a partnership with GVHA would have minimal impact on their day-to-day tasks. The CEO of GVHA even told hospital staff that "a partnership would not disrupt the wonderful community culture of Hope Medical Center." However, only days after the deal was signed, this promise seemed moot. First, a bright-red and purple GVHA banner was hung, overshadowing the Beacon. Next, GVHA administrators sent an e-mail informing Hope employees that as part of the GVHA network, Hope employees must wear the GVHA-approved uniforms or lab coats. Although seemingly a trivial issue, Stella and the rest of the community relations team were upset. Not only were they being forced to wear a uniform, but the demand also meant the Beacon logo could no longer be worn because it wasn't "consistent" with the other GVHA hospitals.

Transformations appeared in the gift shop, too. The Beacon merchandise was still there but on a back shelf where it was hard to see. And several weeks after that, Stella noticed changes to the hospital's website. The Beacon was no longer featured prominently; instead it was a tiny link, buried halfway down the page. Stella was confused; normally, her department managed the website and all changes were made as a team. Yet no one in community relations knew anything about the changes. When Stella called GVHA to find out about the new website, she was told, "Oh, you don't need to worry about maintaining your site anymore. We'll do all of that for you so you have more time to work on fund-raising." Stella felt conflicted. On one hand, no one in community relations liked the tedious task of constantly updating the website; however, she wished the team would have been asked, or at least informed, about this change.

The changes weren't just about logos and merchandise. Hope had always prided itself on its family-like atmosphere where all of the doctors, nurses, and staff knew each other by first name. The cafeteria and elevators were typically jovial places because people would chat with each other. Since the merger, however, physicians and nurses could be required to work at several of GVHA's hospitals, depending on which hospital had the most need. This meant there was an ongoing influx and exodus of medical personnel and more unfamiliar faces. Although always busy, the pace at Hope now felt more intense as doctors dashed from room to room trying to see all of their patients before driving to another location.

Community relations started receiving complaints—first from the nurses, then from the doctors, and even from patients. A letter to the editor was published in the local newspaper, criticizing Hope for "going commercial." Reported medical mistakes had risen since the partnership, and patient satisfaction had declined. Stella's boss, Mathilde, asked the community relations team to start categorizing these complaints. After a month, Mathilde prepared a report and called a meeting with the board of directors. She showed them all of the data along with her conclusion: Hope was losing what had made it such an exceptional hospital. The medical staff felt more overworked than ever, while patients felt like numbers, rather than people. The whole philosophy behind the Beacon had become overshadowed by GVHA's businesslike atmosphere. The board was at a loss. If the hospital's record of medical mistakes was too high, or if too many patients filed complaints, GVHA would void their contract and withdraw hospital funding. Clearly, something had to be done, but what?

Questions for Consideration

1. Compare and contrast the culture of Hope Medical Center (before the merger) with that of GVHA. Make sure to describe the artifacts, values, and assumptions apparent in both organizations. Using Deal and Kennedy's four cultures, which type of culture has Hope historically had? Based on Schein's theory, can the cultures of Hope and GVHA coexist?

2. Using organizational assimilation theory, describe the stages of Stella's adjustment (or failure to adjust) to the "new" hospital after the GVHA merger. Do you believe metamorphosis will occur? Why or why not?

3. What types of control did Hope Medical Center use before the partnership? Compare this with the types of control GVHA uses to manage its hospital network.

4. Using organizing theory, what evidence is there of the use of double interacts? What might sociocultural evolution predict will happen to Hope?

5. Do any of the theories emerge as "better" than the others? Why do you believe this to be the case? How could the story be altered so as to make a different theory or combination of theories better at explaining the situation?

Mediated Communication

After reading this chapter, you will be able to...

1. Explain social media and discuss how social media differ from mass media.
2. Define the terms *innovation, critical mass, rate of adoption*, and *reciprocal interdependence*.
3. Describe the innovation decision process.
4. Articulate which qualities of an innovation will make it more likely to be adopted.
5. Differentiate the characteristics associated with the five categories of adopters.
6. Identify the properties of networks.
7. Explain the properties of network links.
8. Articulate the characteristics of network roles.
9. Explain how social network analysis explains the production and reproduction of memes.
10. Describe the characteristics associated with media richness.
11. Apply the concept of ambiguity to match a communication message to the appropriate communication channel.
12. Identify the gratifications sought by using particular media forms.
13. Summarize major theoretical approaches to mediated communication.
14. Compare and contrast major theoretical approaches to mediated communication.

Is your LinkedIn profile up to date? How often do you tweet? Do you know what time it is if you don't have your smartphone? Are you more likely to watch TV shows and movies on a television set or on a tablet? There are a bewildering array of communication technologies available to us, with new platforms being launched nearly every month and old platforms slowly becoming obsolete (AOL anyone?). With so many communication channels available to us, being a competent communicator requires selecting the appropriate method to share a particular message. This chapter focuses on **mediated communication** channels—how mediated channels become popular as well as how and why we use them.

WHAT IS SOCIAL MEDIA?

When we use the term **media**, we typically are referring to large organizations responsible for producing the content we see on television and in the movies; the recordings we listen to on the radio and on our MP3 players; and the books and periodicals we read in print, on a Kindle, or on the web. By contrast, the term *social media* refers to "digital technologies that allow people to connect, interact, produce and share content" (Lewis, 2010, p. 2). These media forms vary in nature and purpose and include blogs, microblogging sites like Twitter, wikis, social networking websites like Facebook and LinkedIn, podcasting, video and photo sharing sites such as YouTube and Instagram, and discussion forums. Social media are considered distinct from traditional media because social media are based on user-generated content (versus "institutional content") and because the costs of creating and disseminating the content are either free or relatively inexpensive.

The original focus of social media was on its ability to assist individuals with achieving their personal goals (Vorvoreanu, 2009). However, more and more frequently people are pushing for the use of social media to achieve professional, rather than personal, goals. This is particularly evident in the realm of public relations; PR scholars such as Avery, Lariscy, and Sweetser (2010) claim "virtually no organization can afford to neglect its social media presence" (pp. 198–199). In part this is because social media allow for one group or individual to easily persuade other groups or individuals (Blossom, 2009). Yet there is little evidence social media are different from any other channel available to communicators.

A critical understanding of the role of social media in our lives requires us to understand the nature of mediated forms of communication. The first theory we discuss, diffusion of innovations, seeks to explain how and why particular new communication technologies develop and grow. Next, we explain social network theory, which helps to understand the web of connections we develop through social media. Third, we describe media richness theory, which focuses on the choices a communicator must make about the proper channel for disseminating particular messages. Finally, we discuss uses and gratifications theory, which centers on the choices audience members make in order to fulfill their needs.

DIFFUSION OF INNOVATIONS

Why do we all remember VHS tapes for our VCRs, but we have little memory of Betamax? Other than public displays of affection, what else does PDA stand for, and why don't we use them anymore (answer: personal digital assistant)? Is Facebook dead now that your grandmother has a page? Rogers' (2003) diffusion of innovations theory provides a framework for understanding why some inventions become popular and others never really catch on.

An **innovation** is an idea, practice, or object perceived as new. Although we often think of innovations in terms of technology, Rogers was careful to make sure innovations are understood in the broadest sense possible. His own academic background was in agriculture, and his earliest research focused on farmers' use of a new weed spray. Since the development of his model in the early 1960s, diffusion of innovations has been used to understand everything from the spread of particular medical technologies to the adoption of educational practices. Moreover, Rogers was clear in his belief that what is considered innovative varies by place and community. For example, video chatting through Skype or some other service might not be new to you, but for some groups of people and in some parts of the world, seeing someone live while you talk with him or her might seem very futuristic indeed.

Innovation Decision Process

Rogers (2003) identified six stages through which a person, group, or organization progresses in deciding whether to adopt an innovation. The first stage is known as the knowledge stage; here, the potential adopter becomes aware of the innovation and its potential uses. Second, the persuasion stage occurs when the potential adopter goes beyond mere awareness of the innovation and actively seeks information about it. She might do an Internet search, with careful attention to product reviews, or she might talk to people in her social network to assess their perspective of the innovation. The third stage is the decision stage, during which the potential adopter weighs the benefits and costs of the innovation and chooses either to adopt the innovation or to reject it.

Of course, if the innovation is rejected the process ends here, but if the innovation is adopted the process continues with the fourth stage. The implementation stage occurs when the adopter puts the innovation into use. Not surprisingly, this stage might include a lot of uncertainty and frustration. The adopter has to figure out how the innovation works in general, which specific features are useful and which are less than useful for his or her specific needs, and how to incorporate the innovation into an everyday routine. One important part of implementation is called reinvention, wherein the adopter "repurposes" the innovation. For example, voice mail was developed so callers could leave a message if the phone was not answered. However, many people call themselves and leave a message to create an audio reminder for themselves.

The fifth stage is the confirmation stage. During this stage the adopter reconsiders his or her adoption of the technology. Is it worth it? Does it do what the person had hoped it would do? If the answer is yes, the person has finally entered the adoption stage. If not, the person discontinues his or her use of the innovation. Discontinuance can take two forms. **Replacement discontinuance** occurs when an innovation is replaced with either a new version or an older version. For example, many people feel Microsoft Windows 8 is too big of a departure from the typical operating system they feel comfortable with, so they are using an older operating system, even on new machines. The second type of discontinuance is **disenchantment rejection**, or abandonment, which is when the adopter simply stops using the innovation. For example, after the iPhone was introduced, many people abandoned their PalmPilots and other PDAs.

Why Some Innovations and Not Others?

Of course, not every innovation succeeds. Rogers (2003) was concerned not only with the process of adopting an innovation but also with the essential question of why some innovations are adopted and others are not. He identified five qualities that influence the rate and likelihood of an innovation being adopted. The first is **relative advantage**. Simply put, the innovation has to be better at achieving the goals for performance than other, competing technologies. There are a number of ways an innovation might be considered "better." It might be faster, cheaper, easier to use, more effective, or just be "cooler" than other options. For example, for years Apple products were perceived as having an "it" factor that made them cooler than other brands. That image has started to fade recently (see Chen, 2013).

The second factor that influences the adoption of an innovation is **compatibility**. The extent to which an innovation is consistent with a potential adopter's values, lifestyle, or experience makes it a more attractive option. Consider, for example, a new mother who is philosophically opposed to genetically modified food. If she finds out a new product is made from grain grown using genetically engineered seeds, she is not going to purchase that product. On a more basic level, you are not going to purchase software that is only compatible with a Macintosh if you already own a PC.

Third, potential adopters consider **complexity**, which refers to the level of difficulty in understanding or using the innovation. For example, if the learning curve for a new technology is perceived as too steep, that technology will not be used, regardless of the benefits it might provide. On the other hand, an individual doesn't have to actually understand how television broadcasts work if the television set itself is easy to use . . . if you can plug it in, turn it on, and figure out how to change channels without reading a lengthy technical manual, the innovation is likely to be adopted.

Trialability is the next factor that influences the rate and likelihood of adoption. The extent to which potential adopters can "try" the innovation before making a decision can expedite the decision-making process. Whether test-driving a new car or a computer, trying on a new style of clothing, getting a sample pack of a potential new prescription, or sitting in on a graduate class before applying to the school, people are much more likely to adopt an innovation if they have had the opportunity to try it out before being required to purchase it.

The last factor is **observability**. People are much more likely to adopt an innovation if they actually see the innovation in public or if the results of the innovation are visible. If everyone else seems to be using a new technology it becomes much more appealing to those who are not ("Seriously, Mom, I am the only person at school without one."). Similarly, if the innovation's impact is obvious ("Wow! You look great! What new fitness routine are you using?"), people will be more inclined to adopt it.

Time and Diffusion

You have probably heard the old question "If a tree falls in the woods and no one hears it, does it make a sound?" A similar question can be asked regarding the diffusion of innovations. That is, if an innovation is available and no one adopts it, can it have an impact? The answer is no. Even if an innovation exhibits the five qualities just described, ultimately people determine the success or failure of its adoption. The third major contribution diffusion of innovations makes to our understanding of how communication media develop and grow is through a focus on critical mass. **Critical mass** refers to the notion that if a sufficient number of people adopt the innovation, additional adoption of the innovation becomes self-sustaining, assuring future growth (Markus, 1987).

At issue is the **rate of adoption**, or the relative speed with which an individual (or group or organization) adopts the innovation. Rogers (2003) classified people into five categories, from those most likely to embrace the innovation rapidly to those who may never adopt the innovation. Figure 10.1 displays categories of people in the innovation adoption process. Innovators are the first group of any social system to adopt an innovation. They tend to be younger, high in social class, and categorized as risk takers socially connected with other innovators, even if they live in different regions of the world. The next group of people are early adopters. Unlike innovators, early adopters tend to be connected with others more locally. However, they tend to be opinion leaders who have a greater influence on other members of the social system. As such, they play a central role in the diffusion of innovations, since their opinions are respected and they assist others with their uncertainty about the innovation. The early majority is the next group of individuals. Although they do not serve as role models or opinion leaders, they carefully deliberate over the adoption of the innovation, and it is their decision to adopt that allows the diffusion of the innovation to reach a critical mass. The fourth group is called the late majority. These individuals tend only to adopt an innovation because of peer pressure; they tend to be skeptical of innovations and unwilling to take risks. Finally, the laggards rarely, if ever, adopt the innovation. Typically older and more traditional in beliefs, laggards are not only mistrustful of new ideas, products, or services, they also are leery of innovators and early adopters.

Figure 10.1   The Types of People Who Adopt Innovations

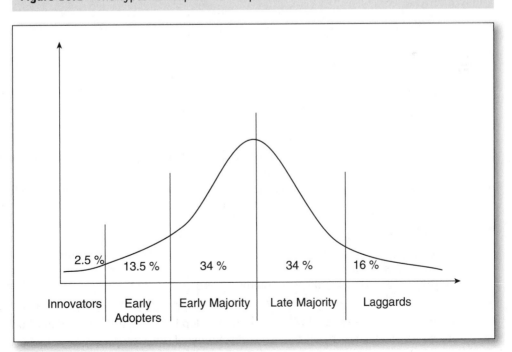

Returning to the notion of critical mass, the process whereby people adopt the use of interactive media is different from the adoption of other types of innovations (Markus, 1987). Interactive media such as the telephone, text messaging, or Facebook entail **reciprocal interdependence**; that is, even if innovators or early adopters have the technology, they need others to adopt the technology in order to receive the maximum benefits. Think about it: What good is having the ability to text on your phone if other people cannot receive your texts? Accordingly, early adopters must actively persuade others to adopt the technology, resulting in a steep increase in the adoption rate. Look at Figure 10.1 again. The first half of the bell curve demonstrates that the rate of adoption is not a straight line but more like a slightly flattened "S" curve.

Diffusion of innovations theory depicts the process whereby new media technologies are adopted in society. The theory details the decision-making process that individuals use in the adoption process and qualities that make a given innovation more likely to be adopted. Finally, the theory classifies people in terms of their likeliness to adopt an innovation, with early adopters playing an important role in persuading others to adopt the innovation.

SOCIAL NETWORK ANALYSIS

In Chapter 9 we introduced you to systems perspectives, which focus on how groups of people interrelate to form a whole. Systems perspectives are used to understand many contexts for communication, although they are used most often to understand organizational communication. Likewise, network analysis has historically been associated with an organizational context, but the growth of social media has led a number of scholars to implement network analysis to understand the relationship patterns of social media users.

In the 1980s Faberge Organics shampoo had a popular commercial featuring Heather Locklear, who was so excited about using the shampoo that she told two friends about it . . . and they told two friends . . . and so on and so on until the screen was filled with people who had heard about the shampoo from one of their friends. In 2012 the same concept was used by the AIDS Council, who developed a public service announcement for Foursquare that focused on safe sex: When you have sex with someone, you are not only having sex with them, you are having sex with everyone they have ever had sex with . . . and so on (because Foursquare identifies "where you have been," the commercial talked about how many other people had "been there already"). Both of these ads feature one of the central concepts of social network analysis: All of us are connected to others, who are connected to others, leading us to "six degrees of separation" from all others around the world (although apparently the popularity of Facebook has now led us to four degrees of separation; see Barnett, 2011).

According to Monge and Contractor (2001), "Communication networks are the patterns of contact between communication partners that are created by transmitting and exchanging messages through time and space" (p. 440). Network analysis involves mapping out those patterns, with a special focus on the types of links between members, the roles members play in the network, the mode or channel by which messages are exchanged, and the content of the messages. At its most basic level, consider your own Facebook network. How many friends do you have? How many of your own friends are also friends with other people on your friends list? How often do you actually message or respond to each of the people on your friends list? Do you primarily share personal information, professional information, or both? How many people do you also talk with using other channels of communication? Social network analysis allows you to develop a picture of how individuals, groups, and organizations are connected with each other to better understand structures of influence and the spread of ideas.

Network Properties

Four attributes of networks are considered in a social network analysis. The first is the **network mode**. Put simply, the network mode involves the channel or channels used by network members. Consider people who work for the same organization but in two different locations; they may have phone and e-mail contact but may never have actually met each other face-to-face. An understanding of which channels are used in the network is important, as each channel has strengths and weaknesses (which we talk about when we discuss media richness theory). The second is the **content** of messages. Gilpin (2010), for example, did a network analysis of the social media content posted by the supermarket chain Whole Foods. She found the content could be classified as focusing either on the core identity of the company or on the well-being of its customers. The third network property is **density**, or the number of interconnections among network members. Highly dense networks involve many connections between network members, such as those between a group of college friends, whereas a less dense network is one of few connections between members. Consider, for example, the informal or social connections between co-workers. Although there may be significant connections among co-workers when considering task-related communication, the co-workers might not have many social connections, making the social network a low-density network. Believe it or not, a lack of a social network among co-workers has been found to negatively predict productivity, so understanding network density can be very important (Litterst & Eyo, 1982). The final consideration is the **level of analysis**. When conducting a social network analysis, is the focus on the individuals in the network, particular groups of organizational members (e.g., departments in an organization or cliques in a friendship circle), or connections among and between organizations?

Properties of Network Links

In addition to considerations of the properties of the network itself, social network analysis also requires uncovering the nature of the connections between network members (Monge & Contractor, 2001). Seven potential links can be assessed: **strength** (the frequency, intimacy, or intensity of the connection), **direction** (the extent to which the link is reciprocal between network members), **symmetry** (whether the two people connected share the same type of relationship with each other), **frequency** (how often the two people communicate with each other), **stability** (the existence of the link over time), **mediation** (whether the connections between network members exist because of a common link), and **multiplexity** (the extent to which two network members are linked together by more than one relationship or type of communication). To illustrate, consider the simple network depicted in Figure 10.2. You can see that network members A, B, C, D, and E seem to have a dense network likely to also be strong, direct, symmetrical, frequent, stable, and demonstrate multiplexity—they are perhaps people who both work together and socialize with each other. Now consider the relationship between B and E; despite being in the same dense network, they are connected only because A, C, and D serve as a mediators. One can easily imagine that at one time B and E might have been directly connected, but their link faded over time. Finally, consider F's relationship with K. The arrow goes in only one direction, perhaps indicating that K's work requires input from F, but F does not require feedback from K to do her job.

Figure 10.2 Exemplar Social Network Graph

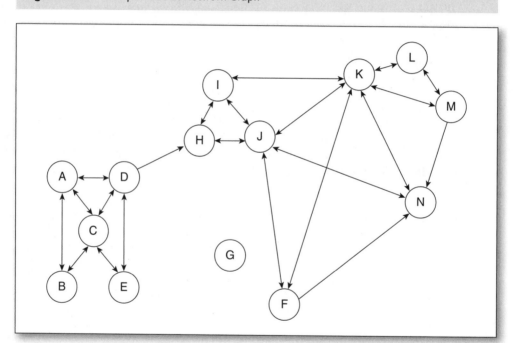

Figure 10.2 includes only a single arrow between network members, but a thorough network analysis might involve multiple types of arrows to demonstrate the different modes of communication between network members. For example, you might have a black arrow to depict face-to-face communication, a blue arrow to depict e-mail, a red arrow to depict Facebook, a green arrow to depict the phone, and so forth. In addition, you might have an unbroken arrow to illuminate links for professional communication and a dashed arrow to show links for social communication. A complete social network analysis is very complex, sometimes requiring 3-D imagery. We encourage you to search online to view images of social network analyses to see the intricacy such work requires.

Network Roles

Social network analysis also requires a consideration of the roles each member plays in the network. Network members are considered **nodes**, since networks are not always comprised of individuals. Five types of roles have been uncovered (Monge & Contractor, 2001). An **isolate** is a node that belongs in a network but has no links. In Figure 10.2, G is an isolate: He or she might work for an organization but does not communicate with others in the organization. Although this sounds improbable, it could be that G's role is a boundary spanner who connects with members of other organizations. A **gatekeeper** is a node that controls the flow of information between one part of the network and another. Consider D in Figure 10.2; he or she is the sole link between members on the left-hand side of the network and those on the right-hand side. A **bridge** is a member of more than one group. J, for example, is a part of the H-I-J group and a member of the J-K-N-F group. A **liaison** has connections with two or more groups that would otherwise not be linked. However, liaisons are not nodes of either of those groups. H, for example, is a liaison for the A-B-C-D-E network and the J-K-N-F network. Finally, a **star** is a node that is highly central to the network. Consider K in Figure 10.2. She or he has six network links, more than anyone else in the network.

In the case of a single organization and talking about individuals, the roles just described make sense, as it is easy to consider individuals playing each role. However, in more sophisticated and extensive social network analyses, we need to recognize that the nodes might be entire organizations. In this case, we need to also consider **hubs**, which are highly dense networks embedded within a larger network. To simplify this notion, consider the Internet as a network. A few heavily used websites, such as Google, Facebook, and YouTube would be considered hubs, whereas very specialized websites might be closer to isolates—they might be password protected and not hyperlinked from any other website.

Implications for Understanding Social Media

Recall that the purpose of social media theory is to uncover the patterns of connections within a system. More than just identifying "who talks to whom," a social network analysis can allow us to uncover large-scale trends in ideas and influences. For example, Kelly (2008) has mapped the blogosphere, uncovering the connections between news (and faux news) sites. Sedereviciute and Valentini (2011) have developed a method for PR practitioners to uncover organizational stakeholders through mapping social media content. Similarly, De Nooy and Kleinnijenhuis (2013) have developed a mechanism to study patterns of support and attack in the political communication arena.

The concepts described earlier (network properties, network links, and network roles) are most often used to investigate the structure of a social network. However, scholars also use social network analysis to investigate **semantic networks**, which particularly focus on the content of the communications (Gilpin, 2010). In this way, researchers can understand the spread of **memes**—ideas, behaviors, or practices that spread from one person to another in a network (Dawkins, 1989). Consider the spread of the Diet Coke and Mentos experiment, the cinnamon challenge, and the "Keep Calm and Carry On" memes in recent years. Social media not only connect each of us in six (or four!) degrees of separation, they also allow for the production and reproduction of significant social trends.

MEDIA RICHNESS THEORY

The decline and ultimate end of Ashton Kutcher and Demi Moore's marriage was on public display through their tweets. And, according to an article in *Vogue*, Katy Perry claimed Russell Brand texted her that he wanted a divorce. In the fictional world, Berger broke up with Carrie using a sticky note on the TV show *Sex and the City*. Most of us have the empathy to realize these might not have been the best media choices to sever a relationship. However, in the professional world sometimes the choice is less obvious. For example, is it okay to conduct layoffs via e-mail? Media richness theory, developed by Daft and Lengel (1984), recognizes that as new communication technologies develop, the decision about the best way to send a message becomes more complex.

What Is a Rich Medium?

The central argument of media richness theory is that communication professionals should match the communication channel to the content of the information (Lengel & Daft, 1988). **Media richness** refers to the information-carrying capacity of the medium. One determines the richness of the media by assessing four characteristics: speed of feedback (related to synchronous or asynchronous capacities), ability to personalize the message, availability of multiple cues, and language variety (Daft & Lengel, 1986). Face-to-face interaction is considered the most "rich" medium. Imagine an organizational training session. A face-to-face trainer can quickly adjust the session if he or she sees that employees do not understand a particular process ("Okay, let me try another way to explain how this new software program is different from the old program"). The trainer can recognize individuals in the group and craft messages to those individuals ("José, your department won't need to be concerned about this next application"). The trainer can use words, facial expressions, gestures, pauses, eye contact, and a host of other possible nonverbal cues in the session. Finally, the trainer can change the vocabulary or jargon usage depending on with whom he or she is talking. Contrast this with a much less rich medium: a DVD. Imagine a group of employees sitting in a room watching a recorded training session. If the employees do not understand something on the recording, little can be done; the DVD cannot be changed in the moment to adapt to audience confusion. Moreover, given production expenses, the DVD likely would be produced for all employees and wouldn't be tailored to particular groups or individuals or to their backgrounds or experiences. As such, it would be considered a "lean" medium. Table 10.1 identifies media from most to least rich based on these characteristics.

How Ambiguous Is the Message?

Of course, the main idea of the theory is that the medium should match the message. As such, the second major consideration is the nature of the message that needs to be sent. Daft and Lengel (1984, 1986) were influenced by the work of Karl Weick (see Chapter 9), so they focused on the notion of ambiguity. **Ambiguity** refers to the possibility of multiple interpretations. If the goal of communication is understanding (as Daft and Lengel

Table 10.1   Media Richness

Richer Media	Face-to-face
↑ ↓	Video conferencing, social networking, interactive websites
	Telephone
	E-mail
	Texting, instant messaging, microblogs
	Video or audio recordings
	Memos, letters
Leaner Media	Bulk mail, brochures, pamphlets, flyers

assumed), then ambiguous messages are those that run a greater risk of being misunderstood. Imagine you are an employee of an organization facing financial crisis. The senior management team of your organization has decided that, rather than layoffs, they will reduce employee benefits. You might have many questions about such a decision. Will this affect all employees? Is it a permanent decision, or will benefits be returned once the crisis is over? Will the elimination of these benefits really solve the financial problems, or might there still be layoffs sometime in the future? Can individuals choose which benefits are reduced? After all, health care might be a major concern to some employees and retirement benefits might be of greater concern to others. In short, this sort of situation is highly ambiguous. Not surprisingly, according to media richness theory, the more ambiguous the message, the richer the medium should be in communicating that message. In the situation just described, media richness theory would suggest using a town hall meeting or even small group meetings to explain the decision and to answer questions; a memo would not be an appropriate choice. On the other hand, using e-mail or a memo might be a perfectly suitable method for announcing the meeting itself, as the time and date of a meeting is not particularly ambiguous.

As asserted earlier, communication effectiveness is assumed to occur because of a match between the ambiguity of the message and the richness of the media. A highly ambiguous message communicated using a lean media form is likely to exacerbate uncertainty and create misunderstanding. Conversely, using a very rich medium to communicate fairly straightforward information is a form of overkill, potentially wasting time and money and possibly contributing to a sense of information overload. Can you imagine having a personal conversation about every bit of information you deal with on an everyday basis? It would be exhausting! As it is, you likely delete some e-mails without reading them because of information overload.

Some scholars have challenged media richness theory because the theory implies there is an objective richness to particular media that does not vary based on individual or organizational variations. After all, we all know people who pick up the phone for even the simplest of questions, whereas others prefer e-mail exchanges. Similarly, organizations have differing cultures related to the preferred ways of communication. However, scholars have found that above and beyond such variations, there are objective differences in the ability of various communication channels to communicate particular types of messages (Trevino, Lengel, & Daft, 1987). As such, a skilled communicator needs to consciously consider media richness in the communication process.

USES AND GRATIFICATIONS THEORY

Uses and gratifications theory (UGT) represents a somewhat different means by which to analyze and explain the use of mediated communication. Rather than look at the media choices made by a message sender, UGT focuses on *why* a receiver uses particular media forms. Specifically, UGT maintains that because humans have options and free will, individuals will make specific decisions about which media to use and when to use them (Katz, Blumler, & Gurevitch, 1973). The choices and decisions you make are based on personal needs and values you wish to fulfill. Thus, you can select among various media for **gratification** of your individual needs.

Three primary assumptions drive our discussion of UGT. First, Katz et al. (1973) believed audience members actively use various media to fulfill certain needs or goals. Thus, media usage isn't passive, involuntary, or coerced. Instead, media technologies represent numerous options available to fulfill a person's social or psychological needs and values. Indeed, the increase in communication technologies available to people in the 21st century only boosts the viability of the notion of choice (Ruggiero, 2000). In this way, UGT suggests media use is active and goal driven based on individuals' needs.

Second, **mass communication** isn't something that happens to you; nor do the media do anything to you. There is no magic spell cast by media owners to coax you into viewing their programming. Instead, UGT maintains a person must identify his or her need and make a media choice (Katz et al., 1973). Individuals *choose* to surf the Internet, tweet, or put together a Pinterest board. In this regard, the term *media effects* is misleading. Katz et al. did not believe in the simple "straight-line effect" whereby a given medium causes people to think or behave differently. According to Katz et al., audience members choose a medium and allow themselves to be swayed, changed, and influenced—or not. You choose to view a YouTube video and watch; You Tube doesn't turn itself on and watch you.

Third, media outlets compete with other available means of satisfying personal needs (Katz et al., 1973). Stated differently, there are many ways to fulfill individual needs. If you feel frazzled after a hectic day at work, you may fulfill your need to relax and unwind by watching a sitcom (mass media) or escaping to the movies. Alternatively, you may meet your needs by taking a run in the park, practicing yoga, or soaking in a warm bath with a glass of wine. Thus, the mass media represent only a handful of alternatives available to you. Next, we present reasons individuals use the media and how media exposure can gratify various social and psychological needs.

Why Do We Watch What We Watch?

McQuail (1987) identified four broad classes of motivations that include several subcategories. For example, we can use the media for entertainment purposes. Under the umbrella term of *entertainment* are some specific subtypes; individuals can relax, escape from daily problems, feel some form of excitement or emotional catharsis, pass time, or simply enjoy an artistic pleasure. You may relax by listening to satellite radio while on your commute home from a long day at the office. You may have watched *The Ring* to experience an eerie thrill or *Casablanca* to experience a romantic heartbreak. Your children may watch *Dora the Explorer* on DVD while riding in the backseat of your car to prevent boredom. Similarly, you may turn on a TV sitcom as a diversion from the daily grind. Table 10.2 provides an overview of gratifications.

Table 10.2   Gratifications

Gratification	Examples
Entertainment	• Listening to a Barry White CD to set a romantic mood • Watching *Psycho* to experience a thrill • Surfing the web because you have nothing else to do
Information	• Seeking advice about practical matters, such as how to cook a turkey (Food Network) • Finding out the weather so you know what to wear to work
Personal identity	• Reading *Vogue* or *Esquire* so you know how to dress and be considered stylish • Putting together a Pinterest board to share your passions
Personal relationships and social interaction	• Listening to the Sports Radio Network on your drive to work so you can talk about it with your co-workers • Watching *Cake Boss* every week to bond with your family

Second, media outlets and content are used to provide information (McQuail, 1987). This media function presents individuals with opportunities to learn about current and historical events, to obtain advice, and to feel secure or satisfy curiosity by acquiring general knowledge. Thus, you may turn on news radio for the weather, traffic updates, and local sports scores. You probably have watched or read about local, national, and world news to find out what is going on in your neighborhood as well as in the world. You may read an advice column for investment strategies or etiquette protocols. You may use the Internet to scour real estate web pages and research the dimensions of your dream home.

Third, people use the media to reflect, reinforce, or contrast their personal identity (McQuail, 1987). In other words, individuals can choose among various media and media content to gain insight into or assist in the development of their own attitudes or beliefs. For example, you might watch Dr. Phil to hear how others struggle with relationship issues. Likewise, a person often acquires a deeper sense of self by comparing, and perhaps contrasting, one's self with characters portrayed in various media. For instance, you are probably familiar with the hit show *The Big Bang Theory.* Although you may find the characters of Sheldon, Leonard, Raj, and Howard to be hilarious with their lack of social skill, you also are apt to compare your own experiences and attitudes with theirs. Are you that self-centered? That neurotic? That immature? That insecure? We hope not! But that is exactly the point of the show—to present extreme personalities audience members can at once relate to and simultaneously ridicule for their triviality.

A fourth and final reason is that people turn to various media for personal relationships and social interaction (McQuail, 1987). Media exposure can help individuals learn about or connect with others through comparisons of interpersonal relationships and social situations. Certain media can even serve as a substitute for real-life relationships by offering companionship. Thursday morning watercooler gossip about the latest twist on *Survivor* creates a sense of community. Following the management blunders on *The Office* allows viewers to compare and commiserate about their own workplace foibles. Reading a magazine article about the growing trend of stay-at-home dads or a newspaper interview with successful single moms may provide readers with an opportunity to consider another type of family arrangement.

UGT maintains people have many options from which they deliberately select to meet personal needs. The question, then, is not what impact the media have on us, but, rather, why people choose the media forms they do and what gratifications they receive from their choices.

Summary and Research Applications

In this chapter, we presented an overview of four theories of mediated communication. First, we described the diffusion of innovations: the process by which people decide to adopt a new media technology, the characteristics that make a new media technology more appealing, and the categories of people most and least likely to adopt the new technology. For example, Chan-Olmsted, Rim, and Zerba (2013) were able to apply the theory to explain the adoption of mobile news services among college students. Second, we explained a social network approach to understanding the factors associated with determining the relationships among members of a social system. Weber and Monge (2011) used a social network analysis in their investigation of digital news sources. They concluded that a few central websites controlled the flow of information across the entire sphere of digital news providers. Next, media richness theory provides advice for choosing particular media to send different types of messages, helpful in understanding media choices within organizations, such as communication preferences between superiors and subordinates (Salmon & Joiner, 2005; Shepherd & Martz, 2006). Pazos, Chung, and Micari (2013) successfully used media richness theory to predict employees would be more likely to use instant messaging for simple tasks (e.g., requesting or supplying information) than for more complex tasks (e.g., to problem solve or resolve a disagreement). Finally, UGT focuses on the choices receivers make. It argues audience members are active and use media forms that provide them with the individual gratifications they seek. As an example, researchers uncovered five gratifications for using MP3 players: control, companionship, entertainment, status, and concentration (Haridakis & Hanson, 2009). Concentration and entertainment were the strongest predictors of using an MP3 player.

Key Terms

Ambiguity   184

Bridge   183

Compatibility   178

Complexity   178

Content   181

Critical mass   179

Density   181

Direction   181

Disenchantment rejection   177

Frequency   181

Gatekeeper   183

Gratification   186

Hub   183

Innovation   177

Isolate   183

Level of analysis   181

Liaison   183

Mass communication   186

Media   176

Media richness   184

Mediated communication   176

Mediation   181

Meme   183

Multiplexity   181

Network mode   181

Node   183

Observability   178

Rate of adoption   179

Reciprocal interdependence   180

Relative advantage   178

Replacement discontinuance   177

Semantic network   183

Stability   181

Star   183

Strength   181

Symmetry   181

Trialability   178

Case Study 10: Casino Controversy

When the Pennsylvania Gaming Control Board approved applications for the development of two casinos within the city limits of Philadelphia, controversy immediately ensued. Before the state had unveiled the approved casino locations, anyone could pick up a newspaper or watch a newscast and see something about the much-awaited casino proposal. These stories emphasized that the casinos would bring jobs and tourism to the city. Suburban residents like June Johnson were thrilled because casino revenue would (at least theoretically) help lower the state's escalating property taxes, and the city's union contractors were eager for the opportunity to bid on the development contracts.

However, these initial news stories never considered the local concerns that would surface, such as traffic congestion and crime. When the announcement hit that the casinos would be built next to residential areas, local homeowners and small-business owners were furious.

Karen Moyer, 52, was a longtime resident and homeowner of the neighborhood adjacent to where the casinos were proposed. Worried about declining home values and the quality of the neighborhood, Karen organized a political action group called CasiNO! Philly. Karen made use of all of her network connections to get people involved with the group; she not only posted on her own Facebook page, she posted on the pages of local businesses, local schools, and other local nonprofit groups. She created a website and posted information such as newspaper articles about the casino proposals along with contact information for the politicians who had supported the initiative. The website also featured an electronic board where registered users could post comments and organize meetings. She started following the Twitter accounts of local politicians and members of the Gaming Control Board, tweeting responses to them with the hashtag #CasiNO!Philly. As the action group's membership grew, CasiNO! Philly began tweeting about potential protests and rallies around historical tourist attractions like Independence Hall and the National Constitution Center. The aim was to attract as much media attention as possible, thereby creating negative publicity for the casino proposals.

CasiNO! Philly's social media outreach was strong, but it didn't actually become successful until one of the members of the action group contacted Karen with an idea. Warren Trembly was a 16-year-old skateboarder who attended a cyber charter school with a focus on new media technologies. Warren introduced Karen to an application called Loke, which provided real-time navigation information to users through their smartphones, also identifying where other network members were at any given time. The app allowed members of the network to see all current CasiNO! Philly activities near the user's current location, as well as all other members' current locations. Warren convinced a core of the activists to start using it to coordinate their efforts, and soon nearly a third of the people who identified with the effort downloaded and used the app.

The coordinated effort worked. Philadelphia newspapers, news radio stations, and TV news stations reported on virtually every protest, which they could easily find because of the information available on Loke. Bloggers wrote about it. The TV news stations even began covering the protests live. The *Philadelphia Times* ran a series of news features examining nearby Atlantic City and its neighborhood collapse due to an increase in robberies, vandalism, and prostitution. A popular local radio talk show held several programs focusing on residents' opinions of the state's proposal. The hashtag #casiNO!Philly trended nearly daily in the social media stats for Philadelphia.

With all of this momentum, CasiNO! Philly members took their plight to city council where they successfully lobbied to have a referendum put on the city's mayoral election ballot. The referendum would give Philadelphia voters a say as to whether or not they wanted casinos in their districts. If passed, the referendum would also prevent slot machines and gaming parlors from being built within 1,500 feet of homes, places of worship, civic centers, public parks, playgrounds, pools, or libraries.

As the election approached, Karen Moyer's city councilman, Chad DeMario, changed his position on the issue. Initially, when the state first proposed that casinos be developed in Philadelphia, Chad supported the measure. However, after several televised protests, he changed his position and helped pass the referendum.

Not to be outmaneuvered, the casino investors' group ran a full-page advertisement in the Sunday *Philadelphia Times* right before the November election. The ad promised their organization would strive to maintain the integrity of the existing neighborhoods while elevating the city's status as a tourist destination. Election Day arrived, and after all the votes were counted, the referendum passed by a slim margin. The issue of finding the "perfect" location for Pennsylvania's casinos was tossed back to the state legislature. Pleased, Karen Moyer updated CasiNO! Philly's website to read "CasiNO! Philly Wins Media Jackpot! No Casinos Here!"

Questions for Consideration

1. Discuss the adoption of Loke using the diffusion of innovations approach. What qualities of the innovation made it likely to be adopted? How might the CasiNO! Philly members be ranked in terms of the qualities of individuals in the adoption process? How did the group reach critical mass?

2. Describe the properties of the networks and network links Karen and CasiNO! Philly evidenced.

3. Explain the differences in media richness between the CasiNO! Philly group and the casino investor group. What advice would you give to the casino investors if they want to make their message less ambiguous?

4. According to UGT, individuals make choices about how they use various media to fulfill different needs. What choices did CasiNO! Philly make? How about the casino investors' group?

5. Do any of the theories emerge as "better" than the others? Why do you believe this to be the case? What situations might surface that would make a different theory or theories better at explaining the situation?

CHAPTER 11

Mass Communication

LEARNING OBJECTIVES

After reading this chapter, you will be able to...

1. Discuss the five characteristics of mass communication/mass media.
2. Explain the assumptions of agenda-setting theory.
3. Apply the two criteria for measuring the media's agenda to current print, digital, and/or broadcast news stories.
4. Explain and apply the framing process to current print, digital, and/or broadcast news stories.
5. Discuss the gatekeeping function of the media.
6. Identify which issues and individuals are most affected by agenda setting.
7. Explain the assumptions associated with cultivation theory.
8. Define television violence and apply this definition.
9. Differentiate between heavy and light viewers.
10. Identify genres other than violence that are influenced by cultivation theory.
11. Explain the process of cultivation via mainstreaming and resonance.
12. Compare and contrast social cognitive theory with cultivation theory.
13. Explain the assumptions associated with social cognitive theory.
14. Differentiate between observational learning and classical learning.
15. Discuss the four processes of observational learning.
16. Compare the direct path and social-mediated path of media influence.
17. Apply the concept of observational modeling to television violence.
18. Compare and contrast social cognitive theory with cultivation theory.

(Continued)

(Continued)

19. Explain the assumptions associated with encoding/decoding theory.

20. Discuss how the media create, transmit, and reinforce cultural ideologies.

21. Identify some of the dominant ideologies in mainstream American media.

22. Differentiate between three ways of reading messages, using preferred, negotiated, or oppositional codes.

23. Discuss the importance of decoding media messages as it pertains to the perpetuation of the dominant cultural ideology.

24. Compare and contrast major theoretical approaches to mass media.

The *Washington Post* reported that 30 years of research examining media effects shows significant connections between media exposure and negative health consequences for children and adolescents (St. George, 2008). According to the article, research concludes exposure to TV, movies, music, and other media forms is associated with childhood obesity, sexual activity, use of tobacco products, drug and alcohol use, low academic achievement, and attention-deficit/hyperactivity disorder. Whew! With such negative consequences, why do we continue to allow the media into our lives? Perhaps it is because such a dismal view oversimplifies our complex relationship with the media. For many of us, the media provide both personal and professional opportunities for development. After all, *Sesame Street* really can teach our children, and the opportunity to surf the web can simplify our quest for information. Moreover, despite the commonly held view of negative media effects, scholarly research often conflicts with popular beliefs and even contradicts other scholars' work. Intellectual and political debate remain over *who* are most affected, *to what extent* these individuals are influenced, and *why* some people are more affected than others. In this chapter, we present four of the most influential and often controversial theories that attempt to explain and predict media use and media effects: agenda-setting theory, cultivation theory, social cognitive theory of mass media, and encoding/decoding theory. First, however, we discuss exactly what we mean by mass media.

CHARACTERISTICS OF MASS MEDIA

Mass communication and mass media are decidedly different from mediated communication and social media. Mediated communication includes all messages in which there is a device, third party, or electronic mechanism that facilitates communication between the sender and receiver. By contrast, **mass communication** "is a process in which professional communicators use technology to share messages over great distances to influence large audiences" (Pearson, Nelson, Titsworth, & Harter, 2008, p. 3). Note the source could be an announcer, reporter, writer, and so on, while the technology used to mediate the mass message could include fiber optics, satellites, cable, radio waves, and printing presses to name a few. In turn, the **mass media** include organizations responsible for using technology to send mass messages to the public. Mass communication and the mass media are intertwined; without organizations and agencies to create, produce, and transmit the message content, reaching a mass audience would be difficult. If all of these distinctions seem confusing, remember this: all mass communication is mediated but not all mediated messages are mass communication.

McQuail (2010) identified five key characteristics of the mass media that have stood the test of time, despite advances in technology and the decrease in some mediums. First, and noted in Chapter 10, the mass media are able to reach an enormous amount of people instantly or almost instantly with information, entertainment, or opinions. However, while the mass communication sender can promptly reach a large audience, feedback from these receivers back to the source is typically much, much slower. For example, if you want to comment on an article written in your local print newspaper or favorite magazine, you need to write a letter or send an e-mail to the editor. The letter may or may not be read, published, or otherwise acknowledged. Likewise, if you want to complain about "lewd" content on a supposed family friendly TV show, you must write, e-mail, or attempt a phone call. Again, the show's producer may or may not receive, read, or otherwise acknowledge your message. With emerging and interactive media technologies, this slow feedback process is not always the case (think about texting your vote to *America's Got Talent* or *The Voice*). Nonetheless, the quality of feedback the audience can provide is often much less rich than in interpersonal communication.

A second characteristic offered by McQuail (2010) argues that the media continue to inspire universal fascination. Again, the popular technologies may change (from sitting around the radio listening to Abbott and Costello to watching streaming video via Netflix), but people's preoccupation with shared stories continues. Likewise, a third feature of mass media is that it can rouse, in equal measure, hope and fear in audiences. Perhaps you might recall watching the hunt for the Boston Marathon bombers . . . it seems almost everyone in the United States watched endless news coverage on television, posted on Facebook, and tweeted their feeling of anxiety during the hunt—and cheered enthusiastically with the successful capture of the surviving bomber as well.

The fourth property of mass media noted by McQuail (2010) concerns the relationship between the media and other sources of societal power. Unlike other types of communication noted in this book, the mass media influence and are influenced by the four sources of social power identified by Mann (2012): economic, ideological, military, and political power. Just consider the role of TV ads during political campaigns. According to Fowler and Ridout (2013), "Record amounts of money went to purchase television advertising during the 2012 election cycle, resulting in unprecedented volumes of advertising," and these ads were overwhelming negative (p. 51). Not only are increased ads evident, analysis of presidential campaign advertising from the 2000 and 2004 elections show the influence of ads is "significant enough to shift election outcomes" (Gordon & Hartmann, 2013, p. 19). We may not like those negative attack ads squeezed in between our primetime TV viewing, but clearly they're influential. In a reverse example of societal power and media influence, the military can wield power over the media. From 1991 to 2009, the U.S. military banned news media from photographing the coffins of dead soldiers as their bodies were returned to the United States.

Economic and ideological power also influence and are influenced by the media. The lack of scrutiny with which commercial journalists reported on subprime mortgages and the housing rise and fall in the United States is believed to have influenced the public's opinions about the safety of home loans and subsequent panic when the bubble burst, contributing to the market collapse (Longobardi, 2009). Conversely, most mass media are funded by advertising. By emphasizing consumerism, either directly through advertisements or indirectly through product placement, sponsoring a national sporting event, or drawing attention to characters' dress, hairstyles, and homes, the media can encourage our shopping and spending habits.

Finally, McQuail's (2010) fifth characteristic of the media is the assumption that it is a source of enormous power and influence. For instance, the media influence social reality—that which we perceive to be true. The 6 o'clock evening news provides viewers with information, but that information is edited and other stories are omitted. The news stories presented may or may not be complete, accurate, or reliable. After the Boston Marathon bombing in 2013, the FBI criticized the Associated Press, the *Boston Globe*, the BBC, CNN, Fox News, and other news organizations for hastily and inaccurately reporting that a Saudi suspect had been apprehended well before any suspects were arrested (Williams, 2013). In a rush to be first with breaking news, imprecise, misleading, or incorrect stories can result, thereby creating unintended consequences. The alleged "Saudi suspect" turned out to be an injured witness, who due to the false reports, ended up receiving threatening e-mails, forcing him to leave his home (Chaudary, 2013). The point here isn't to demonize news organizations; rather, it is to highlight the power the media have.

The theories featured in this chapter focus on the media's power and influence—the ways and the extent to which various media influence receivers. Again, the four theories are agenda-setting theory, cultivation theory, social cognitive theory of mass communication, and encoding/decoding theory. According to these theories of mass communication influence, although mass media can't make us watch, read, or listen, when we do participate as audience members, we are transformed in some way.

AGENDA-SETTING THEORY

McCombs and Shaw (1972) were among the first communication scholars to test and support their ideas of media influence within the realm of political news. Before their study of the 1968 presidential campaign, it was widely held that the news media simply reflected the public's interests, covering issues about which audience members already knew or wanted to understand in more detail. In this way, many assumed the news media simply act as mirrors of public interest. According to this viewpoint, 2012 presidential candidate Mitt Romney's dog was discussed repeatedly during the campaign because the public wanted to know more about his common sense (or lack thereof) about pet ownership.

McCombs and Shaw (1972), however, had a hunch that something wasn't quite right with the "news media as a reflection of society" theory. Instead, they argued that public opinion is shaped, in part, by media coverage—particularly with regard to political news and campaigns. Rather than the news media simply providing a reflection of the public's interests, McCombs and Shaw posited the reverse equation—that is, the public reflects what is presented by the news media. In other words, McCombs and Shaw conceived the news media present audiences with an **agenda** for what events the public should consider as important. Relying on several assumptions, McCombs and Shaw were able to test this "agenda-setting function" of the news media.

Two key assumptions guide agenda-setting theory. First, McCombs and Shaw (1972) argued that the news media have an agenda. That is, the news media tell audiences what "news" to consider as important. However, the media's agenda is viewed as somewhat limited. Using Cohen's (1963) well-known quote discussing the limited effects of media, the agenda-setting function suggests the news media provide "not what to think . . . but what to think about" (p. 13).

Second, McCombs and Shaw (1972) believed most people would like help when trying to understand and evaluate politics and political reality. Because people need assistance with determining their political viewpoints, audience members come to rely on news media to point out topics of importance.

Drawing on these assumptions and using media coverage of the 1968 presidential election as an opportunity to study agenda-setting theory, McCombs and Shaw (1972) predicted a causal relationship between the news media's coverage of the candidates (Richard Nixon and Hubert Humphrey) and subsequent voters' perceptions. In other words, McCombs and Shaw hypothesized that voter perceptions of Nixon and Humphrey and their campaign election issues would form *after* and *based on* the content of campaign coverage presented within various media outlets.

To test their prediction, McCombs and Shaw (1972) derived two primary criteria for measuring the media's agenda: length and position of a news story. Newsprint and broadcast news media (such as TV or radio) contain limited space or time for reporting a given story. Furthermore, on TV and radio, time is money. Similarly, for newspapers and news magazines, space is money; like TV and radio, advertisers and subscribers support the publications to the extent that not every news story can possibly be reported in any one publication.

What McCombs and Shaw (1972) found, and what other researchers have continued to support through numerous studies of the subject, is a clear association between what the news media present to audiences and what the audiences perceive of the issues reported. Their study could only find a correlation, not ascertain causality, however (see Chapter 2 for a discussion of causation). Ten years after McCombs and Shaw's initial hypothesis, Iyengar, Peters, and Kinder (1982) supported the causal relationship through experimental research studies. In other words, these researchers found that what the news media present as important is then perceived by the public as important. This causal notion of agenda setting is further developed through the concept of framing.

"Framing" the News

McCombs and Shaw (1972) hypothesized that the news media's success in telling viewers and readers "what to think about" stems from the media **framing** issues. Much like an art gallery director's choice of which frame to place around a given painting, the media are believed to frame news events. Whereas the gallery director chooses a frame that highlights or deemphasizes certain features of the painting, perhaps nuances in color or angular shaping of objects, news media **gatekeepers**—the handful of news editors who set the agenda—also select, emphasize, elaborate, and even exclude news stories or parts of news stories to create a certain effect for the audience. As Griffin (2003) reported, "75% of stories that come across a news desk are never printed or broadcast" (p. 394). This is probably a good thing because it is estimated the average person can only follow three to five ongoing news stories at a time. However, when considering the large number of news stories, or parts of news stories, left on the editing room floor, it may give you pause to wonder what *has* been left out. Although it is difficult to know which stories or aspects of stories have been excluded, a savvy reader or viewer can take a critical examination of the news event presented. Table 11.1 provides an overview of framing through the processes of **selection**, **emphasis**, **elaboration**, and **exclusion**.

Table 11.1 Framing the News

Process	Example in Action
Selection: What stories are chosen?	• On September 22, 2010, Rutgers University Freshman Tyler Clementi committed suicide by jumping off the George Washington Bridge. Media coverage quickly linked his suicide to cyberbullying and dubbed his suicide a hate crime because Clementi was gay.
Emphasis: What focus is taken?	• "It became widely understood that a closeted student at Rutgers had committed suicide after video of him having sex with a man was secretly shot and posted online" (Parker, 2012). • "America anointed Dharun Ravi as America's Cyberbully No. 1" (Cuomo & Shearn, 2012).
Elaboration: What is added to "beef up" the story?	• Gay activists; politicians such as N.J. governor Chris Christie, President Barack Obama, and Secretary of State Hillary Clinton; and entertainers such as Ellen Degeneres and Nicki Minaj made public statements decrying homophobia. • The situation became a central component of the "It Gets Better" campaign, featuring video messages offering support for bullied or distressed gay teens. • "Clementi's death became an international news story, fusing parental anxieties about the hidden worlds of teen-age computing, teen-age sex, and teen-age unkindness" (Parker, 2012).
Exclusion: What aspects of the situation are not reported?	• Ravi and another new student, Molly Wei, used a webcam to secretly watch Clementi in an embrace with a young man—they did not see a sexual encounter, there was no video, and nothing was ever posted to the Internet (Parker, 2012). • According to Wei, "Ravi was concerned that his iPad might be stolen from the room because Mr. Clementi had asked him to leave for a few hours while he was alone with a man, whom Ms. Wei recalled Mr. Ravi describing as 'an older, shabbier-looking guy'" ("Times Topics," 2012). • Clementi was out as a gay man at the time of the incident. • Ravi apologized to Clementi, saying, "I've known you were gay and I have no problem with it. In fact one of my closest friends is gay and he and I have a very open relationship. . . . I don't want your freshman year to be ruined because of a petty misunderstanding, it's adding to my guilt. You have the right to move if you wish, but I don't want you to feel pressure to without fully understanding the situation" (Cuomo & Shearn, 2012).

We should note that although agenda setting focuses on the gatekeeping ability of the media, other people besides journalists, editors, and broadcasters can influence the media agenda. Public relations professionals, lobbyists, and even the president of the United States can influence what the media cover as news (Huckins, 1999; Peake, 2001). Accordingly, media professionals might, either consciously or unconsciously, frame news coverage, but it can also be deliberately manipulated by other parties.

Issues and Individuals Most Affected

Obviously, the news media do not affect every issue or every audience member, and those who are affected will not necessarily be affected in the same way. As McCombs and Bell (1974) argued, even despite the media's ability to influence, individuals' thoughts, opinions, and actions are not predetermined by the news media's agenda. Certain issues are more likely to influence audience thought, and certain individuals are more likely to be influenced by these issues. First, the media are particularly effective in creating public interest in political issues, such as stories about the candidates and their campaign strategies, and in chronic social issues, such as human rights violations, chronic disease, and teen violence. Topics unlikely to be affected by the media include consumer issues that deal with personal spending, taxes, and personal finance because individuals already have their own opinions of such private matters.

Similarly, individuals have differing needs for external advice or direction, also known as the **need for orientation**. This need for orientation depends both on a topic's relevance as well as on a person's uncertainty about the issue at hand. For example, child care issues are typically more relevant to viewers who are parents—and especially to those who have not yet made up their mind about how to handle child care. Viewers who are not parents or who have their minds made up about the topic are not likely to experience the agenda-setting effect.

Agenda-setting theory states that gatekeepers selectively determine an agenda for what's news. By selecting, excluding, emphasizing, and elaborating certain aspects of the news, public opinions are inevitably shaped and influenced. Thus, the news media influence their audiences to think about selected issues in a certain light.

CULTIVATION THEORY

Like agenda setting, cultivation theory also emphasizes media effects. Unlike agenda-setting theory, which has been used to study the framing of news within a variety of media, the origins-of-cultivation theory focuses almost exclusively on one medium: TV (Gerbner, 1998; Gerbner, Gross, Morgan, & Signorelli, 1980; Signorelli, Gerbner, & Morgan, 1995). Specifically, George Gerbner and colleagues have spent nearly 4 decades specifically examining the portrayal of violence on TV. These researchers argue the inescapable violent content of TV programming influences audiences' view of social reality. Specifically, cultivation theory predicts viewers who watch lots of TV will overestimate the occurrence of real-life violence, thereby perceiving the world as a "mean and scary" place. Before explaining cultivation theory's causal thesis in more detail, we explain several assumptions.

First, cultivation theory assumes TV has become central to American life and culture (Gerbner, 1998). Nearly 99% of Americans have at least one TV in their home and watch, on average, 7 hours of TV programming each day. Because of its ubiquity, Gerbner believes TV has become the principal source of stories and storytelling in the United States. Whereas neighbors and family members used to gather around the dinner table, sit on the front porch, or stand on the street corner sharing stories about what happened during the day or recounting the local gossip, individuals and families now watch endless hours of police procedurals, and watercooler gossip is centered around who got kicked off the reality show du jour. Thus, Gerbner maintains TV has usurped personal conversation, books, religion, and any other medium as the primary source for storytelling and that the stories being told are not "from anyone with anything relevant to tell. They come from a small group of distant conglomerates with something to sell" (Gerbner, 1998, p. 176).

Second, cultivation theory assumes TV influences audience perceptions of social reality, thereby shaping American culture in terms of how individuals reason and relate with others (Gerbner, 1998). In other words, through TV's selective and mass-produced depiction of current events, stories, dramas, comedies, and the like, only certain aspects of social life are presented. Gerbner does not suggest TV programming seeks to persuade audiences to think or act in a particular way; instead, he argues the repetitive representation of commercialized social life is what audiences come to expect and believe as more or less normative.

A final assumption is that TV's effects are limited (Gerbner, 1998), meaning TV is not the only factor—or necessarily the greatest factor—that affects an individual's view of social reality. Although this statement of "limited effects" sounds like backpedaling, Gerbner et al. (1980) argued that the consistency of TV's effect is more telling than its magnitude. In other words, the effects of TV may not be huge, but they are consistently present and do make a significant difference in the way people think, feel, and interact.

Starting With Violence

Although cultivation theory is now focused on issues other than violence, Gerbner and colleagues were originally interested in the extent to which TV fostered a "mean and scary world" thanks to the frequency of violent programming. First, Gerbner and colleagues (Gerbner et al., 1980; Signorelli et al., 1995) have defined violence as the "overt expression of physical force (with or without weapon, against self or others) compelling action against one's will on pain of being hurt and/or killed or threatened to be so victimized as part of the plot" (p. 280). This definition includes cartoon violence, comedic or humorous violence, and so-called accidental violence; the definition excludes more ambiguous messages such as verbal assaults, threats, and inconsequential gestures, such as sticking out one's tongue or giving someone the finger.

Using this definition of violence, Gerbner and his associates (Gerbner et al., 1980; Signorelli et al., 1995) then created the **violence index**, an objective research instrument that uses content analysis to measure the prevalence, frequency, and role of characters involved in TV violence (for an overview, see Chapter 2). Researchers have assessed violence annually and have studied more than 30 years of TV programming (Gerbner, 1998). Year after year, they have repeatedly found that the prevalence, frequency, and role of TV violence during daytime (8:00 a.m. to 2:00 p.m.) and primetime programming (8:00 p.m. to 11:00 p.m.)

differ little. In fact, more than half of primetime programs contain violent content, with about five violent acts per episode; children's programs are worse, averaging 20 violent acts per hour. Heroes and villains alike engage in equal amounts of violence.

Not only does research indicate TV shows are markedly violent, cultivation research also illustrates an imbalance with regard to who is victimized (Gerbner, 1998). Specifically, the victims of TV violence are disproportionately of minority backgrounds; African American, Latino, underprivileged, elderly, disabled, or female TV characters are more likely to be victims of violence than are White, middle-class male characters. Moreover, Gerbner's 30-plus years of research shows these same minority groups are vastly underrepresented during primetime. For example, U.S. census data (updated in 2013) indicate that 16.9% of the population is Latino; however, a study examining racial minorities in the media found Latinos represented only 5% of primetime TV characters (Monk-Turner, Heiserman, Johnson, Cotton, & Jackson, 2010). In other words, a **symbolic double jeopardy** exists in which minority persons are significantly less visible on TV than in real life, and these minority TV characters are much more likely to be portrayed as victims of violence. Not surprisingly, then, minority audience members worry the most about being victimized as a result of TV viewing.

What Effects? For Whom?

The media do not affect everyone; cultivation theory predicts individuals' social attitudes change as their TV viewing increases. In other words, the more TV you watch, the more likely you are to view the world in a way consistent with TV reality. Gerbner et al. (1980) separated heavy viewers, or "television types," from light viewers. Television types average 4 or more hours of TV viewing each day, whereas light viewers report watching 2 hours of TV or less each day. As predicted, television types erroneously believed their chances of being involved with violence were 1,000 times greater than crime statistics suggest; these viewers overestimated criminal and police activity and were more likely to agree with statements such as "most people will take advantage of you if they could" (Gerbner et al., 1980). Gerbner called this phenomenon the **mean-world syndrome**, whereby heavy viewers significantly overestimate real-life danger. Figure 11.1 depicts the differences between heavy and light TV viewers. Televised reality doesn't match actual reality, and heavy viewers are partially influenced by TV reality, whereas light viewers are not. Interestingly, research indicates light viewers select certain programs to watch and then turn the TV off, whereas heavy viewers tend to graze, watching whatever shows catch their attention (Gerbner, 1998).

How Else Is Reality Distorted?

In addition to a focus on violence, more recent research using cultivation theory has focused on differing perceptions of other social issues as a consequence of watching TV. For example, an increasing number of studies have focused on media images of women and how the media influence individuals' perceptions of "healthy" or normal body image. Nabi (2009) assessed the frequency of viewing physical makeover programs and found heavy viewers of such programs were more dissatisfied with their appearance and

Figure 11.1 Heavy Versus Light TV Viewers' Attitudes

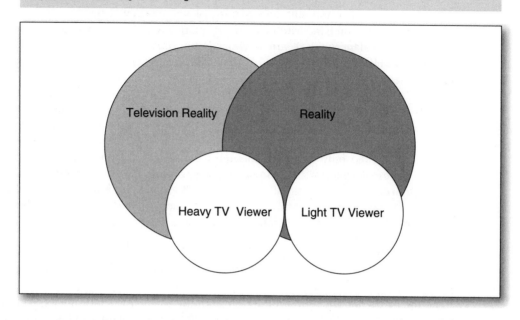

expressed greater likelihood of undergoing plastic surgery than light viewers of this type of programming. Others have looked at the relationship between media images and general beliefs about obesity and disordered eating (Gentles & Harrison, 2006; Hesse-Biber, Leavy, Quinn, & Zoino, 2006).

Moving beyond the effects of TV, still other researchers have looked successfully at other media forms for cultivation effects. To illustrate, Park (2008) found frequent exposure to print advertisements for drugs to treat depression was associated with a distorted sense of the likelihood an individual would develop clinical depression. Vergeer, Lubbers, and Scheepers (2000) found heavy newspaper viewing of ethnic crime was associated with a greater perceived threat by ethnic minorities. Still, other scholars have begun investigating whether cultivation can take place through movies, video games, and even virtual reality experiences.

How Does Cultivation Take Place and With What Effect?

Finally, cultivation theory research suggests viewers' attitudes are cultivated in two ways: mainstreaming and resonance (Gerbner, 1998). **Mainstreaming** implies viewers—heavy viewers in particular—develop a common view of social reality based on their frequent exposure to the repetitive and dominating images, stories, and messages depicted on TV. Thus, these television types are likely to perceive the world in ways that parallel TV's theatrical portrayal of life—as more corrupt, more crime ridden, more attractive, more sexualized, and so on.

Resonance is the second way cultivation is thought to occur (Gerbner, 1998). Resonance involves congruency between viewers' own violent experiences and those they see on TV. In other words, when individuals who have actually faced acts of violence in their own lives then watch violent TV programming, they are forced to replay their own life situations again and again. The TV violence reinforces, or resonates, with their personal experiences and only serves to amplify their suspicion of a mean and scary world while rejecting the vision of a life without such aggression. Similarly, if a person feels as though he or she has been victimized in other ways (being discriminated against because of sex, physical appearance, affectional preference, and so forth), viewing such actions on TV amplifies feelings that such behavior is the norm.

Cultivation theory assumes the power of TV is ubiquitous, with its primary message not reflecting reality in any consistent way. Moreover, TV programming negatively affects heavy viewers by creating a distorted attitude about people and the world.

SOCIAL COGNITIVE THEORY OF MASS COMMUNICATION

Bandura's (1977, 1986, 1994, 2001) social cognitive theory of mass communication, originally developed as an extension of social learning theory, has been widely used to study the media's influence on behavior, particularly to understand the relationship between media use and violent behavior. In contrast to cultivation theory's prediction that heavy television viewing distorts people's attitudes and perceptions of social reality, social cognitive theory posits that the media play a significant role in influencing behavior through observational learning. We discuss several assumptions of social cognitive theory next.

First, whereas social learning theory can apply quite broadly—from learning how to break up with a romantic partner to learning how to perform CPR—Bandura's development of social cognitive theory demonstrates specific concern with mass media's influence on cultural ideology. Like Gerbner, Bandura (2001) was particularly concerned with the mass media's ubiquity and social construction of reality, arguing that "heavy exposure to [television's] symbolic world may eventually make the televised images appear to be the authentic state of human affairs" (p. 282). In other words, the mass media, and TV in particular, are tremendously influential in shaping our view of what is "normal."

A second assumption of social cognitive theory is one's ability to self-reflect (Bandura, 2001). Stated differently, humans are not only actors but also self-examiners of their behavior. This metacognitive activity can be both rightful as well as faulty. You can have accurate self-reflections about the appropriateness of your behavior at the office holiday party, just as you can have wildly distorted ones. The quality of the self-reflection depends in part on the deductive reasoning process, information used in the assessment, and one's own biases.

Beyond the cultivating power of the mass media and humans' self-reflective abilities, Bandura's (1977) most central claim is that "most human behavior is learned observationally through modeling: from observing others one forms an idea of how new behaviors are performed, and on later occasions this coded information serves as a guide for action" (p. 22). In other words, you can learn plenty about relationships, social norms, and acceptable behavior simply by taking note of what others do (and of the consequences) in particular situations. Bandura also maintained that learning through vicarious, observational **modeling** saves individuals time and embarrassment from using a behavioral trial-and-error approach; "learning would be exceedingly laborious, not to mention hazardous, if people had to rely solely on the effects of their own actions to inform them what to do" (p. 22).

This notion of learning through vicarious observation contrasts with classical learning theory. According to classical learning, humans learn primarily through the trial and error of doing, by improving on their own actions, not through observational modeling. Intuitively, however, Bandura's (1977, 1986) idea of learning through observation makes sense. For example, even if you are not a parent right now, you probably have learned quite a bit about raising children from observation—from reflecting on your own parents' child-rearing methods, as well as by watching friends, siblings, and TV parents interact with their children. Thus, social cognitive theorists believe you can learn quite a bit by watching what others do (and don't do) and by noting others' reactions to your behaviors. You can then decide which behaviors to emulate and which to overlook.

Four Processes of Observational Learning

Certainly, not every child who watches *Looney Tunes* or *SpongeBob* lashes out and hits other kids over the head, just as not every adult who watches *Mad Men* or *Scandal* is having an affair with the boss. Other factors come into play. Guided by four processes or "subfunctions," social cognitive theory maintains observational learning is more than monkey see, monkey do (Bandura, 2001). Rather, modeling is based on attention, retention, reproduction, and motivational processes. Figure 11.2 provides an overview.

Figure 11.2   The Observational Learning Process

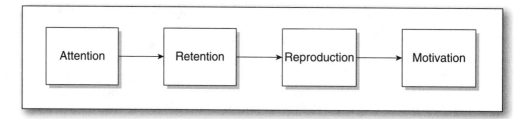

Attention Processes. Using social cognitive theory, you can't learn much if you don't actually observe and pay attention to a particular behavior. Thus, selective attention to a given situation is critical. Bandura (1977, 2001) noted an **attention process** is determined by both the observer's characteristics and the arrangement of intended behaviors. In other words, the observer needs to be attentive, and the actions in question need to be worthy of notice. Obviously, TV stations and other mass media outlets want to make money. To do so, they need audiences. Programmers, scriptwriters, advertisers, and even actors need viewers'

attention. Bright colors, rapid edits, the use of popular songs, dazzling special effects, violence, and sex are just a few of the ways the media seek to gain our attention.

Retention Processes. Learning through observational modeling is not inherently a negative process. In fact, learning by observing has many positive aspects. For example, you can learn how to cook by watching *30-Minute Meals* on the Food Network. Social cognitive theory posits humans can learn without actually engaging in a particular behavior if they can visually and verbally store the images to which they have attended (Bandura, 1977, 2001). In other words, the **retention process** allows you to learn from the observed behaviors.

That said, the modeling process is more complicated than simply watching and mirroring another's behavior. Instead, observational learning is a cognitive process wherein individuals observe, organize, remember, and mentally rehearse behavior (Bandura, 1977). "Observers who code modeled activities into either words, concise labels, or vivid imagery learn and retain behavior better than those who simply observe or are mentally preoccupied with other matters while watching" (p. 26).

Behavioral Reproduction Processes. It only makes sense that to engage in a modeled behavior, one must have the motor skills necessary to reproduce the activity in question. You might attend to and remember how to tie a chicken before roasting, but if you do not have the strength, coordination, or motor skills necessary, you will not be able to replicate the behavior with much success. As Bandura (1977) noted, in the **reproduction process**, individuals can typically execute a fairly accurate demonstration of a new behavior through modeling; they then refine the action through self-corrective adjustments based on feedback and focused demonstrations of behavioral segments only learned in part. Additionally, social cognitive theory maintains that "modeling is not merely a process of behavioral mimicry, as commonly misconstrued. . . . Subskills must be improvised to suit varying circumstances" (Bandura, 2001, p. 275). Think about learning how to parallel park. You might have practiced successfully in an empty parking lot, using orange cones, rather than automobiles, as markers. Now think about parallel parking between real cars in a congested downtown area during rush hour or on a decline with a crying baby in the backseat. The essential principles of parking and mechanics of the behavior are virtually the same; however, the conditions in which the behavior occurs can influence your ability to complete the task. Thus, you must assess and adjust the behavior based on the circumstance.

Motivational Processes. The last piece of observational learning related to social cognitive theory is motivation (Bandura, 1977, 2001). To go from observation to action requires the ability to replicate the behavior as well as the desire, or motivation, to use the learned action. The **motivation process** is inspired by three types of incentives: direct, vicarious, and self-produced (Bandura, 2001). **Direct motivation** is more likely when you perceive you will be rewarded as a consequence of modeling an observed behavior. If, however, you perceive you will be punished as a result, your motivation to use the behavior diminishes. **Vicarious motivation** occurs when individuals "are motivated by the successes of others who are similar to themselves" (p. 274). Conversely, people are typically deterred when they see negative consequences for their peers. Finally, with **self-produced motivation** individuals rely on their own personal standards, engaging in observed activities they find personally worthwhile and refusing to participate in those activities of which they disapprove.

Dual Paths of Influence

Thus far, we've focused on what Bandura (2001) terms a **direct path of influence**. That is, the media influence viewers directly, from creating attention-getting messages, to enabling behavior, to providing incentives to replicate actions so the viewer changes her or his behavior. A second route, the **socially mediated path of influence**, can also link mass media to behavior—through social networks. In the socially mediated path, "media influences are used to link participants to social networks and community settings" (p. 285). Through these social connections, individuals receive guidance, incentives, and social support, making behavioral change more likely. For example, religiously watching *The Biggest Loser* may not provide enough motivation for you to keep up with your low-fat diet and fitness routine. However, *The Biggest Loser* also has an at-home program, offered through the show's website. Here, participants can connect with a community of people with similar goals, get fitness advice from experts, and receive social support from previous contestants, ultimately providing the motivation necessary to keep up with the program. In this case, the media's influence is facilitated by participation in a related social network.

Modeling and Media Violence

As a theoretical construct, observational learning represents an impartial process; it is not inherently negative or positive. As Bandura (1977) argued, observational learning is simply a primary means by which humans learn. When applied within the realm of mass communication, however, research shows such modeled learning can be hazardous, particularly for viewers of media violence (Bandura, 1986). Television is one mass medium in which violent action is both common and frequently rewarded. After all, Superman doesn't save Metropolis from Lex Luther by holding a sit-in.

Remember that for observational learning to occur, the first step is to gain attention. Violent content can be easily found in both entertainment programs and on TV newscasts. In both cases, Bandura (1986) argued violent acts grab viewers' attention. Aggressive behaviors such as kicking, punching, stabbing, shooting, and biting are also easy to remember and reproduce, the second and third steps in the modeling process. Finally, positive motivation is easily introduced when fictitious characters as well as real-life heroes are rewarded (or not punished) for their aggression.

According to social cognitive theory, if viewers know how to do something, they are more likely to do it, particularly when they have positive incentives, such as getting 15 minutes of fame or getting peers' attention and respect. However, the relationship between observation and motivation is a critical determinant in the modeling process. It is not simply the observation of violence that leads one to engage in violent behavior; it is the positive reward associated with aggressive action that entices one to model observed behaviors (Bandura, 1977, 1986; Bandura, Ross, & Ross, 1963; Huesmann, Moise-Titus, Podolski, & Eron, 2003). If violent behavior is denounced, viewers are less likely to copy the aggression. Note it is not enough that "bad guys" are punished on television; many of the "good guys" are rewarded for using violence to triumph over the bad guy. Indeed, as Bandura (1986) argued, "Given that aggressive life styles are portrayed as prevalent, socially acceptable, and highly functional, it is not surprising that viewing violence is conducive to aggressive conduct" (p. 292).

Social cognitive theory predicts the mass media have significant influence because humans learn observationally through a four-step process: attention, retention, motor reproduction, and motivation. For communication scholars, media producers, parents, and viewers, social cognitive theory adds a new level of complexity to TV and media. That is, if individuals are exposed to media aggression that is easily replicable and socially rewarding, viewers, particularly young audience members, are more likely to turn to such violence themselves.

ENCODING/DECODING THEORY

At the same time American scholars were focusing on the extent to which the mass media affect their audience, scholars in other parts of the world were investigating the same issue but with a different focus. You may remember that in Chapter 2 we described the social scientific and humanistic approaches to understanding communication. We also mentioned a third perspective called a critical approach. Theories that take a critical perspective seek to uncover the extent to which communication processes create and reflect differences in power (Craig, 1999). The goal of such theories is to raise awareness of inequities. One critical approach that addresses media effects was created by British sociologist Stuart Hall. Most commonly called encoding/decoding theory, it is also called cultural studies, preferred reading theory, and reception theory.

Assumptions of Encoding/Decoding Theory

Four assumptions set the foundation for understanding encoding/decoding theory (Hall, 1973). First, Hall calls the focus of his work **cultural studies** rather than media studies because he believes the media are simply one mechanism for the development and dissemination of cultural ideologies. An **ideology** is a mental framework used to understand the world; it includes language, concepts, categories, and images we use to make sense out of our experiences (Hall, 1986). Typically, ideologies work at a low level of consciousness. Because we live in a particular culture, we tend not to notice cultural ideologies . . . it is akin to asking a fish to describe water. For fish, water just is. The same is true of ideologies; they are taken-for-granted truisms. Hall believes the media tend to produce messages that support the **dominant ideology**, meaning a view of the world that supports the status quo. For example, an essential U.S. ideology is the power of the individual. Americans believe a single person can make a difference in the world. Now consider successful U.S. films. Whether you consider a political drama like *Zero Dark Thirty*, an historical drama like *Lincoln*, or an action-adventure blockbuster like *The Dark Knight Rises*, Hollywood reasserts the ideology of the individual.

It's individuals, and individuals alone, who matter. In *Zero Dark Thirty*, an isolated, single-minded CIA agent—a loner that no one believes in—is the chief reason the butcher of 9/11 is lost to time at the bottom of the sea. In *Lincoln*, it's only through the singular grace, wisdom, and humanity of the 16th president that the greatest evil in American history, an evil few but he sees with true clarity, is finally put to rest. And in *The Dark Knight Rises*, Gotham is saved by the orphan Bruce Wayne as the pariah Batman. These people do great things. And they do them alone. (Isquith, 2013)

Hall argues mass media messages are a cultural production because they provide a means to create, challenge, reproduce, or change cultural ideologies. According to Hall (1986), the process whereby our cultural ideologies are reinforced is called **articulation**.

The second assumption of encoding/decoding theory is that the meaning of a message is not fixed or determined entirely by the sender (Hall, 1973). In the process of **encoding** or creating a message, the sender typically develops a message using the signs and symbols of a cultural ideology. However, Hall suggests the interpretation, or **decoding**, of the message is not guaranteed. Consider the song "Accidental Racist" performed by Brad Paisley and L. L. Cool J. Paisley intended the song to be an honest dialogue about race (Danton, 2013). However, the song was very controversial, with hoards of listeners claiming it was racist.

Third, encoding/decoding theory assumes all messages are encoded using an ideology (Hall, 1973). That is, there is no such thing as "value-free" communication. Although we might not immediately perceive the meaning system embedded into a television show, song, or movie, Hall assures us that "every language—every symbol—coincides with an ideology" (Becker, 1984, p. 72). Because we are not likely to see the presence of ideologies we endorse, however, we do not often recognize the power built into the messages.

Finally, encoding/decoding theory is grounded in the belief in an active audience. Hall believes audience members can challenge the ideologies embedded in the messages they receive (Hall, 1973). Despite the level of optimism inherent in this belief, Hall does not believe recognizing and wrangling over ideology is easy. After all, it is much easier to become an unthinking recipient of media content than it is to critically confront who benefits and who loses from particular beliefs. Because he comes from a critical tradition, however, he encourages people to do so.

"Reading" a Message

In order to encourage a critical analysis of what we encounter in the media, the central idea of encoding/decoding theory is that even though the media present us with messages that support the dominant ideology, media consumers do not have to interpret the messages in this way (Hall, 1973). Hall describes three ways to interpret—or *read*—a message. To illustrate these ways of interpreting the message, we refer to a news story with which you may be familiar. In 2007 British exchange student Meredith Kercher was murdered in Perugia, Italy. Her American roommate Amanda Knox was arrested, tried, and convicted of her murder. In 2011 the conviction against Knox was overturned, and she was allowed to return home to the United States. More recently, in March 2013 the Italian Supreme Court overturned the acquittal and ordered the case to be retried. Your view of Amanda Knox's guilt or innocence likely depends on the news coverage you viewed and the extent to which you were a critical consumer of the news. Keeping this in mind, let's return to a consideration of the ways to interpret a message.

Encoding/decoding theory says the first way an audience can interpret a message is by engaging in a **preferred reading** (Hall, 1973). In this case, the receiver of the message uses the

dominant code (i.e., the dominant ideology) to interpret the content of the message. That is, the receiver understands and accepts the values and beliefs embedded in the message; this type of reading is considered easy and natural. Returning to the coverage of the Amanda Knox murder case, American news coverage of the story was highly critical of the Italian legal system, endorsing the dominant ideology of the superiority of the United States and its justice system (Annunziato, 2011). In fact, some of the coverage went so far as to suggest that "the Italian judicial system has not 'adapted correctly' the American judicial system" (Annunziato, 2011, p. 74). Accordingly, a dominant-code reading of the news coverage would suggest Amanda Knox was a victim of a corrupt and backward Italian legal system.

In contrast, some receivers use the **negotiated code**. When using the negotiated code, the receiver accepts the dominant ideology in general but engages in some selective interpretation in order to better fit his or her view of the world (Hall, 1973). "Essentially, the receiver only accepts the preferred meanings that he/she wants to accept, while 'misunderstanding' the meanings incompatible with his/her lifestyle" (Platt, 2004, p. 4). In the Amanda Knox murder case, a negotiated reading might be that Amanda Knox was innocent of the murder, but the fact that the trial occurred in Italy played no role in what happened; after all, innocent victims are accused of crimes all around the world. In this case, the interpretation would gloss over the anti-Italian slant that appeared in so many news stories.

Finally, receivers might use the **oppositional code**, in which the receiver recognizes the ideological bias in the message (Hall, 1973). Individuals who use the oppositional code identify the preferred reading, but they deconstruct the message and reconstruct it from a different point of view. Consider a possible oppositional reading of the Amanda Knox case. One interpretation of the Amanda Knox case might be that Knox very cleverly played on stereotypes of Italian corruption (think *The Godfather* or *The Sopranos*) and beliefs that Italians are not very bright (for example, Joey from *Friends* or anyone from *Jersey Shore*) and are obsessed with sex (just look at Silvio Berlusconi) in order to win her freedom, and flag-waving Americans blindly accepted these stereotypes, viewing Knox as a victim.

Decoding Is the Central Process

Although Hall's theory is called encoding/decoding theory, the main thrust of the theory focuses on the decoding process. According to Hall, it is only when mediated messages are decoded that they have any meaning and we can consider possible media effects (Hall, 1973). Hall argues most theories of mass communication ignore the decoding process because decoding tends to happen at a very low level of consciousness. He also points out that a full understanding of decoding is difficult because most people tend to confuse denotative and connotative meaning. **Denotative** meaning refers to a literal meaning; you might think about it as a dictionary definition. **Connotative** meaning refers to all associated meanings. As an example, think about the meaning of the word *terrorist*. As Procter (2004) points out, most people might believe they are interpreting the term in a purely objective way, but it is virtually impossible to separate the meaning of a concept from feelings about the concept, previous experiences associated with it, and value judgments about it. As such, it is the connotative meanings that make up an ideology. According to Hall, media effects are insidious not necessarily because the media encode messages supportive of the status quo but because audience members who use the dominant code to read the messages over and over again eventually come to believe the dominant ideology is "not simply plausible and universal, but common-sense" (Procter, 2004, p. 67). To assist you with being able to read a media message from multiple points of view, select any text (e.g., a newscast, a magazine advertisement, a sitcom) and try to accomplish the tasks associated with each of the three codes in Figure 11.3.

Figure 11.3 Questions to Answer Using Each of the Codes

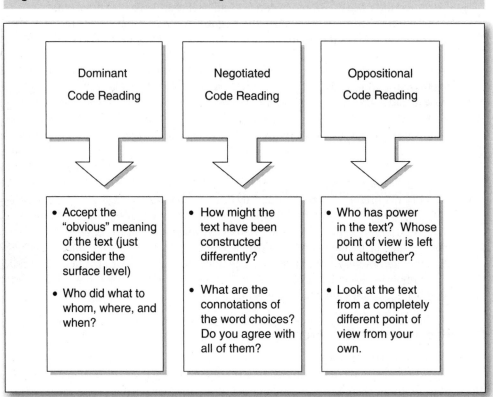

Dominant Code Reading	Negotiated Code Reading	Oppositional Code Reading
• Accept the "obvious" meaning of the text (just consider the surface level) • Who did what to whom, where, and when?	• How might the text have been constructed differently? • What are the connotations of the word choices? Do you agree with all of them?	• Who has power in the text? Whose point of view is left out altogether? • Look at the text from a completely different point of view from your own.

Oppositional Does Not Mean Against

Before concluding our section on encoding/decoding theory, it is important to be clear that the term *oppositional* does not necessarily imply someone is against dominant values or beliefs; it simply means the individual doing an oppositional reading of a message understands the dominant ideology but chooses to interpret the message differently. When messages are reinterpreted in ways not intended by the source, new ideologies are formed and can take root (Pillai, 1992). Similarly, Hall is not concerned with a personal or isolated oppositional reading; he is concerned with the use of an oppositional code among social groups, with a particular focus on minority groups, as a means for increasing power

(Procter, 2004). The use of an oppositional code is likely to be viewed as deviant by those who endorse a dominant ideology, but Hall endorses as a critical approach any cultural resistance that might result in political empowerment.

Summary and Research Applications

In this chapter, we discussed four theories of mass media—specifically, theories about how to understand the power and influence of the mass media. First, agenda-setting theory states that the news media do not tell us what to think, but they do tell us what to think about. Agenda-setting theory continues to be studied within the context of political communication, particularly as interactive media evolve. In a study comparing the agenda-setting effects of traditional, political news media and independent political blogs, Meraz (2011) found that diverse blog networks were able to set traditional news media's online agenda but that the reverse was not true. Agenda-setting research also extends its reach into health communication. To illustrate, researchers found a significant relationship between women who reported viewing TV programs that stressed the importance of routine breast exams and actually obtaining a clinical breast examination (Jones, Denham, & Springston, 2006). Our second mass media theory, the cultivation approach, suggests the social perceptions of individuals who watch large quantities of TV are skewed toward the reality presented on TV. In a study examining the relationship between TV viewing and attitudes about sexual violence toward women, researchers discovered daily television viewers were significantly more likely to accept rape myths—that is, the victim was promiscuous, she "asked for it" by wearing sexy clothing, or that women fabricate the crime after regretting their own misbehavior (Kahlor & Eastin, 2011). Heavy viewers were also more likely to believe rape accusations were false. For example, "one in four respondents indicated that 30% or more of rape accusations are false; only one in eight respondents accurately estimated the number of false accusations to be 5%" (p. 222). Just as agenda-setting theory extends beyond political news, cultivation theory extends beyond media violence. Cultivation research has found that heavy viewers are more materialistic and have less interest in protecting the environment (Good, 2007). Likewise, heavy viewers of credible medical dramas perceived real-life physicians to be more courageous and reported greater satisfaction with their own physicians than light viewers (Quick, 2009).

Discussed third, social cognitive theory is based on learning theory, specifically the idea that when individuals are cognitively aware, motivated, and physically able, they will model their behavior after esteemed others, including people or characters shown in the media. The theory has clear applications to professionals in health communication. Research examining media influences on college women's binge drinking found women who perceive "girls gone wild" images as positive examples of outrageous behavior are significantly more likely to engage in risky, sensation-seeking behavior themselves (Mishra, 2010). Mishra concluded intervention programs could more effectively emphasize the negative consequences of such behavior, thereby reducing women's motivation to conduct themselves in a sensational manner. Similarly, Martins and Wilson (2012) found girls who view social aggression on TV, such as verbally harassing or spreading gossip about a peer, are more likely to engage in these aggressive behaviors themselves.

Finally, Hall's encoding/decoding theory is also concerned with the power and influence of the media, contending the media develop, propagate, and reinforce cultural ideologies. In doing so, audience members who use the dominant code to interpret messages assume this dominant ideology is the "right" or "normal" way of viewing the world, when in fact, other interpretations exist. Perks' (2012) study of satiric and ironic comedy that implicitly pokes fun at racial differences can actually challenge the dominant ideology of racial stereotypes. She contends such critical examinations of ironic comedy can be used to promote media literacy because viewers can learn there are people who critically challenge these ideas. In a similar vein of oppositional interpretation, Espiritu (2011) studied the influx of Korean and Asian television dramas in the Philippines and their perceived effects among young Filipino women. She found the introduction of the Korean dramas challenged the dominant ideology of "American cultural imperialism." Specifically, the young women engaged in negotiated and oppositional readings of the dominant, capitalistic, patriarchal ideology (largely imported from U.S. media) while decoding the Asian dramas in reflexive ways. In other words, Filipino women became more critical of the dominant, American-imposed ideology and identified more with the Korean themes of poverty and class inequality. Espiritu argued "American cultural imperialism was undermined and subverted to some extent" (p. 368) while the viewers could better relate to the family values articulated in the Asian dramas.

Key Terms

Agenda   196
Articulation   208
Attention process   204
Connotative   209
Cultural studies   207
Decoding   208
Denotative   209
Direct motivation   205
Direct path of influence   206
Dominant code   209
Dominant ideology   207
Elaboration   198
Emphasis   198
Encoding   208
Exclusion   198
Framing   197
Gatekeepers   197
Ideology   207
Mainstreaming   202

Mass communication   194
Mass media   195
Mean-world syndrome   201
Modeling   204
Motivational process   205
Need for orientation   199
Negotiated code   209
Oppositional code   209
Preferred reading   208
Reproduction process   205
Resonance   203
Retention process   205
Selection   198
Self-produced motivation   205
Socially mediated path of influence   206
Symbolic double jeopardy   201
Vicarious motivation   205
Violence index   200

Case Study 11: Twerking for Attention

Chestnutville High School students Ginger Lane and Larissa Rogers were nobodies. They weren't part of the in-group, and they weren't in the out-group—they were neither popular nor losers. They were about to graduate from high school, and they were convinced no one would even remember they had attended the school.

They decided they wanted to be remembered. They were aware of all the high school shootings by losers who wanted to make a mark, but they didn't want to be remembered for doing something awful . . . they just sort of wanted to be noticed. They wanted people to know their names. They thought the prom might be the perfect location for getting noticed, but they weren't really sure of what to do.

The administration at Chestnutville has set very strict rules for what girls could and could not wear to the prom—no bare midriffs, no strapless dresses, and no form-fitting dresses. Ginger and Larissa knew they wouldn't be permitted into the gym with any dress that violated those standards, and they figured even if they violated the rules, no one would really care; it certainly wouldn't increase their cool factor.

For a while they considered trying to photobomb the prom court, but then they realized all of the celebrity photobombing episodes they had seen were funny because it was a celebrity doing the prank—random "strangers" would just be perceived as some dork ruining a prom photo.

Sitting around bored one day, they started watching YouTube videos and realized just how many of them featured teenagers twerking. Twerking, a dance move that involves shaking your hips and behind in a bouncing and jiggling motion, caught their attention. They were both good dancers—maybe they could get noticed for their moves on the dance floor? They even found a whole website called youtwerk.com. They started watching all the videos they could, teaching themselves the fine art of twerking.

Just one week before their prom, the local news highlighted a scandal at a rival high school. A group of students had made a video featuring about 30 students twerking. The news coverage reported that the students were suspended for lewd conduct and sexual harassment because the video had been made on school property using video cameras the school owned. The school principal was featured on every broadcast, denouncing the girls who appeared in the video as sexually promiscuous and highlighting the race of the boy who had edited the video.

At first, Ginger and Larissa backed off their plan to twerk at the prom. But then they realized they definitely would get noticed—and people might think they were cool—if they followed through. The scandal a few towns over actually made their idea even better!

Questions for Consideration

1. How did the news media "frame" the twerking incident at the neighboring high school? How would agenda-setting theory explain the fact that, despite the negative news story, Ginger and Larissa continue with their own twerking plan?

2. Based on what you know about Ginger and Larissa, how have the teen's attitudes been cultivated by repeated media exposure? How might mainstreaming and resonance play a part in Ginger and Larissa's cultivation?

3. Apply social cognitive theory's assumptions and observational learning process to the case study. Even after the rival school's scandal, how does the theory explain the fact that Ginger and Larissa still have sufficient motivation to complete their scheme?

4. What is the dominant code presented in the newscast about the twerking scandal? Do Ginger and Larissa rely on the preferred reading, negotiated code, or oppositional code when interpreting the newscast? Why do you think this is the case?

5. Do any of the mass media theories provide "better" explanations than the others? Why do you believe this to be the case? What situations might surface that would make a different theory or combination of theories better at explaining the situation?

CHAPTER 12

What Should a Communicator Do?

LEARNING OBJECTIVES

After reading this chapter, you will be able to...

1. Explain the influences and effects consistently associated with the theories studied.

2. Describe commonalities across the theories studied.

3. Explain how the theories studied can assist in enhancing professional communication skill.

4. Articulate how understanding communication theory can aid in one's own communication competence.

5. Apply individual theories to professional contexts.

In Chapter 1, we asserted that the most competent communicators understand the underlying principles of communication. We proposed that scholarly theory provides a means to obtain that understanding. We proceeded to inundate you with 36 distinct theories, each of which introduced several new concepts, and each of which illuminated a somewhat different aspect of the communication process. Chapter 12 helps you make sense of it all. In the following pages, we identify influences and effects consistently identified in research using the theories. In the end, we genuinely believe application of the individual theories, as well as a synthesis of commonalities across the theories, can assist professionals in enhancing their communication skill.

Before drawing any conclusions, recall that competent communication means being both effective, which means achieving your goals, and appropriate, which means following social expectations for communication (Spitzberg & Cupach, 1989). Research indicates communication competence has profound effects on professional success. It is not surprising that the more communicatively competent a manager is, the more satisfied employees are with that manager (Berman & Hellweg, 1989). More interesting is that strong relationships exist between a supervisor's communication competence and employee job satisfaction (Madlock, 2008) and organizational identification (Myers & Kassing, 1998). In fact, communication competence is a better predictor of job satisfaction than is leadership style (Madlock, 2008). As Madlock concluded, developing professionals' levels of communication competence might be the best way to increase employee satisfaction and performance while reducing absenteeism and turnover.

The theories discussed in this book provide clues about achieving communication competence in the professional setting. In this chapter, we highlight some conclusions we can come to about communication and the influences on communication drawn from intrapersonal/cognitive and individual/social approaches; interpersonal, intercultural, group, organizational, persuasion, and mediated communication; and mass communication theory. We encourage you to pay attention to what the theories say about being both effective and appropriate in your professional communications.

CONCLUSIONS ABOUT COMMUNICATION

As abstractions, theories don't often provide specific templates with stock phrases for those individuals seeking communication advice. They are not topographical maps that can be followed mindlessly from point A to point B. Instead, theories tend to provide general sorts of directions, relying on practitioners to fill in the details. As an analogy, think of a theory as a compass, not as a GPS. Unlike a GPS, a theory will not tell you to follow Bethlehem Pike for four lights, make a left on Dager Road at the BMW dealership, and then take the first left onto Houston Road. Rather, a theory will tell you that you should be traveling north; it is up to the driver to use his or her own creativity in figuring out the best way to go north. Nevertheless, in reviewing Chapters 3 through 11, you will note the theories seem to converge on two general decision points that commonly face communicators: whether communication should be direct or indirect (or some point in between) and whether the communication should be similar to or different from previous communication.

The first decision point is whether communicators ought to assert directly what they are thinking or what they need. Certainly, being direct is likely to be an effective choice because there is less room for misunderstanding (e.g., going "bald on record"). The communication theories discussed in this book suggest, however, numerous influences on whether a direct strategy is also appropriate.

First, as should be clear after reading Chapter 6, different cultures hold different values about clarity and openness. This is true not only for international cultures but also for people in Generation X and those in the Millennial generation, who tend to use (and need) more direct communication (see Chapter 4). Accordingly, to maximize communication competence, you should recognize and adapt to cultural preferences for directness. Second, there are situational influences on the appropriateness of directness. Politeness theory (PT), for example, suggests those in power are more likely to be direct, and those with less power tend to use more indirect strategies. There is also a time and place for directness; expectancy violations theory (EVT) suggests context plays a role in our expectations for communication. Thus, you might expect a co-worker to give a direct answer to a straight-forward question during decision making (e.g., "Did the plant finish production last night?"). You might not expect a direct answer during labor negotiations (e.g., "What is the smallest increase you would accept?").

Finally, there are individual preferences for being direct. Recall our discussion of message design logics (MDLs) in Chapter 4. Individuals using an expressive MDL will value direct communication, whereas those with a conventional MDL will hold stricter expectations for being appropriate. To be a competent communicator you need to consider not only whether you think being direct might be appropriate behavior but also what the culture would expect, what the situation demands, and what your conversational partner might prefer.

The second decision point that emerges from reviewing the theories presented in this book is whether a person should communicate in a similar fashion to previous messages or whether she or he ought to behave differently. This question is at the core of numerous theories. Systems theory makes the general point that patterns of communication can be symmetrical (the same) or complementary (different). EVT projects whether a person will reciprocate or compensate based on the reward valence of the communicator and the valence of the violation. Uncertainty reduction theory (URT) predicts people are more likely to reciprocate during times of high uncertainty. And communication accommodation theory (CAT) suggests converging (behaving more like the other person) can lead to attraction, whereas diverging (behaving in a different fashion) can be a means of asserting power.

Certainly, these factors play a role in whether you choose to behave in a similar or different fashion. What if the issue isn't how you are going to act, however, but getting someone else to act in a particular manner? Beyond the specific advice offered by the theories described here, a wealth of research suggests a strong reciprocity effect (see Burgraff & Sillars, 1987; Sillars, 1980). This means that, over time, people tend to mirror each other's behavior. Therefore, if you want someone to behave in a certain way, you should behave in the fashion you want the other person to behave. Eventually, the other person is likely to reciprocate.

CONCLUSIONS ABOUT INFLUENCES AND EFFECTS

In addition to specific questions that emerge about communication, a review of the theories presented in this book suggests many variables influence communication to numerous effects. Notably, the same variable can be both an influence and an effect. Consider your own values or beliefs. These values can influence how you choose to communicate; being a feminist, for example, might cause you to use gender-neutral language. At the same time, communication can inspire you to change your values or beliefs; someone might persuade you that using the generic *he* is exclusionary, thereby changing your beliefs about the power of language.

Throughout this book, 14 variables emerge as consistent explanations of areas that influence or are affected by the communication process. Table 12.1 provides an overview, but we briefly explain each concept and its importance, providing advice along the way.

Cohesion, Connection, and In-Groups

The degree to which individuals are connected with others is a function of the communication experienced by those individuals. For example, symbolic convergence theory (SCT) suggests particular communication practices, called fantasy chaining, create group cohesion. Organizational assimilation theory (OAT) suggests communication practices socialize employees into becoming members of an in-group. Conversely, many theories focus on the reverse process, suggesting one's connection to an in-group will influence that individual's communication. Uncertainty reduction theory (URT), for instance, suggests shared social networks decrease uncertainty, thereby decreasing uncertainty-reducing messages. Leader–member exchange (LMX) suggests one's in-group status with a manager might increase supportive communication from that manager. And anxiety/uncertainty management theory (AUM) suggests that when in-group members perceive they have power, anxiety about communicating with cultural strangers lessens.

On the other hand, AUM also predicts too much reliance on in-group membership might actually reduce one's mindfulness, such that in-group members rely on stereotypes rather than thinking critically when communicating with cultural strangers. Similarly, organizational identification and control theory (OIC) suggests cohesion can function as a means of controlling employees. Connection is achieved through communication, but once achieved it can have both positive and negative results.

The practical implication of this recognition is an appreciation for when team-building activities are appropriate and when they are not. For example, some amount of team building is often important at the initial stages of group interaction. Team building might be avoided, however, if the group is facing a high-stress decision; such efforts might only lead to groupthink. Moreover, too much cohesion might exacerbate tensions between two groups in a workplace.

Table 12.1   Concepts Appearing in Multiple Theories

Influence or Effect	Theories Identifying the Influence or Effect	
Cohesion, connection, and in-groups	AUM (Chap. 6)	LMX (Chap. 6)
	CAT (Chap. 6)	Networks (Chap. 10)
	Cultural dimensions (Chap. 6)	OAT (Chap. 9)
	Dialectics (Chap. 5)	OIC (Chap. 9)
	DOI (Chap. 10)	SCT (Chap. 8)
	Groupthink (Chap. 8)	URT (Chap. 3)
Context	AST (Chap. 8)	EVT (Chap. 3)
	Attribution theory (Chap. 3)	Groupthink (Chap. 8)
	AUM (Chap. 6)	Organizing theory (Chap. 9)
	CPM (Chap. 5)	

Influence or Effect	Theories Identifying the Influence or Effect	
Expectations	Attribution theory (Chap. 3)	SET (Chap. 5)
	Cultural dimensions (Chap. 6)	SRT (Chap. 4)
	EVT (Chap. 3)	URT (Chap. 3)
Face and self versus other orientation	AUM (Chap. 6)	Interactional perspective (Chap. 4)
	CPM (Chap. 5)	PT (Chap. 5)
	FNT (Chap. 6)	TL (Chap. 4)
Individual qualities	AUM (Chap. 6)	EI (Chap. 4)
	Attribution theory (Chap. 2)	EVT (Chap. 3)
	CPM (Chap. 4)	Narrative paradigm (Chap. 7)
	DOI (Chap. 10)	
Interest and involvement	AUM (Chap. 6)	DOI (Chap. 10)
	AST (Chap. 9)	ELM (Chap. 7)
	Cognitive dissonance (Chap. 3)	Social cognitive theory (Chap. 11)
Needs	AUM (Chap. 6)	PT (Chap. 5)
	DOI (Chap. 10)	SCT (Chap. 8)
	FGDM (Chap. 8)	UGT (Chap. 10)
Power and control	AST (Chap. 8)	Networks (Chap. 10)
	CAT (Chap. 6)	OIC (Chap. 9)
	Cultural dimensions (Chap. 6)	PT (Chap. 5)
	Encoding/decoding (Chap. 11)	TPB (Chap. 7)
	Interactional perspective (Chap. 4)	
Relationships	AST (Chap. 8)	Interactional perspective (Chap. 4)
	DOI (Chap. 10)	Networks (Chap. 10)
	EVT (Chap. 3)	
Rewards	CPM (Chap. 5)	Social cognitive theory (Chap. 11)
	EVT (Chap. 3)	TL (Chap. 4)
	SET (Chap. 5)	URT (Chap. 3)
Rules	AST (Chap. 8)	Interactional perspective (Chap. 4)
	CAT (Chap. 6)	MDL (Chap. 4)
	CPM (Chap. 5)	OIC (Chap. 9)
	Dialectics (Chap. 5)	Organizing theory (Chap. 9)

(Continued)

(Continued)

Influence or Effect	Theories Identifying the Influence or Effect	
Social networks	Dialectics (Chap. 5) DOI (Chap. 10) LMX (Chap. 6)	Networks (Chap. 10) OIC (Chap. 9) Social cognitive theory (Chap. 11)
Uncertainty and ambiguity	Agenda-setting theory (Chap. 11) AUM (Chap. 6) Cultural dimensions (Chap. 6) Dialectics (Chap. 5)	Media richness theory (Chap. 10) OAT (Chap. 9) URT (Chap. 3)
Values and beliefs	AUM (Chap. 6) Cognitive dissonance (Chap. 3) Cultivation theory (Chap. 11) Cultural dimensions (Chap. 6) DOI (Chap. 10) Encoding/decoding (Chap. 11)	Interactional perspective (Chap. 4) MDL (Chap. 4) Narrative paradigm (Chap. 7) OIC (Chap. 9) Organizational culture (Chap. 9) TL (Chap. 4) TPB (Chap. 7)

Note: AST = adaptive structuration theory; AUM = anxiety/uncertainty management theory; CAT = communication accommodation theory; CPM = communication privacy management theory; DOI = diffusion of innovations; EI = emotional intelligence; ELM = elaboration likelihood model; EVT = expectancy violations theory; FGDM = functional group decision making; FNT = face negotiation theory; LMX = leader–member exchange; MDL = message design logics; NP = narrative paradigm; OAT = organizational assimilation theory; OIC = organizational identification and control theory; PT = politeness theory; SCT = symbolic convergence theory; SET = social exchange theory; SRT = social role theory; TL = transformational leadership; TPB = theory of planned behavior; UGT = uses and gratifications theory; URT = uncertainty reduction theory.

Context

Several theories identified contextual influences on communication. Expectancy violations theory (EVT), for example, states that context influences your expectations for how interactions will occur. Organizing theory proposes that the central challenge facing organizations is making sense of an equivocal information environment. Groupthink talks about the role of the situational context in the likelihood of making a poor decision. The context, then, can influence not only the nature of our communication but also our expectations for and understanding of communication. Accordingly, professionals should stop and think about the context in which communication occurs because the same message might be understood very differently in another context. For example, consider how often individuals argue that media stories present them in a negative light because their quotes were taken "out of context."

Expectations

A few theories make special note of individuals' expectations, suggesting these expectations play a role in your evaluation of communication events. To illustrate, both Hofstede's theory of cultural dimensions and social role theory suggest one's biological sex is associated with expectations for appropriate behavior. Attribution theory indicates our expectations for others influence our attributions—say, for example, when a man behaves in a manner not socially prescribed (and therefore expected). Both EVT and social exchange theory (SET) suggest your expectations determine how you evaluate your interactions with others. The practical advice for the professional communicator is to challenge one's own expectations. Knowing why you have certain expectations and making sure to maintain realistic expectations can enhance perceptions of relational and interactional satisfaction. On the other hand, the professional communicator must also make sure the recipients of messages have appropriate expectations. As inoculation theory would suggest, if you want to prevent a potentially damaging counterpersuasive effort, the best thing you can do is to forewarn receivers to expect the persuasive effort.

Face and Self Versus Other Orientation

Several theories implicitly recognize the importance of sustaining individuals' desired images. Not only is protecting one's own self needs warranted, but theories such as politeness theory (PT) and face-negotiation theory (FNT) propose communicators ought to consider others' face needs in interaction. Such efforts are likely to lead to organizational success; transformational leaders, after all, are those skilled at understanding both themselves and others. Accordingly, the advice taken from these theories is to recognize others' needs to protect their image.

Individual Qualities

As indicated earlier, understanding one's self and others is important for effective communication. Several theories explicitly address how qualities of the individual might affect the communication process. For example, expectancy violations theory (EVT) suggests that communicator characteristics (age, sex, and the like) influence your expectations for communication. Attribution theory proposes that one of the ways you answer the question "why?" is by looking for stable internal dispositions of the communicator. Finally, communication privacy management theory (CPM), on the other hand, suggests that one's own individual values and beliefs will determine the privacy rules that he or she creates. The conclusion drawn here is that you cannot presume everyone will respond in the same way to the same message or situation; you need to tailor your communication to match the qualities of the interactants.

Interest and Involvement

Regarding persuasion, the elaboration likelihood model (ELM) maintains the central route is used by people who are motivated—in other words, interested and involved.

Turning to mass media theories, agenda-setting theory states a person's need for orientation and the information's relevance determine whether news media set an agenda for that individual. Social cognitive theory suggests the media must gain our attention in order to influence us to model what we see. Successful communicators cannot presume interactional partners or audience members will naturally be engaged in a given topic.

Needs

One way to engage communication partners is to recognize and seek to meet their needs. Politeness theory (PT), for example, suggests everyone has positive face needs (e.g., the desire to be liked and appreciated) and negative face needs (e.g., the desire to be free from imposition). A different view of needs is proposed by uses and gratifications theory (UGT), which states people select particular media forms to meet particular needs. Symbolic convergence posits that fantasy themes and fantasy chains meet psychological needs of the group. Finally, functional group decision making argues communication in groups must meet four functions (or achieve four needs) to make effective decisions. Professional communicators, then, ought to match particular messages to the needs of those with whom they are communicating. Note that this is receiver focused; certainly meeting one's own needs is important, but competent communication also recognizes the needs of the receiver.

Power and Control

A recurring theme among the theories discussed in this book is that communication is a central means for exerting power; power influences the type of communication used. The link between communication and power can take a macroscopic (big picture) or microscopic focus (individual interactions). On a large scale, Hofstede's cultural dimensions recognize that some cultures accept large differentials in power, whereas others don't. The extent to which a culture tolerates a high power distance influences the perceived appropriateness of particular communication strategies. Also taking a macroscopic perspective, encoding/decoding theory suggests the media's use of the dominant ideology in encoding messages socializes us into adopting that ideology. A slightly different macroscopic view of communication and power is taken by organizational identification and control theory (OIC), which centers on the hidden forms of control in organizations. OIC focuses on the role of unobtrusive (shared values) and concertive control (peer pressure) in organizational life.

Other theories focus on the role of power in more microscopic settings. Both politeness theory (PT) and communication accommodation theory (CAT) suggest people are more likely to adjust their behavior if they have less power than their interactional partner. Accordingly, you will likely engage in more politeness or will converge to your partner if you perceive this person as having more power than you. Finally, the theory of planned behavior (TPB) suggests a person's perceived power over the situation determines whether he or she will be persuaded to act in a particular fashion.

At the beginning of this section, we stated that a number of the theories presented in this book suggest communication is the means by which power is exerted. By now you should recognize that *who* gets to say things, *what* is said, and *how* it is said (or what is *not* said and *why* it is not said) are important questions for uncovering how power is understood and being carried out in any interaction. Competent communicators recognize not only obvious examples of power enactment but also less obvious examples.

Relationships

Just as different contexts call for differing types of communication, diverse relationships call for varied types of communication. To illustrate, expectancy violations theory (EVT) asserts the relationship you have with interactional partners forms your expectations for how an interaction should proceed. Moreover, outside observers may be just as likely to understand a given relationship as are the relational partners; the interactional perspective suggests all communication includes a relationship level that provides clues as to the nature of the relationship between communicators. As practical advice, communication professionals should be mindful of existing relationships (whether agreeable or poor) and monitor the relationship levels of messages to gauge how an interaction is proceeding.

Rewards

One way to understand individualistic cultures using Hofstede's cultural dimensions is to recognize that members of individualistic cultures ask, "What's in it for me?" Many theories discussed in this text explicitly recognize the power of rewards in making sense of communication interactions. Uses and gratifications theory (URT), for example, says the incentive value of an interactional partner can increase your uncertainty about him or her; the more rewarding the person is, the more likely you are to seek to reduce uncertainty. Several other predictions are associated with rewards. Expectancy violations theory (EVT) suggests the reward value of the violator determines in part whether a person will reciprocate or compensate. Communication privacy management theory (CPM) posits individuals will reveal or conceal risky behavior based on the potential rewards for doing so. Social role theory (SET) predicts people seek to maximize rewards and minimize costs in relationships; thus, lack of rewards can lead to dissatisfaction or relational termination. Accordingly, people make choices based on perceived reward power; those who have reward power will be subject to more uncertainty reduction, will have others compensate for perceived negative behaviors, will be privy to more private information, will be perceived as more attractive to relational partners, and will be emulated more often.

Rules

Several of the theories discussed in this book make reference to the rules used to guide communication practices. CPM, for example, explicitly discusses the development of rules for sharing information. Message design logics (MDL) talks about varying perspectives on rules. Individuals using a conventional MDL tend to be rule governed, individuals using an expressive MDL tend to eschew politeness rules, and individuals with a rhetorical MDL learn to bend the rules to meet their own goals. Similarly, the interactional perspective suggests individuals of different generations tend to have different views of rules. Veterans, for example, tend to strictly follow rules, whereas members of Generation X tend to reject rules, and members of the Millennial generation are more likely to ignore any rule that impinges on what they want to do.

Taking a bigger perspective on rules, two theories of organizational communication focus on how contemporary organizations might rethink reliance on rules. Organizational identification and control theory (OIC) discusses how more sophisticated forms of control rely on more implicit, subtle rules than bureaucratic forms of control. Organizing theory also disdains formal rules, suggesting relying on rules rather than creative solutions might serve as the death knell of an organization.

Social Networks

Many theories focus not only on specific relationships we have with others but on the patterns of relationships in which our lives are embedded. Most obviously, the network approach focuses on how we might understand social media through an analysis of links with others. Diffusion of innovations (DOI) also focuses on social networks; this theory suggests early adopters influence others in their network to adopt new innovations. Similarly, social cognitive theory suggests the media can have an indirect path of effects on viewers through a socially mediated process.

Uncertainty and Ambiguity

The notion of uncertainty is frequently proposed as a central motivator for human communication. URT proposes that uncertainty is uncomfortable, so we use communication to reduce it. Indeed, this notion is used within a specific context in organizational assimilation theory (OAT). Agenda-setting theory says a person's need for orientation, which includes his or her uncertainty about an issue, determines the extent of the agenda-setting effect. Media richness theory suggests richer media forms are required when the message is ambiguous. On the other hand, several theories propose a more complex relationship between uncertainty and communication; dialectics argues individuals have conflicting desires for certainty and uncertainty (in the form of the predictability and novelty dialectic). Hofstede's cultural dimensions suggest cultures vary on uncertainty avoidance, with some cultures more tolerant of uncertainty than others. Nevertheless, it seems clear that uncertainty is often perceived as problematic and can drive a person to send or seek specific messages.

Values and Beliefs

Finally, a theme that emerges consistently throughout our presentation of theories is yet another cognitive variable: people's values and beliefs. Suggested earlier in this chapter, values and beliefs have a complex relationship with communication. On one hand, a person's values and beliefs lead that individual to communicate in a particular fashion. On the other hand, communication might be the means by which you reinforce, modify, or change your values and beliefs. At least 14 of the theories discussed in this book address values and beliefs. The theories range from those focusing on individualistic approaches (MDL posits that people's beliefs about communication influence how they communicate); to persuasive settings (the narrative paradigm suggests an individual's values determine in part which stories they find reasonable); to group settings (symbolic convergence states that group members construct a rhetorical vision, which is a system of values or beliefs about how the world works); to organizational settings (Schein's model of organizational culture identifies values and assumptions as abstract ways of understanding how to operate within an organization); to mass-mediated settings (cultivation theory says heavy television viewers are "mainstreamed" into believing television reality); to cultural contexts (members of different cultures hold different values and beliefs that influence how people should communicate with members of that culture). In all cases, the advice to communication professionals is to understand others' values and beliefs and to recognize the difficulty in asking people to change them.

RETURNING TO COMMUNICATION COMPETENCE

At the beginning of this chapter, we asserted that competent communication requires one to be both effective and appropriate. After reviewing the 14 common concepts we have identified, it should be clear that achieving your goals often means considering what the receiver might view as appropriate. If we were to summarize the single biggest piece of advice culled from all the theories discussed in this book, it would be that competent communicators are those who take a receiver orientation to communication; in the pursuit of their own goals they consider what others need to hear (and how they might hear it) so they might accomplish those goals.

According to Spitzberg and Cupach (1984, 1989), the development of communication competence is contingent on three elements: motivation, knowledge, and skill. *Motivation* references your reasons for doing things; knowing what you want is the foundation for being a competent communicator. That you have taken this class and have read this book provides some indication of motivation for improving your communication skill. *Knowledge* refers to knowing how to act. It is not enough to have good intentions; one must also understand *how* to be effective and appropriate in communication. We hope the theories discussed in this book have increased your knowledge in this area.

The final component of competence is skill. *Skill* is the actual behavior. Despite the best of intentions and a wealth of knowledge, we don't always behave competently. As with any skill, however, communication skill can be developed and enhanced. Skill development requires practice, adjustment after evaluation, and being open to constructive criticism. The challenge you will face as a professional communicator is to use your motivation and knowledge as a foundation for increased skill.

Summary

This chapter provided a synthesis of the theories presented throughout the text. First, we identified two decision points communicators face: whether to be direct or indirect and whether to behave in a similar or different manner compared with other communicators. These decisions were framed in the balance of the effectiveness and appropriateness needed to be a competent communicator. Then we turned our attention to 14 important variables that influence the communication process: cohesion, connection, and in-groups context; expectations; face and self versus other orientation; individual qualities; interest and involvement; needs; power and control; relationships; rewards; rules; social networks; uncertainty and ambiguity; and values and beliefs. Specific advice for the professional communicator was interspersed throughout the discussion of these variables.

Case Study 12: Arguments at Amazing Adventures

Selena Framingham is a 24-year-old woman from the South. She was the first in her family to attend college, and she was very proud of the fact that she paid for her entire education by earning scholarships and working summers at a theme park, Amazing Adventures. The hours were long at the theme park, but she and the other workers had a good time despite the oppressively hot weather, cranky children, and obnoxious parents. Besides, she made good money, and she graduated debt free.

After receiving her undergraduate degree, Selena worked full-time doing public relations for a nonprofit company. She quickly became disillusioned with the job, and after doing this work for a little over a year she decided that neither public relations nor the nonprofit world was a good fit for her. She decided to pursue a graduate degree and was excited to be accepted into a prestigious program. However, attending graduate school full-time was even more expensive than funding her undergraduate degree. She received a grant, which paid for part of her tuition, but she found she had to work both part-time during the semester and full-time during the summer to pay for both school and her living expenses.

Selena contacted Bonnie, one of her old friends at Amazing Adventures, and asked if she might be able to get a job at a senior level for the summer.

"Gee Selena, I don't think there are any management-level jobs open, and even if there were, I don't think they would be seasonal. But let me check around and see what I can do," Bonnie replied.

Bonnie had moved up the ladder at Amazing Adventures, starting with Selena at a concession stand at the age of 18 before they were both promoted to ride operators. Bonnie had stayed with the company when Selena took the public relations job, and now she worked in the accounts payable department of the business office.

The next day, Bonnie called Selena. "Hey, would you mind working in the ticket office this summer? I know it isn't management, but I can make sure your seniority is used to calculate your pay grade. Plus the ticket booth is air-conditioned, and best of all, there's no cleaning up involved!"

Serena thought it was a good option to make a decent salary for the summer and decided to go for it.

On her first day back at work, she found a lot of the original management had left, including supervisors who had been there for a long time. Fortunately, Selena was told she would be working for Sam, whom she had known as a ride operator back in the good old days in the park. Sam had always been easygoing, and she figured he would be the same laid-back guy she had hung out with in the past. While at work, Selena did everything she could to be what she considered a good employee. She typically did whatever her supervisors told her to do because she respected authority. And, if she were completely honest, she knew there were bonuses at the end of the summer if a supervisor thought you had been an exemplary employee.

Selena and Sam quickly fell into a habit. Each time he walked by her ticket booth, he would give her a different task to do, which was mainly tedious busywork.

One day, he said, "Straighten up the maps and distribute some of them to the other ticket counters."

Being the good employee she was, Selena hastily agreed and did it immediately.

On another day, Sam demanded, "The glass on these booths has fingerprints all over it. Get the glass cleaner and clean it up."

He didn't even stop to deliver his commands; he just yelled at her as he was walking by. Again, she quickly responded to his request.

This pattern continued for over a week, and Selena began to silently fume about his behavior. *Who the heck does he think he is?* she contemplated. *I've known him for over 5 years, and I'm the one with a college degree and working on my master's degree. I deserve a little more respect!* she thought. But she didn't say anything; she just did what she was told to do.

During her third week on the job, she called Sam over to her booth because she needed more change. He came over to her register with the change, as requested. When he did so he saw several promotional cards piled to the side of the register. The promotional cards were given by local companies, and they worked as discounts to the park.

Sam challenged Selena, "What are these doing here?"

Selena was confused by the question. "Sometimes people want them back after they buy their tickets. I keep a few of them in a pile and throw them out later," she responded.

Sam rolled his eyes and sighed deeply. "Selena, throw these cards out so you don't get them confused with new ones."

Selena was taken aback by his request. "I have never once confused an old card with a new card," she protested.

He rebutted, "Throw them out anyway."

Without thought, Selena argued, "I would have thrown them out *eventually*, and I was going to throw them out soon anyway. I just keep them because some people want them back."

Sam responded sarcastically, "You shouldn't wait until they pile up like that, and obviously you haven't given anyone back their cards because they are sitting there in a pile."

For Selena, it was the straw that broke the camel's back. She couldn't believe Sam was nitpicking about something so trivial!

"Don't tell me how to do my job, Sam. I know what I'm doing. I've been here longer than you," she screamed, her temper rising.

Sam looked at her, laughed, and threw the cards in the bin underneath the register. Walking away, he didn't acknowledge Selena in any way. Selena stood there and sputtered, thinking she would complain to Sam's supervisor. However, before she could do so a human resources representative approached her and told her she was being reassigned to a concession stand.

Questions for Consideration

1. This chapter suggests two decisions each communicator should make: whether to be direct or indirect and whether to compensate or reciprocate. Discuss both Selena's and Sam's behavior in terms of these two decisions, articulating what in each case leads you to the conclusions you draw.

2. Do you believe Selena and Sam are competent communicators? Why or why not? What could they do to improve their communication competence?

3. Discuss how each of the following influenced Selena's and Sam's behavior:
   a. cohesion/connection/in-groups
   b. expectations
   c. face
   d. power/control
   e. relationships
   f. rewards
   g. uncertainty

Glossary

Accommodating: cooperating with others but demonstrating little assertiveness—typically conceding to the partner's requests.

Accommodation: adjusting one's speech and/or conversational patterns.

Accuracy: in evaluating theory, the extent to which systematic research supports the explanations provided by the theory.

Acuity: in evaluating theory, the ability of a theory to provide insight into an otherwise intricate issue.

Agency: a belief in free will.

Agenda: coverage by mass media, which provides an indication of what events the public "should" consider as important.

Agentic qualities: stereotypically male qualities, e.g., being assertive, controlling, confident, ambitious, and forceful.

Aggregate: a set number of individuals—for example, the people standing at a bus stop or the people on an elevator.

Allocative resources: material forms of assistance, such as time and money.

Ambiguity: the possibility of multiple interpretations.

Analogic communication: a message that resembles what it means. Often nonverbal.

Antecedent conditions: factors associated with group decision making that might lead to groupthink.

Anticipatory socialization: the stage of organizational assimilation during which the individual gathers information about a specific vocation, position, and/or organization.

Anxiety: an emotional state of apprehension, worry, or fear of negative consequences.

Articulation: the process whereby our cultural ideologies are reinforced.

Attention process: determined by both the observer's characteristics and the arrangement of intended behaviors. In other words, the observer needs to be attentive and the actions in question need to be worthy of notice.

Attitude: a relatively enduring predisposition to respond favorably or unfavorably toward something.

Attribution: the answer to the question "why did that person behave in that fashion?"

Attributional confidence: appropriately discerning and reducing uncertainty about an interactional partner's behavior.

Authoritative resources: interpersonal characteristics of group members, such as cohesion, experience, and status.

Authority: use of the perception of power or expertise to convince the audience to accept the beliefs or behaviors presented.

Autonomy–connection: the internal dialectical tension focusing on the desire to be alone versus the desire to be in a relationship.

Avoidance: refusing to enact a behavior that might be considered face threatening.

Axiom: a fundamental truth.

Bald-on-record: making no effort to be polite.

Behavioral intention: a plan to act a particular way.

Behavioral uncertainty: uncertainty as to how someone should behave in a given situation.

Behaviorism: in psychology, a narrow focus on cause and effect.

Boundaries: a metaphor for divisions between who has access to private information and who does not.

Boundary coordination: the ways collective boundaries are maintained.

Boundary linkages: alliances between owners of the information.

Boundary ownership: the rights and responsibilities borne by owners of the information.

Boundary permeability: how much information is easily passed through a privacy boundary.

Boundary turbulence: when privacy rules are unclear, making boundary coordination challenging.

Brainstorming: a specific technique used in decision making to generate potential solutions.

Bridge: a member of more than one group.

Bureaucratic control: exerting control over employees by rules and procedures.

Central route: an elaborated route for persuasion. Succeed in long-term attitude change if the audience is motivated and able to process the message.

Change: in a dialectical approach, the assumption that a steady state is impossible to achieve.

Closed-ended questions: in a survey, questions that require the respondent to use selected possible responses.

Closed-mindedness: viewing the world in extremes. For example, things are viewed either as purely good or purely evil.

Cognition: the processes of reducing, elaborating, transforming, and storing stimuli.

Cognitive: in psychology, the focus on the internal processes that occur between cause and effect.

Cognitive uncertainty: uncertainty about how someone should think or feel about a given situation.

Cohesion: the connection between group members.

Collaborating: in conflict, demonstrating a high regard for self and other. Win-win.

Collectivism: a belief that the views, needs, and goals of the group are more important than any individual views, needs, or goals. Focuses on obligation, connection, and cooperation.

Commitment: reliance on a person's dedication to a product, social cause, group affiliation, or political party to craft a persuasive effort.

Commonsense theory: theory in use. Typically created by an individual's own personal experiences or developed from helpful hints passed on from family members, friends, or colleagues.

Communal qualities: stereotypical female attributes, e.g., the expression of affection and exhibiting sympathy, helpfulness, sensitivity, nurturance, and gentility.

Communibiological approach: an approach to communication arguing that neurobiological structures create different temperaments or traits; that these temperaments and traits are genetic; and that temperament and traits are what cause variations in communication behavior.

Communication: a complex process associated with sending, receiving, and interpreting messages. Scholars disagree as to the scope of the process, whether a source or receiver orientation should be taken or whether message exchange need be successful to count as communication.

Communication competence: achieving a successful balance between effectiveness and appropriateness.

Communicator reward valence: an evaluation about the person who has violated expectations; the extent to which the violator is perceived as attractive or rewarding.

Comparison level: rewards a person expects to receive in a particular relationship.

Comparison level of alternatives: the alternatives to staying in the relationship.

Compatibility: the extent to which an innovation is consistent with a potential adopter's values, lifestyle, or experience.

Compensate: making up for someone else's behavior, for example stepping backward if someone steps forward.

Competing: in conflict, a highly assertive style that lacks cooperation. Seeking a win-lose solution.

Complementary pattern: a pattern of communication in which the sender and the receiver use differing styles of communication.

Complete observer: in an ethnography, when the researcher does not interact with the members of the culture or context.

Complete participant: in an ethnography, when the researcher is fully involved in the social setting, and the participants do not know the researcher is studying them.

Complex-cyclic path: when group members cycle through the types of activities identified by functional group decision making but do so in a circular fashion.

Complexity: the level of difficulty in understanding or using the innovation.

Compromising: in conflict, moderate concern for self and others.

Concept: an agreed-upon aspect of reality.

Concertive control: when co-workers develop mechanisms to reward and control behavior that influences the team.

Connotative: associated or subjective meanings of a symbol.

Consensus: the extent to which an individual believes most people would behave in a given fashion.

Consistency: the extent to which an individual believes a target other typically behaves in a particular fashion.

Consonance: when two stimuli or pieces of information are in balance or achieve congruence.

Content: information published by a medium, such as a television show, newspaper article, or video.

Content analysis: a research method that involves creating categories for communication content and counting the number of times each category appears.

Content level: the actual symbols used in a message.

Contexts of communication: the specific frame or focus a scholar seeks to understand. In this book we identify nine contexts: cognitive, individual/social, interpersonal, intercultural, persuasive, group, organizational, mediated, and mass.

Contextual criteria: situations that encourage or dissuade one from sharing private information.

Contradictions: the essential but opposing needs experienced by relational partners.

Contrast: the use of uneven points of comparison in a persuasive effort.

Controllability: the extent to which a given action is within the actor's control.

Conventional logic: the belief that communication is rule governed and that communicators should follow those rules.

Conventionality–uniqueness: an external tension that focuses the desire to behave in ways considered normative versus wanting to emphasize their relationship's distinctiveness by doing something differently.

Convergence: altering speech and behavior so it matches that of the conversational partner.

Corrective facework: messages an individual can use to restore one's own face or to help another restore face after a face-threatening act has occurred.

Costs: lost resources.

Counteractive communication: in functional group decision making, communication that returns discussion toward one of the requisite functions.

Critical mass: if a sufficient number of people adopt the innovation, additional adoption of the innovation becomes self-sustaining, assuring future growth.

Cross-cultural communication: the comparison of two or more cultural communities.

Cultural studies: the study of the role of the mass media in producing and reproducing cultural beliefs. The media are simply one mechanism for the development and dissemination of cultural ideologies.

Culture: one's identification with and acceptance into a group that shares symbols, meanings, experiences, and behavior.

Cyclic alteration (spiralling alteration): managing a dialectical tension by fulfilling one pole or need at one time and then shifting to fulfill the other pole at a later time.

Decoding: the interpretation of a message.

Deductive theory: developed by starting with a theory—or hypothesis—then gathering data to support, reject, or refine the theory.

Denotative: the dictionary-type definition of a symbol.

Density: the number of interconnections among network members.

Dependent variable: the presumed effect.

Descriptive prejudice: stereotype that women have less leadership potential than men because they lack agentic qualities.

Determinism: the belief that causes and effects can be uncovered when studying human communication.

Deviance: behavior that is counter to expectations for typical behavior.

Dialectical tension: opposing forces within relationships that must be managed.

Digital communication: a message that has no direct link between the symbol and its meaning. Often verbal.

Direct motivation: when you perceive you will be rewarded as a consequence of modeling an observed behavior.

Direct path of influence: the media influences viewers directly, from creating attention-getting messages, to enabling behavior and providing incentives, to replicating actions so the viewer changes her or his behavior.

Direction: the extent to which the link is reciprocal between network members.

Discipline: a sense of responsibility to the work group that fosters particular behaviors.

Disenchantment rejection: when individuals stop using an innovation altogether.

Disruptive communication: in functional group decision making, communication not geared toward one of the requisite functions.

Dissonance: incongruence between attitudes and behavior.

Dissonance ratio: the proportion of incongruent beliefs held in relation to the number of consonant beliefs.

Distinctiveness: the extent to which an individual believes a target other has behaved in a similar fashion across different types of situations.

Divergence: differentiating from a partner by seeking to engage in speech and behavioral patterns different from that of the partner.

Dominant code: a preferred reading; interpreting a message using the dominant ideology.

Dominant ideology: a view of the world that supports the status quo.

Double bind: the dilemma women face in leadership. If they behave in a stereotypically female manner they are viewed as ineffective. If they behave in a stereotypically male manner they are viewed as inappropriate.

Double interact: an act, response, and adjustment.

Dramatizing message: a joke, pun, figure of speech, anecdote, double entendre, or metaphor, among other things, that meets emotional needs.

Duality of structure: the idea that group members' actions both create and constrain interaction.

Effective communication: communication that assists the communicator in achieving his or her goals.

Elaborated argument: argument designed to be processed in the central route.

Elaboration: in addenda-setting theory, the elements selected to accompany or build on a news story.

Emotional intelligence: the ability to monitor one's own and others' emotions.

Emotionally expressive: an affective response to conflict as opposed to a cognitive response.

Emphasis: the particular slant taken by a news story.

Enactment: noticing and attending to particular information in the information environment.

Encoding: the process of putting an idea into symbolic form.

Encounter: the stage of organizational assimilation during which the individual begins to learn the norms of the organization.

Equifinality: the idea that there is more than one way to achieve the same goal.

Equivocality: ambiguity of information.

Ethnography: a research method that requires the researcher to immerse himself or herself into a particular context or culture in order to understand communication rules and meanings.

Evaluate and select: in decision making, comparing each solution to the preestablished criteria to ascertain the best solution.

Exclusion: which stories are not covered or which elements of a story are not included.

Expectancy: what an individual anticipates will happen in a given situation.

Experiment: a research method that involves control and manipulation of variables. The only method that allows for a determination of cause and effect.

Expressive logic: the belief that the purpose of communication is to express one's thoughts, feelings, or beliefs.

Extension: when new concepts or ideas are added to a theory.

Exterior locus of control: the belief that an individual does not have control over his or her behaviors; for example, the belief in fate or situational influences.

External consistency: when evaluating a theory, the extent to which the theory is coherent with other widely held theories.

External dialectic: a tension between a dyad and a larger group, including social norms.

Face: desired public image.

Face-threatening act: behaving in a way that challenges another person's face needs.

Facework: specific messages that thwart or minimize face-threatening acts.

Fantasy: a creative understanding of events that fulfils a psychological or rhetorical need.

Fantasy chain: when dramatizing messages are developed further by the group, creating an extended fantasy.

Fantasy theme: a fantasy developed through group interaction that enters group consciousness.

Feminine culture: the cultural belief that norms for behavior should not be determined by biological sex.

Field experiment: an experiment that takes place in a location where people would normally engage in particular communication.

First-order change: changing the behaviors of individuals in a system.

Focus group: a survey method that involves questioning a small group of people at the same time.

Framing: mass media's ability to highlight aspects of news stories by selecting, emphasizing, elaborating on, and even excluding news stories or parts of news stories to create a certain effect for the audience.

Frequency: how often members of a network communicate with each other.

Function: what communication does. For example, an apology serves the function of relationship repair.

Gatekeeper: a node that controls the flow of information between one part of the network and another.

Gatekeepers: in agenda-setting theory, news editors who select which stories run.

Gender: cultural expectations for men and women. Genders are masculine, feminine, androgynous, and undifferentiated.

Gender criteria: sex role norms that encourage or dissuade one from sharing private information.

Generalization: a pattern that holds true across groups, time, and place.

Goal setting: the process in decision making when the conditions that would lead to an ideal resolution are specified.

Good reasons: in the narrative paradigm, that which influence us to accept a narrative. Good reasons are based on an individual's culture, character, history, values, and experience.

Gratification: what an individual seeks to gain from the use of a particular media form.

Group: a system of three or more individuals focused on achieving a common purpose who influence and are influenced by each other.

Group role: a pattern of communicative behaviors performed by one individual in light of expectations held by other group members.

Groupthink: a type of decision making that leads to poor decisions.

Hedonic relevance: the degree to which an individual believes an actor's behavior directly affects him or her.

High-context communication: messages that privilege relational harmony over clarity or directness.

High power distance: cultural beliefs that accept power as a scarce resource; power differences are viewed as natural and inevitable.

Homeostasis: the natural balance in a system.

Hub: highly dense networks embedded within a larger network.

Humanistic approach: the philosophical approach to that study of communication that involves pragmatism, as well as specific theoretical and methodological commitments.

Idealized influence: serving as a role model for employees.

Identification: the sense of oneness with or belongingness to an organization.

Identify alternatives: in decision making, the process of generating possible solutions.

Ideology: a mental framework used to understand the world; it includes language, concepts, categories, and images used to make sense of experiences.

Incentive: the extent to which an individual can provide rewards or punishments.

Inclusion–seclusion: an external tension that focuses on the desire for the dyad to be alone versus spending time with others in their network.

Independent variable: the presumed cause.

Individualism: the belief that the individual is the essential unit of society. Focuses on independence, achievement, and uniqueness.

Individualized consideration: considering each individual's needs and abilities while supporting development and mentoring efforts.

Inductive theory: a theory developed by gathering data first, then drawing conclusions.

Information environment: internal and external information within which an organization exists.

In-groups: social affiliations to which an individual feels he or she belongs.

Innovation: an idea, practice, or object perceived as new.

Inoculation: a method of preventing persuasion.

Inspirational motivation: presenting employees with a clear vision and a desirable future.

Integration: managing a dialectical tension by incorporating aspects of both poles so as to create a more fulfilling experience.

Intellectual stimulation: challenging assumptions and encouraging new approaches.

Intension: a deeper or more nuanced understanding of theoretical concepts.

Intentionality: the extent to which a definition of communication focuses on source intent or receiver interpretation.

Interaction analysis/conversation analysis: a research method that focuses on the nature or structure of interaction.

Intercultural adjustment: a cultural out-group member feels emotionally secure, socially appropriate, and communicatively competent.

Intercultural communication: interaction between members of different cultures.

Interdependence: the notion that all system members are dependent on all other system members.

Interior locus of control: the belief that an individual has control over his or her own behaviors.

Internal consistency: when evaluating a theory, the extent to which the ideas of the theory are logically built on one another.

Internal dialectic: tensions within a dyad.

Interpretation: the understanding someone derives from a message.

Interview: an oral survey method.

Irrelevance: beliefs and behaviors that have nothing to do with each other.

Isolate: a node that belongs in a network but has no links.

Laboratory experiment: an experiment that takes place in a location other than where people would normally engage in particular communication.

Leader–member exchange: relationships between a supervisor and employee characterized by mutual trust, social support, and liking.

Level of analysis: in network analysis, whether the focus is on individuals in the network, particular groups of organizational members, or on connections among and between organizations.

Level of observation: the focus of a definition of communication. The level of observation might be narrow, limiting the focus of what "counts" as communication, or broad, accepting a wide range of activities as communication.

Liaison: a node with connections to two or more groups that would otherwise not be linked.

Liking: persuasive messages that stress affinity toward a person, place, or object.

Logos: the Aristotelian focus on logic as the foundation for persuasion.

Long-term orientation: the cultural belief in thrift, savings, perseverance, and the willingness to subordinate one's self to achieve a goal.

Low-context communication: messages that value direct, explicit expression of ideas.

Low power distance: a cultural belief that values the minimization of power differences.

Mainstreaming: a common view of social reality based on frequent exposure to the repetitive and dominating images, stories, and messages depicted on TV.

Manipulation: in establishing causality, research participants are exposed to varying levels of the independent variable.

Masculine culture: a cultural belief that the appropriate roles for men and women are distinct.

Mass communication: a process in which professional communicators use technology to share messages over great distances to influence large audiences.

Mass media: the organizations responsible for using technology to send mass messages to the public.

Mean-world syndrome: heavy television viewers significantly overestimate real-life danger.

Media: complex organizations that are the source of many mass communication messages.

Media richness: the information-carrying capacity of a medium.

Mediated communication: communication in which there is something in between the sender and receiver. Most often the mediation is a technology.

Mediation: in network analysis, whether the connections between network members exist because of a common link.

Meme: ideas, behaviors, or practices that spread from one person to another in a network.

Message design logic: a belief about how communication should work.

Metamorphosis: the stage of organizational assimilation during which the individual is fully socialized into the organization.

Mindfulness: thoughtful, conscious behavior.

Minimax principle: the assumption that people want to make the most of benefits while lessening costs.

Model: either a synonym to the term *theory*, a precursor to a theory, a physical representation of a theory, or a specific—often mathematical—application of predication.

Modeling: by observing others one forms an idea of how new behaviors are performed, and on later occasions this coded information serves as a guide for action.

Motivational criteria: individual variations that encourage or dissuade one from sharing private information.

Motivational process: to go from observation to action requires the motivation to use the learned action. Motivation is inspired by three types of incentives: direct, vicarious, and self-produced.

Multiplexity: the extent to which two network members are linked together by more than one relationship or type of communication.

Mutual-face concern: recognition of both self- and other-face needs.

Mythos: a collection of stories expressing ideas that cannot be verified or proved in any absolute way.

Narrative: the symbolic words and actions people use to assign meaning.

Narrative coherence: a narrative that appears to flow smoothly, make sense, and be believable.

Narrative fidelity: a narrative that appears truthful and congruent with our own experiences.

Narrative rationality: a logical method of reasoning by which a person can determine how believable another's narrative is.

Need for orientation: relevance of a news story, as well as uncertainty.

Negative face: a person's desire to act freely, without constraints or imposition from others.

Negative politeness: when a speaker makes an effort to recognize another person's negative face needs.

Negotiated code: in decoding a message, the receiver accepts the dominant ideology in general but engages in some selective interpretation in order to better fit his or her view of the world.

Network mode: the channel or channels used by network members.

Node: an individual network member.

Nonrandom sample: a sampling technique in which all members of the population do not have an equal chance of being included.

Nonsummativity: the notion that the system is more than simply a sum of its parts.

Normative beliefs: perceptions about what others in your social network expect you to do.

Normative judgment: whether a definition of communication requires success or accuracy in order for an activity to be considered communication.

Objectivity: the belief that researchers should be value-free when conducting research.

Observability: the extent to which an individual can view the innovation or its effects.

Off-record: subtle hints or indirect mentions of a face-threatening topic.

Open-ended questions: in a survey, questions that allow a respondent to use his or her own words to respond.

Openness–closedness: an internal tension that centers on the desire to share information versus the desire to keep some information private.

Oppositional code: in decoding a message, the individual recognizes the ideological bias in the message. Individuals who use the oppositional code identify the preferred reading but deconstruct the message and reconstruct it from a different point of view.

Organizational assimilation: the process of being socialized into an organization.

Organizational culture: the lived experience of organizational members that consists of values, beliefs, and ways of behaving and communicating.

Organizing: the process of communication that creates an organization.

Other-face concern: demonstrating an awareness of the other person's positive and negative face needs.

Outcome value: in social exchange theory, what an individual receives from the relationship (i.e., rewards minus costs).

Out-groups: social affiliations to which a person feels he or she does not belong.

Overestimation of the group: when group members have an inflated view of the group's abilities.

Participant–observer: in an ethnography, when a researcher becomes fully involved with the culture or context but admits his or her research agenda before entering the environment.

Passive-aggressive: surreptitious attempts to make a partner feel guilty. Passive aggression is more active than avoiding the situation altogether but less active than openly addressing the conflict.

Pathos: Aristotelian focus on emotion as a means of persuasion.

Perceived behavioral control: an inability to behave consistently with one's attitudes. Two components: self-efficacy and controllability.

Peripheral route: a route for processing persuasive messages when motivation or ability is missing. Results in short-term persuasion at best.

Personalism: the belief that an actor specifically and intentionally behaves in ways that are hurtful or helpful.

Persuasion: human communication designed to influence others by modifying their beliefs, values, or attitudes.

Population: everyone or everything that demonstrates a particular characteristic.

Positive face: a person's need to be liked, appreciated, and admired.

Positive politeness: emphasizing the receiver's need to be liked or appreciated.

Postdecision theory: focuses on how people make sense of their decision after they have made it.

Power: the ability to influence others through rewards or punishments. Influences politeness.

Practicality: when evaluating a theory, the extent to which the theory can be used to solve real-world problems.

Pragmatism: the belief that scholars should focus on the communicative choices people make.

Praxis: the assumption that the development of a relationship is neither linear (always moving forward) nor repetitive (cycling through the same things again and again).

Predictability–novelty: an internal tension that centers on the desire to have new experiences versus the desire to manage uncertainty.

Preferred reading: decoding a message using the dominant ideology.

Prescriptive prejudice: actual evaluations of women as less effective than men.

Pressure toward uniformity: Pressure placed on group members by other group members to reach a unanimous agreement.

Prestige: the social distance between communicators. Influences politeness.

Primary research: research reported by the person who conducted it.

Privacy rules: conventions that govern decisions about sharing private information.

Private information: information that is inaccessible to others.

Problem analysis: a realistic examination of the nature, extent, and likely causes of a problem.

Production: in adaptive structuration theory, the idea that the choices group members make create a structure.

Promotive communication: in functional group decision making, communication geared toward one of the requisite functions.

Public–private: a tension between revealing and concealing private information.

Punctuation: the desire to understand the beginnings and endings and causes and effects of communication.

Qualitative: an approach to analyzing data that focuses on rich descriptions of what has been observed, interpreted, or critiqued.

Quantitative: an approach to analyzing data that focuses on numbers or statistics.

Questionnaire: a written survey method.

Random sample: technique in which all members of the population have an equal chance of being in the sample.

Rate of adoption: the relative speed with which an individual (or group or organization) adopts an innovation.

Rationalize: the ability to justify dissonance.

Receiver orientation: the position in the intentionality debate proposing that anything a receiver considers a message should be considered communication.

Reciprocal interdependence: if an innovator or early adopter has the technology, they need others to adopt the technology in order to receive the maximum benefits, e.g., social media.

Reciprocate: engaging in the same behavior as someone else.

Reciprocity: influence of efforts that emphasize a give-and-take relationship.

Refutational preemption: a counterpersuasive effort that involves raising specific challenges and then contesting them.

Relationship level: indicators in a message that suggest how to interpret the message and the nature of the relationship between the communicators.

Relative advantage: an innovation has to be better at achieving the goals for performance than other competing technologies in order to be adopted.

Replacement discontinuance: when individuals reject an innovation after trying it, returning to a different version of the innovation.

Reproduction: in adaptive structuration theory, the idea that the structures group members create constrain future actions, thus being reinforced.

Reproduction process: individuals' demonstration of a new behavior through modeling;

beyond simply mimicry, individuals refine the action through self-corrective adjustments based on feedback and focused demonstrations of behavioral segments that have only been learned in part.

Resonance: congruency between viewers' own violent experiences and that which they see on TV.

Retention: the process by which a double interact gets stored as organizational memory.

Retention process: visually and verbally storing mediated images.

Revelation–concealment: an external tension between keeping some information private within the dyad versus sharing information with the larger network.

Rewards: preferred resources (e.g., time, money, love).

Rhetorical criticism: a research method that involves describing, interpreting, and analyzing texts.

Rhetorical logic: the belief that communication is a cooperative game in which participants pursue multiple goals.

Rhetorical vision: a unified way of viewing the world.

Risk: the extent to which engaging in a face-threatening act will cause harm to another's face needs.

Risk–benefit criteria: an assessment of the rewards and costs for disclosing private information.

Rules: how something should be done.

Sampling: studying only a small group of people or objects and assuming the results hold true of the entire population.

Scarcity: a peripheral persuasive message that preys on people's worry of missing out on something.

Schemata: cognitive structures for organizing new information.

Scholarly theory: one that has undergone systematic research.

Secondary research: research reported by someone other than the person who conducted it.

Second-order change: resolving underlying differences in perspective, most often through the process of reframing.

Segmentation: managing dialectical tensions by compartmentalizing the relationship such that certain issues coincide with one pole or need and other issues are appropriate for the opposite pole.

Selection: in the dialectical perspective, managing dialectical tensions by favoring one pole or need at the expense of the other. In organizing theory, an organization's decision to rely on either a rule or a double interact. In agenda-setting theory, news stories chosen to be printed or aired.

Selective attention: focusing solely on information that reaffirms beliefs.

Selective exposure: actively avoiding information inconsistent with previously established beliefs or behaviors.

Selective interpretation: deciphering ambiguous information so it is perceived to be consistent with established beliefs.

Selective retention: dismissing or forgetting information that creates dissonance.

Self-efficacy: an individual's belief that she or he can perform a behavior.

Self-face concern: being aware of one's own positive and negative face needs.

Self-produced motivation: when individuals rely on their own personal standards, engaging in observed activities they find personally worthwhile and refusing to participate in those activities of which they disapprove.

Semantic network: a particular focus on the content of the communications in a network analysis.

Sex: the biological differentiation between males and females.

Short-term orientation: a cultural belief in immediate gratification.

Simple control: exerting direct authority through commands.

Situational characteristics: problems with the experiences of a group that might lead to groupthink.

Social desirability: consistent with social conventions.

Social proof: persuasive messages that focus on peer pressure.

Social scientific approach: the philosophical approach to that study of communication that involves determinism, as well as specific theoretical and methodological commitments.

Socially mediated path of influence: media influences used to link participants to social networks and community settings. Through these social connections, individuals receive guidance, incentives, and social support, making behavioral change more likely.

Sociocultural evolution: the process of organizational information processing. Organizations that do not go through this process will cease to exist.

Socioemotional communication: communication focused on developing, maintaining, and repairing relationships between group members.

Solution-orientation path: group members make little or no effort to investigate the problem. Rather, group members assume they understand the problem and immediately seek a solution that will satisfy group members.

Source orientation: the position in the intentionality debate proposing the only messages that should be considered communication are those a source intends to send.

Stability: the existence of a network link over time.

Standpoint: a position from which an individual views and understands the world.

Star: a node that is highly central to the network.

Stranger: out-group member.

Strength: the frequency, intimacy, or intensity of a network connection.

Structural flaws: problems with the composition of a group that include homogeneity, biased leadership, and lack of decision-making norms.

Structure: patterns of relationships or interaction.

Subjectivity: the belief that meaning is unique to each person.

Succinctness: when evaluating theory, the extent to which a theory's explanation or description is sufficiently concise.

Supervisory exchange: interaction between a supervisor and subordinate defined entirely by the roles they perform and the contractual obligations provided by the organization.

Survey research: a method that involves asking people what they think or do.

Symbolic convergence: the transformation of a collection of individuals to an identifiable group with a group consciousness.

Symbolic double jeopardy: minority persons are significantly less visible on TV than in real life, and these minority TV characters are much more likely to be portrayed as victims of violence.

Symmetrical pattern: a pattern of communication in which the sender and receiver use similar styles of communication.

Symmetry: whether two people connected in a network share the same type of relationship with each other.

Synergy: the ability to achieve more through group effort than individual effort.

System: a group of people who interrelate to form a whole.

Task communication: communication focused on achieving an instrumental goal.

Team: an ongoing, coordinated group of people working together.

Technological control: exerting control over employees through the use of technology to manage what can and can't be done in the workplace.

Text/data mining: a research method that uses advanced data analysis techniques to uncover patterns in large amounts of information.

Textual analysis: a research method that studies the characteristics or patterns of a written or recorded message.

Theory: any systematic summary about the nature of the communication process.

Third-party help: asking a person outside of the relationship to help manage the conflict.

Threat: a forewarning of a potential persuasive attack on beliefs, making sure the target of the persuasive effort is aware of his or her susceptibility to the attack.

Totality: interdependence between relationship partners.

Transactional leadership: a style that seeks to achieve solid, consistent performance from subordinates through a process of bilateral exchange.

Transformational leadership: a style that seeks to inspire exceptional performance by using subordinates' ideas and actions as a catalyst for transformation.

Trialability: the extent to which potential adopters can "try" an innovation before making the decision to adopt it.

Uncertainty: the inability to explain or predict one's own or others' behavior.

Uncertainty avoidance: cultural preferences for the extent to which ambiguity is tolerated.

Unitary path: when a group uses the same process to generate solutions, regardless of the type of problem they are seeking to solve.

Unobtrusive control: exerting authority over employees by identification with an organizational mission.

Values: core beliefs.

Variable: any concept that has two or more values.

Vicarious motivation: when individuals are motivated by the successes of others similar to themselves.

Violation valence: the positive or negative evaluation of an expectation.

Violence index: an objective research instrument that uses content analysis to measure the prevalence, frequency, and role of characters involved in TV violence.

Vocational anticipatory socialization: the stage of organizational assimilation during which an individual learns what it means to work.

Working theory: generalizations made in particular professions about the best techniques for doing something.

References

Adler, N. J. (1997). *International dimensions of organizational behavior* (3rd ed). Cincinnati, OH: South-Western College.

Ajzen, I. (1988). *Attitudes, personality, and behavior.* Chicago: The Dorsey Press.

Ajzen, I. (1991). The theory of planned behavior. *Organizational Behavior and Human Decision Processes, 50,* 179–211.

Allen, M. W., Coopman, S. J., Hart, J. L., & Walker, K. L. (2007). Workplace surveillance and managing privacy boundaries. *Management Communication Quarterly, 21,* 172–200.

Alsop, R. (2008). *The trophy kids grow up: How the millennial generation is shaking up the workplace.* San Francisco: Jossey-Bass.

An, C., & Pfau, M. (2004). The efficacy of inoculation in televised political debates. *Journal of Communication, 54,* 421–436.

Andersen, J., Nussbaum, J., Pecchioni, L., & Grant, J.A. (1999). Interactional skills in instructional settings. In A. L. Vangelisti, J. A. Daly, & G. W. Friedrich (Eds.), *Teaching communication* (2nd ed., pp. 359–374). Mahwah, NJ: LEA.

Annunziato, S. (2011). The Amanda Knox case: The representation of Italy in American media coverage. *Historical Journal of Film, Radio & Television, 31*(1), 61–78. doi:10.1080/01439685.2011.552697

Armenakis, A., Brown, S., & Mehta, A. (2011). Organizational culture: Assessment and transformation. *Journal of Change Management, 11*(3), 305–328. doi:10.1080/14697017.2011.568949

Ashby, W. R. (1962). Principles of the self-organizing system. In H. von Foerster & G. Zopf (Eds.), *Principles of self-organization* (pp. 255–278). New York: Pergamon.

Avery, A. E., Baradwaj, B. G., & Singer, D. D. (2008). An examination of Hofstede's cultural factors in explanation of differences in Citibank International retail banking web sites. *Journal of Business & Economics Studies, 14,* 73–118.

Avery, E., Lariscy, R., & Sweetser, K. D. (2010). Social media and shared—or divergent—uses? A coorientation analysis of public relations practitioners and journalists. *International Journal of Strategic Communication, 4,* 189–205.

Axley, S. R. (1984). Managerial and organizational communication in terms of the conduit metaphor. *Academy of Management Review, 9,* 428–437.

Aylor, B., & Dainton, M. (2001). Antecedents in romantic jealousy experience, expression, and goals. *Western Journal of Communication, 64,* 370–391.

Aylor, B., & Dainton, M. (2004). Biological sex and psychological gender as predictors of routine and strategic relational maintenance. *Sex Roles, 50,* 689–697.

Bales, R. F. (1970). *Personality and interpersonal behavior.* New York: Holt, Rinehart & Winston.

Banas, J., & Rains, S. (2008, November). *Testing inoculation theory: A meta-analysis.* Paper presented at the annual meeting of the NCA 94th Annual Convention, San Diego, CA. Retrieved February 2, 2009, from www.allacademic.com/meta/p261402_index.html.

Bandura, A. (1977). *Social learning theory.* Upper Saddle River, NJ: Prentice Hall.

Bandura, A. (1986). *Social foundations of thought and action: A social cognitive theory.* Englewood Cliffs, NJ: Prentice Hall.

Bandura, A. (1994). Social cognitive theory of mass communication. In J. Bryant & D. Zillmann (Eds.), *Media effects: Advances in theory and research* (pp. 61–90). Hillsdale, NJ: Lawrence Erlbaum.

Bandura, A. (2001). Social cognitive theory of mass communication. *Media Psychology, 3(3),* 265–299. doi:10.1207/S1532785XMEP0303_03

Bandura, A., Ross, D., & Ross, S. (1963). Imitations of aggressive film-mediated models. *Journal of Abnormal Psychology, 66,* 3–11.

Barbour, J. B., Jacocks, C. W., & Wesner, J. K. (2012). *The message design logics of organizational change: A multisite, multiple message investigation.* Paper presented at the meeting of the International Communication Association, Phoenix, AZ.

Barge, J. K. (1994). *Leadership.* New York: St. Martin's Press.

Barker, J. R. (1999). *The discipline of teamwork: Participation and concertive control.* Thousand Oaks, CA: Sage.

Barker, R., & Gower, K. (2010). Strategic application of storytelling in organizations: Toward effective communication in a diverse world. *Journal of Business Communication, 47*(3), 295–312. doi:10.1177/0021943610369782

Barker, R. T., Rimler, G., Moreno, E., & Kaplan, T. E. (2004). Family business narrative perceptions: Values, succession, and commitment. *Journal of Technical Writing and Communication, 34(4),* 291–320.

Barnett, E. (2011, November 22). Facebook cuts six degrees of separation to four. *Telegraph.* Retrieved May 29, 2013, from www.telegraph.co.uk/technology/facebook/8906693/Facebook-cuts-six-degrees-of-separation-to-four.html.

Bar-On, R. (2006). The Bar-On model of emotional-social intelligence (ESI). *Psicothema, 18*(Suppl), 13–25.

Bass, B. M. (1985). *Leadership and performance beyond expectations.* New York: Free Press.

Bass, B. M. (1997). Does the transactional–transformational leadership paradigm transcend organizational and national boundaries? *American Psychologist, 52,* 130–139.

Bass, B. M. (1998). *Transformational leadership: Industrial, military, and educational impact.* Mahwah, NJ: Erlbaum.

Baumgartner, R. J. (2009). Organizational culture and leadership: Preconditions for the development of a sustainable corporation. *Sustainable Development, 17,* 102–113.

Baxter, L. A. (1988). A dialectical perspective on communication strategies in relationship development. In S. Duck (Ed.), *Handbook of personal relationships: Theory, research, and interventions* (pp. 257–273). Chichester, UK: Wiley.

Baxter, L. A., & Montgomery, B. M. (1996). *Relating: Dialogues and dialectics.* New York: Guilford Press.

Beatty, M. J., & McCroskey, J. C. (2001). *The biology of communication: A communibiological perspective.* Creskill, NJ: Hampton Press.

Becker, E. F. (2012, August 6). Tip sheet: Three tips to fix cross-cultural miscommunications. *PR News* [online]. Retrieved June 26, 2013, from www.prnewsonline.com/featured/2012/08/06/tip-sheet-three-tips-to-fix-cross-cultural-miscommunications.

Becker, S. L. (1984). Marxist approaches to media studies: The British experience. *Critical Studies in Mass Communication, 1*(1), 66–80.

Berger, C. R. (1979). Beyond initial interaction: Uncertainty, understanding, and the development of interpersonal relationships. In H. Giles & R. St. Clair (Eds.), *Language and social psychology* (pp. 122–144). Oxford, UK: Basil Blackwell.

Berger, C. R. (1995). Inscrutable goals, uncertain plans, and the production of communicative action. In C. R. Berger & M. Burgoon (Eds.), *Communication and social processes* (pp. 1–28). East Lansing: Michigan State University Press.

Berger, C. R. (1997). *Planning strategic interaction: Attaining goals through communicative action.* Mahwah, NJ: Erlbaum.

Berger, C. R., & Bradac, J. J. (1982). *Language and social knowledge: Uncertainty in interpersonal relations.* London: Arnold.

Berger, C. R., & Calabrese, R. J. (1975). Some explorations in initial interaction and beyond: Toward a developmental theory of interpersonal communication. *Human Communication Research, 1,* 99–112.

Berman, S. J., & Hellweg, S. A. (1989). Perceived supervisor communication competence and supervisor satisfaction as a function of quality circle participation. *Journal of Business Communication, 26,* 103–122.

Bisel, R. S., Kelley, K. M., Ploeger, N. A., & Messersmith, J. (2011). Workers' moral mum effect: On facework and unethical behavior in the workplace. *Communication Studies, 62*(2), 153–170. doi:10.1080/10510974.2010.551314

Bingham, S., & Burleson, B. (1989). Multiple effects of messages with multiple goals: Some perceived outcomes of responses to sexual harassment. *Human Communication Research, 16,* 184–216.

Blossom, J. (2009). *Content nation: Surviving and thriving as social media changes our work, our lives, and our future.* Indianapolis, IN: Wiley.

Bolkan, S., & Daly, J. A. (2009). Organizational responses to consumer complaints: An examination of effective remediation techniques. *Journal of Applied Communication Research, 31,* 21–39.

Bonito, J. A., & Wolski, S. L. (2002). The adaptation of complaints to participation frameworks. *Communication Studies, 53,* 252–268.

Bormann, E. G. (1982). The symbolic convergence theory of communication: Applications and implications for teachers and consultants. *Journal of Applied Communication Research, 10,* 50–61.

Bormann, E. G. (1996). Symbolic convergence theory and communication in group decision making. In R. Y. Hirokawa & M. S. Poole (Eds.), *Communication and group decision making* (2nd ed., pp. 81–113). Thousand Oaks, CA: Sage.

Bormann, E. G., Cragan, J. E., & Shields, D. C. (1994). In defense of symbolic convergence theory: A look at the theory and its criticisms after two decades. *Communication Theory, 4,* 259–294.

Boudes, T., & Laroche, H. (2009). Taking off the heat: Narrative sensemaking in post-crisis inquiry reports. *Organization Studies, 30*(4), 377–396. doi:10.1177/0170840608101141

Braithwaite, D., Toller, P., Daas, K., Durham, W., & Jones, A. (2008). Centered but not caught in the middle: Stepchildren's perceptions of dialectical contradictions in the communication of co-parents. *Journal of Applied Communication Research, 36,* 33–55.

Broom, C., & Avanzino, S. (2010). The communication of community collaboration: When rhetorical visions collide. *Communication Quarterly, 58*(4), 480–501. doi:10.1080/01463373.2010.525701

Brown, P., & Levinson, S. (1978). Universals in language usage: Politeness phenomenon. In E. Goody (Ed.), *Questions and politeness* (pp. 56–89). Cambridge, UK: Cambridge University Press.

Brown, P., & Levinson, S. (1987). *Politeness: Some universals in language use.* Cambridge, UK: Cambridge University Press.

Bruni, F. (2012, December 8). Bin Laden, torture, and Hollywood. *New York Times.* Retrieved June 19, 2013, from www.nytimes.com/2012/12/09/opinion/sunday/bruni-bin-laden-torture-and-hollywood.html?pagewanted = all&_r = 0.

Bryant, L. E. (2003). Stepchildren's perceptions of the contradictions in communication with stepfamilies formed post bereavement (Doctoral dissertation, The University of Nebraska–Lincoln, 2003). Retrieved June 17, 2009, from Dissertations & Theses: A&I database (Publication No. AAT 3092530).

Bryant, S. E. (2003). The role of transformational and transactional leadership in creating, sharing and exploiting organizational knowledge. *Journal of Leadership and Organizational Studies, 9,* 32–43.

Burgoon, J. K. (1978). A communication model of personal space violations: Explication and an initial test. *Human Communication Research, 4,* 129–142.

Burgoon, J. K. (1994). Nonverbal signals. In M. L. Knapp & G. R. Miller (Eds.), *Handbook of interpersonal communication* (pp. 229–285). Thousand Oaks, CA: Sage.

Burgoon, M., Pfau, M., & Birk, T. S. (1995). An inoculation theory explanation for the effects of corporate issue/advocacy advertising campaigns. *Communication Research, 22,* 485–505.

Burgraff, C. S., & Sillars, A. L. (1987). A critical examination of sex differences in marriage. *Communication Monographs, 54,* 276–294.

Busch, P., Venkitachalam, K., & Richards, D. (2008). Generational differences in soft knowledge situations: Status, need for recognition, workplace commitment and idealism. *Knowledge & Process Management, 15*(1), 45–58.

Caldiero, C. T. (2007). Crisis storytelling: Fisher's narrative paradigm and news reporting. *American Communication Journal, 9* [online]. Retrieved June 28, 2013, from http://ac-journal.org/journal/2007/Spring/articles/storytelling.html.

Calhoun, L. (2008). *One cannot not communicate (unless you are the US and Iran): An interactionist perspective on the foreign policy dilemmas between the US and Iran.* Paper presented at the meeting of the National Communication Association, San Diego, CA.

Canary, D. J., Cody, M. J., & Manusov, V. L. (2003). *Interpersonal communication: A goals-based approach* (3rd ed.). Boston: Bedford.

Canary, D. J., Emmers-Sommer, T. M., & Faulkner, S. (1997). *Sex and gender differences in personal relationships.* New York: Guilford Press.

Canary, D. J., & Hause, K. S. (1993). Is there any reason to research sex differences in communication? *Communication Quarterly, 41,* 129–144.

Canary, D. J., & Zelley, E. D. (2000). Current research programs on relational maintenance behaviors. In M. E. Roloff (Ed.), *Communication Yearbook 23* (pp. 305–339). Thousand Oaks, CA: Sage.

Caruso, D. R., Mayer, J. D., & Salovey, P. (2002). Relation of an ability measure of emotional intelligence to personality. *Journal of Personality Assessment, 79*(2), 306–320. doi:10.1207/S15327752JPA7902_12

Cha, E., Kim, K. H., & Patrick, T. E. (2008). Predictors of intention to practice safer sex among Korean college students. *Archives of Sexual Behavior, 37,* 641–651.

Chan-Olmsted, S., Rim, H., & Zerba, A. (2013). Mobile news adoption among young adults: Examining the roles of perceptions, news consumption, and media usage. *Journalism & Mass Communication Quarterly, 90*(1), 126–147. doi:10.1177/1077699012468742

Characterproducts.com. (2004). *Sesame Street history.* Retrieved August 10, 2004, from www.characterproducts.com/info/character_histories/sesame_st_doorway.htm.

Chaudary, A. (2013, May 21). Boston Marathon Saudi "suspect" speaks out. *The Islamic Monthly* [online]. Retrieved July 2, 2013, from www.theislamicmonthly.com/exclusive-interview-with-the-saudi-man-from-boston.

Chen, B. X. (2013, February 10). Samsung emerges as potent rival to Apple's cool. *New York Times.* Retrieved from www.nytimes.com/2013/02/11/technology/samsung-challenges-apples-cool-factor.html?pagewanted = all&_r = 0.

Chen, S., & Lee, K. (2008). The role of personality traits and perceived values in persuasion: An elaboration likelihood model perspective on online shopping. *Social Behavior and Personality, 36,* 1379–1399.

Cialdini, R. B. (1993). *Influence: Science and practice* (3rd ed.). New York: HarperCollins.

Cialdini, R. B. (1994). Interpersonal influence. In S. Shavitt & T. C. Brock (Eds.), *Persuasion: Psychological insights and perspectives* (pp. 195–218). Boston: Allyn & Bacon.

Cohen, B. C. (1963). *The press and foreign policy.* Princeton, NJ: Princeton University Press.

Cohen, M., & Avanzino, S. (2010). We are people first: Framing organizational assimilation experiences of the physically disabled using co-cultural theory. *Communication Studies, 61*(3), 272–303. doi:10.1080/10510971003791203

Collier, M. J. (1989). Cultural and intercultural communication competence: Current approaches and directions for future research. *International Journal of Intercultural Relations, 13,* 287–302.

Compton, J. A., & Pfau, M. (2004). Use of inoculation to foster resistance to credit card marketing targeting college students. *Journal of Applied Communication Research, 32*(4), 343–364.

The conundrum of the glass ceiling. (2005). *The Economist, 376*(3), 1–6. Retrieved July 8, 2009, from MAS Ultra—School Edition database.

Craig, R. T. (1999). Communication theory as a field. *Communication Theory, 9,* 119–161.

Craig, R. T., Tracy, K., & Spisak, F. (1993). The discourse of requests: Assessment of a politeness approach. In S. Petronio, J. K. Alberts, M. L. Hecht, & J. Buley (Eds.), *Contemporary perspectives on interpersonal communication* (pp. 264–283). Madison, WI: Brown & Benchmark.

Crossen, C. (1994). *Tainted truth: The manipulation of fact in America.* New York: Simon & Schuster.

Cuomo, C., & Shearn. I. (2012, March 13) *Rutgers trial: The political firestorm before the indictment.* Retrieved July 9, 2013, from http://abcnews.go.com/US/clementi-trial-daily-analysis-politics-tyler-clementi-suicide/story?id = 15909031#.UdyW8uChDFI.

Cupach, W. R., & Canary, D. J. (1997). *Competence in interpersonal conflict.* New York: McGraw-Hill.

Cupach, W. R., & Imahori, T. T. (1993). Identity management theory: Communication competence in intercultural episodes and relationships. In R. L. Wiseman & J. Koester (Eds.), *Intercultural communication competence* (pp. 112–131). Newbury Park, CA: Sage.

Cupach, W. R., & Metts, S. (1994). *Facework.* Thousand Oaks, CA: Sage.

Daft, R. L., & Lengel, R. H. (1984). Information richness: A new approach to managerial behavior and organizational design. In L. L. Cummings & B. M. Staw (Eds.), *Research in organizational behavior 6* (pp. 191–233). Homewood, IL: JAI Press.

Daft, R. L., & Lengel, R. H. (1986). Organizational information requirements, media richness and structural design. *Management Science, 32,* 554–571.

Dainton, M., Aylor, B., & Zelley, E. D. (2002, November). *General and relationship-specific social support, willingness to communicate, and loneliness in long-distance versus geographically close friendships.* Paper presented at the National Communication Association annual conference, New Orleans, LA.

Dance, F. E. X. (1970). The "concept" of communication. *Journal of Communication, 20,* 201–210.

Dance, F. E. X., & Larson, C. E. (1976). *The functions of communication: A theoretical approach.* New York: Holt, Rinehart & Winston.

Dansereau, F., Graen, G., & Haga, W. J. (1975). A vertical dyad approach to leadership within formal organizations. *Organizational Behavior and Human Performance, 12,* 46–78.

Danton, E. R. (2013, April 11). Brad Paisley: "Accidental Racist not perfect, but it is honest." *Rolling Stone.* Retrieved June 3, 2013, from www.rollingstone.com/music/videos/brad-paisley-accidental-racist-not-perfect-but-it-is-honest-20130411.

Dawkins, R. (1989). *The selfish gene* (2nd ed.). Oxford, UK: Oxford University Press.

De Nooy, W., & Kleinnijenhuis, J. (2013). Polarization in the media during an election campaign: A dynamic network model predicting support and attack among political actors. *Political Communication, 30*(1), 117–138. doi:10.1080/10584609.2012.737417

Deal, T. E., & Kennedy, A. A. (1982). *Corporate cultures: The rites and rituals of corporate life.* Reading, MA: Addison-Wesley.

Deetz, S. A. (1994). Future of the discipline: The challenges, the research, and the social contribution. In S. A. Deetz (Ed.), *Communication Yearbook 17* (pp. 565–600). Thousand Oaks, CA: Sage.

Deetz, S. A., Tracy, S. J., & Simpson, J. L. (2000). *Leading organizations through transition.* Thousand Oaks, CA: Sage.

DePaulo, B. M., Stone, J. I., & Lassiter, G. D. (1985). Deceiving and detecting deceit. In B. Schlenker (Ed.), *The self and social life* (pp. 323–370). New York: McGraw-Hill.

Dervin, B. (1993). Verbing communication: Mandate for disciplinary intervention. *Journal of Communication, 43,* 45–54.

DeSanctis, G., & Poole, M. S. (1994). Capturing the complexity in advanced technology use: Adaptive structuration theory. *Organization Science, 5*(2), 121–121. Retrieved July 3, 2013, from http://search.proquest.com/docview/213835881?accountid=11999.

Dion, K. K., & Dion, K. L. (1993). Individualistic and collectivistic perspectives on gender and the cultural context of love and intimacy. *Journal of Social Issues, 49,* 53–59.

Dockery, T. M., & Steiner, D. D. (1990). The role of initial interaction in leader–member exchange. *Group and Organizational Studies, 15,* 395–413.

Driscoll, C., & McKee, M. (2007). Restorying a culture of ethical and spiritual values: A role for leader storytelling. *Journal of Business Ethics, 73*(2), 205–217. doi:10.1007/s10551–006–9191–5

Duarte, N. T., Goodson, J. R., & Klich, N. R. (1993). How do I like thee? Let me appraise the ways. *Journal of Organizational Behavior, 14,* 239–249.

Dunleavy, K. N., & Zelley, E. D. (2013, November). *The face of adult female friendships: Examining the relationships between interpersonal competition and facework.* Paper presented at the National Communication Association's annual conference, Washington, DC. Retrieved from http://citation.allacademic.com.

Dyer, W. G. (1987). *Team building: Issues and alternatives* (2nd ed.). Reading, MA: Addison-Wesley.

Eagly, A. H. (1987). Sex differences in social behavior: A social-role interpretation. Hillsdale, NJ: Erlbaum.

Eagly, A. H., & Karau, S. J. (2002). Role congruity theory of prejudice toward female leaders. *Psychological Review, 109*(3), 573–598. doi:10.1037/0033–295X.109.3.573

Eagly, A. H., Karau, S. J., & Makhijani, M. G. (1995). Gender and the effectiveness of leaders: A meta-analysis. *Psychological Bulletin, 117,* 125–145.

Easton, S. S., & Bommelje, R. K. (2011). Interpersonal communication consequences of email non-response. *Florida Communication Journal, 39*(2), 45–63.

Edwards, R. (1981). The social relations of production at the point of production. In M. Zey-Ferrell & M. Aiken (Eds.), *Complex organizations: Critical perspectives* (pp. 156–182). Glenview, IL: Scott, Foresman.

Ellis, D. G. (1999). *Crafting society: Ethnicity, class, and communication theory.* Mahwah, NJ: Erlbaum.

Elsesser, K. M., & Lever, J. (2011). Does gender bias against female leaders persist? Quantitative and qualitative data from a large-scale survey. *Human Relations, 64*(12), 1555–1578. doi:10.1177/0018726711424323

Espiritu, B. (2011). Transnational audience reception as a theater of struggle: Young Filipino women's reception of Korean television dramas. *Asian Journal of Communication, 21*(4), 355–372. doi:10.1080/01292986.2011.580852

Etheridge, J. (2012). Behavior change strategies: Inoculation theory. *SurroundHealth* [online]. Retrieved June 28, 2013, from http://surround-health.net/Topics/Education-and-Learning-approaches/Behavior-change-strategies/Articles/Inoculation-Theory.aspx.

Federal Communications Commission. (2002). *Children's educational television* [online]. Retrieved August 11, 2004, from www.fcc.gov/cgb/consumerfacts/childtv.html.

Feldner, S., & D'Urso, S. C. (2010). Threads of intersection and distinction: Joining an ongoing conversation within organizational communication research. *Communication Research Trends, 29*(1), 4–28.

Festinger, L. (1957). *A theory of cognitive dissonance.* Stanford, CA: Stanford University Press.

Festinger, L. (1962). *A theory of cognitive dissonance.* Stanford, CA: Stanford University Press.

Fishbein, M., & Ajzen, I. (1975). *Belief, attitude, intention and behavior: An introduction to theory and research.* Reading, MA: Addison-Wesley.

Fisher, B. A. (1978). *Perspectives on human communication.* New York: Macmillan.

Fisher, W. R. (1984). Narration as a human communication paradigm: The case of public moral argument. *Communication Monographs, 51,* 1–22.

Fisher, W. R. (1987). *Human communication as narration: Toward a philosophy of reason, value, and action.* Columbia: University of South Carolina Press.

Forman, J. (1998). Mickey Mouse and the French press. *Technical Communication Quarterly, 3,* 247–258.

Forrest, S. (2004). Learning and teaching: The reciprocal link. *The Journal of Continuing Education in Nursing, 35,* 74–80.

Fowler, E. F., & Ridout, T. N. (2013). Negative, angry, and ubiquitous: Political advertising in 2012. *The Forum, 10*(4), 51–61. doi:10.1515/forum-2013-0004

Frey, L. R., Botan, C. H., & Kreps, G. L. (2002). *Investigating communication: An introduction to research methods* (2nd ed.). Boston: Allyn & Bacon.

Frommer's. (2013). *Introduction to Disneyland Paris.* Retrieved June 25, 2013, from www.frommers.com/destinations/disneylandparis/0796010001.html.

Gabrenya Jr., W. K. (2003). Theories and models in psychology [online]. Retrieved July 3, 2013, from http://my.fit.edu/ ~ gabrenya/IntroMethods/eBook/theories.pdf.

Gallois, C., Ogay, T., & Giles, H. (2005). Communication accommodation theory: A look back and a look ahead. In W. Gudykunst (Ed.), *Theorizing about intercultural communication* (pp. 121–148). Thousand Oaks, CA: Sage.

Garcia-Retamero, R., & López-Zafra, E. (2006). Prejudice against women in male-congenial environments: Perceptions of gender role congruity in leadership. *Sex Roles, 55*(1–2), 51–61. doi:10.1007/s11199-006-9068-1

Gardner, L., & Stough, C. (2002). Examining the relationship between leadership and emotional intelligence in senior level managers. *Leadership & Organization Development Journal, 23*, 68–78.

Gass, R. H., & Seiter, J. S. (2003). *Persuasion, social influence, and compliance gaining* (2nd ed.). Boston: Allyn & Bacon.

Gender equality in Sweden. (2013). Swedish Institute [online]. Retrieved December 18, 2013, from http://sweden.se/society/gender-equality-in-sweden/

Gentles, K. A., & Harrison, K. (2006). Television and perceived peer expectations of body size among African American adolescent girls. *Howard Journal of Communications, 17*(1), 39–55.

Gerbner, G. (1998). Cultivation analysis: An overview. *Mass Communication & Society, 1*, 175–194.

Gerbner, G., Gross, L., Morgan, M., & Signorelli, N. (1980). The "mainstreaming" of America: Violence profile no. 11. *Journal of Communication, 30*, 10–29.

Giannetti, L. (1982). *Understanding movies* (3rd ed.). Englewood Cliffs, NJ: Prentice Hall.

Giddens, A. (1979). *Central problems in social theory: Action, structure, and contradiction in social analysis.* Berkeley: University of California Press.

Giles, H., & Coupland, N. (1991). *Language: Contexts and consequences.* Pacific Grove, CA: Wadsworth.

Giles, H., Linz, D., Bonilla, D., & Gomez, M. (2012). Police stops of and interactions with Latino and white (non-Latino) drivers: Extensive policing and communication accommodation. *Communication Monographs, 79*(4), 407–427. doi:10.1080/03637751.2012.723815

Giles, H., Mulac, A., Bradac, J. J., & Johnson, P. (1987). Ethnolinguistic identity theory: A social psychological approach to language maintenance. *International Journal of the Sociology of Language, 68*, 66–99.

Gilpin, D. (2010). Organizational image construction in a fragmented online media environment. *Journal of Public Relations Research, 22*(3), 265–287. doi:10.1080/10627261003614393

Glaser, B. G., & Strauss, A. L. (1967). *The discovery of grounded theory: Strategies for qualitative research.* Chicago: Aldine.

Godbold, L. C., & Pfau, M. (2000). Conferring resistance of peer pressure among adolescents: Using inoculation theory to discourage alcohol use. *Communication Research, 27*, 411–437.

Goffman E. (1959). *The presentation of self in everyday life.* New York: Doubleday.

Goffman, E. (1967). *Interaction ritual: Essays on face-to-face behavior.* New York: Pantheon Books.

Goleman, D. (1995). *Emotional intelligence.* New York: Bantam Books.

Goldfarb, R. S., & Ratner, J. (2008). "Theories" and "models": Terminology through the looking glass. *Econ Journal Watch, 5*(1), 91–108.

Gómez, L. F. (2009). Time to socialize: Organizational socialization structures and temporality. *Journal of Business Communication, 46*, 179–207.

Good, J. (2007). Shop 'til we drop? Television, materialism and attitudes about the natural environment. *Mass Communication & Society, 10*, 365–383.

Gordon, B. R., & Hartmann, W. R. (2013). Advertising effects in presidential elections. *Marketing Science, 32*(1), 19–35. doi:10.1287/mksc.1120.0745

Gouran, D. S., & Hirokawa, R. Y. (1983). The role of communication in decision-making groups: A functional perspective. In M. Mander (Ed.), *Communications in transition* (pp. 168–185). New York: Praeger.

Gouran, D. S., & Hirokawa, R. Y. (1986). Counteractive functions of communication in effective group decision-making. In R. Y. Hirokawa & M. S. Poole (Eds.), *Communication and group decision making* (pp. 81–92). Beverly Hills, CA: Sage.

Gouran, D. S., & Hirokawa, R. Y. (1996). Functional theory and communication in decision-making and problem-solving groups: An expanded view. In R. Y. Hirokawa & M. S. Poole (Eds.), *Communication and group decision making* (pp. 55–80). Thousand Oaks, CA: Sage.

Graen, G., & Uhl-Bien, M. (1995). Development of leader-member exchange theory of leadership over 25 years: Applying a multilevel perspective. *Leadership Quarterly, 6*, 219–247.

Graham, E. E., Papa, M. J., & McPherson, M. B. (1997). An applied test of the functional communication perspective of small group decision-making. *Southern Communication Journal, 62*, 269–279.

Gray, J. (1992). *Men are from Mars, women are from Venus: A practical guide to improving communication and getting what you want in your relationships.* New York: HarperCollins.

Greenberg, P. (2013). The narrative is the thing: the art of corporate storytelling. *Social CRM: The Conversation* [online]. Retrieved December 18, 2013, from http://www.zdnet.com/the-narrative-is-the-thing-the-art-of-corporate-storytelling-7000024315/

Griffin, E. (2003). *A first look at communication theory* (5th ed.). New York: McGraw-Hill.

Griffin, E. (2006). *A first look at communication theory* (6th ed.). New York: McGraw-Hill.

Gudykunst, W. B. (1985). A model of uncertainty reduction in intercultural encounters. *Journal of Language and Social Psychology, 4*(2), 79–98. doi:10.1177/0261927X8500400201

Gudykunst, W. B. (1993). Toward a theory of effective interpersonal and intergroup communication: An anxiety/uncertainty management (AUM) perspective. In R. L. Wiseman & J. Koester (Eds.), *Intercultural communication competence* (pp. 33–71). Newbury Park, CA: Sage.

Gudykunst, W. B. (1995). Anxiety/uncertainty management (AUM) theory: Current status. In R. L. Wiseman (Ed.), *Intercultural communication theory* (pp. 8–58). Thousand Oaks, CA: Sage.

Gudykunst, W. B. (2005). An anxiety/uncertainty management (AUM) theory of strangers' intercultural adjustment. In W. B. Gudykunst (Ed.), *Theorizing about intercultural communication* (pp. 419–458). Thousand Oaks, CA: Sage.

Gudykunst, W. B., & Hammer, M. R. (1988). Strangers and hosts: An uncertainty reduction based theory of intercultural adaptation. In Y. Y. Kim & W. B. Gudykunst (Eds.), *Cross-cultural adaptation: Current approaches* (pp. 106–139). Newbury Park, CA: Sage.

Guerrero, L. K., & Burgoon, J. K. (1996). Attachment styles and reactions to nonverbal involvement change in romantic dyads: Patterns of reciprocity and compensation. *Human Communication Research, 22,* 335–336.

Guerrero, L. K., Jones, S. M., & Burgoon, J. K. (2000). Responses to nonverbal intimacy change in romantic dyads: Effects of behavioral valence and degree of behavioral change on nonverbal and verbal reactions. *Communication Monographs, 67,* 325–346.

Guerrero, L. K., & Smith, A. (2009, November). *Touch in cross-sex relationships between superiors and subordinates: Perceptions of expectedness, inappropriateness, and sexual harassment.* Paper presented at the National Communication Association's annual conference, Chicago. Retrieved June 29, 2013, from http://citation.allacademic.com/meta/p371597_index.html.

Gunawardena, C. N., Walsh, S. L., Gregory, E. M., Lake, M. Y., & Reddinger, L. E. (2005). Cultural perceptions of face negotiation in online learning environments. *Electronic Journal of Communication, 15*(1/2).

Haigh, M., & Pfau, M. (2006). Bolstering organizational identity, commitment, and citizenship behaviors through the process of inoculation. *International Journal of Organizational Analysis, 14,* 295–316.

Hall, A. D., & Fagen, R. E. (1968). Definition of a system. In W. Buckley (Ed.), *Modern systems research for the behavioral scientist* (pp. 81–92). Chicago: Aldine.

Hall, E. T. (1976). *Beyond culture.* Garden City, NY: Doubleday.

Hall, S. (1973). *Encoding and decoding in the television discourse.* Birmingham, UK: Centre for Cultural Studies.

Hall, S. (1986). Gramsci's relevance for the study of race and ethnicity. *Journal of Communication Inquiry, 10*(2), 5–27.

Handfield-Jones R., Nasmith L., Steinert Y., & Lawn, N. (1993). Creativity in medical education: The use of innovative techniques in clinical teaching. *Med Teacher, 15,* 3–10.

Haridakis, P., & Hanson, G. (2009). Social interaction and coviewing with YouTube: Blending mass communication reception and social connection. *Journal of Broadcasting & Electronic Media, 53,* 317–335.

Hartsock, N. (1983). The feminist standpoint: Developing the ground for a specifically feminist historical materialism. In S. Harding & M. B. Hintikka (Eds.), *Discovering reality* (pp. 283–310). Boston: Riedel.

Heath, R., Brandt, D., & Nairn, A. (2006). Brand relationships: Strengthened by emotion, weakened by attention. *Journal of Advertising Research, 46*(4), 410–419.

Hecht, M. L., Collier, M. J., & Ribeau, S. A. (1993). *African American communication: Ethnic identity and interpretation.* Newbury Park, CA: Sage.

Hegel, G. W. F. (1966). *The phenomenology of mind* (2nd ed., J. B. Braillie, Trans.). New York: Humanities Press. (Original work published 1807)

Heider, F. (1958). *The psychology of interpersonal relations.* New York: Wiley.

Hermann, A. F. (2007). Stockholders in cyberspace: Weick's sensemaking online. *Journal of Business Communication, 44,* 13–35.

Hesse-Biber, S., Leavy, P., Quinn, C. E., & Zoino, J. (2006). The mass marketing of disordered eating and eating disorders: The social psychology of women, thinness and culture. *Women's Studies International Forum, 29,* 208–224.

Hickson, M., & Neiva, E. (2002). Toward a taxonomy of universals in the biology of communication. *Journal of Intercultural Communication Research, 31*(3), 149.

Hirokawa, R. Y. (1994). Functional approaches to the study of group discussion: Even good notions have their problems. *Small Group Research, 25,* 542–550.

Hirokawa, R. Y., & Salazar, A. J. (1999). Task-group communication and decision-making performance. In L. R. Frey, D. S. Gouran, & M. S. Poole (Eds.), *The handbook of group communication theory and research* (pp. 167–191). Thousand Oaks, CA: Sage.

Hofstede, G. (1980). *Culture's consequences.* Beverly Hills, CA: Sage.

Hofstede, G. (1986). Cultural differences in teaching and learning. *International Journal of Intercultural Relations, 10,* 301–319.

Hofstede, G. (2001). *Culture's consequences: International differences in work-related values* (2nd ed.). Thousand Oaks, CA: Sage.

Hofstede, G., & Bond, M. H. (1984). Hofstede's culture dimensions: An independent validation using Rokeach's value survey. *Journal of Cross Cultural Psychology, 15,* 417–433.

Huckins, K. (1999). Interest-group influence on the media agenda: A case study. *Journalism and Mass Communication Quarterly, 76,* 76–86.

Huesmann, L. R., Moise-Titus, J., Podolski, C. L., & Eron, L. D. (2003). Longitudinal relations between children's exposure to TV violence and their aggressive and violent behavior in young adulthood 1977–1992. *Developmental Psychology, 39,* 201–221.

Isquith, E. (2013, January 19). Hollywood's real bias is conservative (but not in the way liberals often say). *The Atlantic* [online]. Retrieved June 3, 2013, from w w w . t h e a t l a n t i c . c o m / e n t e r t a i n m e n t / archive/2013/01/hollywoods-real-bias-is-conservative-but-not-in-the-way-liberals-often-say/266960.

Iyengar, S., Peters, M., & Kinder, D. (1982). Experimental demonstrations of the "not-so-minimal" consequences of television news programs. *American Political Science Review, 76,* 848–858.

Jablin, F. M. (1987). Organizational entry, assimilation, and exit. In F. M. Jablin, L. L. Putnam, K. H. Roberts, & L. W. Porter (Eds.), *Handbook of organizational communication: An interdisciplinary perspective* (pp. 679–740). Newbury Park, CA: Sage.

Jablin, F. M. (2001). Organizational entry, assimilation, and disengagement/exit. In F. M. Jablin & L. L. Putnam (Eds.), *The new handbook of organizational communication* (pp. 732–818). Thousand Oaks, CA: Sage.

Jameson, J. K. (2004). Negotiating autonomy and connection through politeness: A dialectical approach to organizational conflict management. *Western Journal of Communication, 3,* 257–277.

Jandt, F. E. (2004). *An introduction to intercultural communication: Identities in a global community.* Thousand Oaks, CA: Sage.

Janis, I. L. (1972). *Victims of groupthink: A psychological study of foreign-policy decisions and fiascoes.* Boston: Houghton Mifflin.

Janis, I. L. (1982). *Groupthink: Psychological studies of policy decisions and fiascoes.* Boston: Houghton Mifflin.

Jeong, S. (2009). Public's responses to an oil spill accident: A test of the attribution theory and situational crisis communication theory. *Public Relations Review, 35*(3), 307–309. doi:10.1016/j.pubrev .2009.03.010

Johnson Avery, E., & Kim, S. (2008). *Preparing for pandemic while managing uncertainty: An analysis of the construction of fear and uncertainty in press releases of major health agencies.* Paper presented at the International Communication Association, Montreal, Québec. Retrieved June 29, 2013, from Communication & Mass Media Complete, EBSCOhost.

Johnson, C. A. (2009, February 11). *Cutting through advertising clutter.* CBSNews.com [online]. Retrieved June 27, 2013, from www.cbsnews. com/8301–3445_162–2015684.html.

Johnston, J., & Breit, R. (2010). Towards a narratology of court reporting. *Media International Australia, 137,* 47–57.

Jones, E. E., & Davis, K. E. (1965). From acts to dispositions: The attribution process in person perception. In L. Berkowitz (Ed.), *Advances in experimental social psychology* (Vol. 2, pp. 220–266). Orlando, FL: Academic Press.

Jones, K. O., Denham, B. E., & Springston, J. K. (2006). Effects of mass and interpersonal communication on breast cancer screening: Advancing agenda-setting theory in health contexts. *Journal of Applied Communication Research, 34,* 94–113.

Kahlor, L., & Eastin, M. S. (2011). Television's role in the culture of violence towards women: Study of television viewing and the cultivation of rape myth acceptance. *Journal of Broadcast and Electronic Media, 55*(2), 215–231. doi:10.1080/08838151.2011 .566085

Kaplan, A. (1964). *The conduct of inquiry.* San Francisco: Chandler.

Katz, E., Blumler, J. G., & Gurevitch, M. (1973). Uses and gratifications research. *Public Opinion Quarterly, 37,* 509–523.

Kelley, H. H. (1967). Attribution theory in social psychology. *Nebraska Symposium on Motivation, 15,* 192–238.

Kelley, H. H. (1973). The processes of causal attribution. *American Psychologist, 28,* 107–128.

Kelly, J. (2008). Mapping the blogosphere: Offering a guide to journalism's future. *Nieman Reports, 62*(4), 37–39.

Kerssen-Griep, J., Hess, J. A., & Trees, A. R. (2003). Sustaining the desire to learn: Dimensions of perceived instructional facework related to student involvement and motivation to learn. *Western Journal of Communication, 67,* 357–381.

Kilmann, R. H., & Thomas, K. W. (1977). Developing a forced-choice measure of conflict-handling behavior. The MODE instrument. *Educational and Psychological Measurement, 37,* 309–325.

Kim, E. Y. (2001). *The yin and the yang of American culture: A paradox.* Yarmouth, ME: Intercultural Press.

Kiyomiya, T. (2006). *Transformation of organizational identity in corporate hegemony: Critical perspectives to Japanese corporate misconduct.* Paper presented at the meeting of the International Communication Association, Dresden, Germany.

Kramer, M. W. (1993). Communication and uncertainty reduction during job transfers: Leaving and joining processes. *Communication Monographs, 60,* 178–197.

Kramer, M. W. (1994). Uncertainty reduction during job transitions: An exploratory study of the communication experiences of newcomers and transferees. *Management Communication Quarterly, 7,* 384–412.

Kramer, M. W. (1999). Motivation to reduce uncertainty: A reconceptualization of uncertainty reduction theory. *Management Communication Quarterly, 13*(2), 305–316.

Lam, C., & O'Higgins, E. E. (2012). Enhancing employee outcomes: The interrelated influences of managers' emotional intelligence and leadership style. *Leadership & Organization Development Journal, 33*(2), 149–174. doi:10.1108/01437731211203465

Lamke, L. K., Sollie, D. L., Durbin, R. G., & Fitzpatrick, J. A. (1994). Masculinity, femininity, and relationship satisfaction: The mediating role of interpersonal competence. *Journal of Social and Personal Relationships, 11,* 535–554.

Lämsä, A.-M., & Sintonen, T. (2006). A narrative approach for organizational learning in a diverse organisation. *Journal of Workplace Learning, 18*(1/2), 106–120. Retrieved June 29, 2013, from http://search.proquest.com/docview/198493402?accountid = 11999.

Lancaster, L. C., & Stillman, D. (2003). *When generations collide.* New York: HarperBusiness.

Landler, M., & Barbaro, M. (2006, August 2). Wal-Mart finds that its formula doesn't fit every culture. *New York Times* [online]. Retrieved June 18, 2013, from www.nytimes.com/2006/08/02/business/worldbusiness/02walmart.html?pagewanted = all&_r = 0.

Larkey, L. K. (1996). Toward a theory of communicative interactions in culturally diverse workgroups. *Academy of Management Review, 21,* 463–491.

Leeds-Hurwitz, W. (1992). Forum introduction: Social approaches to interpersonal communication. *Communication Theory, 2*(2), 131–139.

Lemarié, L., & Chebat, J. (2013). Resist or comply: Promoting responsible gambling among youth. *Journal of Business Research, 66*(1), 137–140. doi:10.1016/j.jbusres.2012.09.005

Lengel, R.H., & Daft, R.L. (1988). The selection of communication media as an executive skill. *Academy of Management Executive, 2*(3), 225–232.

Lewin, K. (1951). *Field theory in social science: Selected theoretical papers.* New York: Harper & Row.

Lewis, B.K. (2010). Social media and strategic communication: Attitudes and perceptions among college students. *Public Relations Journal, 4.* Retrieved from www.prsa.org/Intelligence/PRJournal/Documents/2010Lewis.

Lewis, R. D. (2000). *When cultures collide: Managing successfully across cultures.* London: Nicholas Brealey.

Light, T. (2002). *Thinking ahead about buyer's remorse.* RealEstate ABC. Retrieved November 20, 2003, from http://content.realestateabc.com/homebuying/remorse.htm.

Litterst, J. K., & Eyo, B. (1982). Gauging the effectiveness of formal communication programs: The search for the communication-productivity link. *Journal of Business Communication, 19*(2), 15–26.

Littlejohn, S. W. (1989). *Theories of human communication* (3rd ed.). Belmont, CA: Wadsworth.

Littlejohn, S. W. (2002). *Theories of human communication* (7th ed.). Belmont, CA: Wadsworth.

Longobardi, E. (2009). How "subprime" killed "predatory." *Columbia Journalism Review, 48*(3), 45–49.

Lopez-Zafra, E., Garcia-Retamero, R., & Martos, M. (2012). The relationship between transformational leadership and emotional intelligence from a gendered approach. *The Psychological Record, 62*(1), 97–114.

Maccoby, E. E. (1990). Gender and relationships: A developmental account. *American Psychologist, 45,* 513–520.

Madlock, P. E. (2008). The link between leadership style, communicator competence, and employee satisfaction. *Journal of Business Communication, 45*(1), 61–78.

Mael, F., & Ashforth, B. E. (1992). Alumni and their alma mater: A partial test of the reformulated model of organizational identification. *Journal of Organizational Behavior, 13,* 103–123.

Mann, M. (2012). *The sources of social power: Globalizations, 1945–2011* (Vol. 4). New York: Cambridge University Press.

Manzoni, J. F., & Barsoux, J. L. (2002). *The set-up-to-fail syndrome: How good managers cause great people to fail.* Boston: Harvard Business School.

Markus, M. L. (1987). Toward a "critical mass" theory of interactive media: Universal access, interdependence and diffusion. *Communication Research, 14,* 491–511.

Martins, N., & Wilson, B. J. (2012). Social aggression on television and its relationship to children's aggression in the classroom. *Human Communication Research, 38*(1), 48–71. doi:10.1111/j.1468-2958.2011 .01417.x

Matusitz, J., & Breen, G. (2007). *Addressing the negative aspects of pack journalism to media reporters.* Paper presented at the meeting of the National Communication Association, Chicago.

Mayer, J. D., Caruso, D. R., & Salovey, P. (1999). Emotional intelligence meets traditional standards for an intelligence. *Intelligence, 27*(4), 267–298. doi:10.1016/S0160-2896(99)00016-1

Mayer, J. D., & Salovey, P. (1997). What is emotional intelligence? In P. Salovey & D. J. Sluyter (Eds.), *Emotional development and emotional intelligence: Educational implications* (pp. 3–34). New York: Basic Books.

Mayer, J. D., Salovey, P., & Caruso, D. R. (2008). Emotional intelligence: New ability or eclectic traits? *American Psychologist, 63*(6), 503–517. doi:10.1037/0003-066X.63.6.503

McCombs, M., & Bell, T. (1974). The agenda-setting role of mass communication. In M. Salwen & D. Stacks (Eds.), *An integrated approach to communication theory and research* (p. 100). Hillsdale, NJ: Erlbaum.

McCombs, M., & Shaw, D. (1972). The agenda-setting function of the mass media. *Public Opinion Quarterly, 36,* 176–187.

McCroskey, J. C. (2006). The role of culture in a communibiological approach to communication. *Human Communication, 9*(1), 31–35.

McGuire, D., Todnem By, R., & Hutchings, K. (2007). Towards a model of human resource solutions for achieving intergenerational interaction in organizations. *Journal of European Industrial Training, 31*(8), 592–608.

McGuire, W. J. (1961). Resistance to persuasion conferred by active and passive prior refutation of the same and alternative counterarguments. *Journal of Abnormal and Social Psychology, 63,* 326–332.

McGuire, W. J. (1962). Persistence of the resistance to persuasion induced by various types of prior belief defenses. *Journal of Abnormal and Social Psychology, 64,* 241–248.

McGuire, W. J. (1964). Inducing resistance to persuasion: Some contemporary approaches. In L. Berkowitz (Ed.), *Advances in experimental social psychology* (Vol. 1, pp. 191–229). New York: Academic Press.

McGuire, W. J., & Papageorgis, D. (1961). The relative efficacy of various types of prior belief-defense in producing immunity against persuasion. *Public Opinion Quarterly, 26,* 24–34.

McLellan, H. (2006). Corporate storytelling perspectives. *Journal for Quality and Participation, 29*(1), 17–20.

McMullin, L. (2001). 1969: First broadcast of *Sesame Street.* In D. Schugurensky (Ed.), *History of education: Selected moments of the 20th century* [online]. Retrieved August 10, 2004, from http://schugurensky.faculty.asu.edu/moments/1969sesamestreet .html.

McPhee, R. D. (1985). Formal structure and organizational communication. In R. D. McPhee & P. K. Tompkins (Eds.), *Organizational communication: Traditional themes and new directions* (pp. 149–178). Beverly Hills, CA: Sage.

McQuail, D. (1987). *Mass communication theory: An introduction* (2nd ed.). Newbury Park, CA: Sage.

McQuail, D. (2010). *McQuail's mass communication theory* (6th ed.). Thousand Oaks, CA: Sage.

Meraz, S. (2011). Using time series analysis to measure intermedia agenda-setting influence in traditional media and political blog networks. *Journalism & Mass Communication Quarterly, 88*(1), 176–194.

Metzger, M. J. (2007). Communication privacy management in electronic commerce. *Journal of Computer-Mediated Communication, 12*(2), 1–27.

Mieder, W. W. (1986). *Encyclopedia of world proverbs: A treasury of wit and wisdom through the ages.* Englewood Cliffs, NJ: Prentice Hall.

Millar, F. E., & Rogers, L. E. (1976). A relational approach to interpersonal communication. In G. R. Miller (Ed.), *Explorations in interpersonal communication* (pp. 87–203). Beverly Hills, CA: Sage.

Miller, A. N., & Samp, J. A. (2007). Planning intercultural interaction: Extending anxiety/uncertainty management theory. *Communication Research Reports, 24*(2), 87–95. doi:10.1080/08824090701304717

Miller, G. R. (1978). The current status of theory and research in interpersonal communication. *Human Communication Research, 4,* 164–178.

Miller, K. (2002). *Communication theories: Perspectives, processes, and contexts.* New York: McGraw-Hill.

Miller, K. (2003). *Organizational communication: Approaches and processes* (3rd ed.). Belmont, CA: Wadsworth.

Mishra, S. (2010). Unleashing the wild self: Exploring media influence and drinking among college women. (Doctoral dissertation, Temple University, 2010). Retrieved July 2, 2013, from http://digital.library.temple.edu/cdm/compoundobject/collection/p245801c01110/id/59328/rec/1.

Moideenkutty, U. (2006). Supervisory downward influence and supervisor-directed organizational citizen behavior. *Journal of Organizational Culture, Communication and Conflict, 10,* 1–9.

Monge, P. R., & Contractor, N.S. (2001). Emergence of communication networks. In F. M. Jablin & L. L. Putnam (Eds.), *Handbook of organizational communication: Advances in theory, research, and methods* (pp. 440–502). Thousand Oaks, CA: Sage.

Monk-Turner, E., Heiserman, M., Johnson, C., Cotton, V., & Jackson, M. (2010). The portrayal of racial minorities in prime time television: A replication of Mastro and Greenberg's study a decade later. *Studies in Popular Culture, 32*(2), 101–114.

Montgomery, B. M. (1993). Relationship maintenance versus relationship change: Dialectical dilemma. *Journal of Social and Personal Relationships, 10,* 205–224.

Morley, D. D., & Shockley-Zalabak, P. (1991). Setting the rules: An examination of organizational founders' values. *Management Communication Quarterly, 4,* 422–449.

Morton, T. D. (1999, October). Understanding organizational culture. *Ideas in Action, a publication of the Child Welfare Institute.* Retrieved July 16, 2003, from www.gocwi.org/pdf/ideas1999October.pdf.

Myers, S. A., & Kassing, J. W. (1998). The relationship between perceived supervisory communication behaviors and subordinate organizational identification. *Communication Research Reports, 15,* 71–81.

Nabi, R. L. (2009). Cosmetic surgery makeover programs and intentions to undergo cosmetic enhancements: A consideration of three models of media effects. *Communication Research, 35*(1), 1–27.

Neisser, U. (1967). *Cognitive psychology.* New York: Appleton-Century-Crofts.

Ni, L., & Wang, Q. (2011). Anxiety and uncertainty management in an intercultural setting: The impact on organization-public relationships. *Journal of Public Relations Research, 23*(3), 269–301. doi:10.1080/1062726X.2011.582205

Nudd, T. (2013, April 8). How Subaru fell in love and never looked back. *AdWeek* [online]. Retrieved June 30, 2013, from www.adweek.com/news/advertising-branding/how-subaru-fell-love-and-never-looked-back-148475.

Nystrom, P. C. (1990). Vertical exchanges and organizational commitments of American business managers. *Group and Organizational Studies, 15,* 296–312.

Odland, J. (2004). Television and children. *Childhood Education, 80,* 206B.

Oetzel, J. G., & Ting-Toomey, S. (2003). Face concerns in interpersonal conflict: A cross-cultural empirical test of the face negotiation theory. *Communication Research, 30,* 599–624.

O'Keefe, B. J. (1988). The logic of message design: Individual differences in reasoning about communication. *Communication Monographs, 55,* 80–103.

O'Keefe, B. J. (1997). Variation, adaptation, and functional explanation in the study of message design. In G. Philipsen & T. L. Albrecht (Eds.), *Developing communication theories* (pp. 85–118). Albany: State University of New York Press.

O'Keefe, B. J., & Delia, J. G. (1988). Communicative tasks and communicative practices: The development of audience-centered message production. In B. Rafoth & D. Rubin (Eds.), *The social construction of written communication* (pp. 70–98). Norwood, NJ: Ablex.

O'Keefe, B. J., Lambert, B. L., & Lambert, C. A. (1997). Conflict and communication in a research and development unit. In B. D. Sypher (Ed.), *Case studies in organizational communication 2* (pp. 31–52). New York: Guilford Press.

O'Keefe, D. J. (1990). *Persuasion: Theory and research.* Newbury Park, CA: Sage.

O'Neil, J., & Schenke, M. (2007). An examination of factors impacting athlete alumni donations to their alma mater: A case study of a U.S. university. *International Journal of Nonprofit and Voluntary Sector Marketing, 12,* 59–74.

Palmer, B., Walls, M., Burgess, Z., & Stough, C. (2001). Emotional intelligence and effective leadership. *Leadership & Organization Development Journal, 22,* 5–11.

Park, H. S., & Smith, S. W. (2007). Distinctiveness and influence of subjective norms, personal descriptive and injunctive norms, and societal descriptive and injunctive norms on behavioral intent: A case of two behaviors critical to organ donation. *Human Communication Research, 33,* 194–218.

Park, J. S. (2008). The social reality of depression: DTC advertising of antidepressants and perceptions of the prevalence and lifetime risk of depression. *Journal of Business Ethics, 79*(4), 379–393.

Parker, I. (2012, February 26). The story of a suicide: Two college roommates, a webcam, and a tragedy. *The*

New Yorker. Retrieved July 10, 2013, from www .newyorker.com/reporting/2012/02/06/120206fa_ fact_parker.

Parks, M. R., & Adelman, M. B. (1983). Communication networks and the development of romantic relationships: An expansion of uncertainty reduction theory. *Human Communication Research, 10,* 55–79.

Pattee, H. H. (Ed.). (1973). *Hierarchy theory: The challenge of complex systems.* New York: Braziller.

Pazos, P., Chung, J. M., & Micari, M. (2013). Instant messaging as a task-support tool in information technology organizations. *Journal of Business Communication, 50*(1), 68–86. doi:10.1177/0021943612465181

Peake, J. S. (2001). Presidential agenda setting in foreign policy. *Political Research Quarterly, 54,* 69–86.

Pearson, J., Nelson, P., Titsworth, S., & Harter, L. (2008). *Human communication* (3rd ed.). New York: McGraw-Hill.

Pederson, P. E. (2005). Adoption of mobile internet services: An exploratory study of mobile commerce early adopters. *Journal of Organizational Computing and Electronic Commerce, 15,* 203–222.

Perks, L. (2012). Three satiric television decoding positions. *Communication Studies, 63*(3), 290–308. doi:10.1080/10510974.2012.678925

Peters, R. S. (1974). Personal understanding and personal relationships. In T. Mischel (Ed.), *Understanding other persons.* Oxford, UK: Rowman & Littlefield.

Petronio, S. (2002). *Boundaries of privacy: Dialectics of disclosure.* Albany, NY: SUNY Press.

Petronio, S., & Durham, W. T. (2008). Communication privacy management theory: Significance for interpersonal communication. In L. A. Baxter & D. O. Braithwaite (Eds.), *Engaging theories in interpersonal communication: Multiple perspectives* (pp. 309–322). Thousand Oaks, CA: Sage.

Petronio, S., Sargent, J., Andea, L., Reganis, P., & Cichocki, D. (2004). Family and friends as healthcare advocates: Dilemmas of confidentiality and privacy. *Journal of Social and Personal Relationships, 21,* 33–52.

Petty, R. E., & Cacioppo, J. T. (1986). *Communication and persuasion: Central and peripheral routes to attitude change.* New York: Springer-Verlag.

Pfau, M. (1997). The inoculation model of resistance to influence. In F. J. Boster & G. Barnett (Eds.), *Progress in communication sciences* (Vol. 13, pp. 133–171). Norwood, NJ: Ablex.

Pillai, P. (1992). Rereading Stuart Hall's encoding/decoding model. *Communication Theory, 2*(3), 221–233.

Platt, C. (2004). *A culture of thinness: Negotiated and oppositional decoding of eating disorder discourse by anorectics.* Paper presented at the meeting of the International Communication Association, New Orleans, LA.

Poole, M. S. (1985). Communication and organizational climates: Review, critique, and a new perspective. In R. D. McPhee & P. K. Tompkins (Eds.), *Organizational communication: Traditional themes and new directions* (pp. 79–108). Beverly Hills, CA: Sage.

Poole, M. S. (1988). *Communication and the structuring of organizations.* Unpublished manuscript, University of Minnesota, Minneapolis.

Poole, M. S. (1999). Group communication theory. In L. R. Frey, D. S. Gouran, & M. S. Poole (Eds.), *The handbook of group communication theory and research* (pp. 37–70). Thousand Oaks, CA: Sage.

Poole, M. S., & McPhee, R. D. (1983). A structurational approach to organizational climate. In L. L. Putnam & M. E. Pacanowsky (Eds.), *Communication and organizations: An interpretive approach* (pp. 195–220). Beverly Hills, CA: Sage.

Poole, M. S., & Roth, J. (1989). Decision and development in small groups IV: A typology of group decision paths. *Human Communication Research, 15,* 323–356.

Poole, M. S., Seibold, D. R., & McPhee, R. D. (1985). Group decision-making as a structurational process. *Quarterly Journal of Speech, 71,* 74–102.

Poole, M. S., Seibold, D. R., & McPhee, R. D. (1986). A structurational approach to theory-building in group decision-making research. In R. Y. Hirokawa & M. S. Poole (Eds.), *Communication and group decision-making* (pp. 237–264). Beverly Hills, CA: Sage.

Prada, P., & Orwall, B. (2002, March 12). Parlez-vous Disney? Oui, ja, yes—Mickey's bosses learn from past mistakes in opening new park in France. *The Wall Street Journal,* p. A12. Retrieved July 6, 2009, from ProQuest Central. (Document ID: 110371846).

Procter, J. (2004). *Stuart Hall.* New York: Routledge.

Putnam, L. L. (1983). The interpretive perspective: An alternative to functionalism. In L. L. Putnam & M. E. Pacanowsky (Eds.), *Communication and organizations: An interpretive approach* (pp. 13–30). Beverly Hills, CA: Sage.

Putnam, V. L., & Paulus, P. B. (2009). Brainstorming, brainstorming rules and decision making. *The Journal of Creative Behavior, 43*(1), 23–39.

Quick, B. L. (2009). The effects of viewing *Grey's Anatomy* on perceptions of doctors and patient satisfaction. *Journal of Broadcasting & Electronic Media, 53,* 38–55.

Ragins, B. R., Townsend, B., & Mattis, M. (1998). Gender gap in the executive suite: CEOs and female executives report on breaking the glass ceiling. *Academy of Management Executive, 12,* 28–42.

Rahim, M. A. (1986). *Managing conflict in organizations.* New York: Praeger.

Randazzo, S. (2006). Subaru: The emotional myths behind the brand's growth. *Journal of Advertising Research, 46*(1), 11–17. doi:10.2501/S002184990606003X

Rapoport, A. (1968). The promises and pitfalls of information theory. In W. Buckley (Ed.), *Modern systems research for the behavioral scientist* (pp. 137–142). Chicago: Aldine.

Reinard, J. (1998). *Introduction to communication research* (2nd ed.). New York: McGraw-Hill.

Reynolds, P. D. (1971). *A primer on theory construction.* New York: Bobbs Merrill.

Rhodes, V. W. (2008). Temporary organizational change and uncertainty: Applying uncertainty reduction theory and style analyses to email. (MA dissertation, Clemson University, 2008). Retrieved June 17, 2009, from Dissertations & Theses: A&I database. (Publication No. AAT 1462019).

Riordan, M. A., Markman, K. M., & Stewart, C. O. (2013). Communication accommodation in instant messaging: An examination of temporal convergence. *Journal of Language & Social Psychology, 32*(1), 84–95. doi:10.1177/0261927X12462695

Ritter, B. A., & Yoder, J. D. (2004). Gender differences in leader emergence persist even for dominant women: An updated confirmation of role congruity theory. *Psychology of Women Quarterly, 28*(3), 187–193. doi:10.1111/j.1471–6402.2004.00135.x

Rogers, E. M. (2003). Diffusion of innovations (5th ed.). New York: Free Press.

Rogers, P. S., & Lee-Wong, S. M. (2003). Reconceptualizing politeness to accommodate dynamic tensions in subordinate-to-superior reporting. *Journal of Business and Technical Communication, 17,* 379–412.

Rosenberg, S. (2004). Inoculation effect in prevention of increased verbal aggression in schools. *Psychological Reports, 95*(3 Pt2), 1219–1226. doi:10.2466/PR0.95.7.1219–1226

Rothwell, J. D. (1998). *In mixed company: Small group communication* (3rd ed.). New York: Harcourt Brace.

Rubin, R. B. (1999). Evaluating the product. In A. L. Vangelisti, J. A. Daly, & G. W. Friedrich (Eds.), *Teaching communication* (2nd ed., pp. 425–446). Mahwah, NJ: LEA.

Ruggiero, T. E. (2000). Uses and gratifications theory in the 21st century. *Mass Communication and Society, 3*(1), 3–37.

Runes, D. D. (Ed.). (1984). *Dictionary of philosophy.* Totowa, NJ: Rowman & Allanheld.

Rusbult, C. E. (1980). Commitment and satisfaction in romantic associations: A test of the investment model. *Journal of Experimental Social Psychology, 16,* 172–186.

Salant, P., & Dillman, D. A. (1994). *How to conduct your own survey.* New York: Wiley.

Salazar, A. J. (1995). Understanding the synergistic effects of communication in small groups: Making the most out of group member abilities. *Small Group Research, 26,* 169–199.

Salmon, S., & Joiner, T. A. (2005). Toward an understanding of communication channel preferences for the receipt of management information. *Journal of American Academy of Business, 7,* 56–62.

Salovey, P., Caruso, D., & Mayer, J. D. (2004). Emotional intelligence in practice. In P. Linley & S. Joseph (Eds.), *Positive psychology in practice* (pp. 447–463). Hoboken, NJ: John Wiley & Sons.

Salovey, P., & Mayer, J. D. (1989). Emotional intelligence. *Imagination, Cognition and Personality, 9*(3), 185–211.

Schein, E. H. (1985). *Organizational culture and leadership.* San Francisco: Jossey-Bass.

Schein, E. H. (1992). *Organizational culture and leadership* (2nd ed.). San Francisco: Jossey-Bass.

Schiller, S. Z., & Mandviwalla, M. (2007). Virtual team research: An analysis of theory use and a framework for theory appropriation. *Small Group Research, 38*(1), 12–59. doi:10.1177/1046496406297035

Sedereviciute, K., & Valentini, C. (2011). Towards a more holistic stakeholder analysis approach. Mapping known and undiscovered stakeholders from social media. *International Journal of Strategic Communication, 5*(4), 221–239. doi:10.1080/1553118X.2011 .592170

Seifert, J. W. (2007, January 18). *Data mining and homeland security: An overview.* Congressional Research Service Report for Congress, order code RL31798. Retrieved March 23, 2010, from www.fas.org/sgp/crs/intel/RL31798.pdf.

Shepherd, M. M., & Martz W. B. (2006). Media richness theory and the distance education environment. *Journal of Computer Information Systems, 47,* 114–122.

Sherry, J. L. (2004). Media effects theory and the nature/nurture debate: A historical overview and directions for future research. *Media Psychology, 6*(1), 83–109.

Signorelli, N., Gerbner, G., & Morgan, M. (1995). Violence on television: The cultural indicators project. *Journal of Broadcasting and Electronic Media, 39,* 278–283.

Sillars, A. L. (1980). Attributions and communication in roommate conflict. *Communication Monographs, 47*(3), 180–200. doi:10.1080/03637758009376031

Simons, H. W. (1976). *Persuasion: Understanding, practice, and analysis.* Reading, MA: Addison-Wesley.

Sivanathan, N., & Fekken, G. C. (2002). Emotional intelligence, moral reasoning, and transformational leadership. *Leadership & Organization Development Journal, 23,* 198–204.

Smith, E. B., & Kuntz, P. (2013, April 30). CEO pay 1,795-to-1 multiple of wages skirts U.S. law. *Bloomberg* [online]. Retrieved June 25, 2013, from www .bloomberg.com/news/2013-04-30/ceo-pay-1-795-to-1-multiple-of-workers-skirts-law-as-sec-delays.html.

Smircich, L. (1983). Concepts of culture and organizational analysis. *Administrative Science Quarterly, 28,* 339–358.

Smola, K. W., & Sutton, C. D. (2002). Generational differences: Revisiting generational work values for the new millennium. *Journal of Organizational Behavior, 23,* 363–382.

Spitzberg, B. H., & Cupach, W. R. (1984). *Interpersonal communication competence.* Beverly Hills, CA: Sage.

Spitzberg, B. H., & Cupach, W. R. (1989). *Handbook of interpersonal competence research.* New York: Springer-Verlag.

St. George, D. (2008, December 2). Media bombardment is linked to ill effects during childhood. *The Washington Post,* p. C7. Retrieved June 30, 2009, from www.washingtonpost.com/wp-dyn/content/article/2008/12/01/AR2008120102920.html.

Staton, A. Q. (1999). An ecological perspective on college/university teaching: The teaching/learning environment and socialization. In A. L. Vangelisti, J. A. Daly, & G. W. Friedrich (Eds.), *Teaching communication* (2nd ed., pp. 31–47). Mahwah, NJ: LEA.

Tannen, D. (1990). *You just don't understand: Women and men in conversation.* New York: Morrow.

Texter, L. A. (1995). Attribution theory. In R. L. Hartman & L. A. Texter (Eds.), *Advanced interpersonal communication* (pp. 53–68). Dubuque, IA: Kendall Hunt.

Thibaut, J. W., & Kelley, H. H. (1959). *The social psychology of groups.* New Brunswick, NJ: Transaction Books.

Thomas, K. W., & Kilmann, R. H. (1974). *Thomas-Kilmann conflict mode instrument.* Tuxedo, NY: Xicom.

Times topics: Tyler Clementi. (2012, March 16). *New York Times.* Retrieved July 10, 2013, from http://topics.nytimes.com/top/reference/timestopics/people/c/tyler_clementi/index.html.

Ting-Toomey, S. (1988). Intercultural conflicts: A face-negotiation theory. In Y. Kim & W. Gudykunst (Eds.), *Theories in intercultural communication* (pp. 213–238). Newbury Park, CA: Sage.

Ting-Toomey, S. (1991a). Cross-cultural communication: An introduction. In S. Ting-Toomey & F. Korzenny (Eds.), *Cross-cultural interpersonal communication* (pp. 1–7). Newbury Park, CA: Sage.

Ting-Toomey, S. (1991b). Intimacy expression in three cultures: France, Japan, and the United States.

International Journal of Intercultural Relations, 15, 29–46.

Ting-Toomey, S. (1992, April). *Cross-cultural face-negotiation: An analytical overview.* Paper presented at the meeting of the Pacific Region Forum on Business and Management Communication, Vancouver, British Columbia.

Ting-Toomey, S. (1994). Managing intercultural conflicts effectively. In L. Samovar & R. Porter (Eds.), *Intercultural communication* (7th ed., pp. 360–372). Belmont, CA: Wadsworth.

Ting-Toomey, S. (2005). The matrix of face: An updated face-negotiation theory. In W. B. Gudykunst (Ed.), *Theorizing about intercultural communication* (pp. 71–92). Thousand Oaks, CA: Sage.

Ting-Toomey, S., & Oetzel, J. (2002). Cross-cultural face concerns and conflict styles: Current status and future directions. In W. Gudykunst & B. Mody (Eds.), *Handbook of international and intercultural communication* (2nd ed., pp. 143–164). Thousand Oaks, CA: Sage.

Tomkiewicz, J., & Bass, K. (2008). Attitudes of business students toward management generation cohorts. *North American Journal of Psychology, 10*(2), 435–444.

Tompkins, P. K., & Cheney, G. E. (1985). Communication and unobtrusive control in contemporary organizations. In R. D. McPhee & P. K. Tompkins (Eds.), *Organizational communication: Traditional themes and new directions* (pp. 179–210). Beverly Hills, CA: Sage.

Trevino, L. K., Lengel, R. H., & Daft, R. L. (1987). Media symbolism, media richness, and media choice in organizations. *Communication Research, 14*(5), 553–574.

Triandis, H. C. (1995). *Individualism and collectivism.* Boulder, CO: Westview Press.

Tulgan, B. (2003). *Managing Generation X.* New York: Capstone.

Twenge, J. M., & Campbell, S. M. (2008). Generational differences in psychological traits and their impact on the workplace. *Journal of Managerial Psychology, 23*(8), 862–877.

Twenge, J. M., Campbell, S. M., Hoffman, B. J., & Lance, C. E. (2010). Generational differences in work values: Leisure and extrinsic values increasing, social and intrinsic values decreasing. *Journal of Management, 36*(5), 1117–1142. doi:10.1177/0149206309352246

U.S. Bureau of Labor Statistics. (2008, October). *Highlight of women's earnings in 2007.* Retrieved July 08, 2009, from www.bls.gov/cps/cpswom2007.pdf.

Vecchio, R. P., Griffeth, R. W., & Hom, P. W. (1986). The predictive utility of the vertical dyad linkage approach. *Journal of Social Psychology, 126,* 617–625.

Vergeer, M., Lubbers, M., & Scheepers, P. (2000). Exposure to newspapers and attitudes toward ethnic minorities: A longitudinal analysis. *Howard Journal of Communications, 11*(2), 127–143.

Vivero, V. N., & Jenkins, S. R. (1999). Existential hazards of the multicultural individual: Defining and understanding "cultural homelessness." *Cultural Diversity and Ethnic Minority Psychology, 5,* 6–26.

von Bertalanffy, L. (1968). *General system theory: Foundations, development, applications* (Rev. ed.). New York: Braziller.

Vorvoreanu, M. (2009). Perceptions of corporations on Facebook: An analysis of Facebook social norms. *Journal of New Communications Research, 4,* 67–86.

Wadsworth, A., Patterson, P., Kaid, L., Cullers, G., Malcomb, D., & Lamirand, L. (1987). "Masculine" vs. "feminine" strategies in political ads: Implications for female candidates. *Journal of Applied Communication Research, 15*(1/2), 77.

Wan, H., & Pfau, M. (2004). The relative effectiveness of inoculation, bolstering, and combined approaches in crisis communication. *Journal of Public Relations Research, 16,* 301–328.

Wang, Y., & Huang, T. (2009). The relationship of transformational leadership with group cohesiveness and emotional intelligence. *Social Behavior and Personality, 37,* 379–392.

Waters, R. D. (2009). Examining the role of cognitive dissonance in crisis fundraising. *Public Relations Review, 35*(2), 139–143. doi:10.1016/j.pubrev.2008.11.001

Watzlawick, P., Bavelas, J. B., & Jackson, D. D. (1967). *Pragmatics of human communication: A study of interactional patterns, pathologies, and paradoxes.* New York: Norton.

Watzlawick, P., Weakland, J., & Fisch, R. (1974). Change: Principles of problem formulation and problem resolution. New York: Norton.

Weber, M. S., & Monge, P. (2011). The flow of digital news in a network of sources, authorities, and hubs. *Journal of Communication, 61*(6), 1062–1081. doi:10.1111/j.1460-2466.2011.01596.x

Weick, K. E. (1969). *The social psychology of organizing.* Reading, MA: Addison-Wesley.

West, R., & Turner, L. H. (2007). *Introducing communication theory: Analysis and application* (3rd. ed.). Mountain View, CA: Mayfield.

Westermann, J. W., & Yamamura, J. H. (2007). Generational preferences for work environment fit: Effects on employee outcomes. *Career Development International, 12*(2), 150–161.

Williams, M. (2013, April 17). FBI urges media to "exercise caution" after inaccurate arrest reports. *The Guardian* [online]. Retrieved July 2, 2013, from www.guardian.co.uk/world/2013/apr/17/fbi-media-exercise-caution-bombings.

Wood, J. T. (1993). Gender and moral voice: From woman's nature to standpoint theory. *Women's Studies in Communication, 15,* 1–24.

Wood, J. T., & Dindia, K. (1998). What's the difference? A dialogue about differences and similarities between women and men. In D. J. Canary & K. Dindia (Eds.), *Sex differences and similarities in communication: Critical essays and empirical investigations of sex and gender in interaction* (pp. 19–39). Mahwah, NJ: Erlbaum.

Yudell, M. (2012, March 14). *Mr. mayor, try for that soda tax again!* Philly.com. Retrieved July 1, 2013, from www.philly.com/philly/health/Mr-Mayor-try-for-that-soda-tax-again.html.

Zhang, H., & Poole, M. (2007). *A multiple case study of media use in workplace virtual teams.* Paper presented at the meeting of the International Communication Association, San Francisco.

Zimbardo, P. G., Ebbesen, E. B., & Maslach, C. (1977). *Influencing attitudes and changing behavior.* New York: Random House.

Index

About the Authors

Marianne Dainton (MA, PhD, The Ohio State University; BA, Villanova University) is professor of communication at La Salle University in Philadelphia. She teaches communication theory, interpersonal communication, group communication, and organizational communication. Marianne's research focuses on communication that facilitates relationship maintenance. She has published in Communication Monographs, the Journal of Social and Personal Relationships, Family Relations, and Communication Quarterly, among other places. She has also published numerous book chapters, and is the coeditor (with Daniel Canary) of the Erlbaum book Maintaining Relationships Through Communication.

Elaine D. Zelley (MA, PhD, The Pennsylvania State University; BA, Ursinus College) is an associate professor of communication at La Salle University in Philadelphia. She teaches communication theory, interpersonal communication, group communication, and communication ethics. Elaine's research also focuses broadly on the communication of relationship maintenance. She is particularly interested in women's friendships and the messages used to sustain such relationships. She has published in Communication Yearbook and has also coauthored several book chapters dealing with the topics of relationship maintenance and friendship.

⊗SAGE research**methods**

The essential online tool for researchers from the world's leading methods publisher

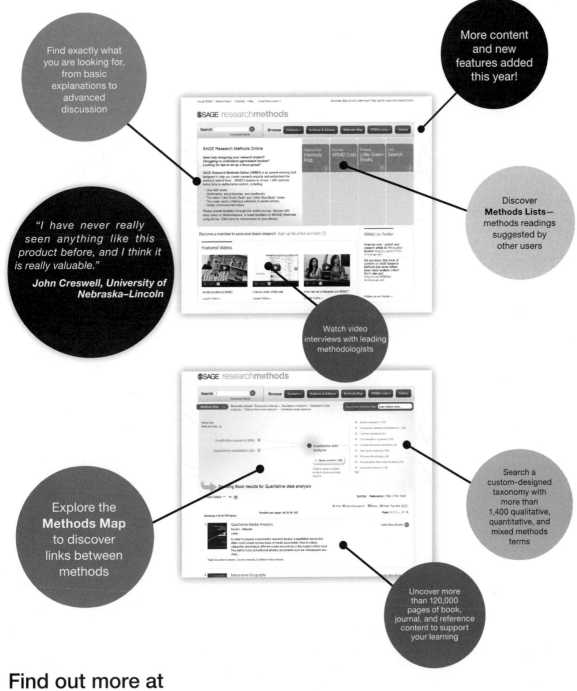

Find exactly what you are looking for, from basic explanations to advanced discussion

More content and new features added this year!

"I have never really seen anything like this product before, and I think it is really valuable."

John Creswell, University of Nebraska–Lincoln

Discover **Methods Lists**— methods readings suggested by other users

Watch video interviews with leading methodologists

Search a custom-designed taxonomy with more than 1,400 qualitative, quantitative, and mixed methods terms

Explore the **Methods Map** to discover links between methods

Uncover more than 120,000 pages of book, journal, and reference content to support your learning

Find out more at
www.sageresearchmethods.com